Parker's Modern Wills Precedents

Parker's Modern Wills Precedents

Seventh edition

by

Michael Waterworth MA (Cantab)
Barrister

Bloomsbury Professional

Bloomsbury Professional, an imprint of Bloomsbury Publishing Plc
Maxwelton House
41–43 Boltro Road
Haywards Heath
West Sussex
RH16 1BJ

© Bloomsbury Professional Ltd, 2011

All rights reserved. No part of this publication may be reproduced in any material form (including photocopying or storing it in any medium by electronic means and whether or not transiently or incidentally to some other use of this publication) without the written permission of the copyright owner except in accordance with the provisions of the Copyright, Designs and Patents Act 1988 or under the terms of a licence issued by the Copyright Licensing Agency Ltd, Saffron House, 6–10 Kirby Street, London, EC1N 8TS, England. Applications for the copyright owner's written permission to reproduce any part of this publication should be addressed to the publisher.

Warning: The doing of an unauthorised act in relation to a copyright work may result in both a civil claim for damages and criminal prosecution.

Crown copyright material is reproduced with the permission of the Controller of HMSO and the Queen's Printer for Scotland. Parliamentary copyright material is reproduced with the permission of the Controller of Her Majesty's Stationery Office on behalf of Parliament. Any European material in this work which has been reproduced from EUR-lex, the official European Communities legislation website, is European Communities copyright.

British Library Cataloguing-in-Publication Data

A CIP Catalogue record for this book is available from the British Library.

ISBN 978 1 84766 688 8

Typeset by Kerrypress Ltd, Luton, Beds

Printed and bound in Great Britain by Martins the Printers, Berwick-upon-Tweed, Northumberland

Preface

This is the seventh edition of *Parker's Modern Wills Precedents*. It comes not long after the sixth edition, but necessarily so. That edition was brought about in response to the introduction of transferrable nil-rate bands between spouses and civil partners in the Pre-Budget Report of 9 November 2007. Since the sixth edition the economic uncertainty afflicting the economy of England and Wales has continued and legislation has, yet again, affected the way in which Will draftsmen operate.

On 6 April 2010, the Perpetuities and Accumulations Act 2009 came into force. This Act does not affect Wills made before that date but, as regards Wills made since the commencement of the new Act, there is now a perpetuity period of 125 years and this is the only period permissible. The rule limiting excessive accumulations has also been ended after some 200 years and it is now possible to accumulate income throughout the duration of a trust. The immediate result of both of these changes is that precedents need no longer be peppered with those obscure references to periods of 21 years that so often perplexed clients who thought that they had asked for 'simple and straightforward' Wills.

This change comes on top of the introduction of transferrable nil-rate bands between spouses and civil partners which has done much by itself to simplify Will-drafting following the radical changes made by Finance Act 2006. The significance of earlier changes such as the introduction of civil partnerships and the legal recognition of gender changes should not be forgotten but the more recent developments have done much to return to a simplicity of Will-drafting. It is, of course, important for the Will-draftsman to retain sight of the client's particular objectives without becoming distracted by the latest legislative changes but this is now a much easier task than was the case five or so years ago.

This book continues to be aimed at Will draftsmen including general private client solicitors dealing with Wills. Wills are among the most important documents which a client will ever complete although, as with conveyancing, most clients want the job done at a rate which is of marginal profitability for the practitioner. In this practically unregulated area the successful draftsman should have sufficient background legal knowledge and a focused proficiency in his subject. Given the ever-increasing complexity of the law and the time and other pressures under which a practitioner has to work, a degree of specialisation is nowadays essential.

Preface

The draftsman must be aware not only of relevant legal points but also of pitfalls and drafting problems thrown up by the client's requirements. Bewildered clients shy away from legal detail and glaze over if inundated with excessive legal theory, often of only peripheral relevance. They want practical advice and a practical approach from their Will draftsman. At the same time they expect and deserve accuracy of drafting and need to have essential points explained to them. Often points of fundamental importance such as the difference between a joint tenancy and a tenancy in common, or the consequences of a discretionary trust can be the hardest to explain and some time has to be devoted to getting the point across.

The draftsman must be clear and to the point and not pave the way to dispute and uncertainty. He should thoroughly cover the legal, fiscal and other more practical implications both in the draft and in any associated advice given to the client. Having done that, the client ought to understand the terms of his Will and raise queries at an early stage.

It is to be hoped that, as with previous editions, this book enables the draftsman to fulfil that goal and that the effect of changes in the law apart, it will stand as well as previous editions. This is a practical book for practical readers. Paul Sharpe, Chairman of the Institute of Professional Willwriters, made a large number of helpful suggestions, many of which were taken up in previous editions and can be found in this new edition. There is always room for improvement and comments and suggestions from other readers and users which might affect the form and content of future editions are welcomed.

Finally, I would like to thank those who helped in various ways towards the production of this edition. Thanks to Richard Wallington of 10 Old Square for the help that he has given me over the years and to my former pupilmasters Francis Barlow QC and Simon Taube QC for teaching me rather more than I am able to remember. I am also grateful for the patience and support of my clerks Keith Plowman and Marc Schofield and the staff at Bloomsbury. Last, but not least, thanks to my wife Caroline for her continued tolerance and her proofreading.

The law is stated as at January 2011.

Michael Waterworth,

10 Old Square, Lincolns Inn, London WC2A 3SU

e-mail: michaelwaterworth@tenoldsquare.com

Contents

Preface v

Table of Statutes xvii

Table of Statutory Instruments xxiii

Table of Cases xxv

1 **Introduction** 1
A short word about drafting 3

2 **General considerations** 5
Severance of a joint tenancy 5
The intestacy rules 6
Capacity and probate claims 8
Claims under the Inheritance (Provision for Family and Dependants) Act 1975 11
Foreign issues 13

3 **Opening and revocation** 15
Identity of the testator 15
Revocation 16
    Form 3.1 Usual opening with revocation 19
    Form 3.2 Opening with revocation where the testator has an alias, has changed his name or has sometimes used the name appearing on his birth certificate which is not the name by which he is informally known 19
    Form 3.3 Opening with revocation where the testator needs to be distinguished from a relative having the same name living at the same address 19
    Form 3.4 Opening where Will is to remain in force after marriage or civil partnership 19
    Form 3.5 Opening where Will is to remain in force after marriage or civil partnership but is not to apply until then 20
    Form 3.6 Opening of Scheduled Will: first schedule immediately operative; second schedule to apply on revocation of first by marriage or civil partnership 20
    Form 3.7 Opening where Will is made in contemplation of divorce etc 20

Contents

4 Declarations concerning joint, mutual and reciprocal Wills 21
    Form 4.1 Clause reciting the creation of reciprocal but not mutual Wills 23
    Form 4.2 Clause creating a mutual Will 23
    Form 4.3 Agreement underpinning a mutual Will 23

5 Declarations Part I 25
Declarations as to jurisdiction and exclusion 25
Directions concerning the disposal of the testator's body and funeral arrangements 25
Cremation 26
Donation of the body 26
    Form 5.1 Foreign element 27
    Form 5.2 Declaration of exclusion 27
    Form 5.3 Objection to cremation 28
    Form 5.4 Direction for cremation with deposit of ashes 28
    Form 5.5 Direction for cremation with ashes scattered 28
    Form 5.6 Direction for funeral service followed by cremation 28
    Form 5.7 Direction for funeral service 28
    Form 5.8 Funeral arrangements: prepaid funeral 28
    Form 5.9 Direction for burial 29
    Form 5.10 Direction for burial with reference to specific plot 29
    Form 5.11 Donation of the body 29

6 Appointment of executors and trustees 30
Different executors and trustees 30
Power to charge 30
Appointment of solicitors 31
Incorporation and solicitors' limited liability partnerships 32
Common appointments 32
    Form 6.1 Appointment of a sole executor with alternative provision 34
    Form 6.2 Appointment of the testator's widow as executor with children as alternatives 34
    Form 6.3 Appointment of the testator's surviving civil partner as executor with friend as alternative 34
    Form 6.4 Appointment of whoever are beneficially entitled as executors 35
    Form 6.5 Appointment of two executors where there is no possibility of a trust arising 35
    Form 6.6 Appointment of executors and trustees where a trust may arise 35
    Form 6.7 Contingent appointment of a minor as executor 35
    Form 6.8 Appointment of executor with a contingent appointment of a minor as a second executor 36
    Form 6.9 Appointment of the Public Trustee as executor and trustee 36
    Form 6.10 Appointment of the Public Trustee to act with an individual with wish expressed regarding solicitors to be employed 36
    Form 6.11 Appointment of bank as executors and trustees 36
    Form 6.12 Appointment of members of a solicitors' firm including successor practice whether incorporated or of limited liability as executors where there is no possibility of a trust arising 37
    Form 6.13 Appointment of members of a solicitors' firm etc as executors and trustees 37

Form 6.14 Appointment of members of a solicitors' firm etc and another individual as executors and trustee 38
Form 6.15 Appointment of members of a solicitors' firm and an accountants' firm as executors and trustees 39
Form 6.16 Appointment of executors with two others as trustees 40
Form 6.17 Professional charges clause 40

7 Appointment of testamentary guardians 41
Form 7.1 Appointment of testamentary guardians 43
Form 7.2 Appointment of testamentary guardians by surviving parent 43
Form 7.3 Appointment of testamentary guardians by surviving parent 43
Form 7.4 Appointment of testamentary guardians with their having power to appoint successors 43

8 Legacies 44
Legacies and identity of legatees 44
Types of legacy 44
Gifts free of inheritance tax 44
Gifts to charities 45
Form 8.1 Declaration that legacies are free of inheritance tax and other duties 46
Form 8.2 Pecuniary legacy 46
Form 8.3 Specific pecuniary legacy 46
Form 8.4 Demonstrative pecuniary legacy 46
Form 8.5 Legacy subject to inheritance tax 47
Form 8.6 Priority legacy 47
Form 8.7 Legacies to two beneficiaries with provision for accruer 47
Form 8.8 Legacy to be divided between two or more beneficiaries 47
Form 8.9 Legacy to a minor – provision for payment to minor if over 16 and otherwise to parent or guardian 48
Form 8.10 Legacy to grandchildren 48
Form 8.11 Legacy to grandchildren – alternative method 48
Form 8.12 Legacy of specific amount to each grandchild 48
Form 8.13 Legacy to grandchildren with substitution of great grandchildren 49
Form 8.14 Legacy to executor 49
Form 8.15 Legacy to employee if still employed 49
Form 8.16 Gift to charity 49
Form 8.17 Purpose gift to particular charity 50
Form 8.18 Inflation-proof legacy 50
Form 8.19 Gift of a number of inflation-proof legacies 50

9 Specific gifts of chattels and other personal property 51
Need for a gift of chattels 51
Inheritance tax and gifts of chattels 51
Gifts of personal chattels 51
Collections 52
Rights of selection of chattels 52
Chattels subject to a charge 53
Releases and gifts of debts 54
Gifts of shares 54
Gift of a family business 54

Contents

      Form 9.1 Bequest of car owned at date of Will   56
      Form 9.2 Bequest of car owned at date of death   56
      Form 9.3 Bequest of Baxter Prints   56
      Form 9.4 Bequest of collection by reference to inventory   56
      Form 9.5 Bequest of specific items by reference to inventory – alternative method   56
      Form 9.6 Bequest of chattels as defined by Administration of Estates Act 1925   57
      Form 9.7 Bequest of personal chattels as defined by Administration of Estates Act 1925 with additions   57
      Form 9.8 Bequest of personal chattels as defined by Administration of Estates Act 1925 with exceptions   57
      Form 9.9 Bequest of personal chattels as defined by Administration of Estates Act 1925 with additions and exceptions   58
      Form 9.10 Bequest of furniture and household effects   58
      Form 9.11 Bequest of jewellery and personal effects   58
      Form 9.12 Bequest of contents of house   58
      Form 9.13 Bequest of contents of house – alternative form   59
      Form 9.14 Bequest of personal chattels selected by beneficiaries   59
      Form 9.15 Gift of jewellery to daughter with right of selection and distribution, default gift into residue   60
      Form 9.16 Gift of pictures to children to select with provision for disagreement   60
      Form 9.17 Absolute gift of personal chattels to children with non-binding request as to distribution in accordance with memorandum   60
      Form 9.18 Bequest of personal chattels as defined by Administration of Estates Act 1925 – gift to trustees for distribution equally among children   61
      Form 9.19 Bequest of chattels in possession of testator but not owned by him   61
      Form 9.20 Bequest of chattels subject to financial agreement   61
      Form 9.21 Cost of delivery to or vesting in beneficiary   62
      Form 9.22 Gift of a debt   62
      Form 9.23 Release of simple debt   62
      Form 9.24 Release of security   62
      Form 9.25 Release of debt and the debtor's estate   63
      Form 9.26 Gift of shares   63
      Form 9.27 Gift of shares – alternative form   63
      Form 9.28 Gift of shares and loan account in family company – provision for amalgamation reconstruction and takeover   63
      Form 9.29 Gift of option to purchase farming business and freehold farm   63
      Form 9.30 Gift of interest in partnership   64
      Form 9.31 Gift of business of which testator is sole proprietor   65

10 Specific gifts of real property and rights of occupation   66
   Simple gifts of land (devises)   66
   Settled gifts of land   67
      Form 10.1 Simple gift of house free of mortgage   73
      Form 10.2 Simple gift of house to two or more persons as tenants in common   73
      Form 10.3 Simple gift of house to two or more persons as joint tenants   74

Contents

   Form 10.4 Gift of immovable property – provision for description   74
   Form 10.5 Gift of house – subject to inheritance tax   74
   Form 10.6 Gift of interest in a house held as tenant in common   74
   Form 10.7 Settled gift of immovable property   74
   Form 10.8 Gift of testator's residence   75
   Form 10.9 Gift of house to trustees to permit occupation as a residence   75
   Form 10.10 Gift of house to trustees to permit occupation as a residence – alternative   76
   Form 10.11 Gift of a furnished house to trustees to permit occupation as a residence   77

11 Residuary gifts   78
   Survivorship clause   78
   Form 11.1 Creation of trust for sale with debts, inheritance tax etc to be paid out of proceeds   85
   Form 11.2 Gift to spouse or civil partner to be followed by substitutional gift   86
   Form 11.3 Gift to spouse or civil partner for life   86
   Form 11.4 Gift to spouse limited for life or until remarriage or formation of civil partnership   87
   Form 11.5 Gift to civil partner limited for life or until marriage or formation of another civil partnership   87
   Form 11.6 Vested gift to children with substitutional gift to grandchildren   87
   Form 11.7 Vested gift to children with substitutional gift to any surviving spouse of deceased child but otherwise to grandchildren   88
   Form 11.8 Gift to children at 25 with substitutional gift to grandchildren   88
   Form 11.9 Gift to children at 21 with substitutional gift to issue   88
   Form 11.10 Gift to those of issue whom spouse or civil partner with life interest appoints with default gift to children   88
   Form 11.11 Gift to brothers, sisters, brothers-in-law and sisters-in-law with substitutional gift to nephews and nieces   89
   Form 11.12 Gift to specified charities   89
   Form 11.13 Gift among charities to be selected by trustees   89
   Form 11.14 Gift for specified charitable objects   90
   Form 11.15 Division of residue among a number of persons in fractional shares   90
   Form 11.16 Division of residue among a number of persons in percentage shares with gift over to children   91
   Form 11.17 Division of residue among a number of persons in percentage shares with gift over to children and provision for accruer of lapsed shares   91
   Form 11.18 Division of residue among a substantial number of exempt and non-exempt beneficiaries   92
   Form 11.19 General discretionary trust   93
   Form 11.20 Discretionary trust of residue for testator's children   94

12 Powers of executors and trustees   95
   Maintenance and advancement   95
   Administrative powers   96
   Investment powers and duties   96
   Delegation to investment managers and nominees   98

xi

Contents

    Insurance   101
    Duty of care   101
    STEP provisions   102
    I   Forms extending statutory dispositive powers of maintenance and advancement   103
        Form 12.1 Maintenance   103
        Form 12.2 Maintenance – alternative form   103
        Form 12.3 Advancement   103
        Form 12.4 Advancement – alternative form   103
        Form 12.5 Advancement in favour of life tenant   104
        Form 12.6 Minors – receipts   104
    II   Forms extending statutory administrative powers of investment and management of property   104
        Form 12.7 Introductory clause   104
        Form 12.8 Investment   104
        Form 12.9 Appointment of agents   105
        Form 12.10 Use of nominees   105
        Form 12.11 Loans to life tenant   105
        Form 12.12 Borrowing power   105
        Form 12.13 Power to carry on testator's business   106
        Form 12.14 Improvement of property   106
        Form 12.15 Purchase of trust assets by trustee   106
        Form 12.16 Retention for tax liabilities   107
        Form 12.17 Appropriation   107
        Form 12.18 Ancillary powers   107
    III   Forms restricting and excluding statutory duties   107
        Form 12.19 Exclusion of duty of care   107
        Form 12.20 Exclusion of duty to consult   108
        Form 12.21 Exclusion of duty to review acts of agents and nominees   108
        Form 12.22 Exoneration of trustees from liability   108

13 Declarations Part II   109
    Form 13.1 Immovable property bought by trustees to be held on trust for sale   110
    Form 13.2 Restriction on trustees' right to sell assets   110
    Form 13.3 Lapse   110
    Form 13.4 Survivorship   110
    Form 13.5 No account to be taken of advances   110
    Form 13.6 Account to be taken of advances   111
    Form 13.7 Excluding doctrine of satisfaction   111
    Form 13.8 Excluding ademption   111
    Form 13.9 Intermediate income   111
    Form 13.10 Illegitimate, legitimated and adopted children   112
    Form 13.11 Precatory trust   112
    Form 13.12 Provision for accrual in equal shares   112
    Form 13.13 Provision for proportional accrual   113

14 Attestation   114
    Will draftsman's duty in relation to attestation   115
    Will draftsman's duty in relation to capacity   116
        Form 14.1 Standard form of testimonium and attestation clause   117
        Form 14.2 Form of testimonium and attestation clause to a codicil   117
        Form 14.3 Where the testator is unable to read or write   117

Contents

Form 14.4 Where the testator is able to sign but unable to read 118
Form 14.5 Where the testator is able to read but unable to sign his name 118
Form 14.6 Where Will is made by an authorised person under Mental Capacity Act 2005 119

15 Inheritance tax mitigation 120
The transferable nil-rate band 122
Inheritance tax planning in other cases 127
Inheritance tax planning through gifts and the equalisation of estates 127
Use of testamentary trusts 129
Options for inheritance tax mitigation including those using the matrimonial (or civil partnership) home where a nil-rate band will still be wasted because one or both of the couple is entitled to an enhanced nil-rate band following a previous marriage 131
Post-death rearrangements 133
Precedents 136
Form 15.1 Gift to children of inheritance tax nil-rate band 136
Form 15.2 Capped gift of inheritance tax nil-rate band to children 137
Form 15.3 Gift on discretionary trust of [capped] inheritance tax nil-rate band in favour of issue 137
Form 15.4 Gift on short-term discretionary trust of amount of inheritance tax nil-rate band for benefit of spouse and issue 138
Form 15.5 Gift on discretionary trust of amount of inheritance tax nil-rate band for benefit of spouse and issue 139
Form 15.6 Contingent gift of amount of inheritance tax nil-rate band 140
Form 15.7 Gift to children of testator's beneficial interest in residence 141
Form 15.8 Specific gift of property attracting business property relief and the balance of the inheritance tax nil-rate band 141
Form 15.9 Clauses enabling use of a promissory note to satisfy the nil-rate band gift 141

16 Complete Wills 143
Non-dispositive Will forms 145
Codicil 145
Form 16.1 Non-dispositive clauses of complete Will incorporating STEP provisions 145
Form 16.2 Non-dispositive clauses of complete Will in the (recommended) longer form 146
Form 16.3 Codicil 148
Form 16.4 Codicil revoking nil-rate band legacy 149

17 Single adults 150
Wills for single adults 151
Form 17.1 Will of single adult leaving everything to a single adult who is appointed executor 151
Form 17.2 Will of single adult leaving everything to a single adult who is appointed executor with gift over only on beneficiary predeceasing testator 152
Form 17.3 Will giving residue to nephews and nieces with funeral arrangement, specific gifts and legacies 152

Contents

        Form 17.4 Will of widow or widower in favour of children or their spouses or, alternatively, the grandchildren with specific and pecuniary legacies   154

18 Wills for married couples or civil partners with no children   158
    Wills for married couples or civil partners with no children   159
        Form 18.1 Will in favour of surviving spouse or civil partner with substitutional gift to brothers, sisters, brothers-in-law and sisters-in-law   159
        Form 18.2 Will leaving spouse or civil partner life interest in the entire estate with remainder to collaterals as above   160

19 Wills for married couples or civil partners with children   164
    Wills for married couples or civil partners with children   168
        Form 19.1 Will of married adult with adult children leaving everything to spouse with substitutional gift to children   168
        Form 19.2 Will leaving everything to spouse or civil partner creating discretionary trust for children if spouse or civil partner has predeceased   171
        Form 19.3 Will of married adult with adult children leaving everything to spouse for life with gift of remainder to children   174
        Form 19.4 Will creating capped 21-year capped nil-rate band discretionary trust with residue to spouse or civil partner   177
        Form 19.5 Will as one of reciprocal Wills creating nil-rate band discretionary trust with residue to spouse or civil partner for life   180
        Form 19.6 Will creating trust for a disabled child with residue to the testator's spouse or civil partner   183
        Form 19.7 Will giving testator's interest in residence to children with residue to spouse or civil partner   185
        Form 19.8 Will for those previously married whose spouse has an enhanced nil-rate band either for use alone or as one of reciprocal Wills creating nil-rate band discretionary trust with residue to spouse or civil partner absolutely. Will including promissory note provisions   186

20 Unmarried couples with children   189
    Wills for unmarried couples with children   190
        Form 20.1 Legacies; residue equally between children and partner   190
        Form 20.2 Will providing for right of residence and legacy for partner with residue to children   193

21 Second marriages or civil partnerships   196
    Wills where there is a second marriage or civil partnership   197
        Form 21.1 Will in favour of testator's second spouse with legacies to children of first marriage   197
        Form 21.2 Will giving residence to surviving spouse with half residue to spouse or civil partner and half residue to children of first marriage or civil partnership   198
        Form 21.3 Will giving right of residence to surviving spouse with half residue to spouse or civil partner and half residue to children of first marriage etc   201
        Form 21.4 Will giving right of residence and life interest in residue to surviving spouse or civil partner with remainder to children of first marriage etc   202

Form 21.5 Will sharing estate between the testator's second spouse or civil partner and the brothers and sisters of his first spouse or civil partner   203

22   Variations after death   205
Disclaimer   206
Deed of Variation   206
  Form 22.1 Deed of Disclaimer   210
  Form 22.2 Simple Deed of Variation   210
  Form 22.3 Deed of Variation – longer alternative   211
  Form 22.4 Deed of Variation – original beneficiary surviving but subsequently dying intestate   213
  Form 22.5 Deed of Variation – use of nil-rate band where previously married widow with enhanced nil-rate band has absolute interest   214
  Form 22.6 Deed of Variation – intestacy, simple form   215
  Form 22.7 Deed of Variation – where some of the property passes by survivorship   216

23   Oaths for executors   219
Need for an oath   219
Reference to Registries   219
Description by address   219
Female deponents   220
Power reserved   220
Size of the estate   220
Drafting variants   221
  Form 23.1 Oaths for Sole Executor; Sole Surviving Executor; Sole Proving Executor (Power reserved to the other)   222
  Form 23.2 Oath for two named Executors and two Executors – power reserved to a third   223
  Form 23.3 Oath for Partner in Solicitors' firm or its successor   225
  Form 23.4 Oath for Two Partners in firm of Solicitors and two Partners in its successor firm   227
  Form 23.5 Oath for a Partner in each of a Solicitors' and an Accountants' firm or a Partner in a Solicitors' firm and a layman appointed, power reserved to either the Accountant or the layman   229
  Form 23.6 Oath for Minor contingently appointed with an adult: having attained eighteen; still not having attained eighteen   231
  Form 23.7 Notice to Non-Proving Executor(s)   232
  Form 23.8 Deposition for non-believers and non-Christians   233

24   Letters and other support materials   234
1. Basic procedure note   234
2. Will draftsman's Guidance Notes   235
3. Will and related matters – checklist   235
4. Matters to be considered at interview and beyond   241
5. Letter about a Life Interest Trust   243
6. Letter about a Discretionary Trust   244
7. Letter submitting a draft Will and Notice of Severance   245
8. Notice of Severance   246
9. Letter enclosing Wills for completion   247
10. Will enabling Promissory Note – Procedure after completion of administration of the estate   249

Contents

    11. Promissory Note   249
    12. Appointment ending a discretionary trust within two years of death   250

Appendix   251

Appendix Part 1: Attestation, construction and interpretation   255

Appendix Part 2: Powers   273

Appendix Part 3: Intestacy Rules   303

Appendix Part 4: Inheritance tax and capital gains tax   309

Index   *319*

Table of statutes

	PARA
Administration of Estates Act 1925	9.20; 12.1, 12.23; 22.25
Pt I	25.17
Pt IV	25.17
s 3(4)	2.3
25	23.11
33(4)	2.12
34	6.6
(3)	6.6; 26.54, 26.59
35	10.2; 25.16
41	12.23; 16.6; 17.2; 18.2; 19.12; 20.2; 21.3
46	2.7, 2.12; 11.11; 15.40; 27.1
(3)	11.11
47	2.7, 2.14; 27.2
(1)	15.40
47A	2.7; 27.3
(2)	27.3
49	2.11
55	9.6, 9.20; 25.17
(1)(x)	2.14; 9.6, 9.8, 9.20; 18.2; 19.12; 20.2; 21.3
Administration of Justice Act 1970	
s 1	27.3
Sch 2	27.3
Administration of Justice Act 1977	
s 28(1)	27.1
(3)	27.3
32	27.3
Sch 5, Pt VI	27.3
Administration of Justice Act 1982	3.13
s 17	14.1; 25.3
18(1)	25.5
(2)	3.10; 25.6
19	25.14
20	25.19
21	25.20
Administration of Justice Act 1985	
s 9	6.11; 12.16; 26.46
Adoption Act 1976	13.2
Pt 4	25.27

	PARA
Adoption Act 1976 – *contd*	
s 42	25.25
Adoption and Children Act 2002	7.1, 7.3; 13.2
Pt I Ch IV (ss 66–76)	25.24
s 51(2)	25.28
s 66	25.27
67	25.28, 25.29, 25.30
s 67(1)–(3)	25.30
s 68	25.29
s 69	25.25, 25.30
s 69(2)	25.31
70	25.31
72	25.32
73	25.33
Sch 4	25.28, 25.30
Anatomy Act 1984	5.7
Banking Act 1987	26.55
Capital Transfer Tax Act 1984	
s 4, 32, 32A, 126	28.4
Sch 1	
Table 1	28.4
Sch 2	28.4
Charities Act 1993	26.60
Charities Act 2006	
s 75(1)	26.19, 26.46
Sch 8	
para 182	26.19
197	26.46
Children Act 1989	7.1; 26.24
s 3(3)	12.23
4, 4A, 4ZA	7.3
5(3)	7.3
7(4)	7.7
108(5)	25.1
Sch 13	
para 1	25.1
Civil List Act 1910	27.1

Table of statutes

	PARA
Civil Partnership Act 2004	1.12; 2.14; 6.20; 15.2; 19.12
s 71	3.9, 3.10; 25.4, 25.7, 25.8, 25.17, 25.18, 27.1, 27.2, 27.3
Pt V Ch III (ss 219–238)	25.8
s 261(1)	26.2, 26.4
Sch 4	
para 2	3.9, 3.10; 25.7, 25.8
3	25.4, 25.18
7	27.1
8(2)–(4)	27.2
9	27.3
12	25.17
Sch 27	
para 5(1)	26.2
(2)(a), (b)	26.2
(3), (5)	26.2
6	26.4
Commonhold and Leasehold Reform Act 2002	
ss 21, 22, 68	26.20
Sch 5	
para 8	26.20
Constitutional Reform Act 2005	
s 59(5)	27.3
Sch 11	
Pt I	27.3
Consumer Credit Act 1974	9.12
Corporation Tax Act 2010	
s 1124	12.16, 26.46
County Courts Act 1959	
s 192	25.17
County Courts Act 1984	
s 145	25.17
148(1)	25.17
Sch 2	
Pt III	
para 15	25.17
Courts Act 1971	
s 56(4)	25.17
Sch 11	
Pt II	25.17
Enduring Powers of Attorney Act 1985	26.22
Family Law Act 1986	
Pt II	25.6
s 53	25.6
Family Law Act 1996	
s 66(1)	25.6
Sch 8	
para 1	25.6
Family Law Reform Act 1969	
s 1(3)	26.2
3(1)(a)	25.2
(2)	27.2

	PARA
Family Law Reform Act 1969 – *contd*	
Sch 1	
Pt I	26.2
Family Law Reform Act 1987	
Pt III (ss 18–21)	25.31
s 1	13.2; 25.24, 25.25; 26.4
19	13.2; 25.25
(1)	26.4
33(1)	26.4
Sch 2	
para 2	26.4
Sch 3	
para 1	26.4
Family Provision Act 1966	
s 1	27.1
(2)	27.1
9, 10	27.2
Sch 2	27.2
Finance Act 1894	
s 17	28.4
Finance Act 1969	
Sch 17	
Pt I	28.4
Finance Act 1975	
s 22, 37	28.4
Sch 5	
para 1(3)	28.8, 28.9
3(6)	28.8
para 4(9)	28.9
para 6(3)	28.9
Sch 9	
para 2	28.4
Finance Act 1976	
s 78	28.4
Finance Act 1978	
s 62	28.4
68(1)–(5)	28.5
Finance Act 1980	
s 93(3)	28.5
Sch 15	28.4
Finance Act 1982	
s 108(1)(b)	28.8
Finance Act 1986	
s 101, 102	28.5
103	15.56
Sch 19	
Pt I	
para 24	28.5
Finance Act 1998	
s 121(3)	28.10
Sch 21	
para 5	28.10
Finance Act 2002	
s 52	28.10
120	28.5
Finance Act 2003	
s 49	22.18

Table of statutes

	PARA
Finance Act 2003 – *contd*	
Sch 3	
para 4	22.18
Finance Act 2006	11.14, 11.30; 15.7, 15.10, 15.34, 15.35, 15.37, 15.38, 15.40, 15.41, 15.44, 15.64, 15.65; 18.2; 19.6, 19.12
s 156	28.7
Sch 20	
para 7, 27	28.7
Finance Act 2008	11.5, 15.8
s 8	28.10
Sch 2	
paras 23, 29	28.10
Sch 4	28.4
para 9	15.10
Gender Recognition Act 2004	1.13; 24.4
Human Fertilisation and Embryology Act 2008	7.3
s 42	25.24
s 43	25.24
s 43(b)	25.24
s 56, 139	25.24
Sch 6, Pt I	
paras 24(1)–(3)	25.24
Human Tissue Act 2004	5.7, 5.8
s 4, 56	25.1
Sch 6, para 1	25.1
Income and Corporation Taxes Act 1988	
s 840	26.46
Income Tax (Trading and Other Income) Act 2005	
s 624, 625, 629	22.7
Inheritance (Provision for Family and Dependants) Act 1975	2.1, 2.2, 2.30, 2.32, 2.33, 2.34, 2.37; 4.5, 4.6; 11.30;18.2; 19.9; 19.12; 24.4; 25.6, 25.8
s 4	2.30
Inheritance Tax Act 1984	11.8, 11.30
s 4	15.11; 28.3, 28.4
8A	15.8, 15.9, 15.10; 28.1, 28.2, 28.3, 28.4
(1)(a), (b)	28.3
(2)	15.11
(3), (4)	15.11, 28.3
(7)	15.11
8B	15.8; 28.2
8C	15.8; 28.1, 28.3, 28.4
10	28.4
17(a)	22.16
18	15.2
32, 32A	28.3, 28.4

	PARA
Inheritance Tax Act 1984 – *contd*	
s 41	11.30
43(3)	28.8, 28.9
Pt III Ch II (ss 49–57A)	10.16
s 49(1)	28.5
s 49A	15.44; 18.2; 19.12
50(6)	28.8
52(3), (4)	28.9
Pt III Ch III (ss 58–85)	28.7
s 64	28.7
65(1)(b)	28.8
(4)	15.65
71	11.18; 15.35, 15.39
71A	15.39, 15.40, 15.43, 15.64, 15.65, 28.7
71D	11.18; 15.36, 15.39, 15.41, 15.64, 15.65; 19.6, 19.12, 28.7
75, 76, 79	28.7
89	15.35
(4)–(6)	19.12
89B(1)	19.12
92	11.8
126	28.3, 28.4
141	11.4
142	22.7, 22.16, 22.19; 28.5
(1)	15.58; 22.2, 22.4, 22.6, 22.9, 22.11, 22.16, 22.25
(2)	22.13, 22.25
(3)	22.6
143	9.11, 9.20; 13.2; 28.6
144	9.11, 9.20; 15.60; 22.22; 28.7
(1)	15.63
160, 168	9.20
218A	22.5
267	2.41
Sch 1	15.7; 28.1
Sch 2	28.3, 28.4
Sch 4	
para 16(1)	28.7
Sch 5	
para 1	28.4
Insolvency Act 1986	
Sch 6	26.59
Interpretation Act 1978	10.10; 26.35
Law of Property Act 1925	25.17; 26.60, 27.1
s 4(3)	26.6
s 29	26.22
s 36(2)	2.6, 24.8
164–166	11.19
184	11.11; 25.15
196(4)	24.8
Law of Property (Miscellaneous Provisions) Act 1994	
s 21(2)	25.17
Sch 2	25.17

Table of statutes

	PARA
Law Reform (Succession) Act 1995	3.11; 6.20
s 1(1)	27.1
(2)(a)	27.2
3	3.10; 25.1, 25.6
5	25.6; 27.2
Sch	27.2
Legitimacy Act 1976	13.2
s 1	25.24
s 5	13.2; 25.26
10	25.24
Limited Liability Partnerships Act 2000	
s 1	6.11
Mental Capacity Act 2005	2.21, 2.22; 14.14; 26.22
s 1	25.21
s 4	25.21
s 16	14.14; 25.21, 25.22
18	14.14; 25.22, 25.23
67(1)	25.17; 26.22
Sch 2	25.22, 25.23
paras 1–4	14.14
Sch 6	
para 5	25.17
42(1), (2)	26.22
Partnership Act 1891	
s 33	9.18
Perpetuities and Accumulations Act 1964	11.16
s 1	26.5
4	11.19
9(2)	26.5
Perpetuities and Accumulations Act 2009	1.14; 11.15, 11.30; 17.2; 19.11, 19.12
s 1	26.6, 26.12
s 1(1)–(6)	26.8
s 2	26.6, 26.12
s 3	26.6
ss 4–11	26.12
5	26.7
s 5(1)	11.15
s 6	26.8
s 7	11.16, 26.9, 26.10
s 8	26.9, 26.10
s 11	26.11
s 12	26.12
s 13	11.19; 12.3, 12.23, 26.12
s 14, 15	26.12
s 20	26.13
s 22(2)	26.12
Prescription Act 1832	25.4, 25.18
Public Trustee Act 1906	26.60
s 4(3)	25.17
Senior Courts Act 1981	
s 109	23.9

	PARA
Senior Courts Act 1981 – *contd*	
s 127	27.3
152(1)	27.3
(4)	25.17
Sch 5	27.3
Sch 7	25.17
Settled Land Act 1925	10.7; 25.17; 26.3, 26.15, 26.60
s 1	26.18
s 27	26.29
s 67(1)	26.15
Statute Law (Repeals) Act 1969	25.1
Statute Law (Repeals) Act 1981	27.1
Statute Law Revision Act 1893	25.1
Statute Law Revision (No 2) Act 1888	25.2, 25.4, 25.12
Taxation of Chargeable Gains Act 1992	
s 10A	28.10
s 17	28.10
s 62	28.10
(6)	22.2, 22.4, 22.9, 22.11, 22.25
(7)	22.25
64	28.10
67(7)	22.13
s 87	28.10
s 89(2)	28.10
92, 225	11.21
Trustee Act 1925	12.1, 12.5; 17.2; 18.2; 26.60
s 15	26.61
16	12.23
19	12.19; 26.1, 26.58, 26.61
(1)(a), (b)	12.19
(2)	12.19
(3)(a), (b)	12.19
(5)	12.19
22(1), (3)	26.61
31	11.18, 11.19; 12.3, 12.23; 26.2
s 31(2)	12.3
32	12.4, 12.23; 26.3
(1)	13.2
33	25.25; 26.4
61	12.23
69(2)	12.3, 12.4
Trustee Act 2000	6.20; 10.8, 10.9; 12.1, 12.5, 12.6, 12.11, 12.12, 12.18, 12.19, 12.20, 12.23; 16.6; 17.2; 18.2
s 1	12.5, 12.20, 12.23; 17.2; 18.2; 19.12; 20.2; 21.3; 26.19, 26.23, 26.30
(1)(a), (b)	12.20
(2)	26.60
2	10.9, 10.12; 12.20; 26.31
ss 3–6	12.5

xx

Table of statutes

Trustee Act 2000 – *contd*	PARA
s 3	10.11; 12.6; 26.32
(1)	12.6
(2)	12.6; 26.60
(3)	10.11; 12.6
4	12.6, 12.7, 12.8; 26.33, 26.40, 26.61
(1), (2)	12.7
(3)	26.60
(a), (b)	12.7
5	12.6, 12.9; 26.34, 26.61
(1)	12.9, 12.10
(2)–(4)	12.9
6	12.8, 12.10; 26.35
s 6(1)	12.6
(2), (3)	26.60
8	26.19; 26.32, 26.36, 26.61
(1)	10.10, 10.11
(1)(b)	26.59
(2)	10.10
9	10.9, 10.11; 26.37
Pt IV (ss 11–26)	12.5, 12.11; 26.55, 26.56, 26.57
s 11	26.1; 26.38, 26.39, 26.40, 26.46, 26.48, 26.61
(1)	12.12
(2)	12.12
(a)–(d)	12.12
12	26.39
(1)	12.13; 26.52
(2)	12.13
(3)	12.13; 26.52
13	26.40
(1), (2)	12.12
14	26.41
(1), (2)	12.13
(3)(a)–(c)	12.13
15	26.42, 26.49, 26.61
(1)	12.14
(2)	26.41
(a), (b)	12.14
s 15(3)	26.49
(4)	12.14; 26.49
(5)	26.60
(a)–(c)	12.14
16	26.39, 26.43, 26.46, 26.47, 26.48, 26.61
(1)(a), (b)	12.15
(2)	12.15
17	26.39, 26.44, 26.46, 26.47, 26.48, 26.61
(1)	12.15
(2)	12.15; 26.60
(3)	12.15
18	26.39, 26.45, 26.46, 26.47, 26.48, 26.52, 26.61
(1), (2)	12.15

Trustee Act 2000 – *contd*	PARA
s 19	26.46
(1)	12.16
(2)(a)–(c)	12.16
(5)	26.52
(5)(a), (b)	12.16
(6), (7)	12.16
20	26.47
(1), (2)	12.15
(3)(a)–(c)	12.15
21	12.17; 26.48
22	12.23; 16.6; 17.2; 18.2; 19.12; 20.2; 21.3; 26.42, 26.48, 26.49, 26.50, 26.61
(1)(a)–(c)	12.17
(2)(a)–(c)	12.17
(4)	26.60
23	12.17; 26.48, 26.50
24	12.17; 26.51
25	26.52
26	26.53
(a), (b)	12.18
28	12.5; 26.54, 26.59
(1), (2)	6.4, 6.20
(4)	6.6; 14.4
(b)	6.6
(5), (6)	6.4; 26.60
ss 29–32	26.41, 26.47
s 29	12.5; 26.55, 26.59
(1), (2)	6.4, 6.20
31	26.56
32	12.13, 12.15; 26.57
33(2)(a)	14.4
34	12.19; 26.58
(1)	26.1
35	12.5; 26.59
(2)(a)	26.60
(3)(a)	6.6
39	26.60
40(1)	26.2, 26.23
Sch 1	10.9, 10.12; 12.5, 12.20; 26.31, 26.61
para 3	26.50
7	10.9; 12.21
Sch 2	
Pt II	26.2
para 45	10.9; 26.19
46	26.22
47	26.23
Trustee Investments Act 1961	12.5, 12.6
Trusts of Land and Appointment of Trustees Act 1996	10.7, 10.8, 10.9, 10.15, 10.23; 12.1, 12.23
s 1	26.14
(1)(a)	10.7

Table of statutes

Trusts of Land and Appointment of Trustees Act 1996 – contd	PARA
(2)(a)	10.7
2	10.6, 10.23; 26.14, 26.15, 26.29
(1)	10.7
3	26.16
(1)	10.7; 26.28
4	11.2; 26.17, 26.40
(1)	10.7
5	26.18
6	10.8; 26.19, 26.21
(1)	10.9
(2)	26.25
(3)	10.10
(9)	10.9
7	26.20, 26.21
8	26.21
(1), (2)	10.11
9	10.8; 26.22, 26.23
(1), (7)	10.12
9A	10.8; 26.23
(1)	10.12
(2)(b)	10.12
(3)(a)–(c)	10.12
10	10.8; 26.24, 26.28
11	10.8; 16.6; 17.2; 18.2; 19.12; 20.2; 21.3; 26.25, 26.28
(1)	10.13; 12.23; 26.40
(a), (b)	10.13
(2)(a)	10.13
12	10.8; 26.26, 26.27
(1)	10.15, 10.16
(a), (b)	10.15
(2)	10.16
13	10.8; 26.26, 26.27
(1), (2)	10.17
(3)	10.17, 10.23
(4)(a)–(c)	10.18
(5)(a), (b)	10.17

Trusts of Land and Appointment of Trustees Act 1996 – contd	PARA
(6)	10.17
(a), (b)	10.17
(7)	10.18
(a), (b)	10.18
(8)	10.18
14	26.28
18	10.9; 26.28
25(1)	25.17; 26.3
(2)	25.10.1, 25.17
Sch 1	10.6; 26.15, 26.29
Sch 2	26.18
Sch 3	
para 3(8)	26.3
6(5)	25.17
Sch 4	25.1, 25.17
Universities and College Estates Act 1925	26.14
Variation of Trusts Act 1958	22.3
Wills Act 1837	3.13; 14.3; 25.23
s 1	3.6; 23.10; 25.1, 25.4
7	25.2
9	14.1; 24.9; 25.3, 25.23
15	6.6; 14.4; 25.4, 25.18; 26.54
18	3.9, 3.12, 3.13; 25.5
18A	3.10, 3.11, 3.13; 6.20; , 25.6
18B	3.13; 25.7
(1)	3.9
(3)	3.12
18C	3.10, 3.11, 3.13; 25.8
20	3.5, 3.6; 25.9
21	14.2; 25.10
22	25.11
24	9.4; 25.12
29	25.13
33	11.25, 11.26; 13.2; 19.11; 21.3; 24.4; 25.14
Wills Act 1968	
s 1	14.4; 25.4, 25.18

Table of statutory instruments

	PARA
Family Provision (Intestate Succession) Order 1993, SI 1993/2906	27.1
HMRC Inheritance Tax Manual	
IHTM35060	22.17
IHTM43000 et seq	15.16
Inheritance Tax (Delivery of Accounts) (Excepted Estates) Regulations 2004, SI 2004/2543	23.9
Intestate Succession (Interest and Capitalisation) Order 1977, SI 1977/1491	
art 2	27.1
3	27.3
Intestate Succession (Interest and Capitalisation) Order 1983, SI 1983/1374	27.1
Land Registration Rules 2003, SI 2003/1417	
Sch 4	
form A	24.8
Limited Liability Partnerships Regulations 2001, SI 2001/1090	6.11
Mental Capacity Act Code of Practice	2.21
Non-Contentious Probate Fees Order 2004, SI 2004/3120	
Sch 1	23.3
Non-Contentious Probate Rules 1987, SI 1987/2024	
r 13	14.6

	PARA
Non-Contentious Probate Rules 1987, SI 1987/2024 – *contd*	
27(1A)	23.8
Rules of the Supreme Court 1965, SI 1965/1776	
Order 65	
r 14B	9.20
Solicitors' Incorporated Practices Order 1991, SI 1991/2684	6.11
Solicitors' Incorporated Practice Rules 1988	6.11
Solicitors' Recognised Bodies Order 1991, SI 1991/2684	6.11
Solicitors' Recognised Bodies (Amendment) Order 2009, SI 2009/500	6.11
Stamp Duty (Exempt Instruments) Regulations 1987, SI 1987/516	12.23; 22.17
Schedule	
category M	22.17, 22.25
Tax and Civil Partnership Regulations 2005, SI 2005/3229	15.2
Inland Revenue Press Release 6 August 1975	28.9
Inland Revenue Statement of Practice SP10/79	28.8
Hague Convention on InterCountry Adoption	
Art 23(1)	25.27

Table of cases

	PARA
Allhusen v Whittell (1867) LR 4 Eq 295, 36 LJ Ch 929, 16 LT 695 ......, [1861–1873] All ER Rep 149, Vice-Chancellor's Ct	11.30; 16.6; 17.2; 18.2; 19.12; 20.2; 21.3
Banks v Goodfellow, Re (1869–1870) LR 5 QB 549, 39 LJQB 237, 22 LT 813, [1861–73] All ER Rep 47	2.19
Barry v Butlin (1838) 2 Moo PCC 480, 12 ER 1089	2.26
Bartlett v Barclay's Bank Trust Co Ltd (No 1) [1980] Ch 515, [1980] 2 WLR 430, [1980] 1 All ER 139, (1979) 124 SJ 85	12.20
Benham's Will Trusts, Re [1995] STC 210, [1995] STI 186, ChD	11.30; 24.4
Birmingham v Renfrew [1937] HCA 52, (1937) 57 CLR 666, Australia	4.5
Blewitt, In the Goods of (1880) LR 5 PD 116, 49 LJP 31, 42 LT 329, 44 JP 768, PDA	14.2
Bowen-Buscarlet's Will Trusts, Re [1972] Ch 463, [1971] 3 WLR 742, [1971] 3 All ER 636, (1971) 115 SJ 872	2.10, 2.11
Buckenham v Dickinson (1997) [2000] WTLR 1083, [1997] CLY 4733, QBD	2.25
Burgess v Rawnsley [1975] Ch 429, [1975] 3 WLR 99, [1975] 3 All ER 142, (1975) 30 P & CR 221, (1975) 119 SJ 406	2.6
Cattermole v Prisk [2006] 1 FLR 693, [2006] Fam Law 98, ChD	2.25
Chesterfield's (Earl) Trusts, Re (1883) LR 24 Ch D 643, 49 LT 261, [1881–5] All ER Rep 737, ChD	11.30; 16.6; 17.2; 18.2; 19.12; 20.2; 21.3
Cleaver (deceased), Re; Cleaver v Insley [1981] 1 WLR 939, [1981] 2 All ER 1018, (1981) 125 SJ 445	4.5
Dale (deceased), Re; Proctor v Dale [1994] Ch 31, [1993] 3 WLR 652, [1993] 4 All ER 129, [1994] Fam Law 77, (1993) 137 SJLB 83, ChD	4.5
Dove v Reynolds see Reynold's Will Trusts, Re	
Esterhuizen v Allied Dunbar Assurance plc [1998] 2 FLR 668, [1998] Fam Law 527, (1998) The Times, June 10, QBD	14.9
Gould v Kemp (1834) 2 My & K 304, 39 ER 959, LC	2.5
Gray & others v Richards Butler (a firm: supervision of execution) (1997) [2000] WTLR 143	14.8, 14.9, 14.10; 24.9
Green (deceased), Re [1951] Ch 148, [1950] 2 All ER 913, 66 TLR (Pt 2) 819, (1950) 94 SJ 742	4.5
Hall v Hall (1868) LR 1 P & D 481, P&D	2.28
Heys (Mary) (deceased), Re; Walker v Gaskill [1914] P 192, 83 LJP 152, 111 LT 941, 30 TLR 637, 59 Sol Jo 45, PDA	2.6
Hoff v Atherton [2004] EWCA Civ 1554, [2005] WTLR 99, [2004] All ER (D) 314 (Nov)	2.25
Holmes v McMullan; sub nom Ratcliffe (Deceased), Re [1999] STC 262, [1999] BTC 8017, (1999) 96 (11) LSG 70, ChD	11.30

Table of cases

PARA

Howe v Earl of Dartmouth (1802) 32 ER 56, (1802) 7 Ves Jr 137 .. 11.30; 16.6; 17.2; 18.2;
19.12; 20.2; 21.3
Kenward v Adams [1975] CLY 3591, (1975) *The Times*, 29 November, ChD ... 2.25; 14.11
Kinch v Bullard [1999] 1 WLR 423, [1998] 4 All ER 650, [1999] 1 FLR 66,
[1998] 3 EGLR 112, [1998] 47 EG 140, [1998] Fam Law 738, [1998] EG 126
(CS), [1998] NPC 137, (1999) 77 P & CR D1, ChD 24.8
Knox v Till [2000] Lloyd's Rep PN 49, [2000] PNLR 67, [2002] WTLR 1147,
NZCA 14.12
McKee, Re; Public Trustee v McKee [1931] 2 Ch 145, 100 LJCh 325, 145 LT
605, CA 2.11
Martin v Nicholson [2004] EWHC 2135 (Ch), [2005] WTLR 175 .... 22.15, 22.23
Palmer v Bank of New South Wales (1975) 7 ALR 671, 133 CLR 150, (1976) 50
ALJR 320, Australia 4.5
Parker v Felgate (1883) LR 8 PD 171, 52 LJP 95, 47 JP 808, 32 WR 186 .... 2.24
Phillips, Re [1938] 4 All ER 438 .... 9.20
Public Trustee v Till [2001] 2 NZLR 508, [2002] WTLR 1169, NZHC 14.12
Ratcliffe (deceased), Re *see* Holmes v McMullan
Recher's Will Trusts, Re [1972] Ch 526, [1971] 3 WLR 321, [1971] 3 All ER
401, (1971) 115 SJ 448 .... 8.13
Reynold's Will Trusts, Re; Dove v Reynolds [1966] 1 WLR 19, [1965] 3 All ER
686, (1965) 109 SJ 903 .... 9.8
Rogers (deceased), Re [2006] EWHC 753 (Ch), [2006] 1 WLR 1577,
[2006] 2 All ER 792, [2006] WTLR 691, (2005–2006) 8 ITELR 886, (2006)
103 (18) LSG 30, (2006) 156 NLJ 644, [2006] NPC 45 .... 6.14, 6.20
Russell v IRC [1988] 1 WLR 834, [1988] 2 All ER 405, [1988] STC 195, (1988)
132 SJ 659 .... 22.19
Sansom v Peay (Inspector of Taxes) [1976] 1 WLR 1073, [1976] 3 All ER 375,
[1976] STC 494, 52 TC 1, [1976] TR 205, (1976) 120 SJ 571 .... 11.21
Scammell v Farmer [2008] EWHC 1100 (Ch), [2008] WTLR 1261, (2008) 152
(23) SJLB 31 .... 2.21
Selby-Bigge (deceased), Re [1950] 1 All ER 1009, 66 TLR (Pt 1) 993, [150] WN
231, (1950) 93 SJ 287 .... 14.5, 14.14
Sharp v Adam [2006] EWCA Civ 449, [2006] WTLR 1059, 10 ITELR 419 .... 2.20
Simpson, Re (1977) 121 Sol Jo 24 .... 2.25; 14.11
Sinclair, (deceased) Re [1985] Ch 446, [1985] 2 WLR 795, [1985] 1 All ER
1066, [1985] Fam Law 227, (1985) 82 LSG 1567, (1985) 135 NLJ 363, (985)
129 SJ 206 .... 3.11
Soutter's Executry v IRC [2002] STC (SCD) 385, [2002] WTLR 1207, [2002]
STI 1259, Special Commissioner 22.16
University College of North Wales v Taylor [1908] P 140, 77 LJP 20, 98 LT 472,
24 TLR 29, 52 Sol Jo 44, CA 9.20
Wilford's Estate, Re; Taylor v Taylor (1879) LR 11 Ch D 267, 48 LJ Ch 243 .... 2.6
Williams v Williams (1882) 20 Ch D 659, [1881–1885] All ER Rep 840, ChD 5.3
Wilson v Bell (1843) 5 Ir Eq R 501 .... 2.6
Woolnough, Re; Perkins v Borden (1999) [2002] WTLR 595, ChD 2.5
Zehr, Re [1944] 2 DLR 670 .... 15.65; 19.12; 21.3

1 Introduction

1.1 Many clients visit their solicitor or call on the services of a Will draftsman for the express purpose of 'making a Will' and have not thought of anything beyond that. They often do not contemplate achieving their aims by means other than a Will but, despite recent falls and uncertainty in the housing market, with increasing personal wealth through increased property values, there are often other considerations which ought to be the subject of considered advice. The solicitor is, of course, more than just a Will draftsman. Increasingly, however, the Will draftsman, whether a solicitor or not, is expected to advise how the client can best achieve his objectives. More often the draftsman must consider how the *clients* can best achieve their objectives, for Will making, particularly among the young or middle aged, is largely the domain of couples. When dealing with couples it is increasingly important to take account of second marriages or relationships after an earlier marriage and the desire to make provision for children of only one half of a couple.

1.2 The clients' wishes and their desire to make provision for their dependants' needs are paramount. No two cases are alike. A young couple can make their Wills on a 'long-term' basis but, even so, the considerations applicable to them will be quite different from those of their middle-aged parents or elderly grandparents. It is important in all cases to think about what can be done and what should be done for the clients. On no account should a Will draftsman rely on precedents without regard to what is appropriate. The draftsman must, therefore, consider alternative solutions for his clients and the possible disadvantages of using a Will as the only method of fulfilling their wishes. A Will is often only one instrument in a composite plan and, however 'long-term' the clients' view might be, Wills should be reconsidered more frequently than most people anticipate.

1.3 Even in small and relatively simple estates, there will often be other related matters to consider such as pension provision and life assurance, the question whether the matrimonial home should be held as joint tenants or tenants in common and the further question as to how to discharge any outstanding mortgage on death. At the same time, the draftsman must not ignore the fact that there are many cases in which the client's wishes can be accommodated in a straightforward Will. He must guard against becoming obsessive about the use of alternative methods with the result that he provides a complicated solution where a simple solution is satisfactory; or devises a plan which is tax effective but fails to meet the needs of the client's family or to accommodate the client's wishes.

1.4 The draftsman should nonetheless consider, discuss and give advice about those difficult questions such as the entitlement to life assurance and which of the, to many clients confusing, descriptions of 'joint tenancy' or 'tenancy in common' should apply to a jointly owned home (and other properties).

1.5 *Introduction*

1.5 In doing so it should be remembered that clients usually underestimate the value of their estates and do not take into account contingent assets, such as death in service benefits, which can often be dealt with outside the Will in a tax-efficient way. Neither are they aware of the need to ensure that the trustees of policies of assurance and death benefits should be kept informed about their circumstances.

1.6 Clients can also fail to take into account special considerations which apply to certain assets. Some property, like the matrimonial home, may be required for personal use and occupation; some may be easy and some difficult to realise; some may attract special relief from inheritance tax; some property may not pass under the Will and yet form part of the estate for inheritance tax purposes; other property may not form part of the estate at all if appropriate steps are taken during the client's lifetime. In the case of a business, immediate steps might need to be taken to secure its future but that should not be done in such a way as to diminish the enjoyment or value of the business during the lifetime of the client(s). A farmer's or businessman's Will might be tax efficient by virtue of agricultural property relief but become hopelessly inefficient upon retirement.

1.7 There are, in most cases, a raft of questions which the draftsman ought to ask before even putting pen to paper or, as is now the case, searching through a database of precedents. For example, it is advisable to make a point of asking whether the client has made any lifetime gifts, as experience shows that many clients fail to mention such gifts which, of course, may influence the tax payable on death. In order to assist with this process, this edition, like the last, incorporates a section of support materials including a sample checklist and a list of points which ought to be covered when the client is interviewed. A checklist and interview are intended to discover the intentions and principal concerns of the client including the size and nature of the estate, the identity of the intended beneficiaries and any difficulties which might be encountered in attempting to put the client's intentions into practice. It is also a useful means of securing an understanding of what steps might be taken to minimise inheritance tax liability[1].

1   Reference is made here to estate planning. Any detailed consideration of it is outside the scope of this introduction. The reader is referred to the section dealing with inheritance tax mitigation (**chapter 15**) and the list of points to consider at interview and beyond (**chapter 24**).

1.8 In all cases it should be remembered that a well-devised scheme, whether of distribution amongst family or of inheritance tax mitigation, may be ruined by altered circumstances or legislative changes[1] between the date on which the Will is made and the date of death. The client needs to be warned of this. It is a fact of life with which both clients and solicitors have to cope. So long as it continues to be possible to vary a Will after death in a tax-effective manner, some, but not all, of the problems created by legislative changes may be resolved. It is, of course, much better to resolve those difficulties before death by reviewing Wills from time to time.

1   As dramatically underlined by the introduction of the pre-owned assets regime, the 2006 Budget and the contents of the 2007 Pre-Budget Report concerning transfer of the nil-rate band between married couples and civil partners.

1.9 Many clients are conscious of this but it is worthwhile reminding the client that his Will has been drafted on the basis of the law at the date of his Will and the circumstances existing or reasonably foreseeable at that time. A well-organised draftsman might notify clients of relevant changes in the law but busy practitioners do not always find this possible, however profitable this repeat business might be. If the relationship between draftsman and client is such that the client can expect to be informed of changes in the law then terms of business should record that. The draftsman on the other hand is unlikely to become aware of changes in a client's personal circumstances. Clients should be made aware of the fact that they ought to review their Wills if their personal family circumstances or wishes change and they should be encouraged to contact their solicitors for advice if a Budget indicates changes in inheritance tax.

A short word about drafting

1.10 The draftsman will not be judged on literary content but on precision, accuracy and effectiveness of communication. The discipline of using tried and tested set forms is an enormous benefit to clients and draftsmen alike and the use of plain language can help a clear thinker to express himself precisely and a muddled thinker to focus his mind. Certainly, the muddled thinker should not attempt to excuse himself by hiding behind dated drafting practices and language. Such practices, including sheltering behind tortuous or unnecessary technical words and phrases, often serve only to conceal a lack of thought.

1.11 In a good Will a complicated provision should be expressed simply, clearly and concisely in a manner which can be understood by clients and lawyers alike. However, the draftsman should remember that the client is mainly, if not exclusively, interested in the destination rather than the fine technical detail of the vehicle and the route used to get there. The draftsman, on the other hand, must take care to ensure that what he produces will achieve the client's aims: sloppy, vague, ambiguous and ill thought out attempts to impose plain language in place of meaningful and precise technical phrases does much more harm than good. The draftsman should, in all cases, exercise clear-headed, independent judgment in selecting and tailoring precedents for he who tries to force an ill-fitting precedent onto a client is also forcing a client into a precedent. That is a terrible sin.

1.12 The advent of civil partnerships and of gender recognition has, unfortunately, added to the difficulty of adapting a suitable Will precedent. Very little needs to be said about civil partnerships, because the effect of the Civil Partnership Act 2004 is to make civil partners equivalent to heterosexual spouses[1]. However, a point which many draftsmen miss is that in the case of a widowhood interest (ie an interest which terminates on death or remarriage) express provision should also be made for termination on the formation of a civil partnership. Similarly, if it is to be effective, an interest limited in favour of a surviving civil partner ought to be made terminable on that civil partner 'dying, forming a new civil partnership or marrying'.

1   Civil partners are not necessarily homosexual, there being no concept or possibility of sexual consummation (exclusively by male–female vaginal penetration) in the formation of a civil partnership, nor of adultery (likewise) in the ending of it.

1.13 In deference to the Gender Recognition Act 2004 the Will draftsman should now steer clear of unspecific class gifts to 'daughters' or 'sons'[1] in order to avoid the accident of including or excluding a person who has changed gender when the testator did not intend that result. By way of example, a gift to 'my daughter's born female' probably does the trick. Likewise a gift of 'my farm to my eldest son' should be clarified by naming the son lest his elder sister alter her gender and take the gift[2].

1   Or to nephews, nieces, grandsons, granddaughters etc.
2   An absurd example, perhaps, but the point is, I hope, clear.

1.14 In respect of Wills made on or after 6 April 2010 drafting is simplified by Perpetuities and Accumulations Act 2009 in two respects. First, this Act has abolished the statutory restrictions on accumulations that, over the last two centuries, have curtailed the power of trustees to accumulate income. This means that it is no longer

1.15 *Introduction*

necessary to restrict the power to accumulate to a period of 21 years, a formulation which tended to confuse clients. Accumulation is now permitted throughout the period of any trust and all that is needed is a power to accumulate in general terms. The second change brought about by Perpetuities and Accumulations Act 2009 is that, for Wills made on or after 6 April 2010, the perpetuity period is now 125 years. This also serves to simply Will drafting by removing the need to consider lives in being and the like. Whereas previously, a gift to children might have specified that it should vest at the age of 30 but the gift over to their children would have had to vest at the age of 21 years, it is no longer necessary to draft trusts with those discrepancies. Both of these matters are discussed further in **chapter 11**.

1.15 Finally, a cautionary note. Many of the precedents in this book give alternatives in square brackets and some optional additions are bordered by obliques[1]. When using these precedents the draftsman should take the greatest care in the choice (and printing) of alternatives and additions. Wills in which these vital points have been overlooked make their way to the Probate Registry via the bowels of Lincoln's Inn. That a Will should undertake such a journey is embarrassing, expensive and can be source of great distress to the relatives of the testator.

1   Particular cases in point are the alternatives [husband]/[wife]/[civil partner] and [children]/[daughters]/[sons] and the optional contingency provisions such as /and attain 25.

2 General considerations

2.1 There are a number of general matters to take into account before taking instructions for the drafting of a Will. In this chapter some space is given over to:
- Severing a joint tenancy.
- The intestacy rules and the likely consequences of a testator making no Will.
- The capacity of a testator to make a Will and other challenges which might be made by way of probate claim.
- The potential for claims to be made under the Inheritance (Provision for Family and Dependants) Act 1975 by claimants who consider that the testator has not made reasonable provision for them.
- Consideration of issues of domicile and foreign property.

2.2 For the most part the Will draftsman need only be alert to the problems which might arise in relation to these matters. It is not necessary for him to consider the hypothetical consequences and it is not the purpose of this book to delve too deeply into any of these areas so only a brief account is given of each of them. However, it is important that the Will draftsman obtains proper instructions and to do so he must consider such matters as whether property is held on a joint tenancy and, if so, whether the joint tenancy ought to be brought to an end. Further information, particularly in connection with the litigious aspects of probate and administration of estates claims including claims under the Inheritance (Provision for Family and Dependants) Act 1975, can be found in a variety of more specialised texts.

Severance of a joint tenancy

2.3 Property of any sort (whether land or personal property) held jointly with another does not form part of the estate (except for inheritance tax purposes) if held under a joint tenancy. It is important, therefore, for the Will draftsman to establish whether there is any property held on a joint tenancy when the Will is drawn since a gift that purports to dispose of an interest in property held on a joint tenancy will fail. This is because on the death of one of two or more persons entitled to property under a beneficial joint tenancy, the whole of the beneficial interest in the property accrues to the surviving joint tenant(s) by right of survivorship. It does not pass by Will and no part of it devolves on the personal representatives of the deceased joint tenant. It is not that the beneficial interest of the deceased person passes to others, but that it simply ceases to exist as an asset at all[1].

1 Administration of Estates Act 1925 s 3(4).

2.4 Not all property held by persons jointly is held on a joint tenancy and this is something that many people find difficult to grasp. There is a fundamental distinction

2.5 *General considerations*

between property held by two or more persons on a joint tenancy and property held by them as tenants in common and this is all the more important in land law where the asset in question may be very valuable. The distinction, though usually encountered in relation to land, also applies to other property (such as bank accounts), which may also be held either jointly or in common yet recorded as held by persons in joint names.

2.5 When one is concerned with land owned by more than one person the title (which is the legal registered interest) must be held by them jointly because a legal estate in land cannot be held on a tenancy in common. The joint title holders are only trustees holding the legal interest in the land. Usually, in the case of land, the trustees and the beneficiaries are the same people but the distinction remains important. It is the nature of the beneficial interests that is of concern to the Will draftsman because these may be held either as joint tenants beneficially (where the survivor takes all), or as tenants in common beneficially (where each beneficial owner has a 'share' which can be disposed of by Will). Because the distinction is not widely understood, many clients talk about having 'a share' of a property even though they own it as beneficial joint tenants. If the Will draftsman simply takes the client's word at face value and includes a gift of 'my share of the property at ...' he can get into serious trouble when it turns out that the property in question was owned by the client and another as beneficial joint tenants so that nothing passes under the gift in the Will[1]. It is important that the draftsman appreciates that, in the case of land, the absence of a restriction on the title is not determinative of the question whether the property is held as joint tenants or as tenants in common.

1   A Will does not bring a joint tenancy to an end (*Gould v Kemp* (1834) 2 My & K 304) although, in an extreme case, it is possible that instructions given by joint owners in connection with Will-making might amount to a course of dealing or mutual agreement (*Re Woolnough, Perkins v Borden* [2002] WTLR 595).

2.6 The solution to the uncertainty that sometimes arises where the nature of the beneficial ownership of property is not known is to 'sever' the beneficial joint tenancy. This process does not alter the way in which legal title is held, but affects the devolution of the beneficial interests by converting the beneficial interests into shares held on a tenancy in common. There are various means of doing this including:

- an act of any one of the persons interested operating upon his own share;
- mutual agreement[1]; and
- a course of dealing between the joint tenants sufficient to intimate that their interests were mutually treated as constituting a tenancy in common[2].

In the case of land, a beneficial joint tenancy is most often severed by giving a notice in writing in accordance with Law of Property Act 1925 s 36(2)[3]. This course is recommended wherever there is uncertainty as to whether a gift will pass by survivorship or under a Will and the result is important. Of course, where the testator is leaving the whole of his estate or the entire interest in the property in question to the surviving joint tenant, severance is not important but it will remain a relevant consideration where the ultimate destination of the property is intended to vary depending upon the order in which the joint tenants die.

1   As in *Burgess v Rawnsley* [1975] Ch 429.
2   See, for example, *Wilson v Bell* (1843) 5 I Eq R 501. An agreement to make mutual Wills is effective for this purpose: *Re Wilford* (1879) 11 Ch D 267; *Re Heys* [1914] P 192.
3   An example and further discussion of service of a notice of severance can be found in **chapter 24**.

The intestacy rules

2.7 The statutory intestacy rules laid down in Administration of Estates Act 1925 ss 46 to 47A are set out in the appendix[1]. The intestacy rules are currently the subject

General considerations **2.14**

of a thorough review by the Law Commission as part of its tenth programme of law reform (2008–11). Results are not expect to be available until mid-2011 and any legislation brought in as a result should not be expected to take effect until 2011–12.

1   **Appendix 27.1 to 27.3**.

2.8 An intestacy occurs where there is no disposition or an incomplete disposition of a person's estate either because he has not left a Will or has left a Will which fails to dispose of all of his property or the whole of the beneficial interest in that property.

2.9 The latter case is called a partial intestacy. A partial intestacy is apt to describe the case of a Will which fails to dispose of property of a particular physical description such as that of the testator who disposes of all of his money and other personal property but fails to dispose of his house. This is easily avoided by the Will draftsman making use of a comprehensive gift of residue.

2.10 A partial intestacy also occurs in the more subtle case where a testator disposes of an interest in his property but fails completely to dispose of all interests. Thus, a testator who makes provision for the disposition of a capital interest in property but fails to dispose of the intermediate income (or vice versa) may inadvertently create a partial intestacy. Similarly, a testator might dispose of property on the happening of a contingency but comprehensively fail to include provisions disposing of the property in the event of the contingency not being satisfied[1]. It is this kind of partial intestacy which the Will draftsman should be jealous to avoid.

1   As in *Re Bowen-Buscarlet's Will Trusts* [1972] Ch 463 where, as a result of a drafting mishap, the testator's Will gave a life interest in residue to his widow but did not provide for what was to happen thereafter.

2.11 Cases of apparent partial intestacy, particularly of the latter kind, can give rise to difficult questions of construction which the Will draftsman should strive to avoid and, where there is a genuine partial intestacy, are prone to giving rise to even more difficult problems of distribution[1].

1   The application of the intestacy rules to cases of partial intestacy is governed by Administration of Estates Act 1925 s 49 but, as *Re Bowen-Buscarlet's Will Trusts* [1972] Ch 463 and *Re McKee* [1931] 2 Ch 145 show, the outcome can be difficult to fathom. Section 49 is not reproduced in the appendix: a Will draftsman should not have cause to look at it.

2.12 The intestacy rules make provision for the residuary estate of an intestate[1] to be distributed in the manner or held according to the trusts described in Administration of Estates Act 1925 s 46[2]. The distribution varies in the first instance according to whether or not the intestate leaves a spouse or civil partner.

1   Residuary estate is defined at Administration of Estates Act 1925 s 33(4). It is the property remaining after all debts etc have been paid.
2   Reproduced in **appendix 27.1**.

2.13 If there is a spouse or civil partner but no issue and no parent or brother or sister or nephew or niece then the spouse or civil partner takes the whole of the residuary estate absolutely. In every other case the interest taken by the spouse or civil partner is cut down to some extent, even if there are no children or parents of the intestate but, for example, one sister survives.

2.14 Thus, if the intestate leaves a wife and children the rules dictate that the spouse will take the personal chattels[1] absolutely, a fixed sum (irrespective of the value of the estate), a life interest in one-half of the remainder of the residuary estate with the remainder (including the interest falling in on the wife's death) being held on trusts prescribed by Administration of Estates Act 1925 s 47[2] for the children. Where there are children, this fixed sum is £250,000 but if there are no children the fixed sum is

2.15 *General considerations*

£450,000[3]. For the most part people who die intestate leaving a spouse and children have either given the question of the disposition of their estate no thought at all or mistakenly believe that their spouse will inherit everything[4]. Practically nobody dies intestate intending the result achieved by the intestacy rules.

1   Defined at Administration of Estates Act 1925 s 55(1)(x): see **appendix 20.17**. The spouse takes these irrespective of value.
2   See **appendix 22.2**.
3   Prior to 1 February 2009, the sums were £125,000 and £200,000.
4   By far the worst offenders are unmarried cohabiting couples, a surprisingly large proportion of whom believe that they acquire rights as 'common law husband and wife'; a belief which has only been encouraged by the title of the Civil Partnership Act 2004. Mere cohabitees are, of course, complete strangers to the intestacy rules. At the time of writing the Law Commission has been consulting about what protection might be afforded to unmarried cohabiting couples and this is under review.

2.15 The restrictive nature of these provisions and the fact that they do not apply to unmarried cohabiting couples is often not appreciated by the layman and the avoidance of their inflexible impact is often the best reason a Will draftsman can give for his employment.

Capacity and probate claims

2.16 A Probate Claim is a claim for the grant of probate of a Will, or letters of administration of the estate, of a deceased person; the revocation of such a grant; or a decree pronouncing for or against the validity of an alleged Will; not being a claim which is non-contentious (or common form) probate business. It is hostile Chancery litigation which, even with the best 'will' in the world, a Will draftsman cannot necessarily avoid. However, it is possible for a Will draftsman to minimise the risk of a Probate Claim being brought.

2.17 Probate Claims usually involve allegations of one or more of the following:
(1) That the testator did not properly execute his Will.
(2) That the testator lacked testamentary capacity to make a Will.
(3) That the testator did not know or approve the contents of his Will.
(4) That the testator was acting under undue influence when the Will was made.
(5) That the Will was made by fraud.

Will draftsmen can minimise the risk of these allegations being made out by taking the following steps.

2.18 Execution of the Will under the supervision of the Will draftsman or some other person properly equipped and qualified to supervise execution (see **chapter 14**) will usually suffice to extinguish any claim that the Will was not properly executed. A full attendance note should be kept.

2.19 The test of testamentary capacity derives from the well-known statement of Cockburn CJ in *Banks & Goodfellow*[1], as follows:

> 'It is essential to the exercise of such a power that a testator shall understand the nature of the act and its effects; shall understand the extent of the property of which he is disposing; shall be able to comprehend and appreciate the claims to which he ought to give effect; and with a view to the latter object, that no disorder of the mind shall poison his affections, pervert his sense of right, or prevent the exercise of his natural faculties – that no insane delusion shall

influence his will in disposing of his property and bring about a disposal of it which, if the mind had been sound, would not have been made.'

That classic statement provides the test of capacity today and is repeatedly cited in Probate Claims.

1   (1870) LR 5 QB 549 at 565.

2.20   This means that four things must exist at one and the same time[1]:

(1) the testator must be capable of understanding that he is giving his property to one or more objects of his regard;
(2) he must be capable of understanding and recollecting the extent of his property;
(3) he must also be capable of understanding the nature and extent of the claims upon him both of those who he is including in his Will and those who he is excluding from his Will; and
(4) no insane delusion shall influence his Will in disposing of his property and bring about a disposal of it which, if the mind had been sound, would not have been made.

1   *Sharp v Adam* [2006] WTLR 1059.

2.21   The Mental Capacity Act 2005 and the Code of Practice provide a new definition of capacity. As the Code of Practice explains, this new definition is not intended to replace the common law tests but to build on them. As cases come before the court, it may be that judges will consider the new statutory definition and they may use it to develop common law rules in particular cases. Testamentary capacity is one of those referred to in the Mental Capacity Act Code of Practice but it is not at all clear that that Act and the Code are intended to apply to everyday Will-making. In *Scammell v Farmer* [2008] WTLR 1261, the court declined to apply the test laid down by the Mental Capacity Act 2005 in so far as it differs from the common law test (if at all).

2.22   Mental Capacity Act 2005 provides that the starting point should be that there is a presumption of capacity and lack of capacity is determined by reference to a 'functional' approach which is 'decision specific'. Thus, under the Act a person lacks capacity in relation to a matter if at the material time he is unable to make a decision for himself in relation to the matter because of an impairment of, or a disturbance in the functioning of, the mind or brain. It does not matter whether the impairment or disturbance is permanent or temporary.

2.23   For these purposes, a person is unable to make a decision for himself if he is unable:

(a) to understand the information relevant to the decision;
(b) to retain that information;
(c) to use or weigh that information as part of the process of making the decision; or
(d) to communicate his decision (whether by talking, using sign language or any other means).

2.24   The test focuses on how the decision is made rather than the outcome of it. The Act says that a person is unable to make a decision if he is unable to satisfy any of those tests. It may be some time before one is able to say whether these new provisions have any effect on contentious probate claims and the peculiar nature of some aspects of probate claims – such as the rule in *Parker v Felgate*[1].

2.25 General considerations

1   (1883) 8 P & D 171. The rule is that if a testator has given instructions to a solicitor at a time when he was able to appreciate what he was doing in all its relevant bearings, and if the solicitor prepares the Will in accordance with these instructions, the Will will stand good, though at the time of execution the testator is capable only of understanding that he is executing the Will which he has instructed, but is no longer capable of understanding the instructions themselves or the clauses in the Will which give effect to them.

2.25 In cases in which the Will draftsman is doubtful about a testator's capacity there is a limit to what he can do. It is said that there is a 'golden rule' that where there is a doubt as to the capacity of an old and infirm testator's capacity, a medical practitioner should be present both to witness the Will and to examine the testator and make a record of his findings[1]. However, that is not, of itself, a touchstone of validity, but only a means of minimising disputes[2]. At the very least a Will draftsman should ascertain whether a testator has made a Will before (and discover the terms of that Will)[3] and ask open questions such as 'why, what, who or when' in order to elucidate the true intentions of the testator[4]. It is important, also, that a Will draftsman should take and retain an accurate note of his instructions. A Will draftsman can do no more than that in an area which, when questions arise, is always subject to serious disputes of fact.

1   *Re Simpson* (1977) 121 Sol Jo 24; *Kenward v Adams* [1975] CLY 3591.
2   *Cattermole v Prisk* [2006] 1 FLR 693.
3   *Hoff v Atherton* [2005] WTLR 99.
4   *Buckenham v Dickenson* [2000] WTLR 1083.

2.26 Taking instructions for the Will exclusively from the testator and in the absence of any person who might benefit thereunder and reading the Will over to the testator before execution generally provides an adequate defence to any allegation that a testator did not know or approve the contents of the Will[1]. An appropriate attestation clause[2] is of presumptive importance.

1   *Barry v Butlin* (1838) 2 Moo PCC 480.
2   See **chapter 14**.

2.27 At the other extreme, a Will draftsman who takes instructions by telephone from the principal beneficiary and posts a Will to him for the testator to execute could not possibly give evidence that the testator knew or approved the contents. There are many scenarios in between but a Will draftsman should always avoid taking instructions for a Will with the principal beneficiary present. In a perfect world the Will draftsman would only ever take instructions from the testator, having first satisfied himself that the testator is who he claims to be.

2.28 In the case of Wills, undue influence means coercion. As Sir J P Wilde put it[1]:

> 'Persuasion is not unlawful, but pressure of whatever character if so exerted as to overpower the volition without convincing the judgment of the testator, will constitute undue influence, though no force is either used or threatened.'

Undue influence, even in the form of coercion, is often well hidden from third parties. The best that a Will draftsman can do is to see the testator alone and have his instructions confirmed in that way but there is no plain and obvious means of avoiding undue influence where it occurs.

1   *Hall v Hall* (1868) LR 1 P&D 481 at 482.

2.29 Fraud is a serious matter which, in the case of Wills, usually involves falsifying the testator's signature. That is not something which should concern a Will draftsman provided he is satisfied that the person instructing him is who they claim to be.

Claims under the Inheritance (Provision for Family and Dependants) Act 1975

2.30 Testators have unrestricted freedom of testamentary disposition in England and Wales in name only. Under the Inheritance (Provision for Family and Dependants) Act 1975, a variety of individual classes of individual applicant may make an application to the court for an award on the basis that the testator's Will[1] fails to make reasonable financial provision for them. A claim lies only where the testator died domiciled in England and Wales and should ordinarily be made within six months of the grant of representation being obtained[2] although permission may be given to make a claim out of time[3]. A large number of such claims are made every year. The vast majority arise in cases of intestacy and, of those, most are brought by the survivor of two cohabitees, for whom the intestacy rules make no provision whatsoever. Some claims, however, are brought by persons who believe that a Will has failed to make reasonable financial provision for them. Often these arise in cases of second marriages where there is conflict between the surviving spouse and the children of a previous marriage either because the children perceive that their inheritance is being paid to a stranger or because the testator has made substantial provision for the children without appreciating what effect this might have on the surviving spouse.

1 The Act also applies on intestacy.
2 Inheritance (Provision for Family and Dependants) Act 1975 s 4.
3 This book is not concerned with technical or procedural aspects of such claims. Reference should be made to specialist texts where appropriate.

2.31 For the purposes of the Will draftsman it is important only to be alert to the possibility that a claim might be made under the Act and to advise the testator accordingly. It is not the job of the Will draftsman to seek to persuade the testator to make provision for potential claimants even where it is apparent that a testator is set on a course likely to provoke a potential claimant to make a claim. However, it is always sensible to keep an attendance note of the advice given in order to avoid or minimise future difficulty for the Will draftsman.

2.32 Not everyone is a potential claimant but the following persons may make an application for reasonable financial provision under the Act as of right:
(1) the husband or wife or civil partner of the testator;
(2) the former husband or wife or civil partner of the testator who has not remarried or formed a new civil partnership[1];
(3) in the case of persons dying after 1 January 1996, a person who during the whole period of two years ending immediately before the testator's death was living in the same household as the testator as the husband or wife or civil partner of the testator;
(4) a child of the testator;
(5) a person treated by the testator as a child of the family in respect of a marriage or civil partnership to which the testator was a party; and
(6) any other person not included in the above categories who immediately before the testator's death was being maintained wholly or partly by the testator.

In order to avoid difficulty after death and as a matter of good practice the Will draftsman should inquire whether there is anyone in those categories and ask the testator to consider whether and what provision is being made for those persons by his Will.

1 More often than not the court makes an order on the determination of ancillary relief proceedings following dissolution or annulment which has the effect of preventing a former spouse from claiming under the Act. As yet no civil partnerships have been dissolved or annulled but the practice in such cases is likely to be similar.

2.33 General considerations

2.33 It does not follow that a person who is within one of the recognised classes of applicant will be able to make out a claim under the Act. When considering an application under the Act, the court may only make an order if it concludes that the testator's Will fails to make reasonable financial provision for the applicant. Sometimes it is reasonable to make no provision for a potential applicant. Mature adult children with their own financial security and to whom the testator owes a moral obligation no greater than the paternal or maternal bond ordinarily requires will have considerable difficulty in maintaining a claim. There is, however, nothing that can be done to stop a determined applicant from pursuing a claim against the estate even if that claim is ultimately unsuccessful.

2.34 If the court is satisfied that the testator's Will fails to make reasonable financial provision for the applicant it must then go on to consider what reasonable financial provision for the applicant would be in all of the circumstances. The Act sets out a number of factors which the court must take into account at both stages of this process. These are:

(1) the size of the net estate;
(2) the financial needs and resources of the applicant, or which the applicant is likely to have in the foreseeable future;
(3) the financial needs and resources of the beneficiaries of the estate, or which such beneficiaries are likely to have in the foreseeable future;
(4) the financial needs and resources of any other applicant under the Act;
(5) the obligations and responsibilities owed by the testator to any applicant under the Act or to any beneficiary of the estate;
(6) any physical or mental disability of any applicant for an order or any beneficiary; and
(7) any other matter which the court may consider relevant, including the conduct of the applicant or the testator.

2.35 There are other factors which depend upon the identity of the applicant. Thus:

- Where an application is brought by a spouse, former spouse, civil partner or former civil partner the court must take into account the age of the applicant, the duration of the marriage or civil partnership and the contribution made by the applicant to the welfare of the family. In the case of an application by a spouse or civil partner where there has not been a decree of judicial separation, the court must have regard to the provision which the applicant might have expected to receive on divorce.
- In the case of an application made by a co-habitee, the court must consider the age of the applicant, the length of time that the applicant lived as the husband or wife or civil partner of the testator and any contribution made to the welfare of the testator's family.
- In the case of an application by a child or a person treated as the child, the court must consider whether the testator had assumed responsibility for the applicant's maintenance, the basis upon which he had done so, the length of time for which he had maintained the applicant and, in the latter case, whether or not he did so knowing the applicant was not his child and whether or not anyone else had responsibility for the applicant's maintenance. The court must also consider the manner in which the applicant was being or was expected to be educated or trained.
- In the case of an application by a person who was being maintained by the testator, the court must have regard to the length of time for which the person had been maintained by the testator, and the basis upon which the testator had assumed responsibility for the applicant's maintenance.

2.36 The factors set out above are to be determined at the date of the hearing of the application and so there is a limit to what the testator might do to mitigate the prospects of a claim when making a Will and an obvious limit to the sort of cautionary advice which a Will draftsman might give when taking instructions for the preparation of a Will, but it is still important to consider whether the testator might be making a Will which makes little or no provision for his wife or for someone being maintained by him by, for example, the provision of free accommodation.

2.37 Partly as a result of the ability of applicants to claim under the Act it is no longer considered sensible or appropriate to provide a surviving spouse or civil partner with no more than an interest under a discretionary trust – which is no interest at all – or with a mere right of residence in the matrimonial home or with an income interest which determines on marriage or on the formation of a civil partnership[1].

1   A different test of reasonable financial provision is applied depending upon whether or not the application is made by the surviving spouse/civil partner or another. In the case of an application by a surviving spouse or civil partner, 'reasonable financial provision' means such provision it would have been reasonable for the testator to have made, whether or not that provision is required for the surviving spouse's or civil partner's maintenance. In all other cases, 'reasonable financial provision' means such provision as it would have been reasonable for the applicant to receive for his maintenance (a term in respect of which there is no statutory definition). A discretionary trust might be appropriate for a class of children but often leaves a spouse with no security, especially in the case of second marriages where the identity of the trustees may cause friction. This and other complicated structures are best avoided.

2.38 Testators often find the concept of their wishes being challenged and the uncertain nature of the challenge difficult to grasp. In providing this basic advice to the testator it is important to explain that the test of 'reasonable financial provision' is entirely objective. The question is not whether the testator has been unreasonable in his own mind in the way he has acted, but whether or not the provision made for the applicant is in fact unreasonable.

Foreign issues

Domicile

2.39 Most people have an obvious domicile but, for some, it can be difficult to determine. No person may have more than one domicile and everybody has one from the moment of their birth to the moment of their death. In England and Wales a person's domicile is, for practical purposes, synonymous with his permanent home. All are born with a domicile of origin as a matter of law but domicile may change through choice or dependency.

2.40 Foreign jurisdictions may have a radically different concept of domicile and many are more reliant on concepts of residence or nationality which are quite different and, from the English and Welsh perspective, less permanent.

2.41 In the UK there is also a concept of fiscal domicile[1] for inheritance tax purposes by which a person who does not have a domicile in England and Wales under the general law – either through not having acquired it or through having lost it – may nonetheless be deemed domiciled in the UK for inheritance tax. The importance of this is that UK inheritance tax is charged on the worldwide estate of a person with domicile in the UK. Where questions of inheritance tax mitigation are concerned the deemed domicile of a testator is as important as his actual domicile.

1   Inheritance Tax Act 1984 s 267.

2.42 *General considerations*

Wills and foreign property

2.42 The English private international law of succession is a non-trivial jurisprudence derived from a number of sources but the essential rules can be found in *Dicey, Morris & Collins, The Conflict of Laws* and, although *Dicey* is not an authority per se, it is generally treated as such and the rules relating to succession are not seriously questioned. *Dicey* includes the following rules in relation to the English[1] private international law treatment of succession:

- The material or essential validity of a Will of movables or of any particular gift of movables contained therein is governed by the law of the testator's domicile at the time of his death.
- The material or essential validity of a Will of immovables or of any particular gift of immovables contained therein is governed by the law of the country where the immovables are situated.
- A Will is to be interpreted in accordance with the law intended by the testator. In the absence of indications to the contrary, this is presumed to be the law of his domicile at the time when the Will is made.

The meaning of these rules is largely self-evident.

1   *Dicey* records the view from the English perspective. An additional complication is that foreign jurisdictions may not draw the same distinction between movable and immovable property or apply rules of domicile (as opposed to residence or nationality) in determining which legal system to apply.

2.43 In addition to the validity of Wills there may be questions as to the succession to movable and immovable property in different jurisdictions. Many foreign jurisdictions, including most continental jurisdictions in which English and Welsh domiciled testators are likely to own property, have entrenched concepts of forced succession which severely restrict the testamentary freedom of testators.

2.44 These considerations are of the utmost importance to the Will draftsman who is considering making a Will for a testator with foreign domicile or for a testator domiciled in England and Wales who owns immovable property abroad. In either case, but particularly in the latter (more common) scenario, it is extremely foolish to draft a Will with international scope without taking advice from a lawyer in the correct jurisdiction. Great care should also be taken with revocation clauses in Wills, whether intended to deal with a testator's worldwide estate or to dispose of property in a more limited territory. It is all too easy for a carelessly drawn Will to revoke a foreign Will by mistake although the mistake is usually not so much in the drafting but in taking instructions. The questionnaire in **chapter 24** asks explicit questions about foreign property in order to minimise this risk but there is nothing in this book which ought to lead a Will draftsman to set about drafting a foreign Will. That is a specialist topic which requires specialist advice.

3 Opening and revocation

3.1 The practice followed here is to begin a Will with the name and address of the testator, a statement that all testamentary dispositions are revoked and a statement that the document constitutes the testator' last Will. In this book the date of the Will appears at the end in the testimonium and attestation clause because it is thought that insertion of the date is less likely to be forgotten if it is located there. There is, however, nothing wrong with inserting the date elsewhere, although it would be a little perverse to choose somewhere other than the beginning or end of the document.

Identity of the testator

3.2 The full name and address of the testator should be given for clarity. It is sometimes necessary to state an alias. The draftsman should consider whether the circumstances require this. Where a testator is generally known by the name he commonly uses, it is usually unnecessary to state his alias in the Will and reference to his alternative name may create problems which would not otherwise exist. Reference to the alias will be desirable where it has been used in his birth certificate, marriage certificate or documents of title.

3.3 There are five fairly common situations in which care should be taken:
(1) Where the testator has used two names fairly indiscriminately. In this case, it is important that both names are stated in the Will, because it will probably be found that some documents of title are in one name and some in another.
(2) Where the testator has changed his name by assuming another name, with or without formalities. In these circumstances it is usually desirable to make reference to his former name but it is not necessary to describe how the name came to be changed, for example, by reciting that it was effected by deed poll or the particular date on which it was changed.
(3) Where the testator has habitually used his forenames in a different order from that in which they were given, for example, George Albert instead of Albert George[1].
(4) Where the testator has never used the full names he was given at birth but has, throughout his life, been known by a different name[2]. In this case, much depends on whether he has ever used his given name in documents of title or, for example, when marrying. Often it transpires that in formal documents the testator has always used his given name and only used the name by which he is commonly known informally. In this case it may not be necessary to refer to the names by which he is commonly known, although it would be sensible to do so.

3.4 *Opening and revocation*

In each of the above situations **Form 3.2** is suitable.

(5) Where the testator has anglicised a foreign name. There is little point in referring to the testator's original name in the Will especially where there is the practical difficulty of its not being expressed in the Roman alphabet. In such a case **Form 3.1** suffices.

> 1 This is quite common. For example, both the author's father and his mother-in-law are habitually known by their second names.
> 2 This is also quite common. For example, the author's sister has been known since birth by a name that makes no appearance on her birth certificate.

3.4 There are families in which it is customary to give the eldest son the same name as his father so that there are John Smiths covering three or even four generations. In the fullness of time 'the younger' or 'junior' becomes 'the elder' or 'senior'. The simplest way of dealing with this problem is to give the address but occasionally the two will live at the same address and it will be necessary to state the date of birth after the testator's name. This is a sensible way of distinguishing between two persons of the same name who belong to the same family or have the same address. **Form 3.3** is an example.

Revocation

By act of the testator

3.5 A Will is revoked by destruction either by the testator or by some other person in his presence and by his direction with the testator having the intention of revoking it[1]. A Will is only revoked by a subsequent Will to the extent that the later Will is inconsistent with the earlier one. For this reason, and also because the testator may have forgotten having made an earlier Will, it is desirable to include an express revocation clause in a new Will.

> 1 Wills Act 1837 s 20, **appendix 25.9**. The section refers to 'burning, tearing, or otherwise destroying'.

3.6 It is sometimes contended that 'testamentary disposition' is a wider term than 'Will' because it extends to a Will made by a serviceman on active service. Wills Act 1837 s 1[1], however, provides that:

> 'The word "Will" shall extend to a testament and to a codicil and ... to any other testamentary disposition.'

and s 20[2] provides (as to written revocation):

> 'No Will ... shall be revoked otherwise than by ... some writing declaring an intention to revoke the same and executed in the manner in which a Will is hereinbefore required to be executed.'

This book, therefore, eschews any form of revocation other than the simple clauses appearing in this section using express words of revocation. However, care should be taken where the testator has property overseas which devolves according to a Will taking effect in a different jurisdiction. In such a case the words of revocation used should not have universal effect[3].

> 1 For Wills Act 1837 s 1 see **appendix 25.1**.
> 2 For Wills Act 1837 s 20 see **appendix 25.9**.
> 3 See **5.2** and **Form 5.1** at **5.9**.

3.7 Not all property which passes on death will be governed by the Will. For example, there may have been nominations. These, although not in the form of a Will, will be effective to dispose on death of monies due from National Savings accounts, friendly societies, industrial and provident societies and other property such as death in service benefits. The Will does not alter these. If they are to be changed, new nominations will be required.

3.8 Similarly, if the testator's interest in property held under a beneficial joint tenancy is to pass under the Will and not by survivorship, the joint tenancy must be severed. See the commentary in **chapter 2** at **2.3** to **2.6**.

By marriage or civil partnership

3.9 A Will is, of course, revoked by marriage[1] or by the formation of a civil partnership[2] unless it was made in expectation of that marriage or civil partnership. In such a case the Will is not revoked by the contemplated act. See **3.12**.

1   Wills Act 1837 s 18, see **appendix 25.5**.
2   Wills Act 1837 s 18B(1), added by Civil Partnership Act 2004 s 71, Sch 4 para 2, see **appendix 25.7**.

By decree of divorce or nullity or dissolution of civil partnership

3.10 Wills Act 1837 s 18A[1] provides that, if the testator's marriage is dissolved or annulled, gifts to a former spouse will fail. Wills Act 1837 s 18C[2] provides that gifts to a former civil partner will fail if the civil partnership is dissolved. The appointment of the spouse or civil partner as executor is also rendered ineffective. The Will itself is not revoked.

1   Wills Act 1837 s 18A, inserted by Administration of Justice Act 1982 s 18(2) with effect from 1 January 1983 but subsequently substituted by Law Reform (Succession) Act 1995 s 3 (see below) with effect from 1 January 1996 see **appendix 25.6**.
2   Wills Act 1837 s 18C, added by Civil Partnership Act 2004 s 71, Sch 4 para 2, see **appendix 25.8**.

3.11 In its original form, s 18A provided that divorce or annulment would result in any gift by a testator to his spouse lapsing. In *Re Sinclair*[1], the testator had given the whole of his estate to his wife, with a gift over to charity if she failed to survive him. His marriage was dissolved and he subsequently died without changing his Will. The Court of Appeal held that, although the gift to his former wife failed, the gift over to the charity was contingent on her predeceasing the testator and not on its merely lapsing. Consequently the gift over was inoperative and the estate fell to be distributed as an intestacy. Section 18A was amended by the Law Reform (Succession) Act 1995 so that divorce or annulment results in the testator's spouse being treated as having died on the date of the divorce or annulment. Section 18C is in like terms where a civil partnership is dissolved or a court makes a nullity order in respect of it. This means that, if *Re Sinclair* came before the court now, the charity would take the gift.

1   [1985] Ch 446, [1985] 1 All ER 1066, CA.

Will made in expectation of marriage or civil partnership

3.12 The marriage of, or formation of a civil partnership by the testator revokes an existing Will unless it appears from the Will itself that it was made in expectation of that marriage[1] or civil partnership[2] and is not to be revoked by it. The phrase

3.12 *Opening and revocation*

'expecting to marry' or 'expecting to form a civil partnership' is used in the following forms but no magic formula is needed so long as the Will indicates the expected marriage or civil partnership. The Will can be of unlimited duration but it is not possible to make a Will in the expectation of marrying or forming a civil partnership with the world in general. The testator must be expecting to marry a specific person or to form a civil partnership with a specific person for the Will not to be revoked by the occurrence of that event.

1   Wills Act 1837 s 18, see **appendix 25.5**.
2   Wills Act 1837 s 18B(3), see **appendix 25.7**.

PRECEDENTS

3.13

FORM 3.1

Usual opening with revocation[1]

I, [*full name*] of [*home address*] revoke all earlier Wills and declare this to be my last Will.

1   For a discussion, see **3.2** and **3.5**.

FORM 3.2[1]

Opening with revocation where the testator has an alias, has changed his name or has sometimes used the name appearing on his birth certificate which is not the name by which he is informally known

I, [*more common name*] [*otherwise*]/[*formerly*]/[*commonly*] known as [*alias or original name*] of [*home address*] revoke all earlier Wills and declare this to be my last Will.

1   For a discussion of the various possibilities see **3.2**.

FORM 3.3[1]

Opening with revocation where the testator needs to be distinguished from a relative having the same name living at the same address

I, [*John Smith*] (born on [*date*]) of [*home address*] revoke all earlier Wills and declare this to be my last Will.

1   See the note at **3.4**.

FORM 3.4[1]

Opening where Will is to remain in force after marriage or civil partnership

I, [*full name*] of [*home address*] revoke all earlier Wills and declare this to be my last Will. This Will is not to be revoked by my intended [*marriage*]/[*civil partnership*] to [*name*] taking place[2].

1   See note at **3.12**.
2   Although the earlier legislation contained no provision that it should appear from the Will that the intended marriage was not to revoke the Will, Administration of Justice Act 1982 (which amended Wills Act 1837) requires it. See Wills Act 1837 ss 18, 18A and 18B, **appendix 25.5**, **25.6** and **25.7**.

3.13 *Precedents*

FORM 3.5

Opening where Will is to remain in force after marriage or civil partnership but is not to apply until then[1]

I, [*full name*] of [*home address*] make this Will expecting to [*marry*]/[*form a civil partnership with*] [*name*]. My Will dated [*date*][2] shall remain in force until my intended [*marriage*]/[*civil partnership*] revokes it after which this document constitutes my last Will.

1   Note that no general words of revocation should be included in this clause. See the notes at **3.9** and **3.12**.
2   Insert the date of the testator's existing Will.

FORM 3.6

Opening of Scheduled Will: first schedule immediately operative; second schedule to apply on revocation of first by marriage or civil partnership[1]

I, [*full name*] of [*home address*] revoke all earlier Wills and declare that I make this Will expecting to [*marry*]/[*form a civil partnership with*] [*name*]. The first schedule constitutes my Will until my intended [*marriage*]/[*civil partnership*] revokes it after which the second schedule constitutes my Will.

1   See the notes at **3.9** and **3.12**.

FORM 3.7

Opening where Will is made in contemplation of divorce etc[1]

I, [*full name*] of [*home address*] revoke all earlier Wills and declare that I make this Will expecting my [*marriage to*]/[*civil partnership with*] [*name*] to be [*dissolved*]/[*annulled*]. My Will dated [*date*][2] shall remain in force until the [*dissolution*]/[*annulment*] after which this document constitutes my last Will.

1   See the notes at **3.10**. Dissolution or annulment of a marriage does not revoke a Will but some testators will want to make provision for their erstwhile spouse or civil partner either until the moment of divorce or nullity but not thereafter or after the divorce or nullity notwithstanding that by statute the spouse or civil partner is excluded (by virtue of being treated as having died) by Wills Act 1837 ss 18A and 18C.
2   Insert the date of the testator's existing Will.

4 Declarations concerning joint, mutual and reciprocal Wills

4.1 A joint Will is a single document which embodies the Wills of two (or more) persons. On the death of each testator probate is obtained of the joint Will in respect of that deceased. Joint Wills are very unusual in this jurisdiction. They are more common (but not very common) in continental civil law jurisdictions. The draftsman should actively discourage testators from requiring the preparation of a joint Will (and for this reason no precedent is supplied). Whatever is the objective of those who suggest the making of a joint Will, it can be better achieved by individual Wills, for example, by mutual Wills. Even if the purpose of a joint Will is to exercise a joint power of appointment, this can be achieved by individual Wills in which each testator exercises the power in the same terms.

4.2 It is common for married couples to make reciprocal (or mirror) Wills where each wishes to leave his or her estate to the survivor or to the children if the testator is the survivor. Civil partners are also likely to make reciprocal Wills. Each of two reciprocal Wills is separate and there is no binding agreement as to revocation or alteration. These are quite distinct from mutual Wills.

4.3 Mutual Wills have a precise technical meaning. They are separate Wills executed under an agreement that they will not be revoked[1] or altered at least after one of the parties to the agreement has died. The agreement may, however, permit the alteration of some terms if the other provisions are retained.

---

1   Strictly the Will may be revoked whatever the agreement might provide. However, the personal representatives or executors of a later Will are subject to the terms of the agreement as expressed in the revoked Will.

4.4 An agreement for mutual Wills between the parties may be oral or in writing in a separate document but it is clearly desirable that the precise terms of the agreement should be expressed in the Will itself. Mutual Wills, like joint Wills, should be discouraged if possible. They are often much more restrictive (or less effective) than testators suppose, may be affected by factors beyond the control of the testators and, in the author's experience, are very much more likely to spawn litigation than more conventional testamentary instruments.

4.5 Clients who suggest the preparation of a joint or mutual Will have rarely foreseen the problems which may arise, for example:

(1)   a change in the circumstances after the death of one of them;

(2)   the remarriage or subsequent formation of a civil partnership of the survivor which will revoke the Will in spite of the agreement[1];

4.6 *Declarations concerning joint, mutual and reciprocal Wills*

(3) after remarriage or the subsequent formation of a civil partnership, the possibility of a claim under the Inheritance (Provision for Family and Dependants) Act 1975;

(4) the difficulty of preventing the survivor from depriving the ultimate beneficiaries of their prospective inheritance if he takes active steps to circumvent the agreement, for example, by making lifetime gifts[2].

1   If the survivor changes his Will, the executors of his new Will will be entitled to a grant of probate. The remedy of the ultimate beneficiaries under the original Will is to seek a declaration that the executors hold the estate on a constructive or floating trust to give effect to the terms of the original Will. This is a controversial and uncertain area. The remedy is equitable and the result can be highly uncertain. See *Re Green* [1951] Ch 148, [1950] 2 All ER 913. The same applies if the original Will is revoked by remarriage. The remarriage may not deprive the intended beneficiaries of a remedy but they might not obtain the benefit conferred by the revoked Will.

2   An issue addressed in Australia (see, for example, *Birmingham v Renfrew* (1936) 57 CLR 666 and *Palmer v Bank of New South Wales* (1975) 7 ALR 671) but, as yet, unresolved in this jurisdiction; see: *Re Dale (deceased)* [1994] Ch 31 and *Re Cleaver* [1981] 1 WLR 939.

4.6 Taking account of the problems and difficulties of mutual Wills and the cost of seeking to enforce the underlying agreement, many clients will decide that it would be better to trust the other party to honour a moral obligation, but even the recital of a moral obligation can encourage a claim under the Inheritance (Provision for Family and Dependants) Act 1975 by a disgruntled intended beneficiary[1].

1   Provided he falls into one of the classes of applicant contemplated by the Inheritance (Provision for Family and Dependants) Act 1975, briefly discussed in **chapter 2** at **2.30** to **2.38**.

4.7 Clients may insist on mutual Wills or require a provision to be included which imposes a moral obligation on the survivor to give effect to their joint intention so far as is practicable. **Forms 4.2** and **4.3** should be used together to create mutual Wills, although it is preferable if the terms of the agreement might be recited in the Will itself.

4.8 These precedents have been drafted on the basis that the instructions are from a married couple or two civil partners but reciprocal and mutual Wills are not restricted to married couples, civil partners or cohabitees nor need they confer a benefit on the survivor. For example, each may give the whole of the testator's estate to a third party.

PRECEDENTS

4.9

FORM 4.1

Clause reciting the creation of reciprocal but not mutual Wills[1]

This Will is not one of two mutual wills. [*Name*] is making a will in similar terms to this Will but we have agreed that our wills are not mutual wills and each of us shall be free to revoke his or her will at any time whether before or after the death of the other and be under no obligation or trust to dispose of any of his or her property in accordance with the terms of these wills.

1   It is suggested that this clause appears immediately after the revocation clause.

FORM 4.2

Clause creating a mutual Will[1]

This Will is made by agreement with my [*wife*]/[*civil partner*] [*name*] that we will make mutual Wills each of which is a mirror image of the other and that except by agreement between us neither Will shall be revoked or altered except in respect of administrative provisions.

1   It is suggested that this clause appears immediately after the revocation clause.

FORM 4.3

Agreement underpinning a mutual Will[1]

This Agreement dated   is made between:

(1) [Husband]/[First Civil Partner]; and

(2) [Wife]/[Second Civil Partner].

    1.1   We are making reciprocal Wills which will constitute mutual Wills but we have recognised that circumstances may change and that it is desirable that the survivor of us should be able to change his or her Will within certain limits.

    1.2   It is our intention that our residuary beneficiary [*name*][2] shall take the bulk of the estate passing under the Will of the survivor but a change of circumstances may make that impracticable.

2.   We have therefore agreed that:

    2.1   During our joint lives, neither of us will revoke or change the terms of his or her Will except by agreement with the other[3].

    2.2   The survivor will not revoke his or her Will nor vary it except:

4.9 *Precedents*

      2.2.1 to change any administrative provisions of the Will, for example, the appointment of executors and trustees;

      2.2.2 to revoke or reduce any legacy;

      2.2.3 to nominate an alternative beneficiary if the residuary beneficiary dies before the survivor of us.

[1] The precedent assumes that the clients wish to preserve the residue at the expense of legacies. The clients may however wish to preserve legacies rather than the residue and to avoid a pro rata reduction in legacies if the estate of the survivor is insufficient to enable all legacies to be paid in full. Detailed consideration and precise instructions are a prerequisite to the preparation of this agreement.

[2] This is a simple example. More often there are multiple beneficiaries from two family groups and the mutual wills are designed to protect the interests of the relatives of the first to die while giving the survivor more or less complete control of his estate during his lifetime.

[3] Particularly where the Wills are not to be revoked during the lifetime of the testators, a deed should be preferred to an agreement under hand.

5 Declarations Part I

5.1 This section sets out a number of declaratory provisions which often appear at the beginning of a Will. In earlier editions it was suggested that, generally, all declarations should appear at the end of the Will, grouped together as a single clause with each declaration used constituting a subclause of it. Many testators and most draftsmen prefer to include declarations concerning the jurisdictional extent of a Will, exclusion of relatives and directions as to the funeral at the beginning of a Will.

Declarations as to jurisdiction and exclusion

5.2 Two forms are included here as declarations but for a discussion of these topics see the general notes in **chapter 2** at **2.39** to **2.44**.

Directions concerning the disposal of the testator's body and funeral arrangements

5.3 Many testators wish to express wishes concerning their funeral and the disposal of their corpse in their Will although, strictly, it is the executors and not the testator who have the right to dispose of the testator's corpse[1]. Nonetheless, sometimes testators wish to give detailed instructions (occasionally, quite bizarre instructions) for their funeral arrangements. It is quite impossible to prepare precedents to cover detailed personal arrangements but the draftsman ought to inquire whether the testator wishes to give directions.

1   *Williams v Williams* (1882) 20 Ch D 659.

5.4 The testator should, in any event, be reminded that his funeral may well have been put into effect before the Will is found (and certainly before it has been proven) or been taken in hand by persons other than his intended executors, particularly where professional executors are appointed. Therefore, whatever direction the testator wishes to make in his Will, there is much to be said for the same wishes being expressed informally in a letter to the person likely to make the funeral arrangements. The more detailed the instructions required by a testator, the more important it is that his wishes are expressed in a separate document as well. Many draftsmen prefer detailed funeral arrangements to be expressed in a separate document and the Will merely to state:

> 'I have given detailed written instructions concerning my funeral arrangements to [*name*].'

5.5 *Declarations Part I*

A copy of these instructions can be kept with the Will if the testator so wishes.

5.5 Executors may incur all reasonable expenses in connection with the funeral and burial or cremation of the testator as a testamentary expense without any direction in the Will. Exceptional or unusual expenses should be authorised by the Will, although that is not a complete safeguard because the Will might not be proved.

Cremation

5.6 It is the executors and not the testator who have the right to dispose of the testator's corpse. It was formerly the case that the executors could not cremate the corpse if the testator had left a written declaration forbidding this. It is no longer unlawful to cremate the corpse of a testator who has left directions to the contrary.

Donation of the body

5.7 The donation of bodies is now covered by Human Tissue Act 2004[1]. The executors and in some cases others, including certain residential institutions, may make the donation and authorise the use of the body if there is no reason to believe that the deceased or a relative would object. There has recently been a shortage of bodies donated to medical schools for anatomical research which may have been exacerbated by the exposure of the public to the reality of televised dissections and the public exhibition of manipulated human remains.

[1] HTA 2004 repealed and replaced Anatomy Act 1984 with effect from 1 September 2006. Further information can be obtained from the Human Tissue Authority of Finlaison House, 15–17 Furnival Street, London EC4A 1AB; Tel: 020 7211 3400. There is a website at www.hta.gov.uk. The Human Tissue Authority is to be abolished under government cuts but is still in existence at the time of writing.

5.8 For the therapeutic use of human body parts in transplantation see the Human Tissue Act 2004. The inclusion of such directions in a Will is completely pointless because it will be far too late to implement the testator's wishes by the time the Will is read. A testator who wishes to donate organs for therapeutic use should carry a donor card and inform relations and doctors of his intentions.

PRECEDENTS

5.9

FORM 5.1

Foreign element[1]

This Will does not relate to my immovable property in [*name of country*] *or* [outside England and Wales] which is the subject of a separate Will made according to the law of that country.

or

This Will relates only to my property in England and Wales and does not affect any property elsewhere.

or

This Will relates only to my immovable property in England and Wales and does not affect any other property.

1   This form is for use where the testator has a foreign and an English Will. Settling Wills for testators with a foreign domicile is a highly specialised topic in connection with which the assistance of foreign lawyers will normally be required: see **chapter 2** at **2.39** to **2.44**. Even where a testator is domiciled in England and Wales advice from foreign lawyers may be required where there is substantial property situated abroad because although the rule for English conflict of laws purposes is that the law of the testator's domicile applies to movable property it is the law of the state in which immovables are situated which applies to them. Different states may form different views as to what is and what is not an immovable for these purposes and many non-common law jurisdictions impose restrictions on a testator's freedom to dispose of his property. Accordingly, for immovable property, such as a holiday home in France, a local (French) Will should be made on advice from local lawyers.
    The first alternative is for use by a testator who is domiciled in England but has immovable property elsewhere; it is assumed that for the immovable property a local Will applies but for movables wherever they may be, the English Will is to operate. The second alternative is for use in the situation in which a testator has property throughout the world and wishes this Will to dispose only of his property in England and Wales. The third alternative is for use in the situation in which a foreign domiciled testator requires a Will disposing of his English immovable property only.
    If a testator is to have different Wills taking effect in different jurisdictions special care should be taken to limit the scope of a revocation clause in order to avoid revoking foreign Wills which are intended to take effect.

FORM 5.2

Declaration of exclusion[1]

No provision is hereby made for my [*wife*]/[*civil partner*] [*name*] for the reasons set out in a letter signed by me and left with this my Will[2].

1   See **chapter 2** at **2.30** to **2.39**. This form need not refer exclusively to the spouse. It is often useful where no provision is made for a child of some other person who might be expected to be remembered in the Will.
2   It is usually inappropriate to set out the reasons in the Will itself as these may be scandalous and refused probate. However, where the reason is that the testator and the other person have reached an accommodation by deed or court order then there is much to be gained by reciting that agreement or order.

5.9 Precedents

FORM 5.3

Objection to cremation[1]

I do not wish to be cremated.

1   See the note at **5.6**.

FORM 5.4

Direction for cremation with deposit of ashes[1]

I wish to be cremated and to have my ashes deposited at [ ].

1   See the note at **5.6**.

FORM 5.5

Direction for cremation with ashes scattered[1]

I wish to be cremated and to have my ashes scattered over [ ].

1   See the note at **5.6**. It is important to consider whether the direction is capable of fulfilment.

FORM 5.6

Direction for funeral service followed by cremation[1]

I wish my body to be cremated following a funeral service at [*St Peter's Church St Albans*[2]] and to have my ashes [[deposited at [ ]]/[scattered over [ ]].

1   See the note at **5.5**. It is important to consider whether the direction is capable of fulfilment.
2   This is, of course, only an example.

FORM 5.7

Direction for funeral service[1]

I wish that my funeral service shall be held [*using the liturgy set out in the Book of Common Prayer*[2]] at [*St Peter's Church St Albans*[2]].

1   See the note at **5.5**. It is important to consider whether the direction is capable of fulfilment.
2   This is, of course, only an example.

FORM 5.8

Funeral arrangements: prepaid funeral[1]

I direct that my funeral shall be undertaken by [*AB & Co*] of [*address*] with whom I have deposited money for my funeral expenses [*under plan number #*].

1   See the notes at **5.3** to **5.5**. This has been included because it has become quite common for testators to enter into prior financial arrangements with funeral undertakers and it would be most unfortunate if those responsible for disposing of the body were not aware of the fact.

FORM 5.9

Direction for burial[1]

I wish to be buried.

1   See the notes at **5.3** to **5.5**.

FORM 5.10

Direction for burial with reference to specific plot[1]

I wish to be buried [*in the family grave at etc*[2]*]/[in the plot where my wife is buried*[2]*]*.

1   See the note at **5.5**.
2   Although not binding, it is important to consider whether the direction is capable of fulfilment in order to avoid or, at least, reduce the risk of painful and expensive disagreement among the family.

FORM 5.11

Donation of the body[1]

I wish my body to be used by [*name institution*] and I have made arrangements for this with the appropriate authorities.

or

I wish my body to be used for therapeutic purposes including the transplantation of my organs and corneal grafting by [*name of institution*] and I have made arrangements for this with the appropriate authorities[2]. I wish my body or what remains of it to be [*buried*]/[*cremated*][3]. Any expense incurred in giving effect to these wishes shall be an executorship expense.

1   See the note at **5.7**.
2   Including this direction in the Will is usually pointless: it is imperative that the testator should take advice from and make arrangements with the organisation which is to have his body. Often, any benefit is lost if there is a delay (and in some cases a very short delay) in the organisation receiving the body, for example, where organs from the body are to be transplanted. In the latter case the testator should carry a donor card and keep others informed of his intentions.
3   A donation will not necessarily dispose of the body and this will need to be considered either in the event of the donation being declined or after its purpose has been fulfilled. Some schools of anatomy will in the latter case undertake disposal.

6 Appointment of executors and trustees

6.1 Forms **6.1** to **6.12** are intended for use where there is no possibility of a continuing trust arising. In other cases, although the executors would, if a trust arose, ordinarily become trustees by implication and executors have a statutory power to appoint trustees, one of the other forms should be used. Many draftsmen will prefer to appoint 'executors and trustees', even if a trust is unlikely to arise, and then refer to the appointees as 'my Trustees'. Assuming this to be a common practice, the expression 'my Trustees' is used where appropriate in all the forms contained in this book.

6.2 In the headnotes and in many of the precedents the testator is assumed to be a man. This has not been done in order to offend those who subscribe to the doctrine of political correctness but because references to the testator's spouse or civil partner and the benefit conferred upon him or her results in long-winded paragraphs which are not always easy to follow. Similarly, the term 'executor' is used when the holder of that office is or may be a woman because it is found that most clients consider that the person responsible for the administration of the deceased's estate is called an 'executor' irrespective of sex (or gender if you prefer). For those who wish to be accurate, the correct term where a woman is appointed alone is 'executrix' and the plural (used only where all of those appointed are women) is 'executrices'.

Different executors and trustees

6.3 It is usually convenient to appoint the same people as executors and trustees and this is the common practice unless there is a compelling reason not to do so. Examples of such cases include estates where there might be foreign property, estates of authors where separate literary executors may be desirable and estates in which separate trustees might be needed to run a continuing business. Another case in which trustees who are not executors might be appointed is where testamentary guardians are appointed and it is desirable that one or both of them should be a trustee although it would be inconvenient for that person to be an executor. Sometimes a testator will want professional executors to realise his estate but decides that it is better if members of the family are responsible for the administration of the trust created.

Power to charge

6.4 It was formerly the case that, generally, a solicitor or other professional person could not charge for acting as executor or trustee unless the Will authorised him to charge for his services. Now[1], in the absence of an express remuneration clause, a trustee or personal representative acting in a professional capacity and who is not a sole trustee is entitled to receive reasonable remuneration for any services he provides (including services capable of being provided by a lay trustee[2]) if each other trustee has agreed in writing that he may be remunerated. Similarly, in the absence of an express remuneration clause, a trust corporation is entitled to receive reasonable remuneration for any services provided to or on behalf of the trust[3] including services which are capable of being provided by someone who is not a trust corporation[4].

1   Trustee Act 2000 s 29(2), see **appendix 26.55**.
2   Trustee Act 2000 s 28(1), (2), (5)–(6), see **appendix 26.54**.
3   Trustee Act 2000 s 29(1), see **appendix 26.55**.
4   Trustee Act 2000 s 28(1), (2), (6), see **appendix 26.54**.

6.5 Notwithstanding these provisions, where professional trustees or a trust corporation are appointed, express provision enabling the trustees to charge fees is still desirable because, without such a provision, a professional trustee will still have to obtain the consent of his co-trustees before charging; and, in the case of a trust corporation, the statutory reasonable remuneration might not extend to the scale fees often charged by such institutions.

6.6 In the case of an express remuneration clause, professional trustees' remuneration is to be regarded as remuneration, not as a gift[1], for the purposes of Wills Act 1837 s 15[2] and charges made are to be regarded as an administrative expense for the purposes of Administration of Estates Act 1925 s 34(3)[3]. It is no longer necessary for the Will to declare this to be the case.

1   Trustee Act 2000 s 28(4), see **appendix 26.54**.
2   See **appendix 25.4**.
3   Trustee Act 2000 ss 28(4)(b), 35(3)(a), see **appendix 26.54**. Administration of Estates Act 1925 s 34 concerns the order of application of assets and is not reproduced in the appendix.

6.7 The charging clause is often included in the Will as a declaration but a better practice is to incorporate it in the clause appointing executors and trustees as in the forms contained in this chapter. This emphasises its importance to the appointees and ensures that the testator is aware of its significance. The clause might be treated as a declaration if lay executors and trustees are appointed but the possible future appointment of professional trustees is envisaged[1].

1   For an example, see **Form 6.17**.

Appointment of solicitors

6.8 The testator may wish to appoint his solicitors as his executors – a practice encouraged by most firms as it ensures a continuing connection with the client and his estate. Future executorships are regarded almost as part of the goodwill of the practice and so firms are anxious that appointments should relate to the practice rather than to an individual partner.

6.9 The appointment of a solicitors' firm will operate as an appointment of the partners in the firm at the date of the Will unless the clause contains express provision to the contrary. **Form 6.12** provides that the appointment is of the partners in the firm at the date of the death of the testator but, as a convenience, the wish is expressed that not more than two of the partners should take out the grant of probate. **Form 6.12** attempts to overcome some of the problems which can arise where the firm changes its name, amalgamates with another firm, incorporates or becomes a limited liability partnership (as to which, see below) but there is no solution to the difficulty which

6.10 *Appointment of executors and trustees*

arises where an existing partnership is dissolved and the former partners establish two new firms which, between them, take over the existing clients of the old firm. Neither of the new firms is the successor to the practice of the old firm.

6.10 Where named partners in a firm are appointed (which is not generally recommended), the maintenance of a register of executorships by the firm may enable the firm to invite the testator to change his executors after the death or retirement of an appointed partner but, once again, little protection can be afforded against a dissolution of partnership arising from a dispute among the partners. Problems relating to a continuing trust which arise on the death or retirement of a solicitor trustee can usually be overcome without difficulty unless there is animosity between the partners.

Incorporation and solicitors' limited liability partnerships

6.11 Although usually of little or no significance to the testator, solicitors may form incorporated practices or limited liability partnerships. Incorporated practices have existed for some time[1] but have not been very popular whereas limited liability partnerships, a more recent development[2], are becoming increasingly popular amongst the medium to large firms.

1   Under Administration of Justice Act 1985 s 9 and the Solicitors' Incorporated Practice Rules 1988 and Solicitors' Incorporated Practices Order 1991 (SI 1991/2684), renamed Solicitors' Recognised Bodies Order 1991 and amended by Solicitors' Recognised Bodies (Amendment) Order 2009 SI 2009/500. The corporation must be recognised by the Law Society.
2   Under Limited Liability Partnerships Act 2000 s 1 and the Limited Liability Partnerships Regulations 2001 (SI 2001/1090).

6.12 Where solicitors have incorporated the corporate body itself should not be appointed executor because it is not a trust corporation. An appointment should be made of its owners, directors or members. Solicitors who have incorporated will often form a trust corporation as a separate entity and that may be appointed if desired.

6.13 A limited liability partnership is also a form of incorporated practice and so the partnership itself should not be appointed executor. However, its members (who are often somewhat confusingly described as partners) are able to obtain probate and so should be appointed. Limited liability partnerships also increasingly form trust corporations to act as executors and trustees. Where that occurs Wills ought to be reviewed in order to ensure that the appointment of executors and trustees is effective.

6.14 An appointment of the partners in a firm may not be effective if the firm subsequently converts into an incorporated practice or a limited liability partnership. Lightman J has held[1] that in one such case an appointment of the partners in a firm or any successor firm was effective to appoint the profit sharing (but not the salaried) members of a limited liability partnership. However, he added that testators ought to make express provision whether on the conversion of any appointed firm of solicitors or successor firm for the appointment of employee and profit sharing members.

1   *Re Rogers (deceased)* [2006] 2 All ER 792.

Common appointments

6.15 Usually, one or more of the following are appointed executors:
(1)   one or more members of the testator's family;
(2)   a beneficiary, usually the principal beneficiary;
(3)   one of the testator's professional advisers (solicitor, accountant etc);

Appointment of executors and trustees **6.19**

(4) a disinterested family friend when, for example, the interests of minors need to be balanced against those of adult beneficiaries;

(5) a business acquaintance of the testator;

(6) a trust corporation (such as the trust administration arm of a bank) – if the testator insists after being told of the probable cost of administering his estate. In addition, other problems can arise where a trust corporation is appointed: its impersonal nature, its rather cumbersome administrative machinery and, sometimes, the physical distance between its administrative centre and where the beneficiaries live. This is sometimes the most sensible option where, for example, the family are in dispute and professional advisers, business colleagues or family friends will simply be drawn into the dispute if they are appointed. However, trust corporations sometimes renounce probate if made aware of a family dispute.

6.16 If the estate is small and the assets can be administered easily, the principal beneficiary is the obvious choice. There are exceptions: for example, an aged or incompetent beneficiary. In considering a friend or a business acquaintance the testator should remember that the administration may be burdensome to an executor who has no personal interest in the estate and has his own affairs to attend to. Sometimes the appointment of a professional adviser can usefully be combined with that of a responsible member of the family who can, as it were, provide the personal touch. On the other hand, the family executor can sometimes be embarrassed by a conflict of interest.

6.17 When there are interests in succession, the appointment of a beneficiary as trustee has potential to produce a conflict of interest. If the Will gives power to the trustees to use capital for the benefit of a life tenant it is generally unwise to appoint either the life tenant or the remaindermen as trustees because of a possible conflict of interests and paralysis of the administration. The possibility of a conflict should always be a relevant factor in choosing executors/trustees.

6.18 **Form 6.15** includes provision for the appointment of accountants as executors alongside solicitors. This can be sensible where the administration is likely to be complex, involving, for example, the winding up of a business or resolution of difficult tax issues, although it should be borne in mind that taxation issues relating to the administration of trusts and estates are specialist topics in respect of which even the testator's accountants may require separate advice. In the author's experience accountants alone do not make good executors where there is likely to be a continuing trust concerning questions of law, as there often will be, it is advisable to ensure that a solicitor is also appointed. It should be noted, however, that the appointment of a solicitor *and* an accountant from different firms is likely to lead to greatly increased administration charges if both are to do their job properly. In the event of disagreement or dispute between the executors or the beneficiaries the additional expense consequent on appointing both solicitors and accountants can quickly get out of hand.

6.19 Three final points should be mentioned. First, the testator sometimes expresses a wish that the executors should use the services of a particular firm of solicitors. It is convenient to include such a wish in the appointment clause rather than elsewhere in the Will (see **Form 6.10**). The remarks at **6.8** to **6.18** also apply to such a wish. Secondly, the testator may wish to leave a legacy to his executor; this is dealt with elsewhere[1]. Thirdly, there is sometimes concern about the liability of executors/trustees if the estate suffers loss; this too is dealt with elsewhere[2].

1 See **Form 8.14**.
2 See **Form 12.22**.

6.20 *Precedents*

PRECEDENTS

6.20

FORM 6.1

Appointment of a sole executor with alternative provision[1]

I appoint as my executor [*name*] of [*address*] but if he is unable or unwilling to act or if he dies before proving my Will I appoint [*name*] of [*address*].

1   It is undesirable to appoint a sole executor without a substitutional provision and so no precedent for this has been included.
    'Unable' includes the executor's predeceasing the testator but also extends to the executor's inability to act for other reasons, such as mental incapacity.
    It can be said that an executor who neglects to take out a grant and is unco-operative is 'unwilling' but the only remedy is to cite him to take out a grant.
    Where an executor renounces probate, however, the alternative executor can apply. In the absence of an alternative appointment, one of the beneficiaries would have to apply for a grant of letters of administration with Will annexed.
    An executor derives his authority from the Will itself and is able to act as executor prior to obtaining probate. An administrator is empowered by the grant of letters of administration and before obtaining a grant has no authority to deal with the deceased's estate or to make administrative decisions such as the funeral arrangements.
    The draftsman should hesitate before using a clause which combines a gift of the whole of the estate and the appointment of the beneficiary as executor. Invariably, the Will will contain a substitutional gift and the use of the above form will be preferable. This applies particularly to the circumstances envisaged in **Form 6.2** where the gift to the widow is contingent on her surviving the testator by a specified period.
    For oath of executor, see **Form 23.1**.

FORM 6.2

Appointment of the testator's widow as executor with children as alternatives[1]

I appoint as my executor my wife [*name*] but if she is unable or unwilling to act or if she dies before proving my Will I appoint as my executors those of my children who survive me.

1   It is envisaged that the next clause will be:
    'If my wife survives me by thirty days I give the whole of my estate to her but if this gift fails the following provisions of my Will shall apply.'
    The separation of the appointment of the widow as executor from her contingent gift is desirable because otherwise her appointment as executor will also be contingent. The appointment of a spouse will also fail if the marriage is dissolved, annulled or declared void after the date of the Will: Wills Act 1837 s 18A (added by Law Reform (Succession) Act 1995). See **appendix 25.6** and the note at **3.10**.
    For oath of executor, see **Form 23.1**.

FORM 6.3

Appointment of the testator's surviving civil partner as executor with friend as alternative[1]

I appoint as my executor my civil partner[2] [*name*] but if he is unable or unwilling to act or if he dies before proving my Will I appoint my friend [*name*] of [*address*] as my executor.

Precedents **6.20**

1 See the notes to the previous form.
2 For completeness some draftsmen say 'civil partner within the meaning of Civil Partnerships Act 2004'. This book does not do so since in almost all cases the meaning of the term will be obvious to all.

FORM 6.4

Appointment of whoever are beneficially entitled as executors[1]

I appoint my [residuary] beneficiaries as my executors.

or

I appoint as my executors those of my [residuary] beneficiaries [who have attained 18 at my death].

1 This kind of appointment can be useful when the testator wishes the beneficiaries to act as executors but the circumstances import a degree of uncertainty, for example, 'to those of my brothers and sisters who survive me', or where there is a substitutional gift of the residue which may well take effect. The alternative form is desirable if one or more of the residuary beneficiaries may be minors. Consideration should be given to the need to amend this clause if a codicil is executed which changes the [residuary] beneficiaries.
For oath of executors, see **Form 23.1**.

FORM 6.5

Appointment of two executors where there is no possibility of a trust arising[1]

I appoint as my executors [*name*] of [*address*] and [*name*] of [*address*].

1 It may be desirable for the testator to consider the appointment of an alternative executor in the event of one predeceasing him. For oath for executors, see **Form 23.2**.

FORM 6.6

Appointment of executors and trustees where a trust may arise[1]

1 I appoint as my executors [*name*] of [*address*] and [*name*] of [*address*].

2 I appoint as my trustees those of my executors who obtain probate of this Will.

3 In this Will the expression 'my Trustees' means (as the context requires) those of my executors who obtained probate and the trustees for the time being of any trust arising under this Will.

1 See note at **6.3**. For oath of executors, see **Form 23.2**.

FORM 6.7

Contingent appointment of a minor as executor[1]

If he has attained eighteen when I die I appoint as my executor [*name*] of [*address*] but if he has not I appoint as my executors [*name*] of [*address*] and [*name*] of [*address*].

35

6.20 *Precedents*

1 For oath of executor(s), see **Form 23.6**.

FORM 6.8

Appointment of executor with a contingent appointment of a minor as a second executor[1]

I appoint as my executors [*name*] of [*address*] and if he has attained eighteen when I die [*name*] of [*address*].

1 For oath of executor(s), see **Form 23.6**.

FORM 6.9

Appointment of the Public Trustee as executor and trustee[1]

I appoint the Public Trustee as my executor and trustee.

1 An appointment of the Public Trustee does not have effect unless the Public Trustee consents to act so it is advisable for a testator to seek confirmation of a willingness to act in advance by writing with a list of assets and their approximate values to the Public Trustee at 81 Chancery Lane, London WC2A 1DD or by DX to 0012 London/Chancery Lane or fax to 020 7911 7105. The telephone number for general inquiries is 020 7911 7127. The Public Trustee has statutory power to charge for acting as executor/trustee and so no professional charging clause is necessary. If the testator wishes a nominated firm of solicitors to act on behalf of the trustee, see paragraph 4 of the next form.

FORM 6.10

Appointment of the Public Trustee to act with an individual with wish expressed regarding solicitors to be employed[1]

1 I appoint as my executors the Public Trustee and [*name*] of [*address*].

2 I appoint as my trustees those of my executors who obtain probate of this Will.

3 In this Will the expression 'my Trustees' means (as the context requires) those of my executors who obtain probate and the trustees for the time being of any trust arising under this Will.

4 I wish my Trustees to employ as their solicitors [*name*] of [*address*] or any other firm corporation or limited liability partnership[2] which at my death has succeeded to and carries on its practice.

1 An appointment of the Public Trustee does not have effect unless the Public Trustee consents to act so it is advisable for a testator to seek confirmation of a willingness to act. Contact details of the Public Trustee are set out in the footnote to the previous form. The Public Trustee has statutory power to charge for acting as executor/trustee and so no professional charging clause is necessary (unless required for the individual appointed).
2 See the notes at **6.11** to **6.14**.

FORM 6.11

Appointment of bank as executors and trustees[1]

1 I appoint [*name*] Bank plc as my executor and trustee.

2   The conditions on which [*name*] Bank plc acts as executor last published before the date of this Will shall apply and the Bank shall be remunerated in accordance with the scale of fees current at my death as varied from time to time during the administration of any trust arising under this Will[2].

1   See the note at **6.15**. Nevertheless, if a bank is appointed, it may be desirable to use the clause suggested by the bank in its published conditions and to add a preference for the solicitors to be employed as in paragraph 4 of the preceding form.
2   Following the commencement of the Trustee Act 2000 a trust corporation is entitled to receive payment in respect of services provided to or on behalf of the trust even if those services could be provided by a lay trustee: Trustee Act 2000 s 28 (1), (2). However, statute only permits payment of 'reasonable remuneration' (Trustee Act 2000 s 29(1)) so express words such as those used in the second paragraph of this clause should be included if a trust corporation is to be permitted to charge scale fees. See the notes at **6.4** to **6.6**.

FORM 6.12

Appointment of members of a solicitors' firm including successor practice whether incorporated or of limited liability as executors where there is no possibility of a trust arising[1]

1   I appoint as my executors the partners at my death[2] in the firm of [*name*] of [*address*] ('the Firm').

2   The expression 'the Firm' means not only [*name*] but any other firm which at my death has succeeded to and carries on its practice including a firm which has been incorporated or has formed a limited liability partnership.

3   The expression 'partners' means the persons commonly described as partners in the Firm including salaried partners[3] and, in the case of an incorporated practice or limited liability partnership, the directors, members and beneficial owners of any share of the Firm.

4   I wish not more than two of the partners in the Firm to apply for probate of this Will.

5   Any of my executors who is a solicitor may charge fees for work done by him or his firm (whether or not the work is of a professional nature) on the same basis as if he were not one of my executors but employed to carry out the work on their behalf[4].

1   See the notes at **6.8** to **6.14** and, for a variant of the charging clause, **Form 6.17**. For oath of executors, see **Forms 23.3** and **23.4**.
2   In the absence of the words 'at my death' the partners at the date of the Will will be the appointees.
3   Following the decision in *Re Rogers (deceased)* [2006] 2 All ER 792 (see **6.13** to **6.14** above) it is apparent that if salaried partners are to be included the Will must expressly include them.
4   Following the commencement of the Trustee Act 2000 if all of the executors agree, the professionals amongst them will be able to charge fees. Personal representatives (and trustees) acting in a professional capacity are entitled to reasonable remuneration if each other trustee has agreed in writing: Trustee Act 2000 ss 28(2), 29(2). However, in the absence of a provision such as the fifth paragraph of this clause a sole trustee or a professional trustee who cannot obtain the agreement of his co-representative(s) will not be able to charge. See the notes at **6.4** to **6.7**.

FORM 6.13

Appointment of members of a solicitors' firm etc as executors and trustees[1]

1   I appoint as my executors the partners at my death[2] in the firm [*name*] of [*address*] ('the Firm') and I appoint as my trustees those of my executors who obtain probate of this Will.

6.20 *Precedents*

2   The expression 'the Firm' means not only [*name*] but any other firm which at my death has succeeded to and carries on its practice including a firm which has been incorporated or has formed a limited liability partnership.

3   The expression 'partners' means the persons commonly described as partners in the Firm including salaried partners[3] and, in the case of an incorporated practice or limited liability partnership, the directors, members and beneficial owners of any share of the Firm.

4   In this Will the expression 'my Trustees' means (as the context requires) those of my executors who obtain probate and the trustees for the time being of any trust arising under this Will.

5   I wish not more than [two] of the partners in the Firm to apply for probate of this Will.

6   Any of my Trustees who is a solicitor may charge fees for work done by him or his firm (whether or not the work is of a professional nature) on the same basis as if he were not one of my Trustees but employed to carry out the work on their behalf[4].

1   See the notes at **6.8** to **6.10** and, for a variant of the charging clause, **Form 6.17**. For oath of executors, see **Forms 23.3** and **23.4**.
2   In the absence of the words 'at my death' the partners at the date of the Will will be the appointees.
3   Following the decision in *Re Rogers (deceased)* [2006] 2 All ER 792 (see **6.13** to **6.14** above) it is apparent that if salaried partners are to be included the Will must expressly include them.
4   Following the commencement of the Trustee Act 2000 if all of the executors agree, the professionals amongst them will be able to charge fees. Personal representatives (and trustees) acting in a professional capacity are entitled to reasonable remuneration if each other trustee has agreed in writing: Trustee Act 2000 ss 28(2), 29(2). However, in the absence of a provision such as the fifth paragraph of this clause a sole trustee or a professional trustee who cannot obtain the agreement of his co-representative(s) will not be able to charge. See the notes at **6.4** to **6.7**.

FORM 6.14

Appointment of members of a solicitors' firm etc and another individual as executors and trustee[1]

1   I appoint as my executors the partners at my death[2] in the firm ('the Firm') and [*name (AB)*] of [*address*].

2   I appoint as my trustees those of my executors who obtain probate of this Will.

3   The expression 'the Firm' means not only [*name*] but any other firm which at my death has succeeded to and carries on its practice including a firm which has been incorporated or has formed a limited liability partnership.

4   The expression 'partners' means the persons commonly described as partners in the Firm including salaried partners[3] and, in the case of an incorporated practice or limited liability partnership, the directors, members and beneficial owners of any share of the Firm.

5   In this Will the expression 'my Trustees' means (as the context requires) those of my executors who obtain probate and the trustees for the time being of any trust arising under this Will.

6 I wish [AB] and not more than [one] of the partners in the Firm to apply for probate of this Will.

7 Any of my Trustees who is a solicitor may charge fees for work done by him or his firm (whether or not the work is of a professional nature) on the same basis as if he were not one of my Trustees but employed to carry out the work on their behalf[4].

[1] See the notes at **6.8** to **6.12** and, for a variant of the charging clause, **Form 6.17**. For oath of executors, see **Form 23.5**.
[2] In the absence of the words 'at my death' the partners at the date of the Will will be the appointees.
[3] Following the decision in *Re Rogers (deceased)* [2006] 2 All ER 792 (see **6.13** to **6.14** above) it is apparent that if salaried partners are to be included the Will must expressly include them.
[4] Following the commencement of the Trustee Act 2000 if all of the executors agree, the professionals amongst them will be able to charge fees. Personal representatives (and trustees) acting in a professional capacity are entitled to reasonable remuneration if each other trustee has agreed in writing: Trustee Act 2000 ss 28(2), 29(2). However, in the absence of a provision such as the seventh paragraph of this clause a sole trustee or a professional trustee who cannot obtain the agreement of his co-representative(s) will not be able to charge. It is particularly important to retain that paragraph where one of the executors is a professional and the other is not. See the notes at **6.4** to **6.7**.

FORM 6.15

Appointment of members of a solicitors' firm and an accountants' firm as executors and trustees[1]

1 I appoint as my executors the partners at my death[2] in the firm [*name*] of [*address*] ('the Solicitors' Firm') and the partners at my death[1] in the firm [*name*] of [*address*] ('the Accountants' Firm').

2 I appoint as my trustees those of my executors who obtain probate of this Will.

3 In this Will the following expressions have the meanings assigned to them:

3.1 'my Trustees' means (as the context requires) those of my executors who obtain probate and the trustees for the time being of any trust arising under this Will;

3.2 'the Solicitors' Firm' means not only [*name*] but also any other firm which at my death has succeeded to and carries on its practice including a firm which has been incorporated or has formed a limited liability partnership;

3.3 'the Accountants' Firm' means not only [*name*] but also any other firm which at my death has succeeded to and carries on its practice including a firm which has been incorporated or has formed a limited liability partnership;

3.4 the expression 'partners' means the persons commonly described as partners in the Firm including salaried partners[3] and, in the case of an incorporated practice or limited liability partnership, the directors, members and beneficial owners of any share of the Firm.

4 I wish not more than [one] of the partners in the Solicitors' Firm and not more than [one] of the partners in the Accountants' Firm to apply for probate of this Will.

6.20 *Precedents*

> 5 Any of my Trustees who is engaged in a profession may charge fees for work done by him or his firm (whether or not the work is of a professional nature) on the same basis as if he were not one of my trustees but employed to carry out the work on their behalf[4].

1 See the note at **6.8** to **6.12** and the footnote to **Form 6.17**. In the author's experience accountants do not make good executors.
2 In the absence of the words 'at my death' the partners at the date of the Will will be the appointees. For oath of executors see, **Form 23.5**.
3 Following the decision in *Re Rogers (deceased)* [2006] 2 All ER 792 (see **6.13** to **6.14** above), it is apparent that if salaried partners are to be included the Will must expressly include them.
4 Following the commencement of the Trustee Act 2000 if all of the executors agree, the professionals amongst them will be able to charge fees. Personal representatives (and trustees) acting in a professional capacity are entitled to reasonable remuneration if each other trustee has agreed in writing: Trustee Act 2000 ss 28(2), 29(2). However, in the absence of a provision such as the fifth paragraph of this clause a sole trustee or a professional trustee who cannot obtain the agreement of his co-representative(s) will not be able to charge. See the note at **6.4** to **6.7**.

FORM 6.16

Appointment of executors with two others as trustees[1]

> 1 I appoint as my executors [*name*] of [*address*] and [*name*] of [*address*].
>
> 2 I appoint as my trustees 'my Trustees' [*name*] of [*address*] and [*name*] of [*address*].
>
> 3 In this Will the expression 'my Trustees' means the trustees for the time being of this Will and of any trust arising under it[2].

1 It is unusual for the executors not to be appointed as the original trustees but it sometimes occurs. See the note at **6.3**. For oath of executors, see **Form 23.2**.
2 In some cases, the executors will be able to transfer the trust property to the trustees at an early stage of the administration. In other cases, for example, where the trust property is the residuary estate, it will only be transferred when the administration of the estate is complete.

FORM 6.17

Professional charges clause[1]

Any of my Trustees in a profession, including a sole trustee, may charge for work which he or his firm does including work not requiring professional help [*and for a company or firm in any way connected with my estate*] and a trust corporation may be paid fees according to the scale fees which it charges from time to time[2].

1 This clause would normally be added as a paragraph to the clause appointing the executors and trustees as in the above but is sometimes best kept apart.
2 See the notes at **6.4** to **6.7**.

7 Appointment of testamentary guardians

7.1 The appointment of guardians and the rights they have are now governed by the Children Act 1989, as amended by the Adoption and Children Act 2002. A guardian can only be appointed in accordance within the provisions of that Act. A parent with parental responsibility may appoint a guardian by Will or by a document which he dates and signs and which provides that the appointment only takes effect on his death. As the forms in this section relate to appointment by Will, the appointor is referred to as the testator.

7.2 The appointee will become the child's guardian if, at the death of the testator:

(1) no parent with parental responsibility survived the testator; or

(2) there was a residence order in the testator's sole favour relating to the child.

If neither of these conditions is fulfilled, the appointee will not automatically become the child's guardian but the appointment will take effect on the death of the surviving parent, even if the surviving parent with parental responsibility has also made an appointment.

7.3 The unmarried father of a child may acquire parental responsibility for a child if he becomes registered as the child's father; he and the child's mother make a 'parental responsibility agreement'; or the court (on his application) orders that he shall have parental responsibility for the child[1]. Similar provisions apply to a second female parent (i.e. to both members of a same sex female couple) of a child born as a result of artificial insemination[2]. An unmarried father of a child who has parental responsibility is able to appoint a guardian under Children Act 1989 s 5(3) because he is a parent. Under the Children Act 1989, as amended by the Adoption and Children Act 2002, a person married to or in a civil partnership with a child's parent may acquire parental responsibility for a step-child by agreement or if the court (on his application) orders that he shall have parental responsibility for the child[3]. A step-parent is not, however, a parent and so cannot appoint a guardian.

1 Children Act 1989 s 4, as amended by the Adoption and Children Act 2002.
2 Children Act 1989 s 4ZA, as inserted by Human Fertilisation and Embryology Act 2008.
3 Children Act 1989 s 4A, as inserted by the Adoption and Children Act 2002.

7.4 Where a testator has children under the age of 18, the appointment of testamentary guardians should always be considered. The expression 'testamentary guardian', although of ancient origin, now merely indicates that the guardian has been appointed by Will. There is therefore no need to include the word 'testamentary' in the clause of the Will by which the appointment is made.

7.5 *Appointment of testamentary guardians*

7.5 **Form 7.1** is for use where the appointment is not dependent on the testator being the surviving parent, for example, if the parents are divorced or if the testator has a sole residence order in his favour. **Forms 7.2** and **7.3** are for the more usual case where guardians are appointed to act only after the death of the surviving parent. It is still usual (but not essential) that the same persons are appointed guardians of all the testator's minor children. When the guardians are to act only after the death of the surviving parent it is desirable that each parent should appoint the same persons to act as guardian.

7.6 It is, of course, important that the testator should obtain the consent of the proposed guardian before making the appointment.

7.7 The appointed guardian can appoint a successor and **Form 7.4** provides for this. It is strictly unnecessary to make express provision because Children Act 1989 s 7(4) enables a guardian to appoint another individual to take his place in the event of his death. **Form 7.3** makes express provision because the appointed guardian may be unaware of his statutory right.

7.8 Whether guardians should be trustees depends on the circumstances of each case. There are arguments for and against. The guardians are best placed to know the needs of the children and have the task of providing for those needs. On the other hand, the guardians may be regarded as the advocates for the children and the trustees as the judges of their conflicting claims. The problem is particularly acute when the residue is held on discretionary trusts for the children and, in that case, a sensible solution may be to appoint as trustees one of the guardians and, say, two professional trustees.

PRECEDENTS

7.9

FORM 7.1

Appointment of testamentary guardians

I appoint [*name*] of [*address*] and [*name*] of [*address*] as guardians of any of my children under eighteen.

FORM 7.2

Appointment of testamentary guardians by surviving parent

[*If my wife/husband[1] dies before me*][2] I appoint [*name*] of [*address*] and [*name*] of [*address*] as guardians of any of my children under eighteen.

1 This is easily adapted to take account of civil partnerships.
2 Omit if the clause appears in a section of the Will which is only operative if the testator's spouse has predeceased him.

FORM 7.3

Appointment of testamentary guardians by surviving parent

If I am the sole surviving parent with parental responsibility for my children then I appoint [*name*] of [*address*] and [*name*] of [*address*] as guardians of any of my children under eighteen.

FORM 7.4

Appointment of testamentary guardians with their having power to appoint successors

[*If my wife/husband[1] dies before me*[2]] I appoint as guardians of any of my children under eighteen:

(a) [*name*] of [*address*] and [*name*] of [*address*] and

(b) any guardian(s) they appoint to act after their death.

1 This is easily adapted to take account of civil partnerships.
2 Omit if the clause appears in a section of the Will which is only operative if the testator's spouse has predeceased him.

8 Legacies

Legacies and identity of legatees

8.1 Legacies are a means of remembering those friends and relatives who are not intended to participate in a gift of residue. Sometimes, however, the testator uses legacies to make provision for beneficiaries who also take a share of residue in order to increase or guarantee their entitlement. Specific gifts of chattels are considered in the next chapter.

8.2 As in all cases where there may be some doubt as to identity the draftsman should take steps to ensure that there is no ambiguity in the identity of the intended legatee so, if the testator has two nephews called Oliver but intends to make a gift to only one of them, his description must be sufficiently precise to identify which is to take. This can be achieved simply either by describing the relationship, for example, 'my nephew Oliver son of my sister Polly', or by using some other individual description such as 'my nephew Oliver of 34 Acacia Avenue'.

Types of legacy

8.3 A legacy may be general, demonstrative or specific. It is general if the subject matter is not distinguished in the Will from other property included in the estate and which is of the same kind. Most gifts of money are expressed as general pecuniary legacies.

8.4 A specific legacy must be of some thing or of some interest forming part of the testator's estate as distinguished from the whole of his personal property or from the whole of the general residue of his personal estate. The use of a specific legacy for gifts of money should be avoided. Future events often defeat the original intention of the testator and can be a fertile source of family disharmony as well as creating problems relating to their true meaning. Specific legacies are best reserved for bequests of chattels and securities.

8.5 Demonstrative legacies consist of a pecuniary legacy payable out of a particular fund. Such a legacy has the advantage that it is not adeemed by the total or partial failure of the fund out of which it was directed to be paid but then becomes payable out of the general personal estate and it does not abate with the general legacies until after the particular fund is exhausted.

Gifts free of inheritance tax

8.6 Inheritance tax on unsettled UK property is a testamentary expense to be paid out of the estate and not by any particular beneficiary. The Will may vary the incidence of inheritance tax by express direction or make express provision clarifying the position. In the ordinary case the normal direction to pay inheritance tax out of the residue merely makes this clear although in the case of chattels which may be out of the UK an express direction is considered essential.

8.7 If some gifts are expressed to be tax-free and others are not, the problem of 'double grossing-up' may arise. If legacies are subject to double grossing-up a small inheritance tax advantage can result at the expense of time-consuming computations, likely to outweigh any tax saving in cases of low value. This is discussed further in **Chapter 15**.

8.8 Unless the testator desires otherwise, it is advisable to include words expressly freeing pecuniary legacies from inheritance tax, or to include a general declaration freeing legacies from inheritance tax as in **Form 8.1**.

Gifts to charities

8.9 Charitable gifts are exempt from inheritance tax. The forms relating to gifts to charities can be adapted for gifts to non-charitable organisations. With any body of persons whether charitable or not, there is a particular problem if it is not incorporated: a gift to it will take effect as a gift to each member. Accordingly, express provisions concerning receipts are needed. Indeed, where the charitable legatee is relatively small, there could be difficulties unless the Will makes provision for receipts.

8.10 It is usual to provide that the executors are not on inquiry as to the status of the person giving a receipt. There is, however, no need to state that they need not concern themselves with the correct application of the gift: a good receipt for the legacy is sufficient. This is so even if the testator wishes to restrict the application of the gift. Nevertheless, unless the restriction is known to be acceptable to the body concerned, it is preferable to express it as not imposing an obligation on the recipient.

8.11 Where the testator wishes his legacy to be put to a particular use it is advisable to seek the guidance of the institution concerned. Most charities are anxious to give effect to a benefactor's wishes but sometimes there are practical or legal difficulties and sometimes policy decisions of the charity, perhaps because of the influence of the Charity Commission, which are contrary to the testator's wishes. Difficulties arise particularly where the testator wants the bequest to be paid to the local branch of a national charity and in such cases it is advisable to make provision for an effective gift to the national charity coupled with a non-binding expression of desire concerning its local application as in **Form 8.17**.

8.12 Much confusion and expense can result from failing properly to identify the intended donee of a charitable legacy. There are often different organisations sharing similar objects and names and the Will draftsman should take care to ascertain which is to be benefited. It is not adequate to rely on the instructions of the testator who might have confused two charities either by name or address. Now that the Charity Commission maintains a list of registered charities that is freely available online at www.charity-commission.gov.uk the task of ascertaining the correct name and address of a charitable beneficiary or of discovering that there is confusion in the instructions is very much easier. Care should be taken, however, because not all charities are registered.

PRECEDENTS

8.13

FORM 8.1

Declaration that legacies are free of inheritance tax and other duties[1]

The legacies given by this Will shall be paid free of inheritance tax and other taxes or duties payable as a result of my death.

1   See the note at **8.6** to **8.8**.

FORM 8.2

Pecuniary legacy

I give £   to [*name*] [*free of inheritance tax*[1]].

or

I give the following legacies [*free of inheritance tax*[1]]:

    (a)   £   to [*AB*] of [*address*]

    (b)   £   to [*CD*] of [*address*]

etc.

1   It is sensible expressly to provide that legacies are free of inheritance tax if, as is usually the case, that is what the testator intends. See the note at **8.6** to **8.8**.

FORM 8.3

Specific pecuniary legacy[1]

I give to [*name*] [*any money in my safe*] [*free of inheritance tax*[2]].

1   Such gifts are unusual and testators should be advised to avoid them. See the notes at **8.3** to **8.5**.
2   It is sensible expressly to provide that legacies are free of inheritance tax if, as is usually the case, that is what the testator intends. See the notes at **8.6** to **8.8**.

FORM 8.4

Demonstrative pecuniary legacy[1]

I give £   to [*name*] to be paid primarily out of money standing to my credit at my death with [Building Society] but if such credit is insufficient at my death then this gift is payable out of my residuary estate. [*This gift is made free of inheritance tax*[2].]

1   Such gifts have certain advantages but are usually best avoided. See notes at **8.3** to **8.5**.
2   It is sensible expressly to provide that legacies are free of inheritance tax if, as is usually the case, that is what the testator intends. See the note at **8.6** to **8.8**.

FORM 8.5

Legacy subject to inheritance tax[1]

I give £   to [name] subject to his bearing any inheritance tax attributable to it.

1   See the note at **8.6** to **8.8**. If any gifts are expressed to be subject to inheritance tax, the Will ought not to contain a direction (for example, as in **Form 8.1**) for inheritance tax to be paid out of residue as the two provisions relating to inheritance tax will conflict. If a general direction is omitted the inheritance tax on gifts not bearing their own tax will be payable out of residue under statutory provisions.

FORM 8.6

Priority legacy[1]

I give £   to [name] to be paid immediately after my death and to rank in priority to all other gifts made by this Will. [*This gift is made free of inheritance tax*[2].]

1   This provision has three consequences. If the estate is solvent, it requires the executors to pay the legacy as soon as sufficient funds are available without waiting until the estate is ready for general distribution. If the estate is insolvent, the legacy will be payable in full (if possible) out of the moneys available for the payment of pecuniary legacies and will not abate proportionally with other legacies. Finally, interest on the legacy will run from the date of death and not from the first anniversary of the testator's death.
2   It is sensible expressly to provide that legacies are free of inheritance tax if, as is usually the case, that is what the testator intends. See the note at **8.6** to **8.8**.

FORM 8.7

Legacies to two beneficiaries with provision for accruer

I give [£1,500] to each of [AB] and [CD] but if either of them dies before me I give [£3,000] to the survivor. [*This gift is made free of inheritance tax*[1].]

1   It is sensible expressly to provide that legacies are free of inheritance tax if, as is usually the case, that is what the testator intends. See the note at **8.6** to **8.8**.

FORM 8.8

Legacy to be divided between two or more beneficiaries

I give [*free of inheritance tax*[1]] £   to be divided equally among those of the following who survive me:

   [AB]   of   [address];

   [CD]   of   [address];

   [EF]   of   [address];

etc.

1   It is sensible expressly to provide that legacies are free of inheritance tax if, as is usually the case, that is what the testator intends. See the note at **8.6** to **8.8**.

8.13 *Precedents*

FORM 8.9

Legacy to a minor – provision for payment to minor if over 16 and otherwise to parent or guardian[1]

I give [*free of inheritance tax*[2]] £   to [*name*] and if at my death he is under sixteen years old it may be paid to his parent or guardian for his benefit or if he has attained the age of sixteen years it may be paid to the beneficiary himself and either payment shall be a discharge to my Trustees.

1   Although the gift vests on the testator's death, a minor cannot give a valid receipt for it unless married. Without specific authority the trustees would be able to pay the legacy to a person with parental responsibility for the beneficiary while under 18 but in many cases it is desirable to provide that a beneficiary between the ages of 16 and 18 should himself give a good receipt for the legacy.
2   It is sensible expressly to provide that legacies are free of inheritance tax if, as is usually the case, that is what the testator intends. See the note at **8.6** to **8.8**.

FORM 8.10

Legacy to grandchildren

I give [*free of inheritance tax*[1]] £   to be divided equally among [*my grandchildren living at my death*]/[*those of my grandchildren who survive me and attain the age of eighteen years*][2].

1   It is sensible expressly to provide that legacies are free of inheritance tax if, as is usually the case, that is what the testator intends. See the note at **8.6** to **8.8**.
2   In the case of either alternative it is recommended that the executors are given power to pay sums to minor grandchildren or to their parents or guardians, as in **Form 12.6**. If the second alternative is to be used the executors could find themselves holding a fund for the grandchildren for very many years. Where professional executors or trustees are appointed by the Will their charges for the management of the fund may have the effect of depleting it so the provision may only be appropriate where there is a substantial fund for investment. The argument in favour of gifts to children and grandchildren being vested (see **11.14** to **11.24**) suggests that it would be better to exclude an age contingency provision.

FORM 8.11

Legacy to grandchildren – alternative method

(a) I give £   to be divided equally among those children of my son [*AB*] [*who are living at my death*]/[*who survive me and attain the age of eighteen years*][1].

(b) I give £   to be divided equally among those children of my daughter [*CD*] [*who are living at my death*]/[*who survive me and attain the age of eighteen years*][1].

[*This gift is made free of inheritance tax*[2].]

1   See footnote 2 to **Form 8.10**.
2   It is sensible expressly to provide that legacies are free of inheritance tax if, as is usually the case, that is what the testator intends. See the note at **8.6** to **8.8**.

FORM 8.12

Legacy of specific amount to each grandchild

I give [*free of inheritance tax*[1]] £   to each of my grandchildren [*living at my death*]/[*who survives me and attains the age of eighteen years*][2].

1   It is sensible expressly to provide that legacies are free of inheritance tax if, as is usually the case, that is what the testator intends. See the note at **8.6** to **8.8**.
2   See footnote 2 to **Form 8.10**.

FORM 8.13

Legacy to grandchildren with substitution of great grandchildren

I give [*free of inheritance tax*[1]] £   to be divided equally among those of my grandchildren who survive me [*and attain the age of eighteen years*][2] but if any of them dies before attaining a vested interest leaving children then those children shall [*on attaining the age of eighteen years*][2] take the share which their parent would have inherited if he or she had survived me.

1   It is sensible expressly to provide that legacies are free of inheritance tax if, as is usually the case, that is what the testator intends. See the note at **8.6** to **8.8**.
2   See footnote 2 to **Form 8.10**. The more so in the case of the great grandchildren.

FORM 8.14

Legacy to executor

I give [free of inheritance tax[1]] £   to [*name*] and this legacy [*is*]/[*is not*][2] conditional on his acting as my executor [*and trustee*][2].

1   It is sensible expressly to provide that legacies are free of inheritance tax if, as is usually the case, that is what the testator intends. See the note at **8.6** to **8.8**.
2   It is desirable to make clear whether or not the legacy is conditional on the executor/ trustee accepting the appointment as there is a presumption that a legacy to an executor is conditional on acceptance of the office.

FORM 8.15

Legacy to employee if still employed

I give [*free of inheritance tax*[1]] £   to [*name*] if he is in my employment at my death and not under notice whether given by him or me to leave and this legacy is in addition to any sum due to him for wages which I might owe at the date of my death[2].

1   It is sensible expressly to provide that legacies are free of inheritance tax if, as is usually the case, that is what the testator intends. See the note at **8.6** to **8.8**.
2   It is desirable to make clear that the legacy is in addition to any sums owing to the employee if, for example, wages are payable in arrears.

FORM 8.16

Gift to charity[1]

(a) I give £   to [*precise name of charity*][2] ('the charity').

(b) The receipt of a person who appears to be a proper officer of the charity shall be a discharge to my Trustees.

(c) This legacy shall not fail if at my death the charity has changed its name or ceased to exist or has amalgamated with another charity or has become the subject of a scheme and my Trustees shall pay it to the charitable organisation which they consider most nearly fulfils the objects I intended to benefit.

8.13 *Precedents*

1   See the note at **8.9** to **8.11**.
2   A solicitor or Will draftsman is under a duty to ensure that the name of the intended beneficiary is correctly stated. See *Re Recher's Will Trusts* [1972] Ch 526, [1971] 3 All ER 401 and the note at **8.12**.

FORM 8.17
Purpose gift to particular charity[1]

(a) I give £   to the Royal National Lifeboat Institution[2].

(b) It is my wish without creating a binding obligation on the Institution that this gift is used for the benefit of its lifeboat station at [Craster] or if that station is not in existence at my death then for the nearest station of the Institution to it.

(c) The receipt of a person who appears to be a proper officer of the charity shall be a discharge to my Trustees[3].

1   See the note at **8.9** to **8.11**.
2   The RNLI has been chosen merely as an example of a national charity with a local presence. See the note at **8.9**.
3   In the case of the RNLI a receipt clause is not, in fact, essential as the charity is incorporated by Royal Charter.

FORM 8.18
Inflation-proof legacy

I give [*free of inheritance tax*[1]] to   the sum which has the same value at my death as [£1,000] has at the date of this Will to be calculated by my trustees having regard to the Retail Prices Index in the month in which this my Will is executed and in the month of my death having regard to any re-basing of the Index which might have occurred in the meantime[2].

1   It is sensible expressly to provide that legacies are free of inheritance tax if, as is usually the case, that is what the testator intends.
2   The trustees will have to assess the current value of the specified sum by reference to the RPI. It is not sensible to provide a vague direction as to the means of calculation. The clause could go further and set out the mechanics of the calculation but that ought to be obvious. There is no substitute for reconsidering a Will regularly in the light of changed circumstances.

FORM 8.19
Gift of a number of inflation-proof legacies

I give [*free of inheritance tax*[1]] to each of the legatees named below the sum which has the same value at my death as the amount specified against his name had at the date of this Will, such sum to be calculated by my trustees having regard to the Retail Prices Index in the month in which this my Will is executed and in the month of my death having regard to any re-basing of the Index which might have occurred in the meantime.

      [*AB*]: [£1,000]

      [*CD*]: [£2,500]

      [*EF*]: [£5,000].

1   It is sensible expressly to provide that legacies are free of inheritance tax if, as is usually the case, that is what the testator intends. See the note at **8.6** to **8.8**.

9 Specific gifts of chattels and other personal property

Need for a gift of chattels

9.1 In the simple case in which a testator is giving the whole of his estate to his spouse there is no need to include a separate gift of chattels but where the disposition is more complicated a separate gift of chattels is often desirable.

9.2 A settled gift of chattels (for example, for life) should be actively discouraged. Not only is it inconvenient but it raises problems of maintenance, fair wear and tear, insurance, safe-keeping and taking inventories. The case of a settled gift of chattels usually arises where a testator creates a life interest of the whole of the estate. There is much to be said for chattels being excluded from the life interest and being made the subject of an absolute gift. This is particularly so where the life tenant is the testator's widow. Perhaps the one exception is where a right to occupy a house as a residence is given and the testator wishes the contents to remain in the house. Even so, the testator should think hard about whether an absolute gift of the contents is more appropriate. A precedent for this is **Form 10.11**.

Inheritance tax and gifts of chattels

9.3 Inheritance tax on chattels situated in the UK will be borne by residue as a testamentary expense but chattels situated elsewhere will bear their own inheritance tax. As noted in the previous chapter[1], in the ordinary case, the normal direction to pay inheritance tax out of the residue merely makes this clear but where chattels may be out of the UK an express direction should be included. If valuable chattels are to be given subject to inheritance tax an express direction will be required.

1 See **8.6** to **8.8**.

Gifts of personal chattels

9.4 Gifts of chattels are almost always specific. It should always be made clear in the Will whether the gift is to relate to a particular item owned when the Will is made or to any item which, at death, corresponds to the description given in the Will. In default of a clear direction Wills Act 1837 s 24[1] provides that a Will 'speaks from death' unless a contrary intention is expressed. The expression, for example, 'my car' may refer to the

9.5 *Specific gifts of chattels and other personal property*

car the testator owns at the date of his Will or, by virtue of s 24, the car he owns at death. If there may be ambiguity the matter should be put beyond doubt by the terms of the Will (contrast **Forms 9.1** and **9.2**). Forethought should also be given to the possibility of the testator's owning more than one car at his death.

1   Wills Act 1837 s 24, see **appendix 25.12**.

9.5   Problems also arise when the subject matter of the gift is one of a number of similar items, for example, a piece of jewellery. Practitioners are well aware of the difficulties which can arise on distribution in giving effect to inadequate descriptions such as 'my dress ring'. It behoves the draftsman, therefore, to take pains to obtain detailed descriptions of such items, bearing in mind that, even where only one such item exists at the date of the Will, there is the possibility of others being acquired subsequently.

9.6   Where a testator wishes to make a general gift of personal chattels, it is convenient to refer to 'personal chattels as defined by Administration of Estates Act 1925 s 55(1)(x)'[1]. The definition excludes money, securities for money and chattels used for business purposes. Subject to these general exceptions it includes carriages, horses, stable furniture and effects, motor cars and accessories, garden effects, domestic animals, plate, plated articles, linen, china, glass, books, pictures, prints, furniture, jewellery, articles of household or personal use or ornament, musical and scientific instruments and apparatus, wines, liquors and consumable stores. This section also includes a clause providing that the cost of delivering any gift to a beneficiary or vesting it in him shall be an executorship expense[2].

1   Administration of Estates Act 1925 s 55, reproduced at **appendix 25.17**.
2   See **Form 9.21**. Ordinarily it seems that the beneficiary would have to bear these expenses.

9.7   Special care should be taken in the case of chattels which have a business use. Once again a good example is a car which the testator may refer to as 'my car' when in fact it belongs to a company. The use of a car for both business and private purposes may prevent its being a 'personal chattel' as defined. Where a generic description is adopted (as in **Forms 9.9** to **9.13**), care should be taken that the gift will achieve the testator's desires; there are no helpful authorities.

Collections

9.8   There is some doubt about the application of the statutory definition to collections. Probably a collection of items which themselves come within Administration of Estates Act 1925 s 55(1)(x)[1] will be included but the position is uncertain in relation to, for example, stamps, which might pass as 'pictures' or might not[2]. For this reason, collections of items (porcelain, stamps, coins etc) should be expressly included or excluded. Often the testator has a specific idea of what he wants to do with a particular collection but has no idea what to do with ordinary chattels.

1   See **appendix 25.17**.
2   See, for example, *Re Reynolds' Will Trusts, Dove v Reynolds* [1965] 3 All ER 686.

Rights of selection of chattels

9.9   The testator who has little or no idea what to do with ordinary chattels often has some vague desire that friends or relatives should be given a right to select mementoes or keepsakes from his possessions. The author takes the view that a testator who cannot decide what to do with his own bounty is only saving up trouble for others and so the inclusion of rights of selection should be discouraged where possible. Practitioners will be aware that disputes concerning chattels often arise in the context of litigation concerning the administration of estates and can be the cause of the dispute. However, testators can be quite tenacious and so **Forms 9.14** to **9.18** have been included in this section.

9.10 The possibilities covered by these forms include a gift to trustees subject to various alternative rights of selection[1]; a mere right of selection and distribution with the items not selected falling into residue[2]; a gift of such item as is selected with provision for the resolution of disputes where beneficiaries cannot agree[3]; an absolute gift coupled with a non-binding direction to make a distribution in accordance with a memorandum of wishes[4]; and a gift to children in equal shares subject to division and distribution in specie by trustees[5].

1 See **Form 9.14**.
2 See **Form 9.15**.
3 See **Form 9.16**.
4 See **Form 9.17**.
5 See **Form 9.18**.

9.11 These forms are not exhaustive of the variety of possible schemes of distribution which testators dream up. The important thing in each case is to be clear. As with all testamentary dispositions it is important to establish what is given and to whom but there should also be a long-stop date by which rights of selection or powers of distribution must be exercised. The timing may also have inheritance tax consequences: A gift over by a specific legatee in accordance with the testator's wishes within two years of the testator's death will be treated for inheritance tax purposes as having been made by the testator's Will[1] as will a discretionary distribution by trustees within the same period[2].

1 Inheritance Tax Act 1984 s 143 (**appendix 28.6**) and see **Form 9.17**.
2 Inheritance Tax Act 1984 s 144 (**appendix 28.7**) and see **Form 9.14**.

Chattels subject to a charge

9.12 In the case of chattels subject to a charge there are two typical situations: credit sale and hire purchase. With a credit sale, ownership of the chattel is vested in the testator and will pass to the beneficiary under the Will. The amount outstanding under the agreement is a debt which may be payable out of residue unless express provision is made for the beneficiary to discharge it[1]. The ownership of goods held under a hire purchase agreement is not vested in the testator although, where the Consumer Credit Act 1974 applies, the hirer's rights pass on death to the personal representatives who can transfer the rights to the beneficiary. In other cases there is the difficulty that some agreements prohibit a transfer of rights and others even provide for termination of the agreement on the death of the hirer. A gift of 'my personal chattels' will not include any that are subject to a hire purchase agreement or any other agreement under which the testator does not own the goods.

1 See **Forms 9.19** and **9.20**.

9.13 The simple solution is to refer specifically to any goods which the testator holds under a hire purchase or similar agreement and to provide for the outstanding balance to be paid out of the residue. This is best done in the clause constituting the gift[1]. Whatever the strict legal position, it is likely that the finance company will accept payment in full and transfer ownership. The other possibility is to express the gift in such a way that the beneficiary must, if he wishes to take it, accept it subject to

9.14 *Specific gifts of chattels and other personal property*

the liability of the hire purchase agreement, whatever that may be. The problems resulting from such a provision are obvious[2].

1 See **Form 9.19**.
2 See **Form 9.20**.

Releases and gifts of debts

9.14 Debts are choses in action[1] and so can be given by Will. **Form 9.22** is an example. In their benevolence testators often want to release debtors from debts due to them but it is unwise to include a general forgiveness of debts in a Will as this might include debts incurred subsequently and those which the testator does not regard as such: strictly this would include the balance of a current bank account. It is better to take the trouble to identify the debtor and the debt and include a release by way of specific gift. For examples of releases see **Forms 9.23** to **9.25**.

1 Ie the testator does not have immediate enjoyment of the debt, merely a right to recover it by action.

Gifts of shares

9.15 A simple gift of shares should be distinguished from a gift of a business or an interest in a business in which the testator is a participant. The simple gift of a holding in a public company as in **Forms 9.26** and **9.27** does not normally require any special inheritance tax consideration and is no different from any other specific gift.

Gift of a family business

9.16 Where the testator has an interest in a business, it is wise to consider succession and, if possible, to take action during his lifetime rather than to make provision for succession by Will. Otherwise, particularly in the case of a sole proprietor, personal representatives may find the business cannot be effectively carried on after death. Where the business is carried on through the medium of a private limited company there is usually more flexibility in dealing with succession to ownership, although there will always be the practical problem of succession to management.

9.17 The tax complications relating to businesses, whether incorporated or unincorporated, are beyond the scope of this book. The following short observations are merely intended to remind the draftsman of some of the pitfalls.
(1) The valuation of a majority shareholding in a private limited company which is governed by the value of a company's assets will not be proportionate to the shareholding. A 51% holding is worth considerably more than a 49% holding, the difference in value being much greater than 2% of the total value.
(2) The rules governing 'related property' which result in the shares held by husband and wife being added together to determine whether the deceased had a majority shareholding.
(3) The capital gains tax consequences of a lifetime disposal especially if it results in the testator's ceasing to have a controlling interest.
(4) The inhibitions on estate planning resulting from the testator's wish to make specific provisions for a beneficiary or to accommodate the competing interests of beneficiaries.
(5) The need to ensure that the proposed scheme does not contravene the company's memorandum and articles of association.

9.18 The testator cannot transfer his interest in a partnership unless there is an express provision in the partnership agreement permitting him to do so and this is unusual. In any event, it is desirable for the testator to make provision for the future within his partnership agreement rather than by testamentary disposition. In the absence of a partnership agreement providing for continuation of a partnership after death the partnership will be dissolved by the death of a partner[1]. This is not the place to discuss the means whereby a partnership agreement can provide for succession with little or no inheritance tax liability, but it is often possible within a partnership agreement to provide for a capital sum to enable the share of a retiring or deceased partner to be bought out in instalments by the continuing partners. Pension provision can be extended to provide a widow's pension and, in a variety of other ways, a partner in a successful business can, through his partnership agreement, give effect to the substance of the provisions he originally envisaged as being part of his Will.

1   Partnership Act 1891 s 33.

9.19 **Forms 9.28** to **9.31** go some way towards making provision for the disposition of an interest in a family business and in many cases they will suffice but they are far from exhaustive of the situations which can arise in practice. These forms are best used as a starting point for provisions tailored to quite specific circumstances.

PRECEDENTS

9.20

FORM 9.1

Bequest of car owned at date of Will

I give to [name] my car, registered number[1].

1   If the car is not owned at death the gift will, of course, fail.

FORM 9.2

Bequest of car owned at date of death

I give to [name] the car I own at the date of my death[1].

1   The draftsman must guard against the possibility of the testator owning more than one car. If the car may be subject to a hire purchase or finance agreement, see **Forms 9.19** and **9.20**.

FORM 9.3

Bequest of Baxter Prints[1]

I give to [name] my framed Baxter Prints the 'Ascent of Mont Blanc', catalogue numbers 336, 336A, 336B and 336C.

1   This form is used as an example of a precedent in which it is possible to define the subject matter of the gift with great precision.

FORM 9.4

Bequest of collection by reference to inventory[1]

I give to [name] the collection of [antique silver] which is specified in detail in [my insurance policy [No.   ] with   ].

1   Definition by reference to an inventory can sometimes be useful, particularly where it relates to a valuable collection. For insurance purposes, the testator is likely to ensure that additional items acquired are added to the inventory. There are obvious pitfalls and the testator should be warned that the items appearing in the inventory at his death will constitute the gift.

FORM 9.5

Bequest of specific items by reference to inventory – alternative method[1]

The schedule to this Will applies to gifts of chattels

Schedule

1. I have left with this Will a list of chattels (being a valuation prepared for insurance purposes). Each item bears a number and the number shown in brackets after a chattel specified in paragraph 2 of this schedule corresponds

with the number in the list used for insurance purposes. That list is not a testamentary document but has been placed with this Will to assist my Trustees in identifying the gifts specified in paragraph 2.

2. I give to the person named in the first column below the chattel or chattels specified against his name in the second column

   Donee   Chattel

   [name]   (a) My Tissot gold watch and bracelet (42)

            (b) My gold cufflinks (30)

   [name]   My Avis gold watch and bracelet (43)

   [name]   My silver inkstand (23)

etc.

1   Where a testator makes specific gifts of a number of chattels it is convenient to use a schedule for this purpose. In this form the inventory contained in an insurance document has been used. Such inventories usually contain a detailed description of each article and sometimes a photograph.

FORM 9.6

Bequest of chattels as defined by Administration of Estates Act 1925[1]

I give to [name] my personal chattels as defined by Administration of Estates Act 1925 s 55(1)(x) [*except those which are the subject of specific gifts in this Will or in any codicil to it*].

1   See the note at **9.4** to **9.6**.

FORM 9.7

Bequest of personal chattels as defined by Administration of Estates Act 1925 with additions[1]

I give to [name] my personal chattels as defined by Administration of Estates Act 1925 s 55(1)(x) and also:

   1   [all my medical text books];

   2   [all my surgical instruments].

1   This example is used to emphasise that, while items such as books would fall within the general definition of s 55, items for business purposes would be excluded. See the note at **9.4** to **9.6**.

FORM 9.8

Bequest of personal chattels as defined by Administration of Estates Act 1925 with exceptions[1]

I give to [name] my personal chattels as defined by Administration of Estates Act 1925 s 55(1)(x) except the following:

   1   [any pictures and prints];

9.20 *Precedents*

    2   [any car].

[The items excluded from this gift shall form part of my residuary estate[2].]

1   See the note at **9.4** to **9.6**.
2   Alternatively the specific items referred to could be given to another donee.

FORM 9.9

Bequest of personal chattels as defined by Administration of Estates Act 1925 with additions and exceptions[1]

I give to [*name*] my personal chattels as defined by Administration of Estates Act 1925 s 55(1)(x) but this gift:

    1   includes any [car which is used partly for business purposes[2]];

    2   excludes any [pictures and prints].

1   See the note at **9.4** to **9.6**.
2   This can cause complications if the donee does not also receive the business so care should be taken to ensure that the two gifts are not inconsistent.

FORM 9.10

Bequest of furniture and household effects

I give to [*name*] all my furniture curtains carpets and articles of household use or ornament.

FORM 9.11

Bequest of jewellery and personal effects

I give to [*name*] all my clothing jewellery and articles of personal use or adornment.

FORM 9.12

Bequest of contents of house[1]

I give to [*name*] those of my personal chattels [*in any house in which I live at my death*] which constitute:

    1   furniture or articles of household use or ornament;

    2   jewellery or articles of personal use or adornment;

    3   books, photographs and [*physical*]/[*published or written*][2] articles relating to [*any sport hobby or other pastime*][3].

1   This form and the next have been included with some misgivings. The draftsman should strive to find an alternative to 'the contents of my house'. It is an expression used rather glibly by testators and they do not foresee the problems which can arise, for example, where chattels normally contained in the testator's house have been put into storage, have been lost and are recovered after the testator's death or some of which have been used to furnish the testator's room in a nursing home while the rest have been left in his home. In this precedent the reference to the chattels being contained in a testator's residence could well be omitted.

2   Although in the context of the preceding paragraphs the word 'articles' must mean 'physical articles', when placed beside 'books' and 'photographs' a reference to 'articles' might be construed as a reference to 'writings' only. Such ambiguity should be avoided.
3   A greater degree of precision may be required in defining the subject of the gift than the testator has considered.

FORM 9.13

Bequest of contents of house – alternative form[1]

I give to [*name*] the contents of the house in which I reside that are chattels.

1   See footnote to the preceding precedent. It would almost certainly be better to use one of the **Forms 9.5** to **9.8**.

FORM 9.14

Bequest of personal chattels selected by beneficiaries[1]

I give those of my personal chattels which are articles of personal use or adornment or articles of household use or ornament to my Trustees on the following trusts:

1   To transfer to [*name*] such items as in the opinion of my Trustees he reasonably requires for his personal use[2].

or

1   To transfer to [*name*] the items he selects provided that their value does not in the opinion of my Trustees exceed [£   ] *or* [one quarter of the total value of the items from which the selection is made][3].

or

1   To permit my personal friends to select as mementoes one item each[4] from the personal chattels to which this trust relates and in giving effect to this provision my Trustees in their absolute and unfettered discretion:

    1.1   shall decide who are the persons entitled to select mementoes;

    1.2   may permit more than one item to be selected if together they constitute a set or match one another; and

    1.3   shall transfer the ownership of any item selected or allotted to the person concerned.

2   Any personal chattels not transferred under 1 above within one year[5] shall form part of my residuary estate.

1   See the note at **9.9** to **9.11**. Many testators wish one or more beneficiaries to be permitted to select items from their personal chattels. Often the testator is not clear in his own mind what he really intends to happen. Sometimes he intends, for example, that friends and acquaintances should each select a keepsake or that a relative should select items of furniture for use in his own home but not to sell. Practitioners are well aware of the difficulty of drafting a satisfactory provision and the problems which can arise from interpreting such a provision. The author has tried to overcome the problems encountered in practice but every case is different. It should be noted that this form expressly vests the ownership of the personal chattels in the trustees so as to give them a degree of control over the selection and then provides for them to transfer the ownership of the selected items to the beneficiary. This is preferable to a provision such as:
    'I give to AB such of my personal chattels as he selects.'
2   A testator often wants the intended beneficiary to enjoy the chattel and has a strong objection to the beneficiary selecting an item merely to convert it into cash.

9.20 *Precedents*

3   This provision is intended to prevent the avaricious beneficiary selecting virtually all the personal chattels.
4   A provision designed to restrict the selection to personal keepsakes.
5   It is important to introduce a time limit for the completion of an exercise of this sort. One year is generally convenient but a period of up to two years would take advantage of Inheritance Tax Act 1984 s 144: see **appendix 28.7**.

FORM 9.15

Gift of jewellery to daughter with right of selection and distribution, default gift into residue[1]

I give to my daughter [*name*] absolutely such of my jewellery as she may select within six months after my death and any such articles not selected by her within the said time shall be distributed by her within a further six months amongst such of my female relatives and such of the wives, widows and female cohabitees for the time being of such of my male relatives as she shall in her absolute and unfettered discretion select and any such articles not distributed by her within one year of my death shall fall into and form part of my residuary estate[2].

1   See the note at **9.8** to **9.10**.
2   This is only a gift of the jewellery which the daughter wishes to select or distribute. She might select everything but if there is anything which is neither selected nor distributed it will fall into residue.

FORM 9.16

Gift of pictures to children to select with provision for disagreement[1]

I give to each of my children one of my [*Bill Maltman Watercolours of Lake District Hills*] and I direct that my children should agree which painting each of them is to have but in the event that they cannot agree within six months of my death the decision of my trustees[2] as to which child should take which painting shall be final and binding.

1   See the note at **9.8** to **9.10**.
2   If one or more of the children are trustees then provision should be made for an independent trustee or some other independent person to make this decision. For example, in place of 'my trustees' substitute 'my trustees other than any trustee who is one of my children'.

FORM 9.17

Absolute gift of personal chattels to children with non-binding request as to distribution in accordance with memorandum[1]

I give to my children[2] my personal chattels as defined by Administration of Estates Act 1925 s 55(1)(x) not otherwise disposed of[3] by this my Will in equal shares absolutely and without imposing any trust or binding obligation upon my children I request that my personal chattels be distributed in accordance with any existing or future memorandum[4] of my wishes left by me.

1   See the note at **9.8** to **9.10**. This form should *not* be adapted for use by a testator who cannot make up his mind about the identity of legatees and the sums payable to them. It creates a gift to the children coupled with a non-binding indication as to the applicable wishes.

2 This is an absolute gift to the children who are therefore entitled to the chattels if they do not distribute them in accordance with a memorandum of wishes whether one can be found or not. It is unlikely to be appropriate to make a gift in these terms in favour of the trustees. However, the clause could be adapted as a gift to trustees to hold as part of the residuary estate in the following manner:

'I give to my trustees my personal chattels as defined by Administration of Estates Act 1925 s 55(1)(x) not otherwise disposed of by this my Will to hold as part of my residuary estate but without imposing any trust or binding obligation upon them I request that my personal chattels be distributed in accordance with any existing or future memorandum of my wishes left by me.'

If the chattels are distributed in accordance with the testator's wishes within two years of the death this gift will take advantage of Inheritance Tax Act 1984 s 143: see **appendix 28.6**.

3 This gift could be used in conjunction with one of the earlier gifts because it only affects property not otherwise disposed of.

4 The memorandum will not be incorporated into the Will where the Will refers to either an existing or a future document: *University College of North Wales v Taylor* [1908] P 140. It is not desirable that the memorandum should be incorporated in this situation.

FORM 9.18

Bequest of personal chattels as defined by Administration of Estates Act 1925 – gift to trustees for distribution equally among children[1]

I give to my Trustees my personal chattels as defined by Administration of Estates Act 1925 s 55(1)(x) to be distributed among those of my children who survive me as my Trustees shall think fit and without imposing any binding obligation I direct that my Trustees shall endeavour to share them (as nearly as possible) equally having regard to their nature and value.

1 See the note at **9.9** to **9.11**. A gift in these terms does not include a gift over into residue. If the trustees cannot distribute the chattels in specie they will have to sell and divide the proceeds of sale.

FORM 9.19

Bequest of chattels in possession of testator but not owned by him[1]

I give to [*name*] [*any car*] in my possession at my death and I direct that if it is in my possession under the terms of a hire purchase agreement an agreement for lease purchase or similar agreement my Trustees shall take such steps as are practical to vest ownership of [*the car*] in [*name*] at the expense of my residuary estate.

1 See the note at **9.12** to **9.13**. For financial reasons, motor cars in particular are often in the testator's possession under an agreement with a finance company. Testators are inclined to regard the cars as their own property although the ownership is not vested in them. The testator is often unaware of the legal niceties of the agreement he has entered into and this precedent has been drafted to try to cover any such agreement. If the testator insists on the car itself being transferred to the beneficiary, he should be warned that, because of the terms of the agreement, it may be impossible to give effect to his wishes.

FORM 9.20

Bequest of chattels subject to financial agreement[1]

I give to [*name*] [*any car*] owned by me or in my possession at my death but only on condition that he pays to my Trustees

1 Such sum as they are required to pay in order to discharge:

9.20 *Precedents*

    1.1   any credit sale agreement; or

    1.2   any loan obtained to finance the purchase of the car; or

    1.3   any other similar financial obligation.

2   Such sum as they are required to pay under the terms of any hire purchase agreement an agreement for lease purchase or similar agreement in order to enable the ownership of the car to be transferred to him.

[1]   See the note at **9.12** to **9.13**. This form requires the beneficiary to discharge any financial obligation of the testator relating to his acquisition of the car including liabilities which would otherwise be paid out of his residuary estate.

FORM 9.21

Cost of delivery to or vesting in beneficiary[1]

The cost of delivering any gift to a beneficiary or vesting it in him shall be an executorship expense [*as shall be the cost of the upkeep of the gift until delivery or vesting*].

[1]   In the ordinary course, it is for the beneficiaries to make their own arrangements to collect gifts. The extent of this rule is uncertain. Generally it is not treated as requiring, for example, a devisee to bear the cost of an assent in his favour. The words in square brackets oust the usual rule applicable to specific gifts but they may not be appropriate in all cases, for example, to a specific devise or a gift of livestock. In the case of residuary gifts the cost of upkeep is always a testamentary expense.

The cost of tracing a beneficiary is often said to be borne by the beneficiary: *Re Phillips* [1938] 4 All ER 438. However, although in the early 20th century, RSC Ord 65 r 14B did indeed provide that the costs of court inquiries to ascertain the person entitled to a legacy or share be paid out of the legacy unless the court otherwise directed but that provision was repealed and not replaced in 1959 and decisions such as *Re Phillips* may no longer be reliable.

FORM 9.22

Gift of a debt

I give to [*name*] the debt of £   and all interest and arrears owing[1] at the date of my death from [*debtor*].

[1]   See the note at **9.14**. It is important to specify that all interest is included to avoid difficult questions as to the passing of arrears.

FORM 9.23

Release of simple debt[1]

I release [*name*] from the debt of £   and all interest owing.

[1]   See the note at **9.14**. The release of a debt constitutes a legacy in favour of the debtor so that if the debtor dies before the testator, the release will lapse and the debt will remain owing out of the debtor's estate. For a clause also releasing the estate see **Form 9.25**. The release of the debt will enable the debtor to require the release of any security but **Form 9.24** may be preferred where the debt is secured.

FORM 9.24

Release of security[1]

I release [*name*] from the debt of £   and all interest owing on the security of [*property charged*]. [*The cost of discharging the security shall be an executorship expense.*]

[1]   See the note at **9.14** and the footnote to **Form 9.23**.

FORM 9.25

Release of debt and the debtor's estate[1]

I release [name] from the debt of £   and all interest owing and if he dies before me his personal representatives shall have the benefit of this provision.

1   See the note at **9.14**.

FORM 9.26

Gift of shares[1]

I give to [name] [number] [one pound ordinary shares in ABC plc].

1   See the note at **9.15**.

FORM 9.27

Gift of shares – alternative form[1]

I give to [name] my holding of shares in [ABC plc].

1   See the note at **9.15**.

FORM 9.28

Gift of shares and loan account in family company – provision for amalgamation reconstruction and takeover[1]

1   I give to [name]:

   1.1   my holding of shares in [ABC Limited];

   1.2   any loans I may have made to the company which are outstanding at my death;

   1.3   all undrawn remuneration and fees due to me from the company;

   1.4   all dividends and interest accrued at my death.

2   If any of the shares comprised in this gift are as a result of takeover amalgamation or reconstruction represented by a different holding clause 1 above shall take effect as a gift of that holding.

1   For a brief discussion of the tax implications relating to a gift of shares in a family company, see the note at **9.16** to **9.19**.

FORM 9.29

Gift of option to purchase farming business and freehold farm[1]

1   I give to [name] ('the Grantee') the option to buy from my Trustees[2] the business[3] of farmer carried on by me at my death.

2   The purchase if effected shall:

9.20 Precedents

2.1 include all assets of the business and the [freehold] property at which it is carried on known as [*CD Farm*];

2.2 be subject to the Grantee taking over all liabilities in connection with the business and the property and bearing any inheritance tax attributable to this gift.

3 My Trustees shall give written notice to the Grantee of this right within [four][4] weeks of my death.

4 The Grantee shall exercise this option by giving written notice to my Trustees within [# months] of my death[5].

5 The price to be paid by the Grantee shall be:

5.1 [#% of] the market value at my death of the business and property as defined in Inheritance Tax Act 1984 ss 160 and 168;

5.2 paid as to #% upon exercising the option and as to the balance when and on such terms as my Trustees think fit.

6 The cost of any conveyance or transfer required to give effect to this gift shall be an executorship expense.

---

1 See the note at **9.16** to **9.19**. This form will be useful where, for example, the testator wishes his son to carry on his business but the business constitutes the main asset of his estate and he also wishes to provide for his widow and other beneficiaries. Circumstances in general and, in particular, the amount of money required to provide for other beneficiaries, will dictate the terms of the option. It has the advantage of providing cash for those beneficiaries without inheritance tax business or agricultural relief being lost.

2 Whatever the terms of the option, the trustees will require powers to carry on the business and an indemnity during the period between the death of the testator and the exercise of the option. It is probably desirable to incorporate in the option a provision similar to **Form 12.13** rather than to relegate it to the clause dealing with trustees' powers. The trustees will need an indemnity (charged against the business assets) covering the period during which they operate the business.

3 The business constitutes its assets less its liabilities. The balance sheet ought to indicate what constitutes its assets. When obtaining instructions, however, careful inquiry should be made of the testator as to whether he intends the option to exclude some assets or to include others. For example, his car may constitute a business asset and he may not intend that to be included in the option. The business premises are particularly important. They may have been kept out of the business assets although used rent free by the business. In most cases, it is desirable to make express provision for the testator's interest in freehold or leasehold property used in connection with the business.

4 See the previous footnote: The period within which notice of the option ought to be given and accepted should be tailored to the business in question. This example relates to a farming business and there may be issues such as the care and feeding of livestock or sowing and harvesting of crops that require immediate attention and so may demand very rapid action by the executors and/or the option holder. On the other hand the accounts might be in such a state that there is no realistic prospect of ascertaining the price payable until many months after the death. In all cases where there is an option to purchase an ongoing business the Will should include a power enabling the executors/trustees to manage the business as in **Form 12.13**.

5 The trustees will not wish to carry on the business for longer than is necessary. It is therefore desirable that the grantee should be required to exercise the option at the earliest possible time. In some circumstances, the grantee's state of knowledge may be such as to enable him to exercise the option before the precise cost is known but it would be impractical to impose a time limit which takes no account of the date on which the cost of exercising the option will be ascertained.

FORM 9.30

Gift of interest in partnership[1]

1 In the exercise of the power in my partnership agreement dated   *etc* I give to [*name*] my share and interest in that partnership or the price payable for it.

2   This gift:

    2.1   includes my share of all the assets of the business;

    2.2   is subject to [name]

        (a)   indemnifying my residuary estate to the satisfaction of my Trustees from all liabilities of the partnership;

        (b)   accounting for any sum owing to me from the partnership profits at my death or constituting profits to the date of my death;

        (c)   accepting as binding on him so far as is applicable all the terms of the partnership agreement;

        (d)   bearing any inheritance tax attributable to this gift.

1   See the note at **9.16** to **9.19**. A gift of a share in a partnership cannot be made unless there is power to do so in the partnership agreement. If there is no power the testator can only give his share in the proceeds of the dissolution of the partnership to the beneficiary to enable him to have the capital to buy into any succeeding partnership if the other partners agree. This is particularly appropriate where it is a family partnership.

    An option to purchase a partnership share is most unlikely to be required. If it is, **Form 9.29** and this form can be adapted. An option for continuing partners to purchase ought to be dealt with in the partnership agreement itself.

FORM 9.31

Gift of business of which testator is sole proprietor[1]

1   I give to [name] the business of [ABC & Co] carried on by me at my death.

2   This gift:

    2.1   includes the goodwill and all the other assets of the business together with the [leasehold] property known as [xxx] where it is carried on;

    2.2   is subject to [name]

        (a)   taking over all liabilities in connection with the business;

        (b)   bearing any inheritance tax attributable to this gift;

        (c)   observing the provisions of the lease of the property;

        (d)   indemnifying my estate against all liability under the lease whether arising before or after my death.

1   See the note at **9.16** to **9.19**.

10 Specific gifts of real property and rights of occupation

Simple gifts of land (devises)

10.1 As with all gifts of specific property an accurate description is important. In the case of a house it will usually suffice to use the postal address. Sometimes, however, more will be needed. There is no need to extend the description to refer to rights and restrictions that affect the property as it will be taken on the same terms as those on which the testator holds it. Similarly, if the property is subject to tenancies the beneficiary will take subject to them.

Mortgages

10.2 A debt which is charged on the testator's property such as a mortgage is payable out of the property charged, unless the Will expresses a contrary intention[1]. The normal form of direction to pay debts out of residue is not sufficient: there must be an express reference to the mortgage debt[2]. The reference to 'any charge' covers not only a legal but also an equitable charge.

1   Administration of Estates Act 1925 s 35, see **appendix 25.16**.
2   See **Form 10.1**.

10.3 It is important to inquire about mortgages when taking instructions. There may be mortgage protection or other policies, the proceeds of which are intended to go towards the discharge of the debt but which may fall into residue unless express provision is made. This may not accord with the wishes of the testator. Care should also be taken with settled policies of insurance which are payable at the discretion of trustees having regard to a letter of wishes or similar direction of the testator which may be out of date by the time the Will is made. Many testators do not realise that the disposition of settled policies is not something which can be controlled by Will but which must be dealt with by giving a direction to trustees during the testator's lifetime.

Inheritance tax

10.4 Inheritance tax is payable out of residue in the absence of a direction to the contrary. **Form 10.5** is an example of a gift which bears its own inheritance tax. In cases in which the testator directs that any inheritance tax is to be borne by the beneficiary but any mortgage is to be paid out of residue, care should be taken to ensure that the testamentary provision makes it clear whether the beneficiary's inheritance tax liability relates to the value of the house subject to the mortgage or to its value after repayment of the mortgage.

Ademption

10.5 Another feature common to all specific gifts is the risk of ademption. One possible solution is illustrated in **Form 10.8**; the use of the well-known phrase 'principal private residence' is to provide for the testator changing his residence between the date of his Will and the date of his death.

Minors

10.6 A gift of real property to a beneficiary who may be a minor at the death of the testator will normally be effected through an express trust created by the Will. A simple gift to a minor will not be effective to pass the legal estate to the minor but instead operates as a declaration that the property is held in trust for the minor[1].

1 Trusts of Land and Appointment of Trustees Act 1996 s 2 and Sch 1, see **appendix 26.15** and **26.29**.

Settled gifts of land

10.7 Following the commencement of the Trusts of Land and Appointment of Trustees Act 1996[1] it is no longer possible to create a settlement for the purposes of the Settled Land Act 1925[2]. Instead, any trust of property (whether express, implied, resulting or constructive[3]) which consists of or includes land is a trust of land[4]. Furthermore, land held on trust for sale is no longer regarded as personal property[5] and in the case of every trust for sale of land there is implied, despite any provision to the contrary, a power for the trustees to postpone sale of the land[6]. Trusts for sale have not been abolished, but in most cases under the Trusts of Land and Appointment of Trustees Act 1996 it makes no practical difference whether or not there is a trust for sale.

1 The Trusts of Land and Appointment of Trustees Act 1996 commenced on 1 January 1997.
2 Trusts of Land and Appointment of Trustees Act 1996 s 2(1), see **appendix 26.15**.
3 Trusts of Land and Appointment of Trustees Act 1996 s 1(2)(a), see **appendix 26.14**.
4 Trusts of Land and Appointment of Trustees Act 1996 s 1(1)(a), see **appendix 26.14**.
5 Trusts of Land and Appointment of Trustees Act 1996 s 3(1), see **appendix 26.16**.
6 Trusts of Land and Appointment of Trustees Act 1996 s 4(1), see **appendix 26.17**.

10.8 Apart from the appointment of trustees, the Trusts of Land and Appointment of Trustees Act 1996 had four consequences:
(1) it affected powers of management of land[1] which were then further affected by the Trustee Act 2000;
(2) it introduced powers to delegate the powers of management of land to beneficiaries[2];
(3) it introduced consultation with beneficiaries[3]; and
(4) it expressly dealt with rights of occupation of trust land[4].

1 Trusts of Land and Appointment of Trustees Act 1996 s 6, see **appendix 26.19**.
2 Trusts of Land and Appointment of Trustees Act 1996 ss 9 to 9A, see **appendix 26.22** to **26.23**.
3 Trusts of Land and Appointment of Trustees Act 1996 ss 10 to 11, see **appendix 26.24** to **26.25**.

10.9 *Specific gifts of real property and rights of occupation*

4   Trusts of Land and Appointment of Trustees Act 1996 ss 12 to 13, see **appendix 26.26** to **26.27**.

Powers of Management of Land

10.9 Trustees' powers of management of land are derived from the Trusts of Land and Appointment of Trustees Act 1996 and the Trustee Act 2000, which heavily amended the former Act in this regard[1]. Trustees of land have in relation to the land subject to the trust all the powers of an absolute owner[2]. The power also applies to personal representatives[3]. The powers of management of land may be extended or restricted by the Will[4]. The duty of care applies to trustees of land when exercising their powers of management of land[5] but that, too, can be excluded if desired[6].

1   Trustee Act 2000 Sch 2 Part II para 45.
2   Trusts of Land and Appointment of Trustees Act 1996 s 6(1), see **appendix 26.19**.
3   Trusts of Land and Appointment of Trustees Act 1996 s 18, see **appendix 26.28**.
4   Trustee Act 2000 s 9, see **appendix 26.37**.
5   Trusts of Land and Appointment of Trustees Act 1996 s 6(9), Trustee Act 2000 s 2, Sch 1, see **appendix 26.19**, **26.31** and **26.61**. See **10.20** to **10.21**.
6   Trustee Act 2000 Sch 1 para 7, see **appendix 26.61**.

10.10 Trustees may acquire freehold or leasehold land[1] in the UK as an investment, for occupation by a beneficiary, or for any other reason[2]. The term 'freehold or leasehold land' has a specific definition[3] and because of that trustees cannot acquire any undivided share in land in England and Wales under the statutory power, since an undivided share exists only in equity and cannot subsist as a legal estate. Where it is thought that trustees might need to invest in an undivided share of land an express power to that effect should be included[4].

1   'Land' is defined in the Interpretation Act 1978: it includes buildings and other structures; land covered with water; and any estate, interest, easement, servitude or right in or over land.
2   Trusts of Land and Appointment of Trustees Act 1996 s 6(3) and Trustee Act 2000 s 8(1), (2) see **appendix 26.19** and **26.36**.
3   The terms 'freehold or leasehold land' is specifically defined to mean, in relation to England, Wales and Northern Ireland, a legal estate (including in relation to Northern Ireland land held under a fee farm grant), and in relation to Scotland, the estate or interest of the proprietor if the dominium utile, or in the case of land not held on feudal tenure, the estate or interest of the owner, or a tenancy: Trustee Act 2000 s 8(2), see **appendix 26.36**.
4   This is most often necessary where trustees are to hold a share of a property occupied by a beneficiary who is a co-owner. See **Form 10.9** which includes such a power.

10.11 Trustees acquiring land as an investment are under duties to have regard to the standard investment criteria and to obtain and consider proper advice, and also the statutory duty of care, if it has not been limited or excluded by the Will trust instrument[1], but if they are acquiring land for a non-investment purpose, for example, for occupation by a beneficiary, trustees will only be subject to the statutory duty of care. The powers may be restricted or excluded[2] or made subject to consents[3]. As part of general power of investment, trustees may invest in loans secured on land[4].

1   See **12.20** to **12.21**.
2   Trusts of Land and Appointment of Trustees Act 1996 s 8(1) and Trustee Act 2000 s 9, see **appendix 26.21** and **26.37**. Trustee Act 2000 s 8(1) power is more limited than the power in Trustee Act 2000 s 3 in that it only permits trustees to lend on the security of land situated in the UK, but wider in that it permits trustees to lend on the security of land for purposes other than investment.
3   Trusts of Land and Appointment of Trustees Act 1996 s 8(2), see **appendix 26.21**.
4   Trustee Act 2000 s 3(3), see **appendix 26.32**. This power is also subject to the trustees having regard to the standard investment criteria, the requirement to obtain proper advice (unless the exclusion applies), and the statutory duty of care.

Delegation to beneficiaries

10.12 Trustees of land acting together jointly as trustees are given power to delegate by power of attorney to any beneficiary or beneficiaries of full age and beneficially entitled to an interest in possession in land any of their functions which relate to the land, for any period or indefinitely[1]. Beneficiaries to whom functions have been delegated are, in relation to the exercise of those functions, in the same position as trustees with the same duties and liabilities[2]. The duty of care[3] applies to trustees in deciding whether to delegate any of their functions to beneficiaries[4] but, if the delegation is not irrevocable[5], the trustees remain under a continuing duty to keep the delegation under review[6] and, if the circumstances make it appropriate to do so, must consider whether there is a need to exercise any power of intervention that they have[7] and if they consider that there is a need to exercise such a power they must do so[8].

1 Trusts of Land and Appointment of Trustees Act 1996 s 9(1), see **appendix 26.22**.
2 Trusts of Land and Appointment of Trustees Act 1996 s 9(7), see **appendix 26.22**.
3 Trustee Act 2000 s 2, Sch 1, see **12.20** to **12.21** and **appendix 26.31** and **26.61**.
4 Trusts of Land and Appointment of Trustees Act 1996 s 9A(1), see **appendix 26.23**.
5 Trusts of Land and Appointment of Trustees Act 1996 s 9A(2)(b), see **appendix 26.23**.
6 Trusts of Land and Appointment of Trustees Act 1996 s 9A(3)(a), see **appendix 26.23**.
7 Trusts of Land and Appointment of Trustees Act 1996 s 9A(3)(b), see **appendix 26.23**.
8 Trusts of Land and Appointment of Trustees Act 1996 s 9A(3)(c), see **appendix 26.23**.

Consultation with beneficiaries

10.13 In the exercise of any function relating to land subject to the trust[1], trustees of land are under a duty 'so far as practicable' to consult the beneficiaries of full age and beneficially entitled to an interest in possession in the land[2], and so far as consistent with the general interest of the trust to give effect to the wishes of those beneficiaries, or (in the event of a dispute) the majority by value[3]. This applies unless expressly excluded[4].

1 Trusts of Land and Appointment of Trustees Act 1996 s 11(1), see **appendix 26.25**.
2 Trusts of Land and Appointment of Trustees Act 1996 s 11(1)(a), see **appendix 26.25**.
3 Trusts of Land and Appointment of Trustees Act 1996 s 11(1)(b), see **appendix 26.25**.
4 Trusts of Land and Appointment of Trustees Act 1996 s 11(2)(a), see **appendix 26.25**.

10.14 The duty to consult with beneficiaries adds appreciably to the burdens and difficulties of the trustees and in general the author recommends its routine exclusion[1]. The duty to consult is particularly something to exclude in relation to a gift by Will where it is intended that any land shall be sold and the proceeds divided. Sometimes there are special reasons for not doing so such as a co-ownership trust of a house in which the co-owners are going to live, in a trust to provide a residence for a beneficiary, or any other land where it is intended that a beneficiary will occupy it. In such cases it will usually be desirable to provide the occupying beneficiary with the assurance of knowing that trustees must consult him (or, as is usually the case, her).

1 See **Form 12.21** for a form of general exclusion.

The right of occupation

10.15 The Trusts of Land and Appointment of Trustees Act 1996 makes provision for a right of occupation for a beneficiary 'who is beneficially entitled to an interest in possession' in land subject to a trust of land at any time[1] if at that time either the purposes of the trust include making the land available for his occupation (or for the

10.16 *Specific gifts of real property and rights of occupation*

occupation of a class of which he is a member or of beneficiaries in general)[2]; or the land is held by the trustees so as to be so available. This is subject to the right not being available if the land is either unavailable or unsuitable for occupation by him[3].

1   Trusts of Land and Appointment of Trustees Act 1996 s 12(1), see **appendix 26.26**.
2   Trusts of Land and Appointment of Trustees Act 1996 s 12(1)(a), see **appendix 26.26**.
3   Trusts of Land and Appointment of Trustees Act 1996 s 12(1)(b), see **appendix 26.26**.

10.16 The statutory right of occupation is not confined in its application to residential property held on trust, but can be relevant to any kind of land in England and Wales held on trust which is capable of being occupied by a beneficiary, such as a farm or business premises. However, the statutory right is only available in respect of a beneficiary who is beneficially entitled to an interest in possession in the land[1]. No right is conferred on a beneficiary if the land is either unavailable or unsuitable for his occupation[2].

1   Trusts of Land and Appointment of Trustees Act 1996 s 12(1), see **appendix 26.26**. Interest in possession is not defined for these purposes but probably connotes a lesser interest than that contemplated by the use of the same words in Inheritance Tax Act 1984 Part III Chapter II.
2   Trusts of Land and Appointment of Trustees Act 1996 s 12(2), see **appendix 26.26**.

10.17 Trustees may impose reasonable conditions on a beneficiary in relation to his occupation of land[1] including payment of outgoings[2] and assuming any other obligation in relation to the land or any activity conducted there[3]. Where two or more beneficiaries are entitled to occupy land, trustees may exclude or restrict the entitlement to occupy of one or more but not all of them, but may not do so unreasonably or to an unreasonable extent[4]. If a beneficiary is excluded trustees can require compensatory provision to be made for anyone excluded by a beneficiary in occupation[5]. The trustees might also impose conditions on the occupying beneficiary including a condition that a beneficiary who occupies the land may be required to pay a 'rent' to an excluded beneficiary or beneficiaries[6], or a condition that he forgoes benefit from another part of the trust fund so that a compensating additional benefit from that other part is received by the excluded beneficiary or beneficiaries[7].

1   Trusts of Land and Appointment of Trustees Act 1996 s 13(3), see **appendix 26.27**.
2   Trusts of Land and Appointment of Trustees Act 1996 s 13(5)(a), see **appendix 26.27**.
3   Trusts of Land and Appointment of Trustees Act 1996 s 13(5)(b), see **appendix 26.27**.
4   Trusts of Land and Appointment of Trustees Act 1996 s 13(1), (2), see **appendix 26.27**.
5   Trusts of Land and Appointment of Trustees Act 1996 s 13(6), see **appendix 26.27**.
6   Trusts of Land and Appointment of Trustees Act 1996 s 13(6)(a), see **appendix 26.27**.
7   Trusts of Land and Appointment of Trustees Act 1996 s 13(6)(b), see **appendix 26.27**.

10.18 The powers of exclusion or restriction must be exercised having regard to the intentions of the person who created the trust[1], the purposes for which the land is held[2] and the circumstances and wishes of the beneficiaries who are entitled to occupy the land[3]. A testator may include an express declaration of his intentions in a Will and can provide that a property is to be retained in specie for the purpose of providing a particular beneficiary with a home. In doing so the testator will strongly influence what is subsequently done with the land because the powers of exclusion or restriction cannot be exercised so as to prevent a person who is in occupation of land from continuing to occupy the land[4] in a manner likely to result in his ceasing to occupy the land[5] unless he consents or the court has given approval[6]. Should the matter come to court the testator's intentions and the purposes for which the land is held will be taken into account[7].

1   Trusts of Land and Appointment of Trustees Act 1996 s 13(4)(a), see **appendix 26.27**.
2   Trusts of Land and Appointment of Trustees Act 1996 s 13(4)(b), see **appendix 26.27**.
3   Trusts of Land and Appointment of Trustees Act 1996 s 13(4)(c), see **appendix 26.27**.
4   Trusts of Land and Appointment of Trustees Act 1996 s 13(7), see **appendix 26.27**.
5   Trusts of Land and Appointment of Trustees Act 1996 s 13(7)(a), see **appendix 26.27**.

6	Trusts of Land and Appointment of Trustees Act 1996 s 13(7)(b), see **appendix 26.27**.
7	Trusts of Land and Appointment of Trustees Act 1996 s 13(8), see **appendix 26.27**.

Providing for a right of residence by Will

10.19 The precedents in this section providing rights of residence[1] are not designed for inheritance tax mitigation but to serve a practical purpose. The occupant might obtain a beneficiary-taxed interest in possession if, for example, the interest is an immediate post-death interest (see **Chapter 15**) and, in the longer term, no inheritance tax saving will be achieved except, perhaps, in the case of the transfer of nil-rate bands between spouses and civil partners[2]. The precedents can be used to accommodate the wish of the testator to provide a residence for a relative, a friend, an employee, a family retainer or his widow (usually from a second marriage). He wishes the beneficiary to have the right to live in the house during his or her lifetime but not to own it.

1	**Forms 10.7** and **10.9** to **10.11**.
2	In many cases the beneficiary will be of limited means and his estate is not likely to attract inheritance tax. The fact that the beneficiary has an interest in possession will not, therefore, have adverse consequences but the draftsman should bear in mind that the value of the house will aggregate with the beneficiary's free estate which may give rise to an unpredictable inheritance tax liability.

10.20 There are two approaches. One is to create a life interest in the property while the other is to grant a mere right of occupation which may or may not be subject to terms of occupation. Granting a life interest does more than just grant a right of occupation. It entitles the life tenant to the net rents until sale and the income produced by the proceeds of sale of the property if sold[1]. Sometimes the granting of a life interest to the beneficiary is the best way of achieving the testator's wishes. If, for example, the beneficiary's health were to require him to move out of the house to sheltered accommodation or a nursing home, the testator might wish him to have the interest from the sale proceeds to supplement his income. In such cases it is also useful to include a power to advance capital[2] to the life tenant in case the income is not sufficient to pay the fees of a nursing home or similar.

1	See **Form 10.7**.
2	For an example, see **Form 12.5**.

10.21 Where the testator only wants to grant a right of occupation and not a life interest the occupying beneficiary will not be entitled to the net rents until sale or the income produced by the proceeds of sale of the house if sold and so, if it is intended that the proceeds of sale are to be invested in a replacement property, the Will should make express provision for that event[1]. If the intention is that the beneficiary will become entitled to the rents or the interest generated by investment of the proceeds of sale then the testator really intends that he should have a life interest. A problem which often arises is that account is not taken of the liability for outgoings and insurance. If the trustees are to bear these liabilities a separate fund will have to be provided. Even if the liabilities are to be imposed on the beneficiary, if there is no fund held back for the trustees they will not be able to enforce the beneficiary's obligations should that prove necessary.

1	See **Forms 10.9** to **10.11**.

10.22 Often the testator's intention is to provide furnished accommodation. Serious consideration should be given to making an outright gift of the furnishings to the proposed occupant. If this is not done, it is impracticable to place an obligation on the

10.22 *Specific gifts of real property and rights of occupation*

occupant to 'maintain and replace as occasion requires' because, over a period of time, the intended benefit becomes a burden. As ordinary household furniture is not durable, a life interest is also inappropriate. The precedents are not intended to apply to furnishings which constitute valuable assets in themselves.

PRECEDENTS

10.23

FORM 10.1

Simple gift of house free of mortgage

I give to [*name*] my house known as [*postal address*] [and I direct that any charge[1] on my house shall be discharged out of my residuary estate].

1 This will include a statutory charge, an equitable charge or any other financial charge on the property as well as a mortgage.

FORM 10.2

Simple gift of house to two or more persons as tenants in common[1]

I give my house known as [*postal address*] to [AB] and [CD] in equal shares but if one of them dies before me his share shall [form part of my residuary estate]/[be taken by [EF]].

or

I give my house known as [*postal address*] to [AB] and [CD] as tenants in common in equal shares[1] or to the survivor of them.

or

I give my house known as [*postal address*] as tenants in common in equal shares[1] to those of the persons named below who survive me

   [AB];

   [CD];

   [EF].

or

I give my house known as [*postal address*] to the persons named below in the shares indicated:

   [AB] one half;

   [CD] one quarter;

   [EF] one quarter.

If any beneficiary named dies before me then the benefit he would have taken if he had survived me shall be [added proportionally to the other shares]/[shared equally among the surviving beneficiaries][2].

10.23 Precedents

1   A gift to two or more persons without words of severance will constitute a gift to them as joint tenants. If they survive the testator, they can, of course, elect to take the gift as tenants in common. If, however, one of them pre-deceases the testator (or survives the testator and dies before an assent in favour of the beneficiaries as tenants in common has been executed) the whole of the property will pass to the survivor(s). If the gift is to beneficiaries in specified shares they will take as tenants in common and, if one beneficiary pre-deceases the testator, his share will fall into residue. It is better to provide for possible contingencies rather than to allow the position to be regulated by the application of the general law if one beneficiary dies before the testator as it is then clear that the consequence was intended and has not resulted from chance.

2   This can be adapted and used with this or the earlier provisions of this form. In some cases, a suitable adaption may be:

         'shall be taken by his widow [or if his widow does not survive me by those of his children who survive me].'

FORM 10.3

Simple gift of house to two or more persons as joint tenants[1]

I give my house known as [*postal address*] to [AB] and [CD] as beneficial joint tenants [or to the survivor of them].

1   The effect is that if both AB and CD survive the testator but one of them dies before severing the joint tenancy, the survivor will take the whole interest by survivorship. The inclusion of the words in brackets is not essential but is desirable. See footnote 1 to **Form 10.2**.

FORM 10.4

Gift of immovable property – provision for description

I give to [*name*] my [freehold] [leasehold][1] land fronting to [ ] which is [registered at HM Land Registry under title number] *or* [which I hold by a conveyance [*or* assignment, lease *etc*] dated and made between *etc*].

1   Leaseholds are personal property, not real property.

FORM 10.5

Gift of house – subject to inheritance tax[1]

I give to [*name*] my house known as [*postal address*] but subject to his bearing any inheritance tax attributable to its value.

1   See the note at **10.4**.

FORM 10.6

Gift of interest in a house held as tenant in common

I give to [*name*] my beneficial share and interest in the house known as [*postal address*].

FORM 10.7

Settled gift of immovable property[1]

My Trustees shall hold [*description of property*] on trust for [AB] for life[2] and after his death [on the trusts of my residuary estate]/[*insert appropriate gift over*][3].

Precedents **10.23**

1 A strict settlement can no longer be created and the life interest must be held under a trust of land. See Trusts of Land and Appointment of Trustees Act 1996 s 2, **appendix 26.15** and **10.7**.

This clause is silent as to the life tenant's obligations to pay outgoings leaving the matter to the trustees in exercise of their functions under Trusts of Land and Appointment of Trustees Act 1996 s 13(3). In most cases some express provision is required and a more complex form should be used. For example, some may prefer to require the life tenant to undertake obligations of repair or insurance.

Instead of specifying a particular house, it might be preferable to describe it as 'the house that constitutes my residence at my death' or 'the house that at my death constitutes my principal private residence' or 'the house that constitutes the matrimonial home of my wife and myself'. See notes for **Form 10.8**.

It may be necessary to consider giving additional powers to the trustees. If, at some time after the testator's death, the life tenant wishes to occupy another house, he cannot require the proceeds of the sale of the original house to be re-invested in that other house unless the Will gives him an express right to do so. It is thought, however, that where the testator's aim is to provide a home for the beneficiary, one of **Forms 10.9** to **10.11**, rather than this, should be used. A possible exception may be the case in which the testator foresees the beneficiary ultimately requiring sheltered accommodation or a place in a residential home and intends the income from the proceeds of the sale to be available to the life tenant to contribute to his outgoings. In those circumstances a life tenancy may be preferable to a right of residence. See **10.20**.

In addition, where the life tenant might need access to capital in order to pay nursing home fees an express power to advance capital to him ought to be included as in **Form 12.5**.

2 It is not necessary to specify that AB, the life tenant, is entitled to receive the net rents of the property if he does not occupy it and the income generated by investment of the proceeds of sale if it is sold. It is in the nature of his life interest that he is entitled to those things. Similarly, it is not necessary to provide that AB is entitled to occupy the property if it is available for his occupation. As a beneficiary with and interest in possession in the property he is entitled to occupy it in accordance with the provisions of the Trusts of Land and Appointment of Trustees Act 1996, see **10.15** to **10.18**.

3 It is, of course, important to ensure that the testator does not intend that AB is to be the residuary beneficiary or that the gift over is in favour of AB: there is no point in setting out a prior life interest in favour of a person who is also entitled to the whole of the remainder.

FORM 10.8

Gift of testator's residence

I give to [*name*] the house that constitutes at my death my principal private residence[1] [and if doubt exists as to which is my principal private residence the decision of my Trustees shall be final and binding].

1 The term 'principal private residence' has been used because it has a well-established meaning as a result of capital gains tax legislation. There is unlikely to be any doubt as to which constitutes the testator's principal private residence. For capital gains tax purposes he will probably have made an election. If the testator has a house abroad and one or more houses in the UK, it would be as well to describe the property as 'my principal private residence in the United Kingdom'. Where there is no possibility of the testator having a second home, it would be sufficient to refer to 'the house that constitutes my residence at my death'. Although the Will speaks from death it is thought desirable to make it clear that the provision relates to the testator's principal residence at the time of his death and not at the date of the Will.

FORM 10.9

Gift of house to trustees to permit occupation as a residence[1]

I give my house known as [*postal address*] ('the House') to my Trustees on trust [for sale] on the following terms:

1 My Trustees shall permit [AB] ('the Occupant') to live in the House free of charge[2] so long as he wishes.

75

10.23 *Precedents*

2   While the Occupant is living in the House my Trustees shall not sell it without his consent.

3   When the Occupant has ceased to live in the House my Trustees shall hold it [as part of my residuary estate]/[*appropriate gift over*][3].

4   [At the Occupant's request my Trustees may sell the House and buy another to be held on trust [for sale] on the same terms as the House[4].]

5   In purchasing a replacement in accordance with the previous power my Trustees may join with any person in purchasing an undivided share of land.

1   This precedent should not be used for the purpose of inheritance tax mitigation. It serves a practical purpose where inheritance tax savings are not the prime consideration.
2   If terms are to be imposed on the Occupant's right to live in the House, use **Form 10.10**. If not, the testator should consider setting aside a fund out of the residuary estate from which the trustees can pay for repairs and the like.
3   See footnote 3 to **Form 10.7**.
4   The wording of this clause gives the trustees the express power they need to acquire an alternative house. They cannot spend more than the proceeds of the sale of the present house. For a provision enabling them to spend more, see clause 7 of **Form 10.10**.

FORM 10.10

Gift of house to trustees to permit occupation as a residence – alternative[1]

I give my house known as [*postal address*] ('the House') to my Trustees on trust for sale on the following terms:

1   My Trustees shall permit [AB] ('the Occupant') to live in the House without payment to them so long as he wishes and so long as he keeps the House in repair, insures it and pays all outgoings relating to it[2].

2   While the Occupant is entitled to live in the House my Trustees shall not sell it without his consent.

3   When the Occupant has ceased to be entitled to live in the House my Trustees shall hold it [as part of my residuary estate]/[*appropriate gift over*][3].

4   At the Occupant's request my Trustees may sell the House and buy another to be held on trust for sale on the same terms as the House.

5   In purchasing a replacement in accordance with the previous power my Trustees may join with any person in purchasing an undivided share of land.

6   Any surplus arising from the sale and purchase shall [form part of my residuary estate]/[*as in Clause 3*].

7   My Trustees may use money from my residuary estate to make up the difference between the cost of purchase and the cost of sale[4].

1   This precedent should not be used for the purpose of inheritance tax mitigation.
2   It is still sensible, even where a beneficiary is obliged to pay the expenses, for the testator to provide a fund out of which the trustees can pay for the work if the beneficiary fails to do so or take action to compel the beneficiary to comply with his obligations.
3   See footnote 3 to **Form 10.7**.

4   It is only practicable to empower the trustees to use funds from the residuary estate if there is a continuing trust relating to it. It is undesirable that the Occupant should be able to require the trustees to acquire an alternative house and particularly to provide additional funds for it. For that reason the trustees are given a discretionary power only.

FORM 10.11

Gift of a furnished house to trustees to permit occupation as a residence[1]

I give my house known as [*postal address*] ('the House') with the furniture, curtains, carpets and other articles of household use or ornament in it ('the Furnishings') to my Trustees on trust [for sale] on the following terms:

1   My Trustees shall permit [AB] ('the Occupant') to live in the House and have the use of the Furnishings free of charge[2] for so long as he wishes.

2   While the Occupant is living in the House my Trustees shall not sell the House nor the Furnishings without the Occupant's consent.

3   When the Occupant ceases to live in the House my Trustees shall hold the House and the Furnishings [as part of my residuary estate]/[*appropriate gift over*][3].

4   [as in the previous forms][4].

1   This precedent must not be used for the purpose of inheritance tax mitigation.
2   If obligations to repair and insure the House are to be imposed on the Occupant, clause 1 should be amended to read:
    '1   My Trustees shall permit AB ('the Occupant') to live in the House without payment to them so long as he wishes and so long as he keeps the House in repair, insures it and pays all outgoings relating to it and to have the use of the Furnishings free of charge for so long as he wishes.'
    with consequential amendments to 2 and 3 following the wording of clauses 2 and 3 of the preceding form. It is suggested, however, that any maintenance obligation should not extend to the Furnishings.
3   See footnote 3 to **Form 10.7**.
4   The concluding provisions of the preceding forms can be adapted if necessary.

11 Residuary gifts

11.1 The traditional way of dealing with residuary gifts is to vest the residue in the trustees on trust for sale with power to postpone the sale. This often does not accord with what the testator has in mind. He envisages that some of his assets will be retained in specie and others will be sold. In such cases the testator might be better advised to make specific gifts of those assets that he would like to be retained. Where there is an outright gift of the residue and no continuing trust will come into being, it may be better not to vest the residue in trustees but to rely on the powers of executors to give effect to the terms of the Will. There will, of course, have to be provision for administration of the estate so far as is necessary.

11.2 Where the residuary estate will or may be subject to a trust, it is suggested that it is vested in the trustees on an express trust for sale with power to postpone the sale. In the case of land, a power to postpone the sale is implied by Trusts of Land and Appointment of Trustees Act 1996 s 4 but it may be desirable to include an express power to postpone for the personalty which, invariably, will form part of the residuary estate.

11.3 **Form 11.1** sets out standard administration trusts including a trust for sale with power to postpone sale. It is intended to be introductory to the clauses contained in **Form 11.2** and subsequent forms. The form also contains various directions concerning the payment of debts and expenses. In many cases the statutory powers of executors and trustees to pay debts and expenses will suffice. Express provision has been made for the sake of certainty and in order to vary statutory provisions where appropriate. The reader is referred to the notes to the form itself. It is, in many cases, not necessary to include an express trust for sale but many practitioners continue to do so and lay executors often appreciate an express statement of their powers.

Survivorship clause

11.4 It is important to make an informed decision whether a residuary gift[1] should be contingent on the beneficiary's surviving the testator by a stated period. The object of the requirement is to prevent a beneficiary who only survives the testator by a short period from benefiting. In origin, this was also intended to prevent a second levy of estate duty in quick succession, but Inheritance Tax Act 1984 s 141, which gives inheritance tax relief in the event of a beneficiary's dying within five years of the testator, may result in the inclusion of a survivorship clause not being necessary for this purpose. Nevertheless, the inclusion or exclusion of the clause can have inheritance tax consequences and it ought not to be included without thought being given to those consequences.

1   Sometimes this is something which ought to be done in the case of a non-residuary gift.

11.5 The use of survivorship clauses in the case of Wills for married couples and civil partners is likely to be much reduced following the introduction of the transferrable nil-rate band between spouses and civil partners by Finance Act 2008[1]. Prior to this there was sense in including a survivorship condition for the purposes of inheritance tax mitigation in such cases. The following simple example illustrates the point:

> A has an estate of £100,000 in excess of the nil-rate band and B, his spouse or civil partner, a nil estate. By his Will, A gives £100,000 to his children and the residue to B, with a gift over to the children if B fails to survive him by a specified period of, say, one month. If B survives A, but not by the specified period, the spouse or civil partner exemption will not apply and the whole of A's estate will be taxable giving rise to an inheritance tax liability of £40,000 (£100,000 at 40%). If the provision for survival by a specified period had been omitted, no inheritance tax would have been payable on either the estate of A or of B.

This simple example yields the same result both before and after the introduction of the transferrable nil-rate band because the combined estates of A and B are below their combined nil-rate bands. In such a case the inclusion of a survivorship clause could be detrimental whether A died before or after 9 October 2007.

1 The announcement was made in the Pre-Budget Report 2007 with effect from 9 October 2007 and is discussed in detail in **Chapter 15** at **15.8** to **15.22.**

11.6 The introduction of a transferrable nil-rate band between spouses and civil partners has had the immediate consequence that in the case of Wills for married couples and civil partners survivorship clauses are much less important than was previously the case and in many cases their inclusion will be detrimental. This is illustrated by the following example:

> H and W are married with children. Neither has been married before[1]. Their combined estates are taxable. Prior to the introduction of the transferrable nil-rate band H and W might have been advised to make wills including a nil-rate band discretionary trust with debt and/or charge scheme provisions included. This would be done in order to avoid wasting the nil-rate band. As explained in **Chapter 15**, the advice would now be quite different and each of H and W would be encouraged to leave the whole of his or her estate to the other.
>
> Suppose each leaves the whole of his or her estate to the other subject to the other surviving for 30 days. In the alternative each leaves his or her estate to the children. If W survives H but dies within 30 days the gift to W is ineffective and H uses his nil-rate band in full. W then uses her nil-rate band in full on her death and, provided the estates have been equalised, the two dispositions are as tax-efficient as possible.

That situation is now no more advantageous than the case in which there is no survivorship clause because the transferability of H's nil-rate band to W means that H will not waste any of his nil-rate band if his Will leaves everything to W on her surviving him. Indeed, the absence of a survivorship clause may be advantageous if, for example, W dies in a different fiscal year after the nil-rate band has increased. This is because if H does not use any of his nil-rate band W's personal representatives are able to claim double the nil-rate band at the time of her death which will be greater than her nil-rate band plus H's at the time of his death.

11.7 Residuary gifts

1   If either is entitled to an enhanced nil-rate band because of a previous marriage or civil partnership the inclusion of a survivorship clause will remain useful because only one nil-rate band may be transferred.

11.7 Inheritance tax is not the only reason for including survivorship clauses. Administrative convenience might also justify the inclusion of a survivorship clause. More importantly, the testator can have good reasons for including a survivorship clause as a means of controlling the ultimate destination of his estate. In the case of second marriages the use of a survivorship clause is helpful both as a means of controlling the destination of property and as a means of avoiding the waste of an already enhanced nil-rate band. Survivorship clauses are also particularly useful where the testator wishes to confer a benefit on the named person only, as in the case of a pecuniary legacy given as an acknowledgment of friendship or personal services. A survivorship clause under which the gift is deemed to lapse may then be required. One example, which is becoming more common, is the case of an unmarried couple with no children. Each may wish to benefit the other but include a survivorship clause so that his or her estate does not inadvertently end up in the hands of the other's relatives in the event of deaths in quick succession. Similar principles may apply to civil partners.

11.8 Inheritance Tax Act 1984 s 92[1] permits the use of a survivorship clause without adverse inheritance tax consequences if the period for survival does not exceed six months. One month or 30 days is the usual period used. Apart from the factors described above, such provisions are designed to cover the situation which arises where two people are involved in a common calamity and one survives the other by a few days.

1   Where property is held for a person on condition that he survives for a period of not more than six months and he does not do so, the Inheritance Tax Act 1984 applies as if the alternate provision had effect from the beginning of the period.

11.9 It is rare for there to be any advantage in extending the period beyond one month, although inheritance tax mitigation may sometimes require a longer period. The longer the period prescribed the greater the inconvenience and uncertainty because the estate cannot be administered until after the expiry of the period.

11.10 If it is thought desirable to extend the period of survival, it is unwise to apply the survivorship clause to the appointment of an executor as it will not be possible to obtain a grant of probate within the prescribed period.

11.11 If two persons die in circumstances where it is uncertain which of them died first, the following statutory rules apply.

(1) Where the persons concerned are husband and wife or civil partners:

    (a) if the older dies testate, he is presumed to have predeceased the younger[1];

    (b) if the older dies intestate then in the administration of *his estate, the younger is presumed to have predeceased him*[2].

2. Where the persons concerned are not husband and wife or civil partners, the older is presumed to have predeceased the younger whether he dies testate or intestate[3].

1   Law of Property Act 1925 s 184, see **appendix 25.15**.
2   Administration of Estates Act 1925 s 46(3), as amended, see **appendix 27.1**.
3   Law of Property Act 1925 s 184 unaffected by the amendment to Administration of Estates Act 1925 s 46, see **appendix 27.1**.

11.12 The application of the general rule that the elder is presumed to have predeceased the younger is not restricted to spouses or civil partners but it is to those relationships that they most commonly apply. The special rule as to intestate succession applies only to spouses and civil partners.

11.13 In the case of husband and wife or civil partners, if the husband is older than the wife and has left a Will leaving the whole of his estate to the wife or to X if the wife predeceases him and the statutory rules come into operation, the husband will be deemed to have predeceased the wife, his estate will pass to her and her estate will then be applied in accordance with her Will or intestacy. A survivorship clause will avoid this outcome. If the husband had died intestate, his estate would not pass to the wife but would be administered according to the rules of intestacy on the assumption that the wife had predeceased him. The wife's estate would, of course, be administered according to her Will or intestacy without the husband's estate being added to it. For these purposes, it matters not, therefore, whether the younger of the two dies testate or intestate.

Age contingent gifts

11.14 It is usual to make a residuary gift to the testator's children a class gift[1]. The question then arises whether the gift should be made contingent on the beneficiaries attaining a stated age and if so what age. Many testators take the view that they do not want a young beneficiary to have that right to capital which a vested interest confers. It is common, therefore, to provide that a gift does not vest until a beneficiary attains a specified age. The testator's wishes and the circumstances of individual cases will dictate whether gifts to minors would vest on the death of the testator or be made subject to an age contingency. Careful consideration should be given to the inheritance tax consequences of introducing age contingencies as a result of the changes made to inheritance tax by the Finance Act 2006, discussed in **chapter 15**. Before Finance Act 2006 many draftsmen included a common form contingency provision without giving sufficient consideration to its advantages and disadvantages. It is now all the more important to consider what sort of contingency ought to be included but it is thought that most testators' concerns about the inheritance tax regime will be overridden by their concern not to vest interests in immature beneficiaries. As a result, in this chapter age contingencies are employed which may be inefficient for inheritance tax purposes. Some of the matters besides inheritance tax of which the draftsman should take note are considered below.

1   See **Form 11.6**.

11.15 In the case of Wills made on or after 6 April 2010 Perpetuities and Accumulations Act 2009 (which came into force on that day) has the effect of introducing a single perpetuity period of 125 years[1]. No other perpetuity period may be specified and the 125-year period will apply whether or not the Will specifies a perpetuity period. A testator may limit the duration of a trust by specifying that all the income and capital must be distributed within, say, 21 years of his death[2] but this does not have the effect of foreshortening the perpetuity period. For the purposes of age contingencies, the effect of imposing a unitary perpetuity period of 125 years is that there is a much reduced likelihood of a disposition infringing the Rule against Perpetuities. Thus, in previous editions, the delayed vesting of gifts to the testator's children (lives in being at the testator's death) would not contravene the rule that all interests must vest within the perpetuity period but gifts to more remote issue carried the risk (subject to the 'wait and see' provision) of offending the Rule if a vesting age greater than 21 was specified. This meant that Wills made before 6 April 2010 could provide for children

11.16 *Residuary gifts*

to take vested interests at the age of 25 or 30 years but that substitutional gifts to grandchildren required an age contingency of 21 years or less.

1   Perpetuities and Accumulations Act 2009 s 5(1): see **appendix 26.7**.
2   As in **Form 19.4**.

11.16 Perpetuities and Accumulations Act 2009 has continued the 'wait and see' provisions[1] introduced by the 1964 Act so that, unlike the position at common law, a disposition is not void simply because it might not vest until too remote a time. Until it is established that an interest will not vest until after the end of the perpetuity period, the interest is treated as if it were not subject to the Rule against Perpetuities. Furthermore, if it is established that an interest will not vest in time, that does not affect the validity of things previously done in relation to that interest. This, together with a single perpetuity period of 125 years, greatly simplifies the application of the Rule and simplifies will-drafting. It also means that testators need not limit themselves to a 21-year age contingency in substitutional gifts since it is very likely that their grandchildren will attain the age of 30 or 35 years within the 125-year perpetuity period.

1   Perpetuities and Accumulations Act 2009 s 7: see **appendix 26.9**.

11.17 Wills made before 6 April 2010 are still governed by the previous rules even though the testator dies after that date.

11.18 Where the vesting of capital is postponed until an age greater than 18, Trustee Act 1925 s 31 will result in the beneficiary's interest in income vesting at 18. The Will may, of course, provide for income to be used for a contingent beneficiary prior to his attaining 18 or at a prescribed age over 18. There is, however a constraint on the contingent age being greater than 18 in that, if the inheritance tax advantages, such as they are, of a s 71D trust – the successor to the now redundant accumulation and maintenance trust[1] – are to be enjoyed, the right to receive income should not be postponed beyond 25[2].

1   Accumulation and maintenance trusts suffered terribly as a result of the unexpected assault on the taxation of trusts launched by the Chancellor of the Exchequer on 22 March 2006. It is no longer possible to create an accumulation and maintenance trust within IHTA 1984 s 71 and pre-existing trusts have now ceased to come within the section. It may be no great loss to Will draftsmen that these trusts have passed on. They were not easy to draft and probably little used in Wills. Lifetime inheritance tax planning is much more seriously affected.
2   See **chapter 15**.

11.19 Prior to 6 April 2010 there was a second constraint which was that there would be an infringement of the Rule against Accumulations if the right to receive income did not vest within 21 years of the testator's death. This took effect subject to the saving provisions of Perpetuities and Accumulations Act 1964 s 4. Perpetuities and Accumulations Act 2009 has abolished the restrictions on accumulations[1] for Wills made on or after that date. This means that a power to accumulate need not be limited to 21 years and the precedents in this edition have been amended in order to extend the power to accumulate where possible. As a result of this change Will drafting is much simplified and it is now possible to include a clause giving power: 'during the whole of the period in which a beneficiary has a contingent interest to accumulate such income as is not so applied and to invest that income as an addition to the capital of the share to which that beneficiary is entitled'. One consequence is that it is now possible for a Will to provide that Trustee Act 1925 s 31 shall apply with a non-statutory age contingency.

1   Perpetuities and Accumulations Act 2009 s 13 which declares that Law of Property Act 1925 ss 164 to 166 and Perpetuities and Accumulations Act 1964 s 13 cease to have effect.

11.20 The decision whether to create a vested interest or an interest contingent upon age may also be governed by other inheritance tax considerations. The vestiges of the inheritance tax interest in possession regime, 'immediate post death interests', are discussed in **chapter 15**.

11.21 Capital gains tax is also relevant because it is only where an interest in capital is vested in a beneficiary that a disposal by the trustees will be treated as a disposal by the beneficiary under Taxation of Chargeable Gains Act 1992 s 92, ranking for the full yearly exemption from that tax. In *Sansom v Peay*[1], however, it was held that relief from capital gains tax on the sale of a house was available although the occupant did not have a vested interest in the house. The taxpayers were the trustees of a discretionary trust with power to purchase a house and permit one or more of the discretionary beneficiaries to reside in it. They did this and permitted all the discretionary beneficiaries (being a husband, wife and children) to reside there without payment. It was subsequently sold at a profit and the court held that the profit was not subject to capital gains tax because the house was 'the only or main residence of the persons entitled to occupy it under the terms of the settlement'[2]. It is notable that in the circumstances of this case, the beneficiaries (or at any rate the husband and his wife) would almost certainly have had an 'interest in possession' for inheritance tax purposes even though they only had a contingent interest in the house itself.

1   [1976] 3 All ER 375, [1976] 1 WLR 1073. Where the contingent interest carries the right to the intermediate income, the contingent beneficiary is, of course, in the same position (for income tax purposes) as if he had a vested interest.
2   Taxation of Chargeable Gains Act 1992 s 225.

11.22 If tax considerations are the driving force and the gifts are not otherwise significant for inheritance tax purposes (either because the estate is small or because it is very large) it is the liability to income tax which often results in a vested interest being preferred to a contingent interest. Where the interest is vested, the income is, ultimately, treated as that of the beneficiary himself and does not attract income tax at the rate applicable to trusts[1].

1   The rate applicable to trusts is currently 50%. The dividend rate applicable to trusts is now 42.5%. There is now a special trust tax rate in respect of the first £1,000 of income and particular beneficial treatments apply to trusts for vulnerable beneficiaries.

11.23 Where the income is distributed to a contingent beneficiary the beneficiary may, with some inconvenience, offset or reclaim some of the tax but the ability to do so depends upon the beneficiary's circumstances. Where the income is accumulated, it cannot be recovered because when paid over it is treated as capital in the hands of the beneficiary. In most cases this is a financial disadvantage to the beneficiary although, where he is liable to higher rate tax, it may sometimes be better for him to receive the accumulated income as capital.

11.24 A further consideration which may be relevant is that there is greater scope for the variation of a trust where the interests of the beneficiaries are vested rather than contingent or subject to the exercise of a discretion. In making the choice between vested and age contingent gifts the advantages must be weighed against the disadvantages in each case. Some of the main considerations have been mentioned. Others include the risk of a beneficiary inheriting when immature, the personalities of those concerned (both testator and beneficiaries) and the kind of assets that make up the trust fund.

Lapse and class gifts

11.25 A gift (of whatever nature) to a child or remoter descendant of the testator will not necessarily lapse if the beneficiary dies before the testator. Wills Act 1837 s 33, the

11.26 *Residuary gifts*

text of which is set out in the appendix[1], provides for the beneficiary's issue to take. The statutory provisions may be excluded either by an express substitutional provision[2] or by a general declaration[3].

1   See **appendix 25.14**.
2   For example, **Forms 8.13**, **11.6**, **11.8** and particularly **11.9**.
3   For example, **Form 13.3**.

11.26 It is usually better, however, to make express substitutional provision in the Will rather than to rely on the statutory provision in order to avoid difficulty and uncertainty, for example, as to whether the Will expresses a contrary intention so as to exclude the operation of the section. The testator rarely thinks about the possibility without prompting and should always be asked what he intends if a beneficiary dies before him. This is particularly important where the gift is in favour of a child or grandchild. A failure to seek express instructions may result in s 33 applying in a manner which may be contrary to the wishes of the testator.

11.27 Class gifts are subject to the class closing rules. If the class consists of the children of the testator, it must, of necessity, close with his death. In the case of class gifts in favour of the issue of the testator or another, gifts following a prior life interest and contingent gifts, it is essential to make it clear when the class closes and to have regard to the rule against perpetuities.

Discretionary trusts

11.28 A desire for flexibility may result in a discretionary trust being used to give effect to the testator's wishes. The disadvantage of a discretionary trust (sometimes a major disadvantage) is that the testator places outside his own control the detailed disposition of the property. It has, however, many advantages.

11.29 Discretionary trusts are often used for inheritance tax mitigation and the reader is referred to **chapter 15**, but there are other uses for the discretionary trust unrelated to inheritance tax. A discretionary trust can be used where the testator wishes to make provision for his family in the event of his untimely death while the children are still financially dependent on him. An example would be a man in his early forties, married with three teenage children all of whom are at school. He wishes to cover the possibility of his wife and himself being killed in an accident. In that event, he wants his estate to be used for the benefit of the children along the same lines as he and his wife might have used their resources if they had been alive. The requirements of the children are not likely to be identical. At the time of his death one may have completed his education and be in reasonable employment and the other two may still be at school or college. **Form 11.20** is designed for this use of a discretionary trust. **Form 11.19** demonstrates another use for a discretionary trust.

PRECEDENTS

11.30

FORM 11.1

[handwritten: Always]

Creation of trust for sale with debts, inheritance tax etc to be paid out of proceeds

My Trustees shall hold [the rest of[1]] my estate[2] on trust for sale [with power to postpone sale[3]] to pay executorship expenses[4] and debts including mortgages secured on real or leasehold property[5] and any inheritance tax in respect of property passing under this Will or which becomes payable because of my death[6] on any lifetime transfer by me[7] or payable because of my death on property in which I hold a beneficial interest as joint tenant[8]. [All income received after my death shall be treated as income of my estate regardless of the period to which it relates and the statutory rules concerning apportionment and the rules in *Howe v Dartmouth*[9] and *Allhusen v Whittell*[10] [and *Re Earl of Chesterfield's Trusts*[11]] shall not apply[12].] My Trustees shall hold the residue ('my residuary estate') on the trusts of the following clauses.

[Continue with appropriate provisions as illustrated in the following forms.]

1 If the residuary gift is made after legacies then the gift should usually be expressed as a gift of 'the rest of' the testator's estate. If it is a gift of the whole of the estate then the words 'the rest of' can be excluded.
2 If there is a possibility of the testator having a power of appointment exercisable by Will the draftsman might include here the words 'including property over which I have a general power of disposition by my Will'.
3 It will not always be necessary or desirable to include an express trust for sale. In many cases this is now a matter of choice rather than compulsion. The inclusion of an express power to postpone sale is unnecessary but may assist lay executors to comprehend their task.
4 In previous editions the term 'executorship expenses' was preferred to 'testamentary expenses' on the basis that it describes the nature of the expenses more accurately. Indeed, it was the phrase used before 'testamentary expenses' became common. Nonetheless, many draftsmen now prefer 'testamentary expenses'.
5 This provision ought not to be included as a 'catch all'. If it is intended to relate to a specific gift, it is better to include the provision in the clause relating to the gift. If the mortgaged property is part of the residue, the direction serves no useful purpose.
6 The residue will bear inheritance tax in the absence of a direction to the contrary and, therefore, the inclusion of this clause is not strictly necessary. If the testator wishes some gifts to be made subject to inheritance tax and others free of inheritance tax, the draftsman must bear in mind that problems of 'double grossing-up' can arise and advise the testator accordingly.
7 This provision is intended to cover any inheritance tax chargeable on lifetime gifts as a result of the testator dying within seven years of the gift. Its inclusion may be inappropriate. Without it, the donee will be liable for any additional inheritance tax payable.

   It is unwise to include this provision if no potentially exempt transfer has been made by the testator. If potentially exempt transfers have been made, the gifts to which the clause relates should be specified. The danger of including all gifts is that unexpected consequences may ensue. For example, the testator may make future lifetime gifts, intending that the donee should be liable for any inheritance tax which arises, but forgetting the general direction in his Will.
8 As above, this provision should not be included unless it is intended to relate to a particular property. If so, the gift to which the provision relates should ordinarily be specified. In the absence of express provision, the surviving joint tenant will be liable for the inheritance tax of the testator's half share.
9 (1802) 32 ER 56.
10 (1887) LR 4 Eq 295.
11 (1883) 24 Ch D 643.

11.30 *Precedents*

12   In the majority of cases the complicated nature of the technical rules, intended to strike a balance between the interests of the life tenant and the remainderman, justify their exclusion, although there may be cases in which the statutory rules embodied in the Apportionment Act 1870 should be retained. If they are excluded any money received after the testator's death in respect of a period before his death will be treated as the life tenant's income. Similarly, money received after the death of the life tenant in respect of a period before his death will belong to the remainderman.

The rule in *Howe v Dartmouth* requires the notional realisation of the assets of the estate and their reinvestment in authorised securities. This gives the life tenant a notional income and any surplus over actual income is added to the capital and any deficiency made up out of capital.

The rule in *Allhusen v Whittell* results in a proportion of the debts, expenses and legacies being borne out of the first year's income. If it is excluded the life tenant's income will be higher than normal during the first year because the life tenant will be receiving income from capital which is subsequently used to pay debts, expenses and legacies.

Re Chesterfield's Trusts governs the apportionment, between a life tenant and the remainderman, of those of the testator's assets which are of reversionary nature and cannot be realised by the executors on the testator's death, for example, a reversionary interest in the land, a policy of assurance on the life of a person other than the testator, a debt owed to the testator but payable by instalments continuing after death and the right to receive the testator's pension during the residue of a guaranteed period.

In most cases the requirements of convenience will outweigh the need to retain two of the rules but the exclusion of the rule in *Re Chesterfield's Trusts* may cause injustice between the life tenant and the remainderman if the estate has assets of appreciable value which are of a reversionary nature.

FORM 11.2

Gift to spouse or civil partner to be followed by substitutional gift[1]

My Trustees shall pay my residuary estate to my [wife]/[husband]/[civil partner][2] but if this gift fails the following provisions of my Will shall apply[3].

1   In many Wills this primary gift to the surviving spouse or civil partner is not a residuary gift at all but is made without it being necessary to ascertain residue because the spouse or civil partner is the sole executor and universal legatee. That is a different situation from the one contemplated by this clause, which presupposes that other gifts – such as small legacies – have been made before ascertaining residue.
2   If a survivorship clause is desired include the words: 'if [she]/[he] survives me by thirty days'. See the note at **11.4** to **11.12**.
3   Continue with alternative provisions such as those in **Form 11.7**.

FORM 11.3

Gift to spouse or civil partner for life

My Trustees shall pay the income from my residuary estate to my [wife]/[husband]/[civil partner] during [her]/[his] lifetime and after [her]/[his] death [*continue as required with appropriate gift over, for example, as in Form 11.8*][1].

1   The draftsman always has to consider whether the gift over is to be contingent on the remaindermen surviving both the testator and the life tenant or only the testator. Generally it is considered that the remaindermen need only survive the testator. Otherwise it may not be possible to ascertain the remaindermen for many years and it may be difficult to vary the trust if it proves necessary to do so while the life tenancy is in existence so that complicated provisions may need to be included in the Will to accommodate the uncertainty of future events.

FORM 11.4

Gift to spouse limited for life or until remarriage or formation of civil partnership[1]

My Trustees shall pay the income from my residuary estate to my [wife]/[husband] until [her]/[his] death or remarriage or formation of a civil partnership[2] [or [her]/[his] cohabiting with a [man]/[woman][3]] and after [her]/[his] interest ceases [*continue with appropriate gift over, for example, as in Form 11.8*].

1   This form is for use only with a husband and wife. The following form is suitable for civil partners. Because a life interest in favour of a surviving spouse is an immediate post-death interest in possession to which the spouse exemption applies which does not use up any of the testator's nil-rate band, this is now a very tax-efficient means of making provision for a spouse whilst still retaining control over the destination of property.
    Many Will draftsmen advise against providing for the life interest to cease on remarriage or on the formation of a civil partnership because of the difficulties which may ensue. Interests terminable on remarriage or the formation of a civil partnership can give rise to litigation and, in particular, claims under the Inheritance (Provision for Family and Dependants) Act 1975. Nonetheless, such interests are often desired, especially by testators in second marriages.
2   A widowhood interest can end by death, remarriage or the formation of a civil partnership. In order effectively to cater for the demands of a testator it is necessary to provide for all three possibilities.
3   If the testator also wishes the life interest to be terminated by cohabitation, the words in square brackets should be included. The testator should be advised of the practical problems which arise from a cohabitation provision. Whether cohabitation exists is a question of fact and can be difficult to establish with certainty. To provide for the opinion of the trustees to prevail might place a heavy burden on the trustees and could result in the life tenant suffering an injustice. Most draftsmen advise against the inclusion of a cohabitation clause for these reasons and because it can be a fertile source of family disputes.

FORM 11.5

Gift to civil partner limited for life or until marriage or formation of another civil partnership[1]

My Trustees shall pay the income from my residuary estate to my [civil partner] until [his]/[her] death or marriage[2] or the formation by [him]/[her] of a new civil partnership [or [his]/[her] cohabiting with a [man]/[woman][3]] and after [his]/[her] interest ceases [*continue with appropriate gift over, for example, as in Form 11.8*].

1   This form is for use only with civil partners. See note 1 to the previous form.
2   A limited interest such as this can end by death, marriage or the formation of a new civil partnership. In order effectively to cater for the demands of a testator it is necessary to provide for all three possibilities.
3   See note 3 to the previous form.

FORM 11.6

Vested gift to children with substitutional gift to grandchildren

My Trustees shall divide my residuary estate equally among those of my children who survive me [and attain 21] but if any of them dies before me [*or* before attaining 21[1]] his children shall take equally [upon attaining 21][2] the share which their parent would otherwise have inherited.

1   Use the alternative if the gift to the deceased child is age contingent. For a discussion of the inheritance tax consequences of these provisions following the Finance Act 2006, see **chapter 15**.
2   Since the commencement of Perpetuities and Accumulations Act 2009 on 6 April 2010 this age contingency in the substitutional gift need not be fixed at 21 years but could be greater. See **11.19**.

11.30 *Precedents*

FORM 11.7

Vested gift to children with substitutional gift to any surviving spouse of deceased child but otherwise to grandchildren

My Trustees shall divide my residuary estate equally among those of my children who survive me but if any of them dies before me then his spouse shall take the share which he would otherwise have inherited or if he is not survived by his spouse his children shall take equally [upon attaining 21][1] the share which he would otherwise have inherited.

1 Since the commencement of Perpetuities and Accumulations Act 2009 on 6 April 2010 this age contingency in the substitutional gift need not be fixed at 21 years but could be greater. See **11.19**. For a discussion of the inheritance tax consequences of these provisions following Finance Act 2006, see **chapter 15**.

FORM 11.8

Gift to children at 25[1] with substitutional gift to grandchildren

My Trustees shall divide my residuary estate equally among those of my children who survive me [and attain 25] but if any of them dies before me [*or* before attaining a vested interest[2]] his children shall take equally [upon attaining 18][3] the share which their parent would otherwise have inherited.

1 For a discussion of the inheritance tax consequences of these provisions following the Finance Act 2006, see **chapter 15**.
2 Use the alternative if the gift to the deceased child is age contingent.
3 Since the commencement of Perpetuities and Accumulations Act 2009 on 6 April 2010 this age contingency in the substitutional gift need not be fixed at 21 years but could be greater. See **11.19**.

FORM 11.9

Gift to children at 21[1] with substitutional gift to issue

My Trustees shall divide my residuary estate equally among those of my children who survive me [and attain 21] but if any of them dies before me [*or* before attaining a vested interest[2]] his issue[3] shall [upon attaining 21[4]] take equally [per stirpes[5]] the share which my deceased child would otherwise have inherited but none of my issue[3] shall be entitled to benefit while his parent is eligible.

1 For a discussion of the inheritance tax consequences of these provisions following the Finance Act 2006, see **chapter 15**.
2 Use the alternative if the gift to the deceased child is age contingent.
3 'Issue' means children, grandchildren and so on. 'Children' is limited to the first generation.
4 Since the commencement of Perpetuities and Accumulations Act 2009 on 6 April 2010 this age contingency in the substitutional gift need not be fixed at 21 years but could be greater. See **11.19**.
5 Most draftsmen provide for a division per stirpes rather than per capita.

FORM 11.10

Gift to those of issue whom spouse or civil partner with life interest appoints with default gift to children

My Trustees shall pay the income from my residuary estate to my [wife]/[husband]/[civil partner] during [her]/[his] lifetime and after [her]/[his] death divide the capital among those of my issue living at the death of my [wife]/[husband]/[civil partner] as

[she]/[he] by deed or by will appoints or if [she]/[he] makes no appointment [divide it equally among those of my children who survive my [wife]/[husband]/[civil partner]].

FORM 11.11

Gift to brothers, sisters, brothers-in-law and sisters-in-law with substitutional gift to nephews and nieces[1]

(1) My Trustees shall divide one half of my residuary estate equally among those of my brothers and sisters who survive me but if any of them dies before me his or her children shall take equally the share which their parent would otherwise have inherited.

(2) My Trustees shall divide the other half of my residuary estate equally among those of the brothers and sisters of my [wife]/[husband]/[civil partner] who survive me but if any of them dies before me his children shall take the share which their parent would otherwise have inherited.

(3) If the trust in subclause 1 fails then subclause 2 shall apply to the whole of my residuary estate and if the trust set out in subclause 2 fails then subclause 1 shall apply to the whole of my residuary estate.

1 This clause is intended to operate on the death of the survivor of a husband and wife or civil partners without issue. In these circumstances, it is common for them to want what is left from their joint estates on the death of the survivor of them to pass equally to their respective families. Each of their Wills would make a gift to the residuary estate to the other and the above would be the operative clause on the death of the survivor of them.

FORM 11.12

Gift to specified charities[1]

(1) My Trustees shall divide my residuary estate equally among the following charities:

[*List of names and addresses and, if available, registered numbers*].

(2) If at my death any of the above charities has amalgamated with another charity my Trustees shall pay its share to the amalgamated charity.

(3) If at my death any of the above charities has ceased to exist my Trustees shall pay its share to the charitable organisation or organisations the objects of which they in their absolute discretion consider most closely resemble the objects of the charity which has ceased to exist.

(4) The receipt of a person who appears to be a proper officer of a charity shall be a discharge to my Trustees.

1 See note to **chapter 8** at **8.9** to **8.12**.

FORM 11.13

Gift among charities to be selected by trustees[1]

(1) My Trustees shall pay my residuary estate to all or any of the following charities in such shares as my Trustees think fit:

[*List of names, addresses and registered numbers of charities*].

11.30 *Precedents*

(2) If at my death any of the above charities has amalgamated with another charity my Trustees shall apply the provisions of subclause (1) by substituting the charity with which it has amalgamated.

(3) If at my death any of the above charities has ceased to exist my Trustees may (in their discretion) apply subclause (1) by substituting for that charity the charitable organisation or organisations the objects of which they consider most closely resemble the objects of the charity which has ceased to exist.

(4) The receipt of a person who appears to be a proper officer of a charity shall be a discharge to my Trustees.

1 See note to **chapter 8** at **8.9** to **8.11**.

FORM 11.14

Gift for specified charitable objects

(1) My Trustees shall pay my residuary estate in such manner as my Trustees think fit to charities having as their objects:

[Specify the objects, for example, the welfare of handicapped children, medical research, the welfare of the aged, the welfare of animals.]

(2) The receipt of a person who appears to be a proper officer of a charity shall be a discharge to my Trustees.

(3) [If the preceding trusts of this Will fail to apply my residuary estate for general charitable purposes as my Trustees think fit.[1]]

1 This clause can easily be adapted where the general charitable gift is to apply if a particular trust (not being the residue) fails.

FORM 11.15[1]

Division of residue among a number of persons in fractional shares[2]

My Trustees shall divide my residuary estate among the following in the shares specified:

(a) To AB: one half;

(b) To CD: one quarter;

(c) To EF and GH or the survivor of them: one quarter[3].

1 A partial intestacy will occur if any of AB, CD or EF and GH predecease the testator. The following **Forms 11.16** and **11.17** include gifts over in order to counter this possibility and might be adapted in order to minimise the risk of a partial intestacy unless that is what the testator wants. Alternatively, a general disposition of residue to charity might be included as in **Form 11.19** clause (4).
2 Note that if the gifts are to persons who include persons with a mixture of exempt and non-exempt inheritance tax statuses the notes to **Form 11.18** should be heeded.
3 The gift in subclause (c) is a gift to EF and GH as joint tenants which may be useful where they are husband and wife or civil partners. If a gift to residuary legatees as tenants in common is intended it might be expressed, 'to EF and GH in equal shares: one quarter' but in such a case by far the most sensible course is to give each one eighth.

Precedents **11.30**

FORM 11.16

Division of residue among a number of persons in percentage shares with gift over to children[1]

My Trustees shall divide my residuary estate among the following in the shares specified:

- (a) To AB: 25%;
- (b) To CD: 25%;
- (c) To EF: 15%;
- (d) To GH: 15%;
- (e) To IJ: 10%;
- (f) To KL: 10%[2];

but if any of those persons dies before me his children shall take in equal shares the share which their parent would otherwise have inherited.

1 Note that if the gifts are to persons who include persons with a mixture of exempt and non-exempt inheritance tax statuses the notes to **Form 11.18** should be heeded.
2 It is important to ensure that these add up to 100%!

FORM 11.17

Division of residue among a number of persons in percentage shares with gift over to children and provision for accruer of lapsed shares[1]

(1) My Trustees shall divide my residuary estate among the following in the shares specified:

- (a) To AB: 25%;
- (b) To CD: 25%;
- (c) To EF: 15%;
- (d) To GH: 15%;
- (e) To IJ: 10%;
- (f) To KL: 10%[2].

(2) If any of the persons named in subclause (1) dies before me leaving a child or children living at my death then such child or children shall take in equal shares the share of my residuary estate which their parent would otherwise have inherited.

(3) If any share or shares of my residuary estate given by subclauses (1) and (2) hereof shall lapse or fail then such share or shares shall accrue to the other share or shares which have not lapsed or failed in the proportions which they bear to one another so that no share of my residuary estate shall be undisposed of by this subclause.

1 Note that if the gifts are to persons who include persons with a mixture of exempt and non-exempt inheritance tax statuses the notes to the next form should be heeded.
2 Again, it is important to ensure that these add up to 100%.

91

FORM 11.18

Division of residue among a substantial number of exempt and non-exempt beneficiaries[1]

(1) My Trustees shall divide my residuary estate in twenty equal parts (each of which is referred to as a 'share') and to pay:

    (a) four shares to my brother or if he dies before me to his widow or if he has no widow to those of his children who survive me in equal shares;

    (b) four shares to my sister;

    (c) two shares to my nephew or if he dies before me to those of his children who survive me in equal shares;

    (d) two shares to my niece or if she dies before me to her husband [*name*];

    (e) three shares to the NSPCC[1];

    (f) three shares to the RSPCA[1];

    (g) two shares to the [Central Board of Finance of the Church of England][1,2].

(2) If any of the gifts set out above fails it shall be added proportionally to the gifts which do not.

(3) The receipt of a person who appears to be a proper officer of a charity shall be a discharge to my Trustees[1].

[(4) In determining the shares set out above my Trustees shall only make a gross division so that only the shares which are not exempt from inheritance tax shall be reduced by any inheritance tax attributable to them[1].]

[(5) If the preceding trusts of this Will fail to apply my residuary estate for general charitable purposes as my Trustees think fit[3].]

---

1   Where the testator wants to mix exempt and non-exempt shares of residue great care must be exercised. Inheritance Tax Act 1984 s 41 provides that the exempt shares should not bear the tax due in respect of non-exempt shares which means that where the testator wants to make the sort of division contemplated by this form explicit reference should be made to the burden of inheritance tax. No such reference was made in *Re Benham's Will Trusts* [1995] STC 210 or in *Re Ratcliffe* [1999] STC 262. In *Re Benham* it was held that the non-exempt share had to be grossed-up so that the net sums payable to the exempt and non-exempt beneficiaries were equal. In *Re Ratcliffe* it was held that there should be no grossing-up so that the net sums payable to the exempt beneficiaries were greater than those payable to the non-exempt beneficiaries.

    To avoid uncertainty it is recommended that subclause (4) be used whenever there is a mixture of exempt and non-exempt gifts of residue in fractional shares. Gross division is the method adopted in *Re Ratcliffe* whereby the debts and funeral and testamentary expenses (and any legacies legacies) are paid out of the estate and the proceeds divided into equal shares before the payment of inheritance tax due on the non-charitable gifts. Accordingly the non-exempt residuary beneficiaries each receive a lower net benefit (through the deduction of inheritance tax on their shares) than the net benefit received by the charities. This may not be what the testator wants but it is widely accepted that the *Re Ratcliffe* approach is superior to the *Re Benham* approach both as a matter of construction of testamentary documents and as a matter of application of the Inheritance Tax Act 1984.

2   A gift to 'the Church' will not do. The object of the gift must be specified with more precision than that.

3   This clause can easily be adapted where the general charitable gift is to apply if a particular trust (not being the residue) fails.

FORM 11.19

General discretionary trust[1]

(1) In this clause:
- (a) 'the Trust Fund' means my residuary estate.
- (b) 'my Beneficiaries' are the following:

[*specify the discretionary beneficiaries*].

(2) My Trustees shall hold the Trust Fund upon the following trusts:
- (a) For not more than 125 years from my death to apply the capital of the Trust Fund for the benefit of such of my Beneficiaries as my Trustees think fit.
- (b) To apply the income of the Trust Fund for the benefit of such of my Beneficiaries as my Trustees think fit or to accumulate the whole or any part of it.
- (c) Within 125 years of my death to end these trusts by distributing the Trust Fund among such of my Beneficiaries as my Trustees think fit.
- (d) To exercise their discretionary powers over capital or income when and how they think fit without having to make payments to or for the benefit of all my Beneficiaries or to ensure equality among those who have benefited.

(3) My Trustees shall have the following powers[2]:
- (a) To retain or sell any of the assets constituting the Trust Fund;
- (b) To invest as if they were beneficially entitled and this power includes the right to invest:
  - (i) in unsecured interest free loans to any Beneficiary;
  - (ii) in non-income producing assets including policies of life assurance (with power to pay premiums out of income or capital);
  - (iii) in property for the occupation of any Beneficiary;
- (c) To use the income or capital of the Trust Fund for or towards the cost of maintaining or improving any property forming part of the Trust Fund;
- (d) To make loans which may be interest free;
- (e) To insure any asset of the Trust Fund on such terms as they think fit and:
  - (i) to pay premiums out of income or capital, and
  - (ii) to use any insurance money received to restore the asset or to apply it as if it were the proceeds of its sale;
- (f) To borrow money on such terms as they think fit (including the giving of security) and to use it for any purpose for which the capital of the Trust Fund may be used;

11.30 *Precedents*

(g) In exercising the statutory power of appointing new trustees to appoint a professional person and give him the right to charge for work done by himself or his firm.

(4) [If the above trusts fail to divide my residuary estate equally among the following charities:]

1 This residuary gift is designed for a testator who wishes to benefit a comparatively large group of beneficiaries, probably because he has no close relatives. This is certainly a case in which one would expect him to supply his trustees with a written statement setting out in detail the guidelines he wishes his trustees to follow in exercising their discretion.
2 The circumstances of the case will govern the powers given to the trustees. The draftsman should remember that the exercise by the trustees of (3)(b)(iii) might, in the right circumstances, result in the beneficiary so occupying obtaining a post-death interest in possession with the associated inheritance tax consequences. According to the circumstances, this may or may not be relevant but it is, perhaps, a less serious problem post Finance Act 2006 than was the case under the previous regime. See **chapter 15**.

FORM 11.20

Discretionary trust of residue for testator's children[1]

(1) My Trustees shall hold my residuary estate ('the Trust Fund') on the following discretionary trust:

(a) To apply the capital of the Trust Fund for the benefit of such of my children as my Trustees think fit;

(b) To apply the income of the Trust Fund for the benefit of such of my children as my Trustees think fit or to accumulate all or any part of it;

(c) When all my children have attained [25][2] or died under that age to end the trust by distributing the Trust Fund among such of my children as my Trustees think fit;

(d) If any of my children dies before me or while this trust is in existence his children shall be included among those in whose favour my Trustees may exercise their discretion;

(e) My Trustees may exercise their discretionary powers over capital and income when and how they think fit and need not make payments to or for the benefit of all those in whose favour they can exercise their discretion nor ensure equality among those who are benefited.

(2) My Trustees shall have the following powers:

[*Include requisite powers. See, for example,* **Form 11.19**, *subclause (3)*].

1 This is primarily designed to provide for dependent children both of whose parents have died. See the note at **11.27**. It is, however, suitable for other circumstances. As the interests of prospective beneficiaries must vest during the lifetime of the testator's children, the Rule against Perpetuities has no adverse application.
2 If the age specified in subclause (1)(c) is 21 or less these words can be omitted.

12 Powers of executors and trustees

12.1 Personal representatives have by the Administration of Estates Act 1925, Trustee Act 1925, Trusts of Land and Appointment of Trustees Act 1996 and Trustee Act 2000 wide statutory powers, which, in the majority of cases, will suffice. In some cases, however, some extension or restriction of those powers is desirable. Extended powers of investment are most often included when there is a continuing trust but this is not in all cases necessary.

12.2 This section summarises the effects of the various statutory powers and duties set out in the **appendix** at **26.1** et seq. and provides forms which might be employed to alter those powers either by extending the powers or by restricting duties, for example, by excluding the statutory duty of care or relieving the personal representatives from an obligation to consult with beneficiaries in their management of land. A trustee indemnity and exoneration clause is also included here[1].

1 See **Form 12.22**.

Maintenance and advancement

Maintenance

12.3 Trustee Act 1925 s 31[1] applies to all trusts created by Will unless a contrary intention is expressed in the Will[2]. The section enables trustees to pay or apply the income for or towards the maintenance, education or benefit of a minor who has an interest in the property generating the income. Income not paid or applied as above is to be accumulated during the infancy of the beneficiary and, thereafter, is payable to him[3]. The power is subject to prior interests. In the forms which follow two alternatives are offered. The first is a traditional power which amends Trustee Act 1925 s 31 to widen the trustees' discretion[4]. Now that there is no statutory restriction on accumulations a further amendment to s 31 is possible to the effect that income may be accumulated throughout the continuation of the interest in question[5]. This is most easily done by altering the age contingency in s 31 but many testators will not consider it necessary to do this and so the precedents in this book do not amend s 31 in this way as a matter of course. The second makes no reference to Trustee Act 1925 s 31 but is a power to similar effect[6]. It is also useful to include express provision for the trustees exercising this power to accept a receipt from the beneficiary (if over 16 years of age) or a parent or guardian of the beneficiary if younger[7].

1 For the text of Trustee Act 1925 s 31, see **appendix 26.2**.
2 Trustee Act 1925 s 69(2).

12.4 *Powers of executors and trustees*

3   Trustee Act 1925 s 31(2).
4   **Form 12.1.** Using a form such as this has the advantage that s 31 is well understood. The disadvantage is that lay trustees generally do not know what s 31 enables them to do and so either do not use their power to full effect or incur professional fees unnecessarily.
5   This applies to Wills made on or after 6 April 2010. See Perpetuities and Accumulations Act 2009 s 13 (not reproduced in the appendix). See the note concerning perpetuities and accumulations at **11.18** to **11.19**.
6   **Form 12.2.** A form such as this is not tried and tested in the way that Trustee Act 1925 s 31 has been but it does not include a reference to a section which trustees might not understand.
7   See **Form 12.6**.

Advancement

12.4 Trustee Act 1925 s 32[1] applies to all trusts created by Will unless a contrary intention is expressed in the Will[2]. The section provides that trustees have power to pay or apply up to one-half of the presumptive share of a beneficiary in the trusts of the Will for the advancement or benefit of the beneficiary. Most testators incorporate an extended power of advancement because of the increased flexibility which this offers. In the forms which follow three alternatives are offered. The first is a traditional power of advancement which amends Trustee Act 1925 s 32 to create a power in the wider form[3]. The second makes no reference to Trustee Act 1925 s 32 but is a wider power to similar effect[4]. The third is a power to pay or apply capital for the benefit of a life tenant who does not have a presumptive share and so would not benefit from the statutory power[5].

1   For the text of Trustee Act 1925 s 32, see **appendix 26.3**.
2   Trustee Act 1925 s 69(2).
3   **Form 12.3.** Using a form such as this has the advantage that s 32 is well understood. The disadvantage is that lay trustees generally do not know what s 32 enables them to do and so either do not use their power to full effect or incur professional fees unnecessarily.
4   **Form 12.4.** A form such as this is not tried and tested in the way that Trustee Act 1925 s 32 has been but it does not include a reference to a section which trustees might not understand.
5   **Form 12.5.**

Administrative powers

Statutory powers of investment etc

12.5 In many cases expressly extending powers of investment and management will not be necessary because of the wide statutory powers introduced by the Trustee Act 2000 which came into force on 1 February 2001. The Act repealed the Trustee Investments Act 1961 and portions of the Trustee Act 1925 and confers on trustees and personal representatives[1] newer and wider powers of investment[2], powers to delegate investment and investment-holding powers[3] and powers to charge[4], while imposing an excludable statutory duty of care[5].

1   Trustee Act 2000 s 35, see **appendix 26.59**.
2   Trustee Act 2000 ss 3 to 6. See **12.6** to **12.10**. Powers of management of land are dealt with in **chapter 10** at **10.9** to **10.18**.
3   Trustee Act 2000 ss 11 to 26. See **12.11** to **12.18**.
4   Trustee Act 2000 ss 28 to 29. Commentary on the power to charge appears at **chapter 6** at **6.4** to **6.7**.
5   Trustee Act 2000 s 1, Sch 1. See **12.20** to **12.21**.

Investment powers and duties

The general power of investment

12.6 The Trustee Act 2000 has replaced the provisions of the Trustee Investment Act 1961 as the source of trustees' power of investment. One consequence of the Act is that it makes all kinds of investment (apart from equitable interests in land) authorised investments. The power conferred on trustees and personal representatives by the Trustee Act 2000 is referred to as 'the general power of investment'[1]. Essentially, trustees have a power to make any kind of investment, including loans secured on land but otherwise excluding land (power to invest in which is dealt with separately) that trustees could make if they were absolutely entitled to the assets of the trust[2]. The new statutory power of investment is in addition to any other powers conferred on the trustees by the Will but subject to any restriction or exclusion imposed by the Will[3]. The general power of investment is subject to two express duties, the duty to have regard to standard investment criteria[4] and the duty to take advice[5].

1   Trustee Act 2000 s 3, see **appendix 26.32**.
2   Trustee Act 2000 s 3(1)–(3), see **appendix 26.32**. Nonetheless, it is useful to include an express power of investment in the terms of **Form 12.8**. Lay trustees in particular are better equipped to act if the Will sets out their powers than if they have to look elsewhere to discover them.
3   Trustee Act 2000 s 6(1), see **appendix 26.35**.
4   Trustee Act 2000 s 4, see **appendix 26.33**. See **12.7** to **12.8**.
5   Trustee Act 2000 s 5, see **appendix 26.34**. See **12.9** to **12.10**.

Duty to have regard to standard investment criteria: Trustee Act 2000 s 4

12.7   In exercising the general power of investment (or indeed any investment power) trustees or personal representatives must have regard to 'the standard investment criteria'[1]. These criteria are: the suitability to the trust of investments of the same kind as any particular investment proposed to be made or retained and of that particular investment as an investment of that kind[2]; and the need for diversification of investments of the trust, insofar as is appropriate to the circumstances of the trust[3].

1   Trustee Act 2000 s 4(1), (2), see **appendix 26.33**.
2   Trustee Act 2000 s 4(3)(a), see **appendix 26.33**.
3   Trustee Act 2000 s 4(3)(b), see **appendix 26.33**.

12.8   The trustees must also, from time to time, review the investments of the trust and consider whether, having regard to the standard investment criteria, they should be varied[1]. No indication is given as to how often trustees must review the investment, but in the case of a large trust fund or one invested on the stock market at times of particular volatility or depression (such as the present), frequent reviews might be required. Trustee Act 2000 s 4 makes it clear that the requirement of having regard to the standard investment criteria applies to all powers of investment, and that it is not capable of being excluded[2].

1   Trustee Act 2000 s 4, see **appendix 26.33**.
2   Trustee Act 2000 s 6 applies to the general power of investment but does not appear to apply to the standard investment criteria of s 4, which are of general application. For Trustee Act 2000 s 6, see **appendix 26.35**.

Duty to take advice: Trustee Act 2000 s 5

12.9   Before exercising their statutory investment power (or indeed any investment power) and when reviewing their investments, trustees must obtain and consider proper advice about the way in which, having regard to the standard investment criteria, their powers to invest or vary investments should be exercised[1]. They do not need to obtain such advice if they reasonably conclude that in all the circumstances it is unnecessary or inappropriate to do so[2]. Proper advice is the advice of a person who

12.10 *Powers of executors and trustees*

is reasonably believed by the trustees to be qualified to give it by his ability and practical experience of financial and other matters relating to the proposed investment[3].

1 Trustee Act 2000 s 5, see **appendix 26.34**.
2 Trustee Act 2000 s 5(1)–(3), see **appendix 26.34**.
3 Trustee Act 2000 s 5(4), see **appendix 26.34**.

12.10 The duty applies to all types of investment and to the exercise of all powers of investment, not just the statutory one[1]. As with the duty to have regard to the standard investment criteria the duty to take advice cannot be excluded[2].

1 Trustee Act 2000 s 5(1) applies to 'any power of investment', see **appendix 26.34**.
2 Trustee Act 2000 s 6 applies to the general power of investment but does not appear to apply to the duty to take advice under s 5, which is of general application. For Trustee Act 2000 s 6, see **appendix 26.35**.

Delegation to investment managers and nominees

Delegation prior to the Trustee Act 2000

12.11 The conventional power of investment, however wide as to type of investment, confers the power to select investments and decide when to sell them on the trustees only, and is not a power which the trustees can delegate without express power. The Trustee Act 2000[1] now confers on trustees and personal representatives a power to delegate their investment functions to investment managers and to vest trust assets in nominees. The question which the Will draftsman must face is whether he should rely on the statutory powers or whether express provision should still be made. In most cases the statutory powers will probably be sufficient but forms of express power are included in this section[2].

1 Trustee Act 2000 Part IV ss 11 to 26, see **appendix 26.38** to **26.53**.
2 For a form giving power to appoint agents see **Form 12.9** and for a form giving power to use nominees see **Form 12.10**.

The statutory power to delegate

12.12 The statutory power to delegate[1] enables trustees to authorise an agent to exercise any of their delegable functions. Delegable functions are all functions other than those specified in the Trustee Act 2000[2]. The non-delegable functions specified include the exercise of dispositive powers relating to asset distribution such as powers of appointment[3]; power to decide whether fees or other payments should be made out of capital or income[4]; power to appoint new trustees[5]; and powers of delegation and appointment of nominees[6]. These are quite obvious reservations: there are some functions which are fundamental to the character of a trustee and simply cannot be delegated. Agents to whom functions have been delegated are under the same duty in relation to the exercise of those functions as were the trustees themselves[7].

1 Trustee Act 2000 s 11(1), see **appendix 26.38**.
2 Trustee Act 2000 s 11(2), see **appendix 26.38**.
3 Trustee Act 2000 s 11(2)(a), see **appendix 26.38**.
4 Trustee Act 2000 s 11(2)(b), see **appendix 26.38**.
5 Trustee Act 2000 s 11(2)(c), see **appendix 26.38**.
6 Trustee Act 2000 s 11(2)(d), see **appendix 26.38**.
7 Trustee Act 2000 s 13(1), (2), see **appendix 26.40**.

Agents

12.13 In exercise of the power of delegation trustees may authorise one or more of their number to exercise functions as their agent[1] but may not authorise two or more persons to exercise the same function severally. Only a joint exercise of a delegable function is permitted[2]. A beneficiary is not a person who may be appointed to exercise the functions of trustees as their agent even if that beneficiary is also a trustee[3]. Trustees may authorise an agent to receive remuneration[4] but, unless it is reasonably necessary, an agent may not be authorised to appoint a substitute[5], restrict his liability to the trustees or beneficiaries[6] or act in circumstances giving rise to a conflict of interest[7].

1 Trustee Act 2000 s 12(1), see **appendix 26.39**.
2 Trustee Act 2000 s 12(2), see **appendix 26.39**.
3 Trustee Act 2000 s 12(3), see **appendix 26.39**.
4 Trustee Act 2000 s 14(1), see **appendix 26.41**. The trustees may remunerate agents out of the trust fund for services provided the terms of engagement include agreement for remuneration and the amount of the remuneration does not exceed what is reasonable in the circumstances: Trustee Act 2000 s 32, see **appendix 26.57**.
5 Trustee Act 2000 s 14(2), (3)(a), see **appendix 26.41**.
6 Trustee Act 2000 s 14(2), (3)(b), see **appendix 26.41**.
7 Trustee Act 2000 s 14(2), (3)(c), see **appendix 26.41**.

Asset management

12.14 In relation to their functions relating to the investment of assets[1], the acquisition of property[2] and the management of property[3] subject to the trust (the asset management functions) trustees may not authorise a person to act as their agent except by an agreement in or evidenced in writing[4] and may not do so unless they have prepared a statement in or evidenced in writing[5] as to how the asset management functions should be exercised (a policy statement)[6] and their agreement includes a term to the effect that the agent will comply with the policy statement[7].

1 Trustee Act 2000 s 15(5)(a), see **appendix 26.42**.
2 Trustee Act 2000 s 15(5)(b), see **appendix 26.42**.
3 Trustee Act 2000 s 15(5)(c), see **appendix 26.42**.
4 Trustee Act 2000 s 15(1), see **appendix 26.42**.
5 Trustee Act 2000 s 15(4), see **appendix 26.42**.
6 Trustee Act 2000 s 15(2)(a), see **appendix 26.42**.
7 Trustee Act 2000 s 15(2)(b), see **appendix 26.42**.

Nominees and custodians

12.15 Trustees may appoint a person to act as their nominee in relation to the assets of the trust[1] and take such steps to secure that the assets are vested in the nominee as are necessary[2]. The appointment of a nominee must be in or evidenced in writing[3]. Trustees may also appoint[4] a person to undertake safe custody of the assets of the trust or of any documents or records concerning the assets (a custodian)[5]. The appointment of a custodian must also be in or evidenced in writing[6]. If the trustees invest in bearer securities they must appoint a person to act as custodian of the securities[7] unless the trust instrument permits them to invest in bearer securities without appointing a custodian[8]. Trustees may authorise a nominee or custodian to receive remuneration[9] but, unless it is reasonably necessary, a nominee or custodian may not be authorised to appoint a substitute[10], restrict his liability to the trustees or beneficiaries[11] or act in circumstances giving rise to a conflict of interest[12].

12.16 *Powers of executors and trustees*

1 Trustee Act 2000 s 16(1)(a), see **appendix 26.43**.
2 Trustee Act 2000 s 16(1)(b), see **appendix 26.43**.
3 Trustee Act 2000 s 16(2), see **appendix 26.343**.
4 Trustee Act 2000 s 17(1), see **appendix 26.44**.
5 Trustee Act 2000 s 17(2), see **appendix 26.44**.
6 Trustee Act 2000 s 17(3), see **appendix 26.44**.
7 Trustee Act 2000 s 18(1), see **appendix 26.45**.
8 Trustee Act 2000 s 18(2), see **appendix 26.45**.
9 Trustee Act 2000 s 20(1), see **appendix 26.47**. The trustees may remunerate nominees and custodians out of the trust fund for services provided the terms of engagement include agreement for remuneration and the amount of the remuneration does not exceed what is reasonable in the circumstances: Trustee Act 2000 s 32, see **appendix 26.57**.
10 Trustee Act 2000 s 20(2), (3)(a), see **appendix 26.47**.
11 Trustee Act 2000 s 20(2), (3)(b), see **appendix 26.47**.
12 Trustee Act 2000 s 20(2), (3)(c), see **appendix 26.47**.

12.16 A person may not be appointed as a nominee or custodian unless the person carries on a business which consists of or includes acting as a nominee or custodian[1], is a body corporate controlled by trustees[2] or is a body corporate recognised under s 9 of the Administration of Justice Act 1985[3]. Trustees may appoint one of their number if that one is a trust corporation[4] or two or more of their number if they are to act jointly[5]. The trustees may also appoint the same person to be nominee and custodian and their agent[6].

1 Trustee Act 2000 s 19(1), (2)(a), see **appendix 26.46**.
2 Trustee Act 2000 s 19(1), (2)(b), see **appendix 26.46**. This is to be determined in accordance with Corporation Tax Act 2010 s 1124.
3 Trustee Act 2000 s 19(1), (2)(c), see **appendix 26.46**.
4 Trustee Act 2000 s 19(5)(a), see **appendix 26.46**.
5 Trustee Act 2000 s 19(5)(b), see **appendix 26.46**.
6 Trustee Act 2000 s 19(6), (7), see **appendix 26.46**.

Review of and liability for agents and nominees

12.17 Where trustees have authorised a person to exercise functions as their agent or appointed a person to act as their nominee or custodian then, while that person continues to act for the trust, the trustees must keep under review the arrangements by which the agent, nominee or custodian acts and how those arrangements are being put into effect[1] and, if appropriate, consider whether to exercise any power of intervention[2]. If the trustees consider that they need to exercise a power of intervention they must do so[3]. Similarly, where an agent has been authorised to exercise asset management functions the trustees are under a duty to consider whether there is any need to revise or replace the policy statement[4] and must replace it if there is a need to do so[5]. Trustees are also under a duty to assess whether the policy statement is being complied with[6]. Trustees are not liable for the act or defaults of agents, nominees or custodians unless they have failed to comply with their duty of care[7] and a failure by trustees to act within the limits of their powers in authorising a person to act as their agent or in appointing a nominee or custodian does not invalidate the authorisation or appointment[8].

1 Trustee Act 2000 ss 21 and 22(1)(a), see **appendix 26.48** and **26.49**.
2 Trustee Act 2000 s 22(1)(b), see **appendix 26.49**.
3 Trustee Act 2000 s 22(1)(c), see **appendix 26.49**.
4 Trustee Act 2000 s 22(2)(a), see **appendix 26.49**.
5 Trustee Act 2000 s 22(2)(b), see **appendix 26.49**.
6 Trustee Act 2000 s 22(2)(c), see **appendix 26.49**.
7 Trustee Act 2000 s 23, see **appendix 26.50**.
8 Trustee Act 2000 s 24, see **appendix 26.51**.

12.18 The powers to authorise a person to exercise functions as an agent or to appoint a person to act as a nominee or custodian are in addition to powers conferred on trustees otherwise than by the Trustee Act 2000[1] but subject to any restriction or exclusion imposed by the trust instrument[2]. This section includes a form of exclusion[3].

1 Trustee Act 2000 s 26(a), see **appendix 26.53**.
2 Trustee Act 2000 s 26(b), see **appendix 26.53**.
3 See **Form 12.21**.

Insurance

Power to insure

12.19 The Trustee Act 2000 substituted a new Trustee Act 1925 s 19[1]. A trustee may insure any property subject to the trust against risks of loss or damage due to any event[2], and pay the premium out of any income or capital funds of the trust[3]. The power is subject to a contrary direction[4] on the part of beneficiaries of full age and capacity who are absolutely entitled to the property of the trust[5] or each of whom is of full age and capacity and who (taken together) are absolutely entitled to the property subject to the trust[6]. The statutory power is now adequate and no express power of insurance is included in this section.

1 Trustee Act 2000 s 34, see **appendix 26.52**.
2 Trustee Act 1925 s 19(1)(a), see **appendix 26.1**.
3 Trustee Act 1925 s 19(1)(b), (5), see **appendix 26.1**.
4 Trustee Act 1925 s 19(2), see **appendix 26.1**.
5 Trustee Act 1925 s 19(3)(a), see **appendix 26.1**.
6 Trustee Act 1925 s 19(3)(b), see **appendix 26.1**.

Duty of care

Statutory duty of care

12.20 The Trustee Act 2000 imposes a statutory duty of care[1] which applies (unless expressly excluded) not only to trustees or personal representatives exercising the new powers of investment conferred by the Trustee Act 2000, but also to trustees exercising similar powers conferred on them expressly by Will or by other Acts, whether before or after the passing of the Trustee Act 2000, and to the exercise of various other powers. The duty of care requires that a trustee exercise such care and skill as is reasonable in the circumstances having regard in particular to any special knowledge or experience that he has or holds himself out as having[2] and, if he acts in the course of a business or profession, to any special knowledge or experience that it is reasonable to expect of a person acting in the course of that kind of business or profession[3]. Even in the absence of statutory duty, a trustee exercising his powers is subject to fiduciary duties of care arising under the general law, for example, a duty to invest the trust fund as an ordinary prudent man of business, or according to a higher standard if he is a professional trustee[4].

1 Trustee Act 2000 ss 1, 2 and Sch 1, see **appendix 26.30**, **26.31** and **26.61**.
2 Trustee Act 2000 s 1(1)(a), see **appendix 26.30**.
3 Trustee Act 2000 s 1(1)(b), see **appendix 26.30**.
4 *Bartlett v Barclay's Bank Trust Co Ltd (No 1)* [1980] Ch 515.

12.21 *Powers of executors and trustees*

12.21 The statutory duty of care may be excluded or restricted by the Will[1]. A testator may wish to exclude it, particularly if he is appointing family or friends to be his executors and trustees[2].

1   Trustee Act 2000 Sch 1 para 7, see **appendix 26.61**.
2   For a form of exclusion see **Form 12.19**.

STEP provisions

Incorporation of STEP provisions by reference

12.22 An increasing number of practitioners choose to incorporate the standard provisions of the Society of Trust and Estate Practitioners[1] (STEP) in place of a long form of administrative powers and provisions. This is an easy means of setting out lengthy provisions without producing an overly long Will but it must not be used to shorten the thought process involved in choosing powers and other provisions. It is all too easy for the busy draftsman to incorporate unnecessary and perhaps inconsistent provisions in a mechanical way without having due regard to the consequences. The author recommends that if a practitioner is to incorporate the STEP standard provisions, no additional provisions should be incorporated without exercising great care.

1   The STEP standard provisions are available online at www.step.org, as is the clause recommended by STEP for the incorporation of the STEP standard provisions.

PRECEDENTS

12.23

I FORMS EXTENDING STATUTORY DISPOSITIVE POWERS OF MAINTENANCE AND ADVANCEMENT

FORM 12.1

Maintenance

Trustee Act 1925 s 31[1] shall apply to [the trusts of my Will] as if in paragraph (i) of subsection (1) the words 'as the trustees think fit' were substituted for the words 'as may in all the circumstances be reasonable' and there were no provisos to subsection (1).

1   See the note at **12.3**. For the text of Trustee Act 1925 s 31, see **appendix 26.2**.

FORM 12.2

Maintenance – alternative form[1]

My Trustees shall have power to apply for the benefit of any beneficiary who [is under 18[2]] or [has a contingent interest] the whole or any part of the income from any capital to which he is [or may become][3] entitled or to accumulate income[4].

1   This power is intended to replace the statutory provisions of Trustee Act 1925 s 31. See **appendix 26.2**.
2   This need not be limited to the age of 18 years.
3   The alternative should be used if the power is to apply to a contingent beneficiary whether a minor or an adult.
4   There are no statutory restrictions on the accumulation of income in respect of Wills made on or after 6 April 2010 with the result that accumulation will be permitted throughout the duration of the trust either until the beneficiary attains his or her majority or until the contingent interest ends. See Perpetuities and Accumulations Act 2009 s 13 (not reproduced in the appendix). See the note concerning perpetuities and accumulations at **11.18** to **11.19**.

FORM 12.3

Advancement

Trustee Act 1925 s 32[1] shall apply to [the trusts of my Will] as if the words 'the whole of' were substituted for the words 'one half of' in proviso (a) to subsection (1).

1   See the note at **12.4**. For the text of Trustee Act 1925 s 32, see **appendix 26.3**.

FORM 12.4

Advancement – alternative form[1]

My Trustees shall have power to pay or apply for the benefit of any beneficiary who [is under 18]/[has a contingent interest] the whole or any part of the capital to which he is [or may become] entitled.

1   This power is intended to replace the statutory provisions of Trustee Act 1925 s 32. See **appendix 26.3**.

FORM 12.5

Advancement in favour of life tenant[1]

My Trustees shall have power to pay or apply the whole or any part of the capital of [the trust fund]/[my residuary estate] for the benefit of [*life tenant*].

1 The statutory power of advancement under Trustee Act 1925 s 32 (see **appendix 26.3**) is not exercisable in favour of a life tenant. An extended power in this form is primarily for use where the surviving spouse or civil partner is left a life interest and the income from the residuary estate may be insufficient for his needs. It may be particularly useful where a surviving spouse or civil partner has to enter a nursing home or similar, the fees of which may exceed the income generated by the fund. The power to supplement income should be exercised with great care otherwise the payments may be regarded as income in the hands of the recipient and therefore subject to income tax. For this reason it is as important that the power should be to pay over capital and not a power to supplement income.

FORM 12.6

Minors – receipts[1]

My Trustees shall have power to pay any money to which a beneficiary under eighteen is entitled to his parent or guardian for his benefit or to the beneficiary himself once he has attained sixteen and to rely upon the receipt then given by the parent or guardian or the minor himself.

1 Unless there is express provision in the Will the personal representatives cannot normally get a good receipt from a minor beneficiary although a person with parental responsibility for the minor can give a good receipt on the minor's behalf under Children Act 1989 s 3(3). A married minor can give a good receipt for income.

II FORMS EXTENDING STATUTORY ADMINISTRATIVE POWERS OF INVESTMENT AND MANAGEMENT OF PROPERTY

FORM 12.7

Introductory clause

My Trustees shall have the following powers in addition to their powers under the general law[1]:

1 Where very few express powers are incorporated the Will could simply provide that 'My Trustees may'.

FORM 12.8

Investment[1]

Power to invest as if they were beneficially entitled and this power includes the right:

(1) to invest in unsecured loans[2];

(2) to invest in other non-income producing assets including policies of life assurance[2];

(3) to purchase land anywhere in the world[2];

(4) to purchase an undivided share in land[2];

(5) to invest in land for the occupation or enjoyment of any beneficiary[2].

1   The object here is to give the personal representatives the widest possible powers in a way which enables lay trustees to understand that they have such powers.
2   These powers, in particular, ought to be included as an extension of the trustees' powers under the general law.

FORM 12.9

Appointment of agents[1]

Power to delegate their powers of investment and management of trust property to an agent (including one of their number) on such terms including terms enabling the agent to charge remuneration, to appoint a substitute, to limit liability and to act in circumstances giving rise to a conflict of interest as my trustees think fit.

1   See the note at **12.11** to **12.14**.

FORM 12.10

Use of nominees[1]

Power to appoint any person (including one of their number or a beneficiary) to act as their nominee and to take such steps as are necessary to vest any property in such person on such terms including terms enabling the agent to charge remuneration, to appoint a substitute, to limit liability and to act in circumstances giving rise to a conflict of interest as my trustees think fit.

1   See the note at **12.15** to **12.16**.

FORM 12.11

Loans to life tenant[1]

Power to make loans of capital to [*life tenant*[2]] which may be interest free, repayable on demand or repayable at a rate below the market rate.

1   This provision is a useful addition to a power of advancement but loans to an impecunious life tenant may not be recoverable on his or her death and should be made with the benefit of an appropriate exoneration and indemnity as in **Form 12.22**. The overall inheritance tax payable on the estate of the testator and his life tenant will be a relevant consideration.
2   Or the draftsman might substitute the words 'any beneficiary who is entitled to the income of the capital money'.

FORM 12.12

Borrowing power[1]

Power to borrow money on such terms as they think fit including the giving of security and to use it for any purpose for which the capital of my estate [*or* these trusts] may be used[2].

1   The statutory power of borrowing at Trustee Act 1925 s 16 is limited and it is as yet unclear to what extent the statutory powers introduced by the Trusts of Land and Appointment of Trustees Act 1996 and Trustee Act 2000 enable trustees and personal representatives to borrow. It is wise, therefore, to include an express power where that is desired.

12.23 *Precedents*

2   This power can be particularly useful where the trustees are carrying on the testator's business or the trustees require capital and have an investment which can only be realised at a disadvantage or under penalty. The express power to give security overcomes possible problems arising from the statutory limitations on trustees' borrowing powers.

FORM 12.13

Power to carry on testator's business[1]

Power to carry on my business of [*AB & Co*]/[*any business in which I am engaged*] for so long as they think fit and with the same powers as if they were beneficially entitled and in exercise of this power my Trustees shall have the right:

1   to employ in the business any assets of my residuary estate[2];

2   to be indemnified out of my residuary estate for any loss incurred;

3   to be employed in the business and to retain for themselves any reasonable remuneration paid[3];

4   to form a company to carry on the business;

5   to be directors of any such company and to retain for themselves any reasonable remuneration paid[2].

1   In the absence of express provision personal representatives only have power to continue the testator's business so far as that is necessary to enable it to be sold as a going concern.
2   This clause enables assets of the estate generally to be used in the business. Without this express authority, executors and trustees would be restricted to assets used by the testator himself in the business. When trustees carry on a business under a power in a Will they are personally liable for any debts incurred. To prevent their right of indemnity being limited to assets used in the business an express right to resort to the whole of the residuary estate is given but caution should be exercised in including this far-reaching power.
3   The statement that the trustees may carry on the business 'as if they were beneficially entitled' covers most of the trustees' requirements but, because of the general rules that a trustee may not profit from his office, these clauses are included.

FORM 12.14

Improvement of property[1]

Power to use the income or capital of [*my residuary estate*] for or towards the cost of maintaining or improving any property forming part of [*my residuary estate*] or acquired by my Trustees after my death.

1   This power may refer to a specific trust rather than the residuary estate. Trustees have statutory powers to improve property but this form gives wider power and avoids some of the statutory complications. The precedent should be used whenever a specific trust or the residuary estate includes real property. If the income is required to maintain a beneficiary or inheritance tax considerations dictate that an interest in 'possession' must be preserved it may be desirable to restrict this power.

FORM 12.15

Purchase of trust assets by trustee[1]

Power to sell any asset of my residuary estate at its market value to [*any one or more of my Trustees*]/[*named trustee*] [provided that there is at least one other Trustee who is not purchasing any asset or assets from my residuary estate at the same time][2].

1   A trustee cannot purchase trust assets even after he has ceased to be a trustee unless:
    (a) there is an express power in the Will; or
    (b) all the beneficiaries are of full capacity and agree; or
    (c) the consent of the court is obtained.
    An express provision may be particularly useful where a trustee has, perhaps as a member of the testator's family, a personal interest in part of the estate.
2   This proviso is intended as a safeguard where the testator considers it appropriate or necessary.

FORM 12.16

Retention for tax liabilities

Power to make retentions for any taxes for which they may be liable.

FORM 12.17

Appropriation[1]

Power without the restrictions imposed by Administration of Estates Act 1925 s 41:

(1) To appropriate to any beneficiary in satisfaction or partial satisfaction of the gift to him any asset forming part of my residuary estate and not subject to a specific gift.

(2) To appropriate as the assets or part of the assets of any trust created by this Will any asset forming part of my residuary estate and not subject to a specific gift.

1   This provision gives greater power to the trustees to appropriate than their statutory power under the Administration of Estates Act 1925. If the appropriation is made by deed, it may contain a certificate under the Stamp Duty (Exempt Instruments) Regulations 1987 (SI 1987/516) that the document falls within category C or E of the Regulations, which remain in force, notwithstanding the virtual abolition of stamp duty.

FORM 12.18

Ancillary powers

To do anything incidental to the powers which my Trustees have whether given by statute or under this Will.

III   FORMS RESTRICTING AND EXCLUDING STATUTORY DUTIES

FORM 12.19

Exclusion of duty of care[1]

My trustees shall exercise their powers of investment and carry out their duties as trustees without regard to the statutory duty of care and Trustee Act 2000 s 1 shall not apply to the trusts of my Will.

1   See **12.20** to **12.21**.

12.23 *Precedents*

FORM 12.20

Exclusion of duty to consult[1]

My trustees shall be under no duty to consult with beneficiaries in exercising any of their functions in relation to any land held by them on the trusts of my Will and Trusts of Land and Appointment of Trustees Act 1996 s 11(1) shall not apply to the trusts of my Will.

1   The duty to consult beneficiaries in the exercise by trustees of their functions in relation to land held by them is at Trusts of Land and Appointment of Trustees Act 1996 s 11(1), see **appendix 26.25**. For commentary see the note at **12.12**.

FORM 12.21

Exclusion of duty to review acts of agents and nominees[1]

My trustees shall be under no duty to review the acts of agents, nominees and custodians appointed by them and Trustee Act 2000 s 22 shall not apply to the trusts of my Will.

1   For the ability to exclude Trustee Act 2000 s 22 see **12.17**. For the text of the section see **appendix 26.49**.

FORM 12.22

Exoneration of trustees from liability[1]

1.   In the absence of proof of dishonesty or the wilful commission of an act known to be a breach of trust none of my Trustees shall be liable for any loss [*or bound to take proceedings against a co-trustee for any breach of trust*].

2.   My Trustees shall be entitled to be indemnified out of the assets of my estate against all liabilities incurred in connection with the bona fide execution of their duties and powers.

1   The duty of a trustee in the managing of trust affairs is 'to take all those precautions which an ordinary man of business would take in managing similar affairs of his own'. This is not too onerous and Trustee Act 1925 s 61 affords further protection to a trustee acting in good faith. Nevertheless for the cautious a general exoneration provided by this form goes further and provides for indemnity. There is justification for trustees requiring indemnity if they are empowered to continue some trading activity of the testator which may give rise to personal liability, although it is usual to give the indemnity in the clause conferring the power rather than to rely on a general form of indemnity. The Law Commission has issued a consultation paper on trustee exemption clauses. A report was published on 19 July 2006. The principal recommendations are that a professional trustee should not be able to rely on any provision in a trust instrument excluding liability for breach of trust arising from negligence and that, by way of anti-avoidance, the court might disapply such clauses where reliance on such clauses would be inconsistent with the overall purposes of the trust and it would be unreasonable in the circumstances for the trustee to be exempted from liability. It was decided not to recommend a statutory power that all trustees should be able to make payments out of the trust fund to purchase indemnity insurance to cover their liability for breach of trust.

13 Declarations Part II

13.1 This section sets out a number of declaratory provisions which often appear at the end of a Will. It is suggested that, generally, they should appear grouped together as a single clause with each declaration used constituting a subclause of it. A declaration which is relevant to a particular clause in the Will can conveniently be made part of that clause. Indeed, a number of the declarations included in this section are intended to draw the draftsman's attention to the need to accommodate them in the clauses to which they apply or to remind the draftsman that they probably ought to be included in the Will.

PRECEDENTS

13.2

FORM 13.1

Immovable property bought by trustees to be held on trust for sale[1]

Any immovable property acquired by my Trustees shall be held on trust for sale.

1   This declaration is for use where the trustees have power to invest in immovable property.

FORM 13.2

Restriction on trustees' right to sell assets[1]

[*None of my shares in ABC Limited*] shall be disposed of without the consent of [*my wife during her life and after her death of my children who have attained 18 at the date of sale*].

1   A restriction on the exercise of the trust for sale should not be included without the problems its exercise will cause being fully discussed. The proper management of the company may be adversely affected by intermeddling by a person who has no concern with those functions.

FORM 13.3

Lapse[1]

Wills Act 1837 s 33 shall not apply to the provisions of this Will.

or

A gift to any of my children or remoter descendants shall lapse if the intended beneficiary dies before me.

1   The text of s 33 is set out at **appendix 25.14**. This clause is intended as a general declaration but it is better to exclude s 33 in the clause or clauses making gifts to issue. The authors have no preference as to which of the above should be used.

FORM 13.4

Survivorship[1]

Any beneficiary who [*does not survive me*]/[*is not proved to have survived me*] by thirty days shall be treated as having died before me.

1   For a discussion of the rules relating to survivorship, see **11.4** to **11.13**.

FORM 13.5

No account to be taken of advances[1]

In ascertaining the entitlement of any beneficiary no account shall be taken of advances of income or capital made to that beneficiary.

1   If the power to make advances relates to one provision only in the Will, it is better to incorporate the appropriate declaration in the relevant clause. If the trustees are restricted to their statutory powers or any extension does not exclude Trustee Act 1925 s 32(1), proviso (b), then this declaration should be contemplated.

FORM 13.6

Account to be taken of advances[1]

Any advances of income or capital made to a beneficiary shall be taken into account when ascertaining the entitlement of that beneficiary and any capital taken into account shall be net of inheritance tax.

1   See footnote to **Form 13.5**.

FORM 13.7

Excluding doctrine of satisfaction[1]

No gift in this Will is made in satisfaction or part satisfaction of any debt owed by me.

1   An express declaration displaces the equitable doctrine that a legacy is deemed to be in satisfaction or part satisfaction of any debt owed by the testator to the beneficiary.

FORM 13.8

Excluding ademption[1]

No gift in this Will shall be adeemed in whole or in part by any gift made in my lifetime [*unless I expressly declare in writing at the relevant time that I intend the gift to be thereby adeemed*].

1   Equity leans against double portions and if a testator gives a legacy or a share of residue to one of his children and after making the Will makes a substantial gift to him, the gift may be regarded as a portion and as an advance against the child's testamentary benefit. The declaration ought, perhaps, to be treated as common form, especially where it is foreseeable that the testator may make subsequent lifetime gifts as part of an inheritance tax mitigation scheme.

FORM 13.9

Intermediate income[1]

Gifts made by this Will other than those of my residuary estate shall not carry income or bear interest until the expiration of one year from my death and until then my Trustees may in their discretion:

(1)   accumulate the income and add it to the capital of my residuary estate;

(2)   apply it in accordance with their statutory or other powers;

(3)   pay it to the beneficiary of the asset from which the income arises.

1   The rules relating to the application of intermediate income are complex and this form gives added flexibility. If a particular gift, for example, an annuity or a priority legacy, is to take effect from the date of death, it should be excluded from the provision.
    It should also be excluded if the object of a provision of the Will is to confer the right to the intermediate income for inheritance tax purposes.

13.2 *Precedents*

FORM 13.10

Illegitimate, legitimated and adopted children[1]

For the purpose of ascertaining who is entitled to benefit under this Will:

(1) an illegitimate child shall not be treated as if he had been born legitimate and Family Law Reform Act 1987 ss 1 and 19 shall not apply[2];

(2) a legitimated child shall not be treated as if he had been born legitimate and Legitimacy Act 1976 s 5 shall not apply[3];

(3) an adopted child shall not be treated as the child of his adopter[4].

1 This form is for use where it is desired to exclude from inheritance illegitimate, legitimated or adopted children. In the case of a primary gift, this can be done by adapting the wording of the relevant gift. However, where the gift is substitutional, a general declaration along the lines of the precedent may be better. It is less likely that the testator will wish to exclude a relationship derived from adoption or legitimation than an illegitimate child but testators can be capricious creatures.
2 Family Law Reform Act 1987, ss 1 and 19 (see **appendix 25.24** to **25.25**) provides that references in any disposition to a child of a person shall be construed in the absence of a contrary intention appearing as including illegitimate children. There is a similar provision to the effect that in deducing relationships illegitimate links shall be treated as legitimate.
3 The Legitimacy Act 1976 (see **appendix 25.26**) entitles a legitimated person to take any interest to which he would have been entitled if born legitimate.
4 The Adoption and Children Act 2002 (see **appendix 25.27** to **25.33**), which has replaced the relevant provisions of the Adoption Act 1976 with, for practical purposes, identical provisions took effect on 30 December 2005. The Act provides that an adopted child shall be treated as the legitimate child of the adopter(s) and not of his natural parents unless the Will expresses a contrary intention.

FORM 13.11

Precatory trust[1]

It is my wish without imposing any legal obligation that [*name of beneficiary*] shall deal with the gift made to him in accordance with any written directions I may give him [*and that this shall be done within two years of my death*].

1 Although called a precatory trust it is not a trust at all but merely an expression of a wish. Probably it is better to keep out of the Will declarations like this and to rely on the apparent beneficiary fulfilling the moral obligations imposed on him by an extra-testamentary document. The gift made by the apparent beneficiary will be treated as if having been made by the testator for inheritance tax purposes pursuant to Inheritance Tax Act 1984 s 143, see **appendix 28.6**.

FORM 13.12

Provision for accrual in equal shares[1]

If the trust of any share under this clause fails, that share shall be divided equally among the beneficiaries who survive me.

or

If any beneficiary named in this clause dies before me then the benefit he would have taken if he had survived me shall be shared equally among the beneficiaries who survive me.

1 The object of an accruer clause is to avoid a partial intestacy where there is a residuary gift to named persons equally or in fixed proportions. If one of the named persons dies before the testator there will be a partial intestacy as to his share. Accrual clauses also apply to gifts other than of residue and the forms in this section could be used for those gifts. Where the gift is not of residue, however, the inconvenience caused by there being no accrual provision is less inconvenient, because the failed gift falls into residue and does not constitute a partial intestacy.

Prima facie an accruer clause refers only to the original share and not to an augmented share which has already benefited from an earlier accrual. The first clause in **Form 13.13** ensures that the accrual also applies to an augmented share.

FORM 13.13

Provision for proportional accrual[1]

If the trust of any share under this clause fails that share shall be added proportionally to the other shares [*and this provision shall apply to both an original share and an augmented share*].

or

If any beneficiary named in this clause dies before me then the benefit he would otherwise have taken shall be shared proportionally by the beneficiaries who survive me.

1 See footnote to **Form 13.12**.

14 Attestation

14.1 Apart from the cases of a statutory Will of a mental patient or the Will of a person engaged on active service, a Will must comply with the formalities prescribed by Wills Act 1837 s 9[1]. Ordinarily the testator should sign first, either signing in the presence of two witnesses or acknowledging his signature in their presence, and then the two witnesses should sign in the presence of the testator and of one another. Although it is not necessary strictly to adhere to that procedure provided the requirements of s 9 are met, it is essential that the testator should *either* sign *or* acknowledge his signature before *either* witness signs the Will. The Will will be invalid if the signatures are made out of turn or the testator signs the Will before one witness adds his signature and then acknowledges in the presence of two witnesses, one of whom then adds his signature. In the latter case the first witness must also sign again after the acknowledgement.

1   For Wills Act 1837 s 9, as substituted by Administration of Justice Act 1982 s 17, see **appendix 25.3**.

14.2 Alterations made to a Will after its execution are invalid unless properly attested[1]. In the absence of evidence to the contrary, it is presumed that alterations have been made after execution. The initialling of the alterations by the testator and witnesses made before execution is evidence that they were made before execution and the initialling of alterations made after execution will amount to re-execution if the attestation is good[2]. It is preferable to avoid the need for alterations at a late stage. Where the Will covers more than one page, it is useful, but not essential, to number the pages and to have each signed by the testator.

1   Wills Act 1837 s 21, see **appendix 25.10**.
2   *Re Blewitt* (1880) 5 PD 116.

14.3 The witnesses need not be adults, provided that they are old enough to understand what they are doing and have sufficient mental capacity. However, the use of adults, particularly professionals versed in the requirements of the Wills Act, is recommended. Clearly, it is undesirable to use as a witness any person who, for any reason, may prove to be unreliable or untraceable in the event of having to give evidence.

14.4 If a beneficiary under the Will or his spouse or civil partner is an attesting witness, the Will will be valid but the beneficiary will lose the benefit of the gift under the Will. The subsequent marriage or formation of a civil partnership between a beneficiary and an attesting witness will not invalidate the gift. The rule that a witness cannot obtain a benefit under the Will does not extend to a supernumerary witness[1]. The benefit of a professional charges clause will not now be lost if the person entitled, or one of his partners, acts as a witness[2].

1   Wills Act 1837 s 15 and Wills Act 1968 s 1, see **appendix 25.4** and **25.18**.
2   Trustee Act 2000 ss 28(4) and 33(2)(a), see **appendix 26.54**.

14.5 If a Will does not contain an attestation clause indicating that the statutory requirements have been carried out, an affidavit of due execution will be required before probate can be obtained. It is important therefore that a valid attestation clause should appear at the end of the Will because it may be impossible to trace the witnesses or, at best, there will be the inconvenience of obtaining an affidavit. There are hardly any decisions of the courts on what constitutes a valid clause but the wording used in **Form 14.1** is based on that approved in *Re Selby-Bigge*[1]. There is no advantage in using a longer form of words and it is noteworthy that, in *Re Selby-Bigge*, Hodgson J said 'In order to save labour and for the sake of neatness, every skilful practitioner desires to reduce the number of words to the minimum'.

1   [1950] 1 All ER 1009.

14.6 If a testator is unable to read or write, Non-Contentious Probate Rules 1987 r 13 provides:

> 'Before admitting to proof a Will which appears to have been signed by a blind or illiterate testator or by another person by a direction of the testator, or which for any other reason raises doubt as to the testator having had knowledge of the contents of the Will at the time of its execution, the district judge or registrar shall satisfy himself that the testator had such knowledge.'

Usually a special attestation clause will be sufficient to satisfy this requirement.

Will draftsman's duty in relation to attestation

14.7 The duty in relation to the mechanics of attestation has been the subject of two partially inconsistent first instance decisions of the High Court.

14.8 In *Gray & Ors v Richards Butler (a firm)*[1] Lloyd J held that a solicitor is under a duty to advise a testator on the proper procedure to be followed but found in that case that the solicitor's provision of 'most comprehensive' instructions for the execution of the Will was sufficient to ensure that his conduct did not fall short of that required of the reasonably competent solicitor.

1   [2000] WTLR 143.

14.9 Although not reported until 2000, *Gray v Richards Butler (a firm)*[1] was decided in 1997. Sadly, the decision was not cited to Longmore J in *Esterhuizen v Allied Dunbar Assurance plc*[2]. Longmore J asked himself the question whether it was enough for a solicitor or a professional Will maker to provide comprehensive instructions for the execution of a Will and leave it at that. He answered that question in the negative. His words are salutary and should be noted by all practitioners[3]:

> 'The fact is that the process of signature and attestation is not completely straightforward and disaster may ensue if it is not correctly done. Any testator is entitled to expect reasonable assistance without having to ask expressly for it. It is in my judgment not enough just to leave written instructions with the testator. In ordinary circumstances just to leave written instructions and to do no more will not only be contrary to good practice but also in my view negligent.'

1   [2000] WTLR 143.

14.10 *Attestation*

2   [1998] 2 FLR 668.
3   [1998] 2 FLR 668 at 677.

14.10 The view expressed by Lloyd J sets a lower standard but he accepted that a solicitor is under a duty to take proper care in advising the testator as to the procedure to be followed for the valid execution of his Will, in circumstances in which he is not going to be present at that execution and that the solicitor is under a duty, when the Will is returned to him after execution, to examine it and consider whether it appears to be properly executed. If it is not then it is his duty to raise the question with his client in order to check that the Will has been properly executed or, if not, to advise him that it should be re-executed[1]. In this, as in previous editions, **chapter 24** sets out support materials, including instructions for the execution of a Will. The reader is referred to that section for comments on this decision.

1   *Gray v Richards Butler (a firm)* [2000] WTLR 143, see at 157D–157E.

Will draftsman's duty in relation to capacity

14.11 Whether a Will draftsman ought to satisfy himself that the testator has capacity to give instructions for a Will or to execute it is a matter of some doubt. Good practice should require it. Certainly, it has been said that there is a 'golden rule' that where there is a doubt as to a testator's capacity, a medical practitioner should be present: *Re Simpson*[1], following *Kenward v Adams*[2]. Capacity and the golden rule are further discussed in **chapter 2** at **2.25** to **2.26**.

1   (1977) 121 Sol Jo 24.
2   [1975] CLY 3591.

14.12 The question of the solicitor's duty in relation to mental capacity has been considered by the New Zealand Court of Appeal, holding that ordinarily the question of capacity is outside the solicitor's (and, presumably, other Will draftsmen's) professional expertise[1]. The court noted the fact that a solicitor who has suspicions about his testator client's mental capacity will meet confidentiality problems and conflicts of interest. In a subsequent decision at first instance the court accepted that there could be a duty on a solicitor to consider and advise a testator about capacity but ordinarily a solicitor is bound to carry out the testator's instructions and the solicitor may not make inquiries of other persons about his capacity without his authority[2].

1   *Knox v Till* [2002] WTLR 1147.
2   *Public Trustee v Till* [2002] WTLR 1169.

14.13 The question of capacity is sometimes a matter which must be approached with some delicacy. A Will draftsman is always subject to the testator's instructions but if there is reason to doubt his mental capacity it is advisable to stick to the 'golden rule' and arrange for a medical practitioner to certify that he is capable. If the practitioner is satisfied that the testator is of sound mind he should be asked to act as an attesting witness.

PRECEDENTS

14.14

FORM 14.1

Standard form of testimonium and attestation clause[1]

As Witness my hand this [–] day of [———] 20[–].

Signed by the Testator in our presence and attested by us in the presence of the Testator and of each other.

1 The attestation clause approved by the court in *Re Selby-Bigge* [1950] 1 All ER 1009 (see **14.5**) was:
    'Signed by the testator in our presence and attested by us in the presence of him and of each other.'
    'Testator' has been substituted for 'him' only because it gives the clause a better rhythm.

FORM 14.2

Form of testimonium and attestation clause to a codicil[1]

As Witness my hand this [–] day of [———] 20[–].

Signed by the Testator as a codicil to his Will dated [*date of Will*] and attested by us in the presence of him and of each other.

1 In this form 'Testator', 'his' and 'him' might be altered according to the sex of the testator/testatrix.

FORM 14.3

Where the testator is unable to read or write[1]

As Witness my hand this [–] day of [———] 20[–].

The Testator being [blind]/[unable to read or write] this Will was read to him and he stated that he understood it. At the direction[2] of the Testator it was then signed on his behalf by [*name of person signing for testator*] in the presence of the Testator and us and attested by us in the presence of the Testator of [*name of person signing for testator*] and of each other.

1 See the note at **14.6** for rules governing a blind or illiterate testator. If the testator is temporarily blind, this fact can be stated. If this form is used, the signatory can sign in the testator's name or in his own name on behalf of the testator. If the signatory's name is not known when the Will is prepared the following clause can be used:
    'The Testator being [blind]/[unable to read or write] this Will was read over to him and he stated that he understood it. At the direction of the Testator it was then signed on his behalf in the presence of the Testator and us and attested by us in the presence of the Testator of the person signing on his behalf and of each other.'
    Where the signatory's name does not appear in the attestation clause, he should sign the Will in his own name on behalf of the testator, i e 'AB on behalf of CD'.
    Strictly, the Will need not be attested in the signatory's presence but it is desirable and usually convenient that it should be. It is possible for one of the witnesses to act as the signatory but it is the better practice for someone else to sign, in case the validity of the Will is questioned. In all cases in which a special attestation clause is necessary, it is particularly important that the witnesses should be reliable.

14.14 *Precedents*

2   In the previous edition this form used the word 'request', to which some district registries objected. Although other books of precedents continue to use request, this edition uses 'direction' which, it is understood, is preferred by probate registries.

FORM 14.4

Where the testator is able to sign but unable to read

As Witness my hand this [–] day of [———] 20[–].

The Testator being unable to read, this Will was read to him and he stated that he understood it. It was then signed by the Testator [*with his mark*[1]] in our presence and attested by us in his presence and in the presence of each other.

1   A testator who is able to write but unable to read is something of an oddity. Many, but not all, will sign with a mark without the mark being described as a signature.

FORM 14.5

Where the testator is able to read but unable to sign his name[1]

As Witness my hand this [–] day of [———] 20[–].

The Testator being able to read but unable to sign his name this Will was signed by him with his mark in our presence and attested by us in his presence and in the presence of each other.

or

As Witness my hand this [–] day of [———] 20[–].

The Testator being temporarily unable to sign his name [*because of an injury to his hand*] this Will was read by the testator and at his direction[2] signed on his behalf by [*name of person signing for testator*] in the presence of the Testator and us and attested by us in the presence of the Testator of [*name of person signing for Testator*] and of each other[3].

or

As Witness my hand this [–] day of [———] 20[–].

The Testator being temporarily unable to sign his name [*because of an injury to his hand*] this Will was read by the Testator and at his direction[2] signed on his behalf in the presence of the Testator and us and attested by us in the presence of the Testator [*the person signing on his behalf*] and of each other[3].

1   Where the testator's incapacity is temporary, it is desirable that the reason for his incapacity is stated because, if the validity of the Will is disputed, it will be known that the testator was normally able to write. Certainly one should avoid the testator's signature appearing to be different from his normal signature, for example, by his signing with his left hand.
        Even where the inability to write is not temporary many will prefer the Will to be signed at the direction of the testator rather than have the testator sign with a mark.
2   In the previous edition this form used the word 'request', to which some district registries objected. Although other books of precedents continue to use request, this edition uses 'direction' which, it is understood, is preferred by probate registries.
3   See footnote 2 to **Form 14.3**.

FORM 14.6

Where Will is made by an authorised person under Mental Capacity Act 2005[1]

As Witness the hand of [*name of testator*] acting by [*name of the authorised person*] this [–] day of [———] 20[–].

Signed on behalf of the Testator by as an authorised person under the Mental Capacity Act 2005[2] in our presence and attested by us in the presence of [*name of the authorised person*] and of each other.

1   The relevant provisions of the Act are summarised in **appendix 25.21** to **25.32**.
2   Mental Capacity Act 2005 makes provision for the making of Wills for persons who lack capacity. See ss 16 and 18 and Sch 2 paras 1–4 reproduced at **appendix 25.21** to **25.23**.
       The authorised person should sign the Will with the name of the patient and his own name and the Will must be sealed with the official seal of the Court of Protection:

Signature of authorised person

on behalf of

name of testator

15 Inheritance tax mitigation

15.1 This is a book of Will Precedents and so this chapter concentrates on mitigation effected by the Will. However, particularly where Wills are drawn for couples, testamentary inheritance tax mitigation should form part of a planned approach to mitigate the total inheritance tax combining lifetime and post-death planning. The object is legitimately to minimise the inheritance tax otherwise payable on the combined estates of each of the couple be they husband and wife, civil partners or unmarried cohabitees.

15.2 The commentary and forms in this chapter are principally designed to cater for the needs of families with children and perhaps grandchildren who own their own home and intend that the survivor of them will continue to live in that home. In the case of married couples and civil partners whose civil partnerships have been registered[1] as such, property passing to the survivor on the first death will not incur an inheritance tax charge[2] and so there are opportunities for testamentary inheritance tax planning which is now made much more straightforward as a result of the introduction of transferable nil-rate bands between spouses and civil partners.

1   The Civil Partnership Act 2004 came into force on 5 December 2005. The Act regulates relationships between persons of the same sex with the intention that those who enter into civil partnerships governed by the Act will be treated as if married for all purposes. The Tax and Civil Partnership Regulations 2005 (SI 2005/3229), adopting the same approach as the Act, amend existing tax legislation so that registered civil partners are treated in the same way as married couples for tax purposes with effect from 5 December 2005. It should be noted that there is an important distinction between civil partners and married couples which is the absence of any requirement of a sexual relationship between civil partners: a civil partnership is not consummated and adultery is not, of itself, a basis for bringing it to an end. Thus, two people may register as civil partners although they are not, in fact, homosexual lovers. In the text of this chapter a reference to a spouse also includes a civil partner.

2   If the surviving spouse or civil partner is not domiciled in the UK only the first £55,000 is exempt: Inheritance Tax Act 1984 s 18. This has been the case for a quarter of a century.

15.3 The inheritance tax treatment of unmarried couples, whether cohabiting or not, is identical to that of individuals. Unmarried couples and individuals have an inheritance tax free nil-rate band[1] available to them and may make lifetime gifts by way of inheritance tax planning but couples who are unmarried or who are not in a registered civil partnership do not have the benefit of a spouse or civil partnership exemption and without that the opportunity for inheritance tax mitigation is very limited indeed. They might still equalise their estates in order to make maximum use of the nil-rate band but, without a spouse exemption to rely on, there might still be inheritance tax even on the first death. Unmarried couples often face the additional hurdle that, for one reason or another, they have competing desires concerning the ultimate destination of their property which means that where they own a house together the survivor is more likely to be given a limited interest in the first to die's share of the house. This serves to enhance the taxable estate of the survivor without adding any benefit to his or her beneficiaries.

1   The nil-rate band for 2010/11 is £325,000 and is now set to remain at that level for the next fiscal year.

15.4 It should be borne in mind, however, that not all couples rank inheritance tax mitigation as a priority, no matter how obviously important it might seem. Conversely, some may be so concerned with inheritance tax mitigation that they ignore the needs of their dependants. Whilst the job of the Will draftsman is not to impose his views on the testator but to guide the testator to a sensible and measured conclusion, one should not allow patently misconceived instructions to pass without comment. In recent years the sometimes paranoid desire to minimise inheritance tax has been common and has spawned many testamentary and lifetime schemes of dubious effectiveness which were often poorly understood. The introduction of a transferable nil-rate band has helped to reduce the use of such schemes in the vast majority of cases.

15.5 Testators of moderate wealth with families (used in the broad sense described above) will normally be interested in taking steps proportional to their overall family circumstances to reduce their inheritance tax liability for their family's sake. Those who are not should be encouraged to consider inheritance tax mitigation. This is true whether the family is the result of a marriage, a civil partnership, or some other relationship. The exercise of drafting Wills for such persons should start with appraisal of their circumstances including the particular circumstances of whichever of a couple survives[1]. It is important to bear in mind that the factual background, which varies from one client to another, can prove to be very material: There is not a lot of point in producing tax-efficient Wills which leave the survivor with insufficient income or capital to satisfy their needs. At a time when the rate of return on many investments is historically low the point carries even more force.

1   An example of a checklist appears at **24.3**.

15.6 Once it has been established that some form of inheritance tax mitigation ought to be considered advice about appropriate action, including consideration of lifetime planning, should then follow. Lifetime planning is a specialist topic to which a Will draftsman might draw the attention of a testator but, although it should not be considered in isolation, it is not something which a Will draftsman is expected to take on. Lifetime planning is beyond the scope of this book. Briefly, the measures which might immediately (or, in the case of potentially exempt transfers, after seven years) reduce or provide for prospective inheritance tax, include:

(1)   Maximising the use of annual and other lifetime exemptions.
(2)   Giving away the maximum affordable within the nil-rate band but caution should be exercised in doing this because substantial lifetime gifts will detract from the availability of a transferable nil-rate band (see below).
(3)   Giving as much more than the nil-rate band as does not jeopardise the financial independence of the couple and the survivor taking into account the possibility of extreme circumstances such as prolonged illness. Every time the nil rate amount goes up the liability on such a potentially exempt transfer goes down. This is subject to similar concerns to those expressed above.
(4)   Where making gifts is appropriate, giving as early as possible to start the seven-year survival period running.
(5)   Where making gifts is appropriate, making chargeable gifts to relevant property trusts before making potentially exempt transfers.
(6)   Subject to the concerns expressed above, topping up trusts as the nil-rate band increases. Note that the creation of a lifetime discretionary trust is not a

15.7 Inheritance tax mitigation

      potentially exempt transfer and that the cumulative total of chargeable gifts should not exceed the current nil-rate band.

(7) Taking care not to incur capital gains tax in the process of saving inheritance tax by lifetime giving.

15.7 Testamentary inheritance tax planning has tended to concern four principal topics:

(1) The equalisation of estates. This is something done by a couple during their joint lifetime with a view to minimising the inheritance tax due on the death of the survivor of them.

(2) The use of testamentary trusts. This is a subject complicated by the Finance Act 2006 and is discussed below.

(3) Gifts of shares or interests in the matrimonial (or civil partnership) home. The house is usually by far the most valuable asset of a couple and making such a gift is the most effective means of tax planning for many couples.

(4) Post-death rearrangement of dispositions effected by Wills and severance of joint tenancies. Included within this head are two-year discretionary trusts which are discussed below and precatory trusts which are discussed at **9.10** but need not be limited to gifts of chattels. Deeds of variation and disclaimers are discussed in **chapter 22**.

The introduction of a transferable nil-rate band between spouses and civil partners has simplified these topics for most married couples and civil partners so that equalisation of estates and complicated gifts of shares of the matrimonial home are now quite unusual. There are, however, instances in which such schemes remain relevant.

The transferable nil-rate band

15.8 The transferable nil-rate band was introduced in the Pre-Budget Report delivered on Tuesday 9 October 2007 with immediate effect. Finance Act 2008 inserted new ss 8A, 8B and 8C into the Inheritance Tax Act 1984, an Act which has already suffered repeated surgery in the last few years and is now badly in need of rewriting. These new provisions are reproduced in the **appendix** at **28.1** to **28.3**.

15.9 The principal provision is at s 8A entitled 'Transfer of unused nil-rate band between spouses and civil partners'. As the title suggests, the provision only applies as between spouses and civil partners and so, at present, cohabiting couples of whatever orientation cannot take advantage of this provision just as they cannot take advantage of the spouse exemption. Indeed, it remains the case that although suggesting that unmarried cohabitees consider marriage as a form of inheritance tax planning is somewhat outside the usual scope of tax-planning advice, the point can and should be made that, by remaining unmarried, the couple put themselves at a significant inheritance tax disadvantage.

15.10 Section 8A is reproduced at **28.1**. It applies where the survivor of a married couple or of two civil partners dies on or after 9 October 2007 (see Schedule para 9 at **28.4**). Thus, the amendments providing for the transferability of the nil-rate band apply to all deaths of the first of a married couple or civil partnership whether that death occurred before or after 9 October 2007. It is important, however that the survivor of the couple should not have died until on or after 9 October 2007. Where both of a couple died before 9 October 2007 the new provisions are of no benefit but that fact is of only academic interest to Will draftsmen preparing Wills now.

Inheritance tax mitigation **15.12**

The introduction of the transferable nil-rate band with this retrospectivity is most welcome to those who have suffered negative retrospective taxation in the form of the introduction of pre-owned assets charges and an unnatural interference with the taxation of existing trusts under Finance Act 2006. Many people who, because their husband or wife died years ago and have continued to live in a matrimonial home of (apparently) increasing value, would have found satisfactory inheritance tax planning quite impossible now have an opportunity to benefit from the new provisions.

15.11 The important new provisions are set out in s 8A(2)–(4) (at **28.1**). They provide that for the purposes of the statutory transferable nil-rate band a person (the first to die) has unused nil-rate band on death if –

$$M > VT$$

where –

M is the maximum that could be transferred by the chargeable transfer made on death (under IHTA 1984 s 4) on the person's death if it were to be wholly chargeable to tax at the rate of nil per cent; and

VT is the value actually transferred by that chargeable transfer (or nil if there is no such chargeable transfer).

Where a claim is made under the new provisions, the nil-rate band maximum at the time of the survivor's death is to be treated for the purposes of the charge to tax on the death of the survivor as increased by the following percentage:

$$(E \div NRBMD) \times 100$$

Where –

E is the amount by which M is greater than VT in the case of the first to die; and

NRBMD is the nil-rate band maximum at the time of the death of the first of the couple to die.

The term 'nil-rate band maximum' is defined (by IHTA 1984 s 8A(7)) to mean 'the amount shown in the second column in the first row of the Table in Schedule 1 to [IHTA 1984] (upper limit of portion of value charged at rate of nil per cent) and in the first column in the second row of that Table (lower limit of portion charged at next rate)'. This is the figure conventionally known as the nil-rate band.

15.12 The importance of this is best explained by way of examples. Suppose, for example, that Harold died (without making any previous chargeable transfers) in the year 2004/05 (when the nil-rate band) was £263,000. Harold took no advice when making his will and left the whole of his estate of £289,000 to his widow, Winifred. Harold satisfied the basic requirements of the new provisions because he was survived by his widow and she is still alive. Harold had unused nil-rate band and the appropriate calculation is:

M = £263,000

VT = nil

The statute gives a value for E at **E = M – VT**.

In this simple example E is £263,000 because Harold has not used any of his nil-rate band. It is important to note that, because Harold left the entirety of his estate to Winifred, it does not matter whether that estate was £289,000 as in the example, £1 or £1 million[1]. The value of **E** is fixed by the unused nil-rate band.

15.13 *Inheritance tax mitigation*

This means that (after 9 October 2007) Winifred's available nil-rate band is increased. But it is not increased by £263,000 (the nil-rate band at Harold's death) or by £289,000 (the value of Harold's estate). Rather, it is increased by a percentage. Because Harold left the whole of his estate to Winifred we have been able to establish that **E** is £263,000, the percentage increase in Winifred's nil-rate band is therefore:

$$(£263,000 \div £263,000) \times 100$$

(I.e. 100%)

In this simple example the nil-rate band available on Winifred's death will be increased by 100%. Provided she did not die before 9 October 2007, Winifred's nil-rate band is doubled regardless of the size of Harold's estate or the date of his death. This means that Winifred need not worry that she has continued to live in the matrimonial home and that it is too late to vary Harold's will to introduce complex debt and charge scheme provisions.

1   This is confirmed by the guidance notes issued shortly after the 2007 Pre-Budget Report:
   '9. Where a valid claim to transfer unused nil-rate band is made, the nil-rate band that is available when the surviving spouse or civil partner dies will be increased by the proportion of the nil-rate band unused on the first death. For example, if on the first death the chargeable estate is £150,000 and the nil-rate band is £300,000, 50% of the nil-rate band would be unused. If the nil-rate band when the survivor dies is £325,000, then that would be increased by 50% to £487,500.
   10. The amount of the nil-rate band that can be transferred does not depend on the value of the first spouse or civil partner's estate. Whatever proportion of the nil-rate band is unused on the first death is available for transfer to the survivor.'

15.13 It is important to note, however, that the nil-rate band of the survivor (Winifred in the example) is not enhanced unless a claim is made by *her* personal representatives within the 'permitted period' or (if no claim is made by the personal representatives) by any other person liable to the tax chargeable on the survivor's death within such later period as HMRC may specify. Thus, the claim to transfer unused nil-rate band must be made by the accountable persons when the surviving spouse or civil partner dies and not beforehand. In particular, it is not to be made when the first spouse or civil partner dies.

The 'permitted period' is generous. It is the period of two years from the end of the month in which the survivor dies or (if it ends later) the period of three months beginning with the date on which the personal representatives first act as such, or such longer period as HMRC may specify.

15.14 This does mean that on the death of the first to die (Harold in the example), there is no need to make any reference to HMRC. That can, however, give rise to problems later on if evidence of the disposition of the first to die's estate is lost. As the Guidance points out, the personal representatives of the first to die will need to record the proportion of the nil-rate band that goes unused. In the case of a death before 9 October 2007 that information might not be available – because it was not thought to be useful at the time. Therefore, when a person in the position of Winifred comes to make a will and discloses that she is a widow, the will draftsman should take the opportunity to gather as much information as possible about the estate of the first to die so that it may be possible to make a claim when the survivor dies.

15.15 In the simple example given above the exercise is trivial but matters can easily become complicated. Suppose, for example, that Harold owned a lock-up garage worth £6,000 with his brother, George, as beneficial joint tenants. On Harold's death George took the garage by survivorship and for the purposes of these provisions Harold will be treated as having used a portion of his nil-rate band worth £3,000.

This means that, although **M** remains at £263,000, **VT** is £3,000. **E** is therefore £260,000 and the percentage increase in Winifred's estate is not 100% but:

$$(£260,000 \div £263,000) \times 100$$

which is the unhelpful figure of 98.86%

15.16 Further illustrative examples are contained in the Guidance issued with the Pre-Budget Report:

> 'A dies on 14 April 2007 with an estate of £400,000, which he leaves entirely to his spouse, B. B dies on 17 June 2009 leaving an estate of £600,000 equally between her two children. When B dies the nil-rate band is £325,000. As 100% of A's nil-rate band was unused, the nil-rate band on B's death is doubled to £650,000. As B's estate is £600,000 there is no IHT to pay on B's death.'

> 'J dies on 27 May 2007, with an estate of £300,000. She leaves legacies of £40,000 to each of her three children with the remainder to her spouse K. The nil-rate band when J dies is £300,000. K dies on 15 September 2009 leaving his estate of £500,000 equally to his three children; the nil-rate band when K dies is £325,000. J used up 40% of her nil-rate band when she died, which means 60% is available to transfer to K on his death. So K's nil-rate band of £325,000 is increased by 60% to £520,000. As K's estate is only £500,000 there is no IHT to pay on K's death.'

> 'R dies on 14 April 2007 with an estate of £450,000, which he leaves entirely to his spouse, S. S dies on 17 June 2009 leaving an estate of £675,000 which she leaves equally between her two children. When S dies the nil-rate band is £325,000. As 100% of R's nil-rate band was unused, the nil-rate band on S's death is doubled to £650,000. This leaves £25,000 chargeable to IHT on S's death.'

Further examples can be found in HMRC's Inheritance Tax Manual at IHTM43000 et seq which is available online at www.hmrc.gov.uk/manuals.

15.17 The provisions apply even where the death occurred before the introduction of Inheritance Tax. The Guidance is in the following terms:

> '18. Inheritance tax was introduced with effect from 18 March 1986, but before this date other estate taxes (capital transfer tax and estate duty) applied. Where a surviving spouse dies on or after 9 October 2007 and their spouse died before the introduction of the current inheritance tax provisions, a claim may still be made for the nil-rate band of the surviving spouse to be increased by reference to unused allowances of their spouse.

> 19. Where the first spouse died between 13 March 1975 and 18 March 1986 then the estate would have been subject to capital transfer tax. Any transfers to the spouse would have been exempt from tax in the same way as the under the current rules. The transfer of nil-rate band provisions will operate in these cases in the same way as it works for inheritance tax. So that if on the death of the first spouse all their estate was transferred to their surviving spouse, then a claim may be made on the death of the surviving spouse to increase the nil-rate band by 100%.

15.18 *Inheritance tax mitigation*

> 20. Before 13 March 1975 estate duty applied. Under estate duty there was no tax-free transfer permitted between spouses until 21 March 1972 when a tax-free transfer between spouses of up to £15,000 was introduced.
>
> 21. Where the first spouse died between 21 March 1972 and 13 March 1975 a claim to transfer the nil-rate band to the surviving spouse will be based on the amount of the tax-free band that was unused on the death of the first spouse. For example, a husband died in 1973 and left an estate valued at £10,000, which was all transferred to his wife. As this was all within the spouse's exemption, the individual tax-free band was unused. In this case the full amount of that allowance may be transferred, and a claim may be made on the death of the surviving spouse to increase the nil-rate band by 100%.
>
> 22. Where any part of the first spouse's individual tax-free band was used then there will be a proportionate reduction in the amount by which the nil-rate band of the surviving spouse may be increased.
>
> 23. Similarly, where the first spouse died before 21 March 1972 the transfer of nil-rate band will be based on the proportion of the individual tax-free band that was unused on the death of the first spouse. However, as there was no relief from estate duty for transfers to spouses, any transfer made on the death of the first spouse will use up part of the tax-free band and so reduce the amount by which the nil-rate band of the surviving spouse may be increased.'

15.18 An important point for will draftsmen to understand, however, is that the enhanced nil-rate band is capped at 100% so that if a person has already been married and widowed there is still potential for the nil-rate band to be wasted between spouses and civil partners.

On the other hand, an unused nil-rate band can be transferred from one marriage to the next. An example is given in the Pre-Budget Report Guidance:

> '13. The rules allow unused nil-rate band to be transferred from more than one deceased spouse or civil partner, up to a limit of one additional nil-rate band. So if someone has survived more than one spouse or civil partner, then on their death the accountable persons may be able to claim additional nil-rate band from more than one of the relevant estates. A separate claim form should be completed for each spouse or civil partner who died before the deceased. However the total additional nil-rate band accumulated for this purpose is limited to a maximum of the amount of the nil-rate band in force at the relevant time.'

> 'X dies on 14 April 2007 with an estate of £250,000, leaving £120,000 to his son Y and the remainder to his spouse Z. The nil-rate band when X dies is £300,000 so 60% of his nil-rate band is unused. Z later marries W who dies on 14 May 2008 and also leaves 60% of his nil-rate band unused. Z dies on 14 June 2010 with an estate of £700,000 when the individual nil-rate band is £325,000. Z's nil-rate band is increased to reflect the transfer from X and W, but the amount of increase is limited to 100% of the nil-rate band in force at the time. So Z's nil-rate band is £650,000, leaving £50,000 chargeable to IHT on Z's death.'

15.19 The significance of this can be explained by returning to the example of Harold and Winifred but adding the twist that Winifred had previously been married to Hubert who also left the whole of his estate to her. In such a case Winifred is already entitled to a 100% increase in her nil-rate band by virtue of the receipt of Hubert's estate. If Harold leaves his nil-rate band to her he will have 'wasted' it in the manner readily understood before the 2007 Pre-Budget Report.

This is not a problem where the combined estates of Harold and Winifred are modest, because even if Harold leaves the whole of his estate to Winifred she will still have an enhanced nil-rate band so that enhanced inheritance tax planning will not be necessary.

However, where Harold and Winifred have combined estates which are likely significantly to exceed Winifred's enhanced nil-rate band (this is necessarily difficult to predict) there is still sense in ensuring that Harold's nil-rate band is not 'wasted' by employing the methods discussed in the remainder of this chapter. The situations in which this is necessary will, however, be much less common than was previously the case and, for the most part, will apply to elderly second and third marriages where other considerations – such as the desire to make provision for children and grandchildren from a previous spouse – will be paramount.

15.20 It should be noted that if Winifred and Hubert had divorced there would be no prospect of her having a right to claim an enhanced nil-rate band from anyone other than Harold and it is therefore important to establish that the earlier marriage terminated by death.

15.21 It is also significant that a nil-rate band will be regarded as unused for the purposes of the new provisions even where the surviving spouse is given a limited interest in the estate of the first to die. This is readily apparent from the Guidance:

> '16. Where individuals leave assets on trust with a life interest for their surviving spouse or civil partner, with the remainder passing on their spouse or civil partner's death to someone else (for example their children), there is no IHT to pay on the first death because spouse or civil partner exemption applies. So if the entire estate is left in trust to the surviving spouse or civil partner, the nil-rate band would be available for transfer to the estate of the survivor on their eventual death in the same way as if the estate had been left to them absolutely.'

15.22 Thus, where Harold leaves Winifred a life interest in his estate (an immediate post-death interest in possession) the examples given above will still lead to the same result as if he had given her an absolute interest. This is particularly helpful where a couple have previously been married but divorced and wish the survivor to enjoy the income from the combined estates whilst still controlling the ultimate destination of property.

Inheritance tax planning in other cases

15.23 Where the nil-rate band transfer is not available or in cases in which one or both spouses/civil partners has previously been widowed the remainder of this chapter continues to be worthy of consideration just as in cases before 9 October 2007.

Inheritance tax planning through gifts and the equalisation of estates

15.24 Gifts are often made to intended beneficiaries, particularly the couple's children, on the assumption that they will behave honourably and, in some cases, that

15.25 *Inheritance tax mitigation*

they will, if necessary, subsidise the couple and the survivor. The latter may fail as a gift with reservation. An inheritance tax mitigation scheme for a couple (whether married or not) may involve one or both making an outright gift by Will to the children of the share (not exceeding the nil-rate band in value) of the first to die in the matrimonial home on what proves to be the first death and a lifetime gift of a sum of money within the nil-rate band in the expectation (the basis of which should not be such that there is a reservation of a benefit nullifying the lifetime gift) that it will be available, directly or indirectly, to the survivor if necessary. Unfortunately, in the real world as in the tale of Lear and his daughters, that confidence sometimes proves to be misplaced.

15.25 Couples should not make gifts which necessarily are only subject to a moral obligation unless they have complete confidence in the recipients (and their spouses). A balance of power can then be maintained where a child behaves dishonourably towards the couple or the survivor. But while disinheritance may punish the offender, it will not of itself solve the survivor's immediate problems. Therefore, if a couple do not have complete confidence in prospective beneficiaries or a beneficiary, all concerned must accept that the price of the couple's financial security is the payment of inheritance tax. It is particularly the case with inheritance tax that one cannot in reality have one's cake and eat it.

15.26 Further, even if confidence in a beneficiary is entirely justified, the untimely death, divorce or financial problems of a beneficiary may prevent the moral obligation from being discharged. Divorce poses perhaps the greatest problem. Gifts become part of the matrimonial assets of the beneficiary and the beneficiary's spouse. A discretionary trust under which the children are beneficiaries is only a limited part-answer to the problem. The courts adopt a broad brush approach in the matrimonial context and look at the position realistically rather than theoretically. Insolvency is similarly devastating because gifts will result in the beneficiary's assets, including a share of property occupied by a parent, becoming available for creditors.

15.27 Another point to consider is that the approximate equalisation of the two estates is largely guaranteed to minimise inheritance tax no matter what the future structure of the tax. Couples who have engaged in equalisation in recent years may have found it unnecessary following the introduction of the transferable nil-rate band and where one has already been widowed the nil-rate bands may be unequal so equalisation is less attractive and/or sensible. In other cases the practitioner should still tactfully discourage any significant inheritance tax inefficient imbalance between them. One should also prevent gifts reverting to the donor[1]. If each of the two estates is insufficient to enable the maximum within the nil-rate band to be given away without jeopardising the survivor's financial position, consideration should be given as to whether a discretionary Will trust of the nil-rate band under which the surviving spouse is a beneficiary is appropriate.

1   So, for instance, adult donee children should make Wills.

15.28 The object of equalising estates is to make maximum use of the nil-rate band – and thus to avoid wasting it – where a couple's combined estates have a value in excess of the nil-rate band. In the case of a couple who are married or civil partners where there is already and enhanced nil-rate band available the first to die can leave property up to the value of the nil-rate band to others (such as children) and the balance to the survivor without there being any inheritance tax liability on his death. If the property passing into the nil-rate band of the first to die does not form part of the survivor's estate then the survivor's estate is swollen only by the excess and maximum use will have been made of the nil-rate band of the first to die. This is wasteful if the survivor has not previously been widowed but remains useful where the survivor is a widow or widower (or has survived a civil partner) where there has been no wastage of nil-rate band on the first death. If, in the case where one party has previously been widowed, the estates are not balanced so that one of the pair has very little property then there is a risk that the nil-rate band of the first to die will not be utilised with the result that tax is payable on the death of the survivor which might not otherwise have been payable.

15.29 As general rule, if inheritance tax mitigation of this sort is a priority the testator should sever any joint tenancy and ensure that any other joint ownership becomes of independent half shares or is split into two separate ownerships. Particularly in the case of the unmarried, where the joint estates fall between the nil-rate band and twice that limit, the larger estate should not be more than the nil-rate band. Similarly, where the joint estates are above twice the nil-rate band, the smaller estate should be not less than that limit.

15.30 Equalisation of estates is only effective for the moderately wealthy. For inheritance tax purposes there is absolutely no point in equalising the estates of an unmarried couple whose combined estates are worth less than the nil-rate band or a married couple whose estates are worth less than two nil-rate bands because there will be no inheritance tax on the death of the survivor in any event. Balancing the two estates in such cases is unnecessary and wasteful where the principal desire is to leave everything to the survivor.

15.31 Similarly, there is no real inheritance tax advantage in equalising the estates of a very wealthy couple each of whom has assets worth many times the nil-rate band.

15.32 It should be remembered, however, that whilst the equalisation of estates can be beneficial for inheritance tax purposes, it is not necessarily appropriate. In the case of a second marriage, where it may be most sensible for inheritance tax purposes, the husband and wife might well intend to treat their individual property separately so that the ultimate destination of their respective assets is different. In such a case equalisation of the matrimonial estates can be fatal to the testamentary intentions of the parties. Where that is the case ensuring that the testamentary intentions are effectively carried out usually takes priority over inheritance tax mitigation.

15.33 A pension death in service benefit or personal pension or retirement annuity capital benefit can take even a modest estate above the nil-rate band. A testator rarely counts it as part of his assets. Indeed, often its existence does not occur to him in this context. Provision by a nomination can be made under a pension scheme (and as a high priority should be made) for the benefit to be treated in such a way that it does not form part of the deceased's estate for inheritance tax purposes. There is no inheritance tax point in the nomination being in the widow's favour. She is in any event an exempt beneficiary so provision for her should be by Will and the nomination (or trust) in favour of children or issue or to a discretionary trust under which the widow and issue can benefit. If it is not possible for the nomination or trust to constitute the discretionary trust, although a very common form at any rate in the case of a trust involves a trustees' power of appointment with the children as default beneficiaries, the husband can create a lifetime discretionary trust as the prospective receptacle (with only nominal initial assets). Similarly, the benefit under a personal pension or retirement annuity can be put into trust.

Use of testamentary trusts

15.34 The Finance Act 2006 made dramatic and startling changes to inheritance tax and trusts both in respect of lifetime and testamentary trusts. The changes were retrospective in the sense that they affected trusts whether created before or after the 2006 Budget on 22 March 2006.

15.35 *Inheritance tax mitigation*

15.35 Prior to Finance Act 2006 there was a distinction between three kinds of testamentary trusts for inheritance tax purposes. These were:
(1) interest in possession trusts under which the person beneficially interested in the interest in possession (usually a life tenant) was treated as beneficially entitled to the underlying settled property for inheritance tax purposes;
(2) discretionary (relevant property) trusts in which no individual could claim to have a beneficial interest in the underlying settled property for inheritance tax purposes; and
(3) special trusts such as accumulation and maintenance trusts and disabled trusts accorded special treatment for inheritance tax purposes under Inheritance Tax Act 1984 ss 71 and 89.

15.36 Since the 2006 Budget the vast majority of interest in possession trusts are now taxed as relevant property trusts – so that the life tenant is not treated as beneficially entitled to the underlying property – and the inheritance tax advantages which were previously attracted to accumulation and maintenance trusts have been lost. For inheritance tax purposes, other specialist trusts have been reduced to shadows of their former selves. Apart from the disabled trust there are four popular uses of testamentary trust which Will draftsmen ought to consider. These are the discretionary trust (usually used in respect of the nil-rate band), the flexible life interest trust, the trust for bereaved minors (the s 71D trust) and the immediate post-death interest trust.

15.37 Discretionary (nil-rate band) trusts continue to be treated in exactly the same way as before the Finance Act 2006 and, where nil-rate band transfer is not available or desirable, the most tax-efficient Wills for married couples or civil partners will provide for the maximum available nil-rate band to be left to a broad discretionary class of beneficiaries including the surviving spouse or civil partner and the testator's issue with residue passing to the surviving spouse or civil partner absolutely. Such Wills are not liable to inheritance tax on the death of the testator at all.

15.38 Flexible Will drafting with a short-term life interest in favour of the surviving spouse with power to determine the life interest and appoint amongst a discretionary class became extremely inefficient after the Finance Act 2006 because the termination of the life interest is now treated as a gift by the surviving spouse or civil partner for the purposes of the gift with reservation rules so that if the spouse or civil partner has any interest in the property subsequently appointed – as will usually be the case – the gift with reservation rules will apply. However, the introduction of the transferable nil-rate band between spouses has made this a rather more sensible choice than was previously the case.

15.39 Trusts for bereaved minors represent the last vestiges of the former accumulation and maintenance regime. They are trusts drawn in much narrower terms than the former s 71 accumulation and maintenance trusts and comprise two distinct categories of trust: the trust for bereaved minors under s 71A and the so-called s 71D trust for persons aged 18 to 25 years.

15.40 For Will draftsmen, trusts for bereaved minors (under Inheritance Tax Act 1984 s 71A, introduced by the Finance Act 2006) include:
(1) the statutory trusts for the benefit of a bereaved minor contingently on attaining the age of 18 arising on his parent's intestacy under Administration of Estates Act 1925 ss 46, 47(1); and
(2) testamentary trusts for the benefit of a bereaved minor established under the Will of his deceased parent by which the bereaved minor will be fully entitled to the assets in the trust at age 18, and in the meantime income and capital can only be paid to him or for his benefit or, if accumulated, be held for him. In

this context, a parent includes a step-parent or person with parental responsibility where the bereaved minor will be fully entitled to the assets in the trust at age 18, and in the meantime income and capital can only be paid to him or for his benefit.

Property subject to a trust which satisfies these requirements is exempt from the relevant property regime.

15.41 Section 71D trusts are trusts satisfying the requirements of Inheritance Tax Act 1984 s 71D, (introduced by the Finance Act 2006) which might be described as trusts for immature adults. These are trusts for the benefit of a bereaved minor established under the Will of his deceased parent or step-parent where the bereaved minor will certainly be fully entitled to the assets in the trust at age 25, and in the meantime income and capital can only be paid to him or for his benefit.

15.42 Property subject to these trusts is exempt from the relevant property regime until the beneficiary attains the age of 18 years and thereafter the charge on the beneficiary becoming absolutely entitled to the property is limited with the effect that inheritance tax applies as if the property only entered the relevant property regime on the beneficiary attaining the age of 18.

15.43 As with s 71A trusts, the 'favoured' treatment only applies insofar as the trust is made under the Will of a parent.

15.44 The rump of the of interest in possession regime in its traditionally accepted form can be found in the immediate post-death interest provisions arising under Inheritance Tax Act 1984 s 49A (introduced by the Finance Act 2006). These are interests in possession (in the old sense) effected by Will (or on intestacy) by which the person with the interest became beneficially entitled to the interest in possession on the death of the testator which are not, and have never been, trusts for bereaved minors or disabled trusts.

15.45 These immediate post-death interests (IPDIs, as they are becoming known) are important for Will draftsmen because the spouse exemption continues to apply and so, although it is no longer possible to create successive life interests within the IPDI regime, it is possible to maintain the interest in possession treatment of life interest trusts for a surviving spouse or civil partner without incurring inheritance tax. Conversely, because the administration period is ignored for inheritance tax purposes, it is still necessary to consider debt and charge schemes when using discretionary trusts of the matrimonial home occupied by a surviving spouse.

Options for inheritance tax mitigation including those using the matrimonial (or civil partnership) home where a nil-rate band will still be wasted because one or both of the couple is entitled to an enhanced nil-rate band following a previous marriage

15.46 In almost all cases what follows will now be of no interest at all; and mercifully so. There will however be a few situations in which, because one or both of a couple has previously been widowed, an inheritance tax nil-rate band will still be wasted if the whole of the estate of the first to die is left to the survivor. In such cases the lengthy commentary in the previous edition concerning the options available for inheritance tax mitigation in the family situation will remain relevant[1].

1   See the Fifth edition at paras 15.30 et seq.

15.47 *Inheritance tax mitigation*

15.47 Which of the various possibilities might be appropriate in any given case depends, as before, upon the precise circumstances and desires of each client. These include a simple gift of the nil-rate band the children or other beneficiaries, a gift of the nil-rate band on discretionary trusts from which the spouse or civil partner is excluded and a similar gift including the survivor as a beneficiary. It is suggested that, ultimately, the same problem remains after 9 October 2007 as existed beforehand: i.e. such schemes are all very well until one has to include a share of the matrimonial home in the gift, that home is to be occupied by the survivor and it is hoped that no beneficiary taxed interest in possession will arise as a result of the survivor's occupation. In such cases the following analysis remains relevant.

A share of the matrimonial home as an asset of a discretionary trust

15.48 It will now be unusual to want to contemplate schemes as artificial and unwieldy as those discussed below but it remains important to point out that the first and most important point is that even when schemes making use of the matrimonial home as an asset of a discretionary trust were popular they were only ever a last resort. That remains the case. If there are sufficient income-yielding assets to make up a nil-rate band discretionary trust without depriving the surviving spouse or civil partner of a (discretionary) source of income the trust should be constituted out of those assets in the first instance. Indeed, it should be an unusual case where one or both of a married couple has an enhanced nil-rate band and it is still necessary to use a share of the matrimonial home to make up a discretionary trust of the nil-rate band of the first to die.

15.49 Schemes were, nonetheless, devised which vest assets equal to the nil-rate band in such a trust but, directly or indirectly, make them available to the surviving spouse or civil partner if required. In the case of testators who are less well off the inclusion of the matrimonial home within the nil-rate band was attractive because, if a non-income producing asset is hived off, it leaves more income-producing assets available to the survivor. This is sometimes unacceptable because the survivor wishes to retain absolute control of the house while living in it and that is something which needs to be considered.

15.50 Where the testator wishes to constitute a nil-rate band discretionary trust using the matrimonial home or a share in the matrimonial home it is important that the settlement does not create an immediate post-death interest. Practitioners must always bear in mind the dangers of creating such an interest in what, on the face of it, appears to be a discretionary trust. For a discretionary or contingent interest trust to succeed in mitigating inheritance tax, it is crucial that the survivor does not have an interest taxed as an IPDI. There are two schemes, the debt scheme and the charge scheme, which were popular prior to the introduction of transferrable nil-rate bands and, at present, are believed to be accepted by HMRC as not creating an interest in possession or, presumably, an immediate post-death interest.

15.51 The debt or promissory note scheme is highly artificial but popular. It is thought that it continues to be accepted by HMRC.

15.52 In essence, spouses make reciprocal Wills each giving residue to the other absolutely and each giving a nil-rate band legacy on discretionary trusts. Those trusts must include express powers to constitute the fund by accepting a personal obligation from the survivor to pay the value of the legacy to the trustees on demand and interest free.

15.53 When the testator dies the nil-rate band discretionary trust is constituted by this debt and residue, including the testator's share of the matrimonial home, is vested in the survivor so that capital gains tax main residence relief will continue.

15.54 In effect, the trustees of the nil-rate band discretionary trust make a loan to the survivor of the whole or part of the nil-rate band which is repayable out of the survivor's estate and so depletes that estate for inheritance tax purposes. No immediate post-death interest arises because the survivor owes the debt and so cannot have an immediate post-death interest in the property subject to the obligation.

15.55 The charge scheme is a variation of the debt scheme in which the nil-rate band discretionary trust is constituted, not by a promise to repay but by a charge on the testator's share of the matrimonial home which falls into the residuary estate in the way described above. The share of the property subject to the charge can then be held for the survivor with the charge being a deduction from the value of that share of the property.

15.56 When contemplating a gift of the nil-rate band in this way the charge scheme ought to be used if there is a possibility that Finance Act 1986 s 103 might apply to abate the liability of the survivor to the nil-rate band trust on his death. This problem arises for the simple debt scheme where the first to die was given property by the survivor. The charge scheme avoids this by creating a charge on property without the survivor being personally liable.

15.57 Some specific points should be noted:
(1) If the charge scheme is to be used the survivor should not be one of the personal representatives who create the charge although the survivor can be one of the trustees of the nil-rate band trust who accept the charge. In the case of both the debt and the charge scheme the survivor should not be the sole trustee.
(2) Neither scheme can be effected unless there are express powers to constitute the nil-rate band discretionary trust with an investment comprising a debt or a charge and the trustees should be expressly exonerated from liability for loss suffered by the fund as a result of accepting such an investment.
(3) Both schemes are only effective to the extent that the survivor actually receives property from the first estate or the property charged is more valuable than the charge.
(4) HMRC takes the view that the debt scheme is subject to stamp duty and tax but the charge scheme, if properly implemented, is not. See 'Modernising Stamp Duty on land and buildings in the UK' *Practitioners' Newsletter*, Issue 4 (7 December 2004).
(5) Finally, these schemes appear to be accepted by HMRC as effective[1] but officers of HMRC can change their minds from time to time[2]. This area is one in which litigation and/or legislation – perhaps even retrospective legislation – is possible. Clients should be warned accordingly.

1 Mr Twiddy (then of the Capital Taxes Office) accepted, at a CTO open day in late 2000, that these schemes can be effective if carried out correctly.
2 Questions are constantly being raised about these schemes.

Post-death rearrangements

15.58 As discussed in **chapter 22**, the disposition of the deceased's estate may be varied by a deed of variation or by disclaimer. For inheritance tax purposes, a variation or disclaimer which is within Inheritance Tax Act 1984 s 142(1) and which contains a

15.59 *Inheritance tax mitigation*

statement to the effect that it is to be read back into the testator's Will takes effect as if the dispositions effected by it were made by the deceased.

15.59 The variation or disclaimer must be in writing and made within two years of the death by the persons who benefit or would benefit under the dispositions affected. Where two spouses die within two years of one another and the first has not made full use of his nil-rate band but should have done so it may be possible to vary the disposition of the estate of the first to die in order to make maximum use of his nil-rate band. HMRC accepts that a variation can retrospectively sever a joint tenancy thus bringing a severable share of property within the estate which would otherwise pass by survivorship. Where a joint tenancy has not been severed prior to death – whether because a Will draftsman has neglected to advise that it should be or that advice has been ignored or a conveyance subsequent to the Will has created a joint tenancy or for whatever other reason – a deed of variation can be used to rectify the situation in order to make maximum use of the nil-rate band.

A gift of the nil-rate band on short-term discretionary trusts[1]

15.60 Inheritance Tax Act 1984 s 144[2] permits dispositions made by trustees out of a discretionary trust less than two years after the testator's death to be read back into the Will. This has enabled Wills to be drafted with considerable flexibility giving an opportunity for the trustees to take stock before making a decision about the manner in which the estate should be distributed.

1 See **Form 15.4**.
2 Set out at **appendix 28.7**.

15.61 The trustees are able to appoint the capital among the beneficiaries so as to produce the best practical result in the circumstances which have emerged at the time of death or shortly afterwards. In theory the trustees are better placed to do this than the testator was because they know the value of the estate, the current inheritance tax rates and the foreseeable requirements of the widow and other beneficiaries. The short-term discretionary trust requires the trustees to exercise their discretion and bring the trust to an end within two years of the death so that the appointments of capital which they make will be treated as dispositions under the Will for inheritance tax purposes. This has disadvantages. It limits the trustees' scope and, for capital gains tax purposes, the recipient acquires the property appointed at its market value at the date of appointment and not at the date of death. There might also be a cash-flow problem during the administration of an estate in which inheritance tax must be paid at an early stage.

15.62 There will often be a strong case for an 'ordinary' discretionary trust[1] even though the discretion may well be exercised within the two-year period. Of course, whatever is appointed to the surviving spouse of civil partner will increase inheritance tax on his death whether or not an appointment is made within or outside the two years. Subject to the stance taken by HMRC, the surviving spouse of civil partner should ideally rely on benefits from the discretionary trust and not benefit from an appointment.

1 See **Form 15.5**.

15.63 For deaths on or after 22 March 2006 Inheritance Tax Act 1984 s 144(1) applies where property comprised in a person's estate immediately before his death is settled by Will and within two years of that death and before an immediate post-death interest or a disabled person's interest has subsisted in the property, an appointment is made which results in the property ceasing to be settled.

15.64 The section, as amended by the Finance Act 2006, now also has effect (in respect of deaths on or after 22 March 2006) as if the Will had provided that on the testator's death the property should be held as it is held after the event without there being a charge on the property leaving the discretionary trust where property comprised in the person's estate immediately before death is settled by his Will, but no immediate post-death interest or a disabled person's interest has subsisted in the property and within the period of two years after the death there occurs an event that involves causing the property to be held on trusts that would, if they had in fact been established by the Will, have resulted in an immediate post-death interest subsisting in the property, or s 71A or s 71D applying to the property.

PRECEDENTS

FOR USE IN CASES WHERE THE FIRST TO DIE INTENDS TO DIRECT SOME PORTION OF HIS NIL-RATE BAND TO PERSONS OTHER THAN HIS SURVIVING SPOUSE OR CIVIL PARTNER.

15.65

FORM 15.1

Gift to children of inheritance tax nil-rate band[1]

(1) I give the maximum amount which can be given to them under this clause without inheritance tax being payable[2] in equal shares to those of my[3] children who survive me [and attain [25]/[18][4]].

(2) If any of my[3] children dies before me his or her children [who attain 21][5] shall take equally the share which their parent would otherwise have inherited[6].

---

1 The use of the nil-rate band clause has the advantage of avoiding the need to update the Will to accommodate the changes in banding but it has the disadvantage that any change may increase the amount of the legacy beyond that which the testator would wish and so care should be exercised in using a nil-rate band clause, instead of the current ceiling for the nil-rate or a lesser sum, where the size of the testator's estate is such as may not justify automatic increases in the legacy. See **Form 15.2** for a capped nil-rate legacy. However, a better answer may be the use of promissory note provisions, for which see **Forms 15.10** and **16.17**. The survivor can then have what she needs and the children take the full benefit of the nil-rate band.

2 This clause is intended to use the nil-rate band. Where the testator has made no lifetime gifts which bite into the nil-rate band, the gift under this clause will be the amount of the nil-rate band at the date of death. Where there have been gifts (including PETs) during the seven years preceding death, the legacy will be the amount of the nil-rate band less the total of such gifts. The testator should be advised to consult his solicitor or Will draftsman if, at a later date, he contemplates making lifetime gifts because the consequences may require a review of this Will. Care should also be taken if the estate is likely to include agricultural or business property attracting relief at 100%. If so, the nil-rate band gift defined by this clause will include all of that property perhaps leaving nothing in residue.

3 This clause refers expressly to the testator's own children as 'my children'. In circumstances in which the clause is used in one of two Wills for a married couple reference could be made to 'our' children. Where there is only one marriage and it is clear to whom the testator is referring the choice between 'my' and 'our' children will ordinarily pass without comment. Where there is more than one marriage the testator's children will always be included within 'my children'. Illegitimate children will be included unless expressly excluded.

Where there has been more than one marriage care must be taken in defining the relationship between the testator and the beneficiaries. In the Commonwealth, a gift to 'our children' has been held to refer to all children of all marriages of both spouses: *Re Zehr* [1944] 2 DLR 670. In the right context – especially where there are no children of the present marriage – a gift to 'our children' will include all of the children of all marriages of both spouses but in other circumstances may limit the gift to the children of the second marriage.

4 Given the trustees' powers of advancement and maintenance, 25 will be quite soon enough for most testators. Usually beneficiaries will have a satisfactory degree of financial maturity by then. A gift at this age will come within Inheritance Tax Act 1984 s 71D (see above). It has traditionally been quite common for either a greater age, say 30, to be chosen or inheritances to be staggered, for instance one-third at 24, one-third at 27 and the remainder at 30. This arrangement is now prejudiced as a result of the Finance Act 2006.

5 Now that the perpetuity period is 125 years (with a 'wait and see' provision), a greater age contingency might be selected for grandchildren if that is thought desirable.

6 Normally, a substitutional gift in favour of grandchildren will suffice but this provision or a higher age 'wait and see' provision could be included.

FORM 15.2

Capped gift of inheritance tax nil-rate band to children[1]

(1) I give the maximum which can be given to them under this clause without inheritance tax becoming payable in respect of this gift [or the sum of £   ]/[% of my estate]/[% of my Residue]/[£   increased by the percentage by which the latest available figure of the All Items Index of Retail Prices exceeds that last available before today] if that is less in equal shares to those of my children who survive me [and attain [25]/[18]].

(2) If any of [my[2]] children dies before me his or her children [who attain 21][3] shall take equally the share which their parent would otherwise have inherited[4].

1 See footnotes to the last precedent. The only difference between this form and the preceding form is the restriction on the gift.
2 See **Form 15.1** footnote 3.
3 See **Form 15.1** footnote 5.
4 See **Form 15.1** footnote 6.

FORM 15.3

Gift on discretionary trust of [capped] inheritance tax nil-rate band in favour of issue[1]

(1) I give the maximum which can be given to them under this clause without inheritance tax becoming payable in respect of this gift [or the sum of £   ]/[% of my estate]/[% of my Residue]/[£   increased by the percentage by which the latest available figure of the All Items Index of Retail Prices exceeds that last available before today] if that is less to my Trustees on the following trusts.

(2) My Trustees are to hold the assets at any particular time held by them on the trusts of this clause ('the Trust Fund') for not more than 125 years ('the Trust Period') after my death to:

   (a) apply the capital of the Trust Fund for the benefit of whichever of my issue my Trustees think fit;

   (b) apply the income of the Trust Fund for the benefit of whichever of my issue my Trustees think fit or during the whole of the Trust Period to accumulate such income as is not so applied and to invest that income as an addition to the capital of the Trust Fund;

   (c) not later than 125 years after my death to end the trust by distributing the Trust Fund among whichever of my issue are then alive in equal shares;

   (d) if these trusts fail hold the Trust Fund on trust for whichever charity my Trustees think fit.

(3) My Trustees may:

   (a) invest or otherwise apply any part of the Trust Fund and vary investments and applications including by making loans [which may be interest-free or at less than a full market rate and may also be linked to the All Items Index of Retail Prices or its replacement] to any beneficiary;

15.65 *Precedents*

  (b) make retentions to meet any taxes for which they may be liable and pay those taxes and any other expenses of the administration of the Trust Fund out of capital or income;

  (c) not except under subclause (2)(a) or on a distribution of the Trust Fund exercise their powers under this sub-clause so as to create an immediate post-death interest an interest under Inheritance Tax Act 1984 s 71A or 71D or any other interest in possession for a beneficiary.

1 If this gift is to be capped, the words in square brackets in (3)(a) should be included.

FORM 15.4

Gift on short-term discretionary trust of amount of inheritance tax nil-rate band for benefit of spouse and issue

(1) I give the maximum which can be given to them under this clause without inheritance tax becoming payable in respect of this gift [or the sum of £]/[% of my estate]/[% of my Residue]/[£ increased by the percentage by which the latest available figure of the All Items Index of Retail Prices exceeds that last available before today] if that is less ('the Trust Fund') to my Trustees on the following trusts:

  (a) To apply the income and capital of the Trust Fund for the benefit of such of my [wife]/[husband]/[civil partner] and any of my issue who survive me ('my Beneficiaries') as my Trustees think fit.

  (b) To add any undistributed income to the capital of the Trust Fund.

  (c) To end these trusts not earlier than three months[1] nor later than two years after my death by distributing the Trust Fund among whichever of my Beneficiaries then alive or if none whichever charity my Trustees think fit.

(2) My Trustees may:

  (a) invest or otherwise apply any part of the Trust Fund and vary investments and applications including by making loans which may be interest-free or at less than a full market rate and may also be linked to the All Items Index of Retail Prices or its replacement to any beneficiary;

  (b) make retentions to meet any taxes for which they may be liable and pay those taxes and any other expenses of the administration of the Trust Fund out of capital or income;

  (c) not except under subclause (1)(a) or on a distribution of the Trust Fund exercise their powers under this sub-clause so as to create an immediate post-death interest an interest under Inheritance Tax Act 1984 s 71A or 71D or any other interest in possession for a beneficiary.

1 See Inheritance Tax Act 1984 s 65(4).

FORM 15.5

Gift on discretionary trust of amount of inheritance tax nil-rate band for benefit of spouse and issue[1]

(1) I give the amount which at my death equals the maximum which can be given to them on these trusts without inheritance tax becoming payable in respect of this gift to my Trustees on the following trusts:

(2) In this clause:

  (a) 'the Trust Fund' means the assets at any particular time held by my Trustees on the trusts of this clause;

  (b) 'my Beneficiaries' means my [wife]/[husband]/[civil partner] and issue[2].

(3) My Trustees shall hold the Trust Fund on trust:

  (a) For not more than 125 years after my death ('the Trust Period'):

    (i) to apply the capital of the Trust Fund for the benefit of such of my Beneficiaries as my Trustees think fit;

    (ii) to apply the income of the Trust Fund for the benefit of such of my Beneficiaries as my Trustees think fit or during the whole of the Trust Period to accumulate such income as is not so applied and to invest that income as an addition to the capital of the Trust Fund.

  (b) Not later than 125 years after my death to end these trusts by distributing the Trust Fund among such of my Beneficiaries as are then alive in equal shares or if these trusts fail for whichever charity my Trustees think fit.

(4) My Trustees may:

  (a) invest or otherwise apply any part of the Trust Fund and vary investments and applications including by making loans which may be interest-free or at less than a full market rate and may also be linked to the All Items Index of Retail Prices or its replacement to any beneficiary;

  (b) make retentions to meet any taxes for which they may be liable and pay those taxes and any other expenses of the administration of the Trust Fund out of capital or income;

  (c) not except under subclause (3)(a)(i) or on a distribution of the Trust Fund exercise their powers under this sub-clause so as to create an immediate post-death interest an interest under Inheritance Tax Act 1984 s 71A or 71D or any other interest in possession for a beneficiary.

1 This is a long-term discretionary trust giving flexibility to enable the trustees to apply income and capital for the benefit of the surviving spouse so far as is required.
2 In some cases, the beneficiaries will be restricted to the surviving spouse and the children but it is usually desirable to enlarge the class of beneficiaries where a long-term discretionary trust is envisaged. For example, it may be envisaged that on the death of the widow the trust will be ended and the Trust Fund shared equally by the children but one of the children may request that his share

15.65 *Precedents*

or part of his share is appointed to one of his children. Another possibility is that one of the testator's children has died during the lifetime of the survivor and the Trust Fund is needed for the benefit of his children.

FORM 15.6

Contingent gift of amount of inheritance tax nil-rate band[1]

(1) I give the maximum amount which can be given to them without inheritance tax becoming payable ('the Trust Fund') to my Trustees on the trusts set out below.

  (a) My Trustees are to hold the Trust Fund in equal shares for those of my[2] children who survive my [wife]/[husband]/[civil partner] and me [and attain [18/[25][3]] on the following terms:

   (i) If any of my children does not inherit then his or her children shall take in equal shares [on attaining 21[4]] the share of the Trust Fund which their parent would otherwise have inherited.

   (ii) If any of my grandchildren fails to survive my [wife]/[husband]/[civil partner] and me [or dies before attaining 21] then his or her children shall take in equal shares [on attaining 21[4]] the share of the Trust Fund to which their parent would have been entitled.

   (iii) Until the capital of the Trust Fund has been fully distributed my Beneficiaries shall be entitled to any income arising from the Trust Fund and 'my Beneficiaries' means the persons who at the time income is distributed will receive a share of the capital of the Trust Fund if they survive my [wife]/[husband]/[civil partner] and me [and attain the age specified][5].

   (iv) The share of income of each of my Beneficiaries shall be proportional to the share of capital to which he is presumptively entitled.

   (v) The income to which any Beneficiary under 18 is entitled cannot be accumulated but must be applied for his benefit.

(2) My Trustees may:

  (a) invest or otherwise apply any part of the Trust Fund and vary investments and applications including by making loans which may be interest-free or at less than a full market rate and may also be linked to the All Items Index of Retail Prices or its replacement to any Beneficiary[6];

  (b) make retentions to meet any taxes for which they may be liable and pay those taxes and any other expenses of the administration of the Trust Fund out of capital or income;

  (c) not except under subclause (1)(a) or on a distribution of the Trust Fund exercise their powers under this sub-clause so as to create an immediate post-death interest an interest under Inheritance Tax Act 1984 s 71A or 71D or any other interest in possession for a beneficiary.

1   If it is desirable to cap the inheritance tax free gift, see **Form 15.2**.

2   See **Form 15.1** footnote 3.
3   An age contingency will be governed by the testator's family circumstances. The important point is that the children must survive both husband and wife or both civil partners before attaining a vested interest which is designed as a protection to the surviving spouse or civil partner.
4   The age contingency provision at this stage was previously relevant because grandchildren and particularly great grandchildren may not have attained 21 at the death of the survivor of the husband and wife or civil partner. The use of 21 instead of 25 for grandchildren and great grandchildren avoided the need to rely on the 'wait and see' perpetuity provision. Now that the perpetuity period is 125 years (with a 'wait and see' provision), a greater age contingency might be selected for grandchildren etc, if that is thought desirable.
5   This clause will give the intermediate income to the presumptive beneficiaries. This results in their having an immediate post-death interest which, in turn, means that, if one of them dies before attaining a vested interest, the value of his presumptive interest in the trust fund will aggregate with his free estate for inheritance tax purposes.
6   The object of this clause is to enable loans to be made to the surviving spouse or civil partner to provide capital which will bear income for his benefit. If the survivor's needs deplete the capital itself then his own estate will be reduced to the extent of the capital used because, at death, the whole of the loan will have to be repaid to the Trustees.

FORM 15.7

Gift to children of testator's beneficial interest in residence[1]

I give my beneficial interest in the house known as [*postal address*] *or* [the house that constitutes my principal private residence[2] at my death] or if less than an interest whose value is equal to the maximum amount which can be given to them without Inheritance Tax being payable to those of my children who survive me in equal shares.

1   The testator should only make an outright gift to the children if he is completely confident that the surviving spouse or civil partner, as co-owner, will be left in undisturbed possession and is prepared to take a view about the possibility of children's matrimonial or other financial problems.
2   This term is used because it has a well-established meaning for capital gains tax purposes.

FORM 15.8

Specific gift of property attracting business property relief and the balance of the inheritance tax nil-rate band[1]

I GIVE my shares in Waterbow Limited if they still qualify for 100% Business Relief and the maximum amount which can be given to them under this clause without Inheritance Tax being payable to those of my children who survive me and attain 25 in equal shares

1   A form which makes it clear that the property attracting business relief is to form part of the nil-rate band gift.

FORM 15.9

Clauses enabling use of a promissory note to satisfy the nil-rate band gift

(1)   MY Trustees may require [the Discretionary Trustees] to accept from them in full or partial satisfaction of [the Trust Fund] a promise on the part of my [wife]/[husband]/[civil partner] to pay [the Trust Fund] on demand or a charge of any part of my Residue with payment when demanded of all or part of [the Trust Fund][1].

(2)   The promise or charge may include whatever terms my Trustees think fit including terms:

15.65 *Precedents*

- (a) relating to the provision of fixed or floating security;
- (b) requiring the payment of interest; and
- (c) making the sum payable linked to the All Items Index of Retail Prices or any other index.

(3) [The Discretionary Trustees]:

- (a) may refrain from calling in or exercising any rights in relation to any sum the subject of the promise or charge for as long as they think fit;
- (b) will not be liable for any loss which may occur through the exercise of any power under this clause if my Trustees are unable to make payment in full or any security given becomes inadequate.

(4) The powers given under this clause are exercisable even though [the Discretionary Trustees] and my Trustees are one and the same provided that my [wife]/[husband]/[civil partner] must not be the only trustee in either case.

16 Complete Wills

16.1 As in the previous edition, the Complete Wills are divided into five common situations, the purpose and effect of each of which is described where they occur. In this edition each of these cases is considered in a separate chapter. The five situations are:

- single persons (**chapter 17**);

- married couples with no children (**chapter 18**);

- married couples with children (**chapter 19**);

- unmarried couples with children (**chapter 20**); and

- second marriages where there are children of the first marriage (**chapter 21**).

Civil partnerships are treated in the same way as marriages although, unlike marriages, the vast majority of civil partnerships will be childless.

16.2 In addition to those five categories, this chapter sets out two examples of non-dispositive Will forms and two examples of a codicil. The two non-dispositive 'complete' Wills are provided to illustrate how the essential elements of each should appear without the complication of dispositive provisions interfering. As in the previous edition, one of these incorporates the standard provisions of the Society of Trust and Estate Practitioners[1] (STEP) while the other does not. Both do the same job but in different ways. These forms (**Forms 16.1** and **16.2**) show that incorporation of the STEP standard provisions provides a useful shorthand for Will draftsmen but, as pointed out at **12.22**, if a practitioner is to incorporate the STEP standard provisions, no additional powers should be incorporated without exercising great care. Thus, it would be inappropriate to include express provision for trustee charging and exoneration when those matters are already dealt with by the standard provisions. However, the Will draftsman should also take care in including non-administrative powers (such as powers of maintenance and advancement). This is because the STEP provisions contain an unfortunate mix of dispositive and administrative powers.

1   The STEP standard provisions are available online at www.step.org, as is the clause recommended by STEP for the incorporation of the STEP standard provisions.

16.3 There are disadvantages in using the STEP standard provisions. Not all practitioners are familiar with their terms and it is all too easy to incorporate terms which might conflict with those expressly set out in the Will. There is the further problem that incorporation of powers by reference can lead to uncertainty (real or imagined) as to what powers are in fact available. Lay trustees in particular prefer to

16.4 *Complete Wills*

see their powers clearly set out in the Will than to have to look elsewhere to discover what they can and cannot do. This is, of course, true both of the STEP provisions and a reliance on statute and the general law.

16.4 There is a STEP form of incorporation of the standard provisions. However, in the age of the personal computer and cheap laser printer there is really no excuse for failing to set out all of the executors' powers in the Will itself. It is partly for this reason that the form of words recommended to incorporate the STEP provisions is not included in this edition.

16.5 As in the previous edition, a Will's date appears at the end. There is then less chance of the date being overlooked if it is inserted immediately before the signatures are made on the same page. The testator ought to have read through the Will and be happy with it. There are a variety of situations in which that does not happen but analysis and discussion of those situations, the consequences and remedies are outside the scope of this book.

PRECEDENTS

16.6

Non-dispositive Will forms

Form 16.1 Non-dispositive clauses of complete Will incorporating STEP provisions
Form 16.2 Non-dispositive clauses of complete Will in the longer form

Codicil

Form 16.3 Codicil
Form 16.4 Codicil revoking nil-rate band legacy

FORM 16.1

Non-dispositive clauses of complete Will incorporating STEP provisions[1]

I, [*full name*] **of** [*home address*] revoke all earlier Wills and declare this to be my last Will

1. I appoint my [wife]/[husband]/[civil partner] [*name*] as my sole [executrix]/[executor] but if [she]/[he] is unable or unwilling to act or if [she]/[he] dies before proving my Will I appoint as my executors those of my children who survive me.

2. I appoint as my trustees those of my executors who obtain probate of this Will and in this Will the expression 'my Trustees' means (as the context requires) those of my executors who obtained probate and the trustees for the time being of any trust arising under this Will.

3. I give the following legacies free of inheritance tax:

    [(a) ...

    [(b) ...]

4. I give the rest of my property to my Trustees to hold my estate on trust for sale with power to postpone sale to pay executorship expenses and debts including mortgages secured on real or leasehold property and any inheritance tax in respect of property passing under this Will or which becomes payable because of my death on any lifetime transfer by me or payable because of my death on property in which I hold a beneficial interest as joint tenant. All income received after my death shall be treated as income of my estate regardless of the period to which it relates and the statutory rules concerning apportionment and the rules in *Howe v Dartmouth*[2] and *Allhusen v Whittell*[3] and *Re Earl of Chesterfield's Trusts*[4] shall not apply.

5. My Trustees shall hold the residue of my estate ('my residuary estate') on trust ... [*Insert dispositive provisions here*]

16.6 *Precedents*

6. [Administrative powers: Incorporate the Standard Provisions of the Society of Trust and Estate Practitioners (1st edition) by stating, in this clause, that those provisions shall apply. STEP recommend that the provisions apply with the deletion of paragraph 5 and an express exclusion of section 11 Trusts of Land and Appointment of Trustees Act 1996.]

As Witness my hand this [–] day of [———] 20[–].

Signed by the Testator in our presence and attested by us in the presence of the Testator and of each other.

1 This form does not actually do anything other than appoint executors/trustees and give the estate to them to hold on the trusts of clause 4: it is merely an example.
2 (1802) 32 ER 56. See **Form 11.1** footnote 12.
3 (1887) LR 4 Eq 295. See **Form 11.1** footnote 12.
4 (1883) 24 Ch D 643. See **Form 11.1** footnote 12.

FORM 16.2

Non-dispositive clauses of complete Will in the (recommended) longer form[1]

I, [*full name*] **of** [*home address*] revoke all earlier Wills and declare this to be my last Will

1. I appoint my [wife]/[husband]/[civil partner] [*name*] as my sole [*executrix*]/[*executor*] but if [*she*]/[*he*] is unable or unwilling to act or if [*she*]/[*he*] dies before proving my Will[2] I appoint as my executors those of my children who survive me.

2. I appoint as my trustees those of my executors who obtain probate of this Will and in this Will the expression 'my Trustees' means (as the context requires) those of my executors who obtained probate and the trustees for the time being of any trust arising under this Will.

3. I give the following legacies free of inheritance tax:

   [(a) …

   [(b) …]

4. I give the rest of my property to my Trustees to hold my estate on trust for sale with power to postpone sale to pay executorship expenses and debts including mortgages secured on real or leasehold property and any inheritance tax in respect of property passing under this Will or which becomes payable because of my death on any lifetime transfer by me or payable because of my death on property in which I hold a beneficial interest as joint tenant. All income received after my death shall be treated as income of my estate regardless of the period to which it relates and the statutory rules concerning apportionment and the rules in *Howe v Dartmouth* and *Allhusen v Whittell* and *Re Chesterfield's Trusts* shall not apply.

5. My Trustees shall hold the residue of my estate ('my residuary estate') on trust … [*Insert dispositive provisions here*].

6. My Trustees shall have power[2]:

Precedents **16.6**

- (1) to apply for the benefit of any beneficiary who has a contingent interest the whole or any part of the income from any capital to which he may become entitled;

- (2) during the whole of the period in which a beneficiary has a contingent interest to accumulate such income as is not so applied and to invest that income as an addition to the capital of the share to which that beneficiary is entitled;

- (3) to pay or apply for the benefit of any beneficiary who has a contingent interest the whole or any part of the capital to which he may become entitled;

- (4) to pay any money to which a beneficiary under eighteen is entitled to his parent or guardian for his benefit or to the beneficiary himself once he has attained sixteen and to rely upon the receipt then given by the parent or guardian or the minor himself.

7. My Trustees shall have the following powers in addition to their powers under the general law[2]:

- (1) Power to invest as if they were beneficially entitled and this power includes the right:

    - (a) to invest in unsecured loans;
    - (b) to invest in other non-income producing assets including policies of life assurance;
    - (c) to purchase land anywhere in the world;
    - (d) to purchase an undivided share in land;
    - (e) to invest in land for the occupation or enjoyment of any beneficiary.

- (2) Power to delegate their powers of investment and management of trust property to an agent (including one of their number) on such terms including terms enabling the agent to charge remuneration, to appoint a substitute, to limit liability and to act in circumstances giving rise to a conflict of interest as my Trustees think fit.

- (3) Power to appoint any person (including one of their number or a beneficiary) to act as their nominee and to take such steps as are necessary to vest any property in such person on such terms including terms enabling the agent to charge remuneration, to appoint a substitute, to limit liability and to act in circumstances giving rise to a conflict of interest as my Trustees think fit.

- (4) Power to make loans of capital to a beneficiary which may be interest free, repayable on demand or repayable at a rate below the market rate.

- (5) Power to borrow money on such terms as they think fit including the giving of security and to use it for any purpose for which the capital of my estate may be used.

- (6) Power without the restrictions imposed by Administration of Estates Act 1925 s 41:

- (a) To appropriate to any beneficiary in satisfaction or partial satisfaction of the gift to him any asset forming part of my residuary estate and not subject to a specific gift.
- (b) To appropriate as the assets or part of the assets of any trust created by this Will any asset forming part of my residuary estate and not subject to a specific gift.

8. (1) My Trustees shall exercise their powers of investment and carry out their duties as trustees without regard to the statutory duty of care and Trustee Act 2000 s 1 shall not apply to the trusts of my Will[3].

(2) My Trustees shall be under no duty to review the acts of agents, nominees and custodians appointed by them and Trustee Act 2000 s 22 shall not apply to the trusts of my Will[4].

(3) Section 11 Trusts of Land and Appointment of Trustees Act 1996 (consultation with beneficiaries) shall not apply[5].

(4) In the absence of proof of dishonesty or the wilful commission of an act known to be a breach of trust none of my Trustees shall be liable for any loss or bound to take proceedings against a co-trustee for any breach of trust.

(5) My Trustees shall be entitled to be indemnified out of the assets of my estate against all liabilities incurred in connection with the bona fide execution of their duties and powers.

As Witness my hand this [–] day of [———] 20[–].

Signed by the Testator in our presence and attested by us in the presence of the Testator and of each other.

[1] This form does not actually do anything other than appoint executors/trustees and give the estate to them to hold on the trusts of clause 4. It is merely an example.
[2] For a general discussion of trustees' powers see **chapter 12**.
[3] See **12.20** to **12.21**.
[4] See **12.17**.
[5] See **10.13** to **10.14**.

FORM 16.3

Codicil

I, [*full name*] **of** [*home address*] make this [*first*] Codicil to my Will dated [*date*].

1. I REVOKE [AB]'s appointment as one of my Executors and Trustees and appoint [EF] in his place to act jointly with my other Executors and Trustees

2. In Clause [4] of my Will the gift of '£[x]' is to be replaced by '£[y] increased by the percentage by which the latest available figure of the All Items Index of Retail Prices exceeds that last available before today'[1]

3. In all other respects I confirm my Will

As Witness my hand this [–] day of [———] 20[–].

Signed by the Testator in our presence and attested by us in the presence of the Testator and of each other.

1 This is, of course, only an example.

FORM 16.4

Codicil revoking nil-rate band legacy

I, [*full name*] **of** [*home address*] make this [*first*] Codicil to my Will dated [*date*].

1. I revoke Clause […] of my Will by which I give to my trustees [the maximum which can be given to them under that clause without inheritance tax becoming payable in respect of the gift] to hold on the discretionary trusts set out in that clause[1]

2. In all other respects I confirm my Will.

As Witness my hand this [–] day of [———] 20[–].

Signed by the Testator in our presence and attested by us in the presence of the Testator and of each other.

1 This is, of course, only an example. In this example the testator revokes the nil-rate band discretionary trust created by his Will. This is appropriate where the residue passes to the spouse and a nil-rate band trust was inserted in each Will for inheritance tax saving purposes. This ensures that the nil-rate band is not used up (other than in respect of other pecuniary legacies) so that the unused nil-rate band will be available to augment the testator's spouse's nil-rate band on her death.

17 Single adults

17.1 The single adult might be a bachelor, a spinster, a widow, a widower or one half of an unmarried or homosexual couple who have not formed a civil partnership. Each of these situations is different but the appropriate Will is often very similar whichever category a person falls into. Most intend to make provision for another adult or for other adults including, for example, their siblings, and many wish to include gifts in favour of charity. **Forms 17.1** to **17.4** cater for single adults and require no further explanation.

PRECEDENTS

17.2

Wills for single adults

Form 17.1 Single adult leaving everything to a single adult who is appointed executor

Form 17.2 Single adult leaving everything to a single adult who is appointed executor with gift over on beneficiary predeceasing testator

Form 17.3 Will giving residue to nephews and nieces with funeral arrangement, specific gifts and legacies

Form 17.4 Will of widow or widower in favour of children with specific and pecuniary legacies

FORM 17.1

Will of single adult leaving everything to a single adult who is appointed executor[1]

I, [*full name*] **of** [*home address*] revoke all earlier Wills and declare this to be my last Will

1. I appoint [AB] as my sole executor [but if [he]/[she] is unable or unwilling to act or if [he]/[she] dies before proving my Will I appoint [CD] as my executor][2].

2. I GIVE all my real and personal property to [AB] absolutely [if [he]/[she] survives me by 30 days and if [he]/[she] does not survive me by 30 days my executor shall apply the whole of my estate for whatever charitable purposes my executor thinks fit][3].

As Witness my hand this [–] day of [———] 20[–].

Signed by the Testator in our presence and attested by us in the presence of the Testator and of each other.

1   It is unwise for the testator to give the whole of his estate to a single beneficiary without some long-stop provision. There is the possibility of including a survivorship condition with a general gift over to charity by using the words in square brackets at the end of clause 2.

2   If there are children then usually all the children or none should be appointed executors. It can be divisive to do otherwise unless a child has asked or agreed not to act. In the case of a large family, the three eldest children can be appointed jointly with the other spouse with the fourth child being substituted for the first to die on the second death. In the case of a single adult with no children the formula adopted in this form is common.

3   A Will in such simple terms does not really require the inclusion of express powers whether set out in the Will or incorporated by reference. If powers are desired the 'Standard Provisions of the Society of Trust and Estate Practitioners' (1st edition) are suitable and could be incorporated. Alternatively the powers set out in clauses 6 to 8 of **Form 16.2** could be incorporated but many of them are quite unnecessary in this situation.

17.2 *Precedents*

FORM 17.2

Will of single adult leaving everything to a single adult who is appointed executor with gift over only on beneficiary predeceasing testator[1]

I, [*full name*] **of** [*home address*] revoke all earlier Wills and declare this to be my last Will

1. I appoint [AB] as my sole executor [but if [he]/[she] is unable or unwilling to act or if [he]/[she] dies before proving my Will I appoint [CD] as my executor].

2. I give all my real and personal property to [AB] absolutely if [he]/[she] survives me[2].

3. If the gift made by clause 2 of this Will fails I give all my real and personal property to [CD] if [he]/[she] survives me[2].

4. If the gift made by clause 3 of this Will also fails I give all my real and personal property to my personal representatives for whatever charitable purposes they think fit[3].

As Witness my hand this [–] day of [———] 20[–].

Signed by the Testator in our presence and attested by us in the presence of the Testator and of each other.

[1] It is unwise for the testator to give the whole of his estate to a single beneficiary without some long-stop provision.
[2] This form could include a survivorship condition by including here the words 'by [30 days]/[six months]' (see **11.4** to **11.10**). Where a testator intends to leave the whole of his estate to an individual there is usually no requirement.
[3] There is no point in directing that the executor is to decide in these circumstances because the executor [CD] will be dead. As to powers, see footnote 3 to the previous form.

FORM 17.3

Will giving residue to nephews and nieces with funeral arrangement, specific gifts and legacies

I, [*full name*] **of** [*home address*] revoke all earlier Wills and declare this to be my last Will

1. I appoint as my executors my nephew [AB] and my niece [CD] and in this Will the expression 'my Trustees' means (as the context requires) my executors and the trustees for the time being of any trust arising under this Will.

2. I wish my funeral to consist of a requiem mass at St Mary's Roman Catholic Church Nanton followed by burial in the family grave at Nanton cemetery[1].

3. I give:

    (1) my jewellery and articles of personal use or adornment to my niece [CD];

Precedents **17.2**

    (2)   my rosary, my missal and all books of devotion to my goddaughter [MN].

4. I give those of my personal chattels which constitute furniture or articles of household use or ornament to my executors:

    (1)   To transfer to my nephews and nieces such items as each selects provided that the value of the items selected by each does not in the opinion of my executors exceed one-fifth of the total value of the items from which the selection is made.

    (2)   To transfer the ownership of those items selected to the person concerned.

    (3)   To hold the remainder as part of my residuary estate.

5. I give:

    (1)   £5,000 to my goddaughter [MN];

    (2)   £1,000 to the priest in charge of St Mary's Roman Catholic Church Nanton to be applied for such religious purposes as he shall think fit and I declare that the receipt of the priest shall be sufficient discharge for my Trustees[2].

6. I give all the rest of my property to my Trustees to hold my estate on trust for sale with power to postpone sale to pay executorship expenses and debts including mortgages secured on real or leasehold property and any inheritance tax in respect of property passing under this Will or which becomes payable because of my death on any lifetime transfer by me or payable because of my death on property in which I hold a beneficial interest as joint tenant. All income received after my death shall be treated as income of my estate regardless of the period to which it relates and the statutory rules concerning apportionment and the rules in *Howe v Dartmouth* and *Allhusen v Whittell* and *Re Chesterfield's Trusts* shall not apply.

7. My Trustees shall hold the residue of my estate on trust for those of my nephews and nieces who survive me in equal shares.

[8. *Powers*[3]]

As Witness my hand this [–] day of [———] 20[–].

Signed by the Testator in our presence and attested by us in the presence of the Testator and of each other.

1   This is, of course, only an example and can be compared with the examples given in **chapter 5**.
2   This is an additional variety of clause to that which appears in **chapter 8**, where other examples of charitable legacies can be found.
3   In a simple case such as that contemplated by this Will there is no compelling reason to set out express dispositive and administrative powers. This is so even where one or more of the nephews or nieces may be a minor for in such a case the statutory powers under the Trustee Act 1925 and Trustee Act 2000 ought to suffice but there is no harm in taking in either the STEP standard provisions by incorporation (as in **Form 16.2**) or express powers (as in clauses 6 to 8 of **Form 16.2**).

17.2 *Precedents*

FORM 17.4

Will of widow or widower in favour of children or their spouses or, alternatively, the grandchildren with specific and pecuniary legacies

I, [*full name*] **of** [*home address*] revoke all earlier Wills and declare this to be my last Will

1. I appoint as my executors and trustees my son [AB] and my daughter [CD] and in this Will the expression 'my Trustees' means (as the context requires) my executors and the trustees for the time being of any trust arising under this Will.

2. I give to my nephew [EB] the Military Medal and Distinguished Service Order awarded to his grandfather which I inherited under his father's Will and the Georgian table which is kept in my study and which has belonged to members of my family for over 164[1] years.

3. I give the following legacies:

    (1) £1,000 to each of my grandchildren living at my death [who attains the age of 21 years][2];

    (2) £10,000 to my sister [FG];

    (3) £500 each to:

    (a) [LN] of [*address*]

    (b) [PQ] of [address]

    (c) [RS] of [address].

    (4) £1,000 to the Parochial Church Council (the Council) of Linwich for whatever religious purposes in the Parish are charitable and on which the Council decides at its discretion and if the Parish has been united with another Parish or divided into two or more other Parishes or has been dissolved this gift will have effect with the substitution of whatever other Parochial Church Council (or organisation succeeding to the relevant functions of a Parochial Church Council) within a radius of ten miles from Linwich Parish Church my Trustees think fit[3].

4. I give all the rest of my property to my Trustees to hold my estate on trust for sale with power to postpone sale to pay executorship expenses and debts including mortgages secured on real or leasehold property and any inheritance tax in respect of property passing under this Will or which becomes payable because of my death on any lifetime transfer by me or payable because of my death on property in which I hold a beneficial interest as joint tenant. All income received after my death shall be treated as income of my estate regardless of the period to which it relates and the statutory rules concerning apportionment and the rules in *Howe v Dartmouth* and *Allhusen v Whittell* and *Re Chesterfield's Trusts* shall not apply.

5. My Trustees shall hold the residue of my estate on trust for those of my[4] children who survive me in equal shares and if any of my children dies before me [his or her spouse][5]/[his or her children shall take equally [upon

attaining 21][2] the share which their parent would otherwise have inherited] shall take the share of my estate which my deceased child would otherwise have inherited[6].

6. My Trustees shall have power[7]:

   (1) to apply for the benefit of any beneficiary who has a contingent interest the whole or any part of the income from any capital to which he may become entitled;

   (2) during the whole of the period in which a beneficiary has a contingent interest to accumulate such income as is not so applied and to invest that income as an addition to the capital of the share to which that beneficiary is entitled[8];

   (3) to pay or apply for the benefit of any beneficiary who has a contingent interest the whole or any part of the capital to which he may become entitled;

   (4) to pay any money to which a beneficiary under eighteen is entitled to his parent or guardian for his benefit or to the beneficiary himself once he has attained sixteen and to rely upon the receipt then given by the parent or guardian or the minor himself.

7. My Trustees shall have the following powers in addition to their powers under the general law:

   (1) Power to invest as if they were beneficially entitled and this power includes the right:

      (a) to invest in unsecured loans;

      (b) to invest in other non-income producing assets including policies of life assurance;

      (c) to purchase land anywhere in the world;

      (d) to purchase an undivided share in land;

      (e) to invest in land for the occupation or enjoyment of any beneficiary.

   (2) Power to delegate their powers of investment and management of trust property to an agent (including one of their number) on such terms including terms enabling the agent to charge remuneration, to appoint a substitute, to limit liability and to act in circumstances giving rise to a conflict of interest as my Trustees think fit.

   (3) Power to appoint any person (including one of their number or a beneficiary) to act as their nominee and to take such steps as are necessary to vest any property in such person on such terms including terms enabling the agent to charge remuneration, to appoint a substitute, to limit liability and to act in circumstances giving rise to a conflict of interest as my Trustees think fit.

   (4) Power to make loans of capital to a beneficiary which may be interest free, repayable on demand or repayable at a rate below the market rate.

17.2 *Precedents*

(5) Power to borrow money on such terms as they think fit including the giving of security and to use it for any purpose for which the capital of my estate may be used.

(6) Power without the restrictions imposed by Administration of Estates Act 1925 s 41:

(a) To appropriate to any beneficiary in satisfaction or partial satisfaction of the gift to him any asset forming part of my residuary estate and not subject to a specific gift.

(b) To appropriate as the assets or part of the assets of any trust created by this Will any asset forming part of my residuary estate and not subject to a specific gift.

8. (1) My Trustees shall exercise their powers of investment and carry out their duties as trustees without regard to the statutory duty of care and Trustee Act 2000 s 1 shall not apply to the trusts of my Will.

(2) My Trustees shall be under no duty to review the acts of agents, nominees and custodians appointed by them and Trustee Act 2000 s 22 shall not apply to the trusts of my Will.

(3) Section 11 Trusts of Land and Appointment of Trustees Act 1996 (consultation with beneficiaries) shall not apply.

(4) In the absence of proof of dishonesty or the wilful commission of an act known to be a breach of trust none of my Trustees shall be liable for any loss or bound to take proceedings against a co-trustee for any breach of trust.

(5) My Trustees shall be entitled to be indemnified out of the assets of my estate against all liabilities incurred in connection with the bona fide execution of their duties and powers[6].

As Witness my hand this [–] day of [——] 20[–].

Signed by the Testator in our presence and attested by us in the presence of the Testator and of each other.

1   In a previous edition (2006), this table had been in the family for over 159 years. It has not been moved since at least 1997. Long may it continue in family ownership!
2   The use of an age contingency at 21 years in both clause 3(1) and clause 5 is no longer necessary as an upper limit because Perpetuities and Accumulations Act 2009 has introduced a single perpetuity period of 125 years (see **11.15** to **11.17**). In the case of clause 3(1) this could never have been a problem provided that the legacies were payable only to those living at the testator's death (which is obviously the most sensible approach). The residuary gift at clause 5 is absolute and immediate in the first instance and, once again, it only contemplates a gift over to grandchildren in existence at the date of the testator's death. Most testators will want to delay the vesting in possession of a grandchild's interest in a legacy or in residue to a point at which that grandchild might have developed sufficient maturity to cope with the gift. The selection of 21 years as the appropriate age is arbitrary but popular. This does mean, however, that the trustees will have to hold on to a fund to satisfy the gift when the grandchild attains the specified age.
3   This is an additional variety of clause to that which appears in **chapter 8**, where other examples of charitable legacies can be found.
4   A widow or widower is, of course, going to refer to 'my children'. For a discussion of gifts to 'my' children and gifts to 'our' children see **Form 15.1** footnote 3.
5   Where civil partners are intended to be included an express inclusion is required since 'spouse' does not include 'civil partner'.

6 Many testators will want to include gifts over to grandchildren (the second alternative) but where the grandchildren are young or there are no grandchildren at all it is more sensible to make an absolute gift over to the surviving spouse of the child as in the first alternative. For alternatives see **Forms 11.7** to **11.9** and, for a form of accruer, **Form 11.17**, all of which can easily be adapted for use here.
7 These powers at clauses 6 to 8 are taken from **Form 16.2**.
8 Perpetuities and Accumulations Act 2009 has removed the statutory restrictions on accumulations (see **11.18 to 11.19**) so that this power may be expressed even if the specified age in clause 5 is an age in excess of 21 years.

18 Wills for married couples or civil partners with no children

18.1 The case of a married couple or civil partners with no children is similar to that of an individual in many respects. There is usually one principal adult beneficiary (the spouse or civil partner) and then there may be additional pecuniary legacies or substitutional gifts in favour of siblings, friends and charity. If the whole of the estate of the first to die is left to the survivor the nil-rate band of the first to die will be unused and the survivor will be entitled to a nil-rate band enhanced by 100%. This is more fully discussed in **chapter 15. Forms 18.1** and **18.2** cater for married couples and civil partners with no children but **Forms 17.1** to **17.4** could easily be adapted to cater for this situation.

PRECEDENTS

18.2

Wills for married couples or civil partners with no children

Form 18.1 Will in favour of surviving spouse or civil partner with substitutional gift to brothers, sisters, brothers-in-law and sisters-in-law

Form 18.2 Will leaving spouse or civil partner life interest in the entire estate with remainder to collaterals as above

FORM 18.1

Will in favour of surviving spouse or civil partner with substitutional gift to brothers, sisters, brothers-in-law and sisters-in-law

I, [*full name*] **of** [*home address*] revoke all earlier Wills and declare this to be my last Will

1. I appoint my [wife]/[husband]/[civil partner] [AB] as my sole [executrix]/[executor] or if [she]/[he] is unable or unwilling to act or dies before proving my Will I appoint my brother [JC] and my sister-in-law [VL] as my executors and trustees.

2. If [she]/[he] survives me I give the whole of my estate to my [wife]/[husband]/[civil partner] absolutely[1].

3. If the gift at clause 2 fails then I give all my property to my Trustees to hold my estate on trust for sale with power to postpone sale to pay executorship expenses and debts including mortgages secured on real or leasehold property and any inheritance tax in respect of property passing under this Will or which becomes payable because of my death on any lifetime transfer by me or payable because of my death on property in which I hold a beneficial interest as joint tenant. All income received after my death shall be treated as income of my estate regardless of the period to which it relates and the statutory rules concerning apportionment and the rules in *Howe v Dartmouth* and *Allhusen v Whittell* and *Re Chesterfield's Trusts* shall not apply. My Trustees shall hold the residue of my estate:

    (1) As to one half for those of my brothers and sisters who survive me in equal shares and if any of them dies before me his or her children shall take per stirpes the share of my estate which their parent would otherwise have inherited;

    (2) As to the other half for those of my [wife's]/[husband's]/[civil partner's] brothers and sisters who survive me in equal shares and if any of them dies before me his or her children shall take per stirpes the share of my estate which their parent would otherwise have inherited.

18.2 *Precedents*

[4. *Powers²*]

As Witness my hand this [–] day of [———] 20[–].

Signed by the Testator in our presence and attested by us in the presence of the Testator and of each other.

1   The inclusion of a survivorship condition is now of no effect or even detrimental where the gift is in favour of a surviving spouse because of the transferability of the nil-rate band (discussed in **chapter 15**). In the previous edition the survivorship condition appears in the following terms:
        'If [she]/[he] survives me by [30 days]/[six months] I give the whole of my estate to my [wife]/[husband]/[civil partner] absolutely'.
     If the survivor's Will is not in reciprocal terms or the surviving spouse has already been married and has an enhanced nil-rate band by virtue of the previous marriage there will be some justification for including the survivorship condition.

2   In a simple case such as that contemplated by this Will there is no compelling reason to set out express dispositive and administrative powers. However, where the primary beneficiaries under clause 3 die the nephews and nieces (or nephews-in-law and nieces-in-law) might include minors. In such a case the statutory powers under the Trustee Act 1925 and Trustee Act 2000 ought to suffice but there is no harm in taking in either the STEP standard provisions by incorporation (as in **Form 16.1**), or express powers (as in **Form 16.2**).

FORM 18.2

Will leaving spouse or civil partner life interest in the entire estate with remainder to collaterals as above[1]

I, [*full name*] **of** [*home address*] revoke all earlier Wills and declare this to be my last Will

1.   (1)   I appoint my [wife]/[husband]/[civil partner] [AB] and the partners at my death in the firm of   of   ('the Firm') as my executors and trustees and in this Will the expression 'my Trustees' means (as the context requires) my executors and the trustees for the time being of any trust arising under this Will.

    (2)   In this clause:

         (a)   The expression 'the Firm' means not only [*name*] but any other firm which at my death has succeeded to and carries on its practice including a firm which has been incorporated or has formed a limited liability partnership; and

         (b)   The expression 'partners' means the persons commonly described as partners in the Firm including salaried partners and, in the case of an incorporated practice or limited liability partnership, the directors, members and beneficial owners of any share of the Firm.

    (3)   I wish my [wife]/[husband]/[civil partner] and not more than [one] of the partners in the Firm to apply for probate of this Will.

    (4)   If my [wife]/[husband]/[civil partner] is unable or unwilling to act or dies before proving my Will I appoint my brother [JC] as executor in her place to act with the partners in the Firm.

    (5)   Any of my Trustees who is a solicitor may charge fees for work done by him or his firm (whether or not the work is of a professional nature) on the same basis as if he were not one of my Trustees but employed to carry out the work on their behalf.

2. I give to my [wife]/[husband]/[civil partner] my personal chattels as defined by Administration of Estates Act 1925 s 55(1)(x)[2].

3. If my [wife]/[husband]/[civil partner] does not survive me[3] I give legacies of £500 to each of my nephews and nieces and to each of the nephews and nieces of my [wife]/[husband]/[civil partner].

4. I give the rest of my property to my Trustees to hold my estate on trust for sale with power to postpone sale to pay executorship expenses and debts including mortgages secured on real or leasehold property and any inheritance tax in respect of property passing under this Will or which becomes payable because of my death on any lifetime transfer by me or payable because of my death on property in which I hold a beneficial interest as joint tenant. All income received after my death shall be treated as income of my estate regardless of the period to which it relates and the statutory rules concerning apportionment and the rules in *Howe v Dartmouth* and *Allhusen v Whittell* and *Re Chesterfield's Trusts* shall not apply.

5. My Trustees shall hold the residue of my estate ('my residuary estate') on trust to pay the income from my residuary estate to my [wife]/[husband]/[civil partner] during [her]/[his] lifetime with power to pay or apply the whole or any part of the capital of my residuary estate for the benefit of my [wife]/[husband]/[civil partner][4] and subject to any exercise of that power after [her]/[his] death:

    (1) as to one half of my residuary estate in equal shares to those of my brothers and sisters who survive me in equal shares and if any of them dies before me his or her children shall take per stirpes the share of my estate which their parent would otherwise have inherited[5];

    (2) as to the other half of my estate to those of my [wife's]/[husband's]/[civil partner's] brothers and sisters who survive me in equal shares and if any of them dies before me his or her children shall take per stirpes the share of my estate which their parent would otherwise have inherited[5].

6. My Trustees shall have power:

    (1) to apply for the benefit of any beneficiary who has a contingent interest the whole or any part of the income from any capital to which he may become entitled;

    (2) during the whole of the period in which a beneficiary has a contingent interest to accumulate such income as is not so applied and to invest that income as an addition to the capital of the share to which that beneficiary is entitled;

    (3) to pay or apply for the benefit of any beneficiary who has a contingent interest the whole or any part of the capital to which he may become entitled;

    (4) to pay any money to which a beneficiary under eighteen is entitled to his parent or guardian for his benefit or to the beneficiary himself once he has attained sixteen and to rely upon the receipt then given by the parent or guardian or the minor himself.

18.2 *Precedents*

7. My Trustees shall have the following powers in addition to their powers under the general law:

   (1) Power to invest as if they were beneficially entitled and this power includes the right:

   (a) to invest in unsecured loans;

   (b) to invest in other non-income producing assets including policies of life assurance;

   (c) to purchase land anywhere in the world;

   (d) to purchase an undivided share in land;

   (e) to invest in land for the occupation or enjoyment of any beneficiary.

   (2) Power to delegate their powers of investment and management of trust property to an agent (including one of their number) on such terms including terms enabling the agent to charge remuneration, to appoint a substitute, to limit liability and to act in circumstances giving rise to a conflict of interest as my Trustees think fit.

   (3) Power to appoint any person (including one of their number or a beneficiary) to act as their nominee and to take such steps as are necessary to vest any property in such person on such terms including terms enabling the agent to charge remuneration, to appoint a substitute, to limit liability and to act in circumstances giving rise to a conflict of interest as my Trustees think fit.

   (4) Power to make loans of capital to a beneficiary which may be interest free, repayable on demand or repayable at a rate below the market rate.

   (5) Power to borrow money on such terms as they think fit including the giving of security and to use it for any purpose for which the capital of my estate may be used.

   (6) Power without the restrictions imposed by Administration of Estates Act 1925 s 41:

   (a) To appropriate to any beneficiary in satisfaction or partial satisfaction of the gift to him any asset forming part of my residuary estate and not subject to a specific gift.

   (b) To appropriate as the assets or part of the assets of any trust created by this Will any asset forming part of my residuary estate and not subject to a specific gift.

8. (1) My Trustees shall exercise their powers of investment and carry out their duties as trustees without regard to the statutory duty of care and Trustee Act 2000 s 1 shall not apply to the trusts of my Will.

   (2) My Trustees shall be under no duty to review the acts of agents, nominees and custodians appointed by them and Trustee Act 2000 s 22 shall not apply to the trusts of my Will.

   (3) Section 11 Trusts of Land and Appointment of Trustees Act 1996 (consultation with beneficiaries) shall not apply.

(4) In the absence of proof of dishonesty or the wilful commission of an act known to be a breach of trust none of my Trustees shall be liable for any loss or bound to take proceedings against a co-trustee for any breach of trust[6].

(5) My Trustees shall be entitled to be indemnified out of the assets of my estate against all liabilities incurred in connection with the bona fide execution of their duties and powers[7].

As Witness my hand this [–] day of [————] 20[–].

Signed by the Testator in our presence and attested by us in the presence of the Testator and of each other.

1. This Will is not suitable for the younger couple. Binding a young widow, widower or surviving civil partner to a life interest can be overly wasteful and complex. It might also lead to a claim under the Inheritance (Provision for Family and Dependants) Act 1975.
2. It is unwise to settle chattels. They deteriorate over time, require maintenance and their upkeep necessitates expense.
3. This gift is made without a survivorship condition in order to avoid double payment but that is only a concern where the Wills are in reciprocal or mirror terms. As to survivorship conditions generally see **11.4** to **11.10**. The inclusion of a survivorship condition can have a detrimental effect for inheritance tax purposes between spouses, as to which see **chapter 15**.
4. Note that this clause includes an express power to pay or apply capital to the life tenant. This could be important if a capital outlay is needed in connection with the provision of assisted accommodation. The gift of a life interest is an immediate post-death interest within Inheritance Tax Act 1984 s 49A, as added by the Finance Act 2006.
5. In this case the brothers and sisters living at the death of the testator have been chosen but the gift could be limited to those living at the death of the surviving spouse with an increased risk of a partial intestacy.
6. This exoneration clause is broader than that which the Law Commission considers to be appropriate where trustees are professional. See the note to **Form 12.22**.
7. This form deserves full powers. The STEP provisions could be incorporated in place of clauses 6 to 8 if preferred with the added deletion of subclause 1(4).

19 Wills for married couples or civil partners with children

Married couples or civil partners with children

19.1 For most couples with children the overriding requirement is to make provision for the surviving spouse and those children who are not self-sufficient. They are often greatly concerned about the possibility of their both being killed in a common calamity leaving minor children surviving them. In many cases the mitigation of inheritance tax is of little or no significance. Despite these concerns clients rarely contemplate the appointment of testamentary guardians without prompting but invariably accept that such an appointment is highly desirable if both are to die while they have a child under 18. **Forms 19.1** to **19.8** cater for married couples or civil partners with children.

19.2 Couples should be encouraged to discuss the provisions of their Wills with each other and their solicitor or Will draftsman so as to ensure that the provisions are in harmony. Where the assets are vested in the husband he often has to be reminded that, while his wife has 'nothing to leave', the whole of his estate will constitute her intestacy if she were to die shortly after him. It goes without saying that almost invariably (taking no account of the moral issue) it is undesirable for the total assets of a married couple or civil partners to be vested entirely in one or other of them.

19.3 It is a truism to say that the particular circumstance of the client will govern the precise terms of his Will. In the case of married couples and civil partners the variety of possible situations is broader and more subtle. What is a sensible provision for a married man in his early thirties will be quite different from that of the same man in his early seventies. There are, however, certain family situations which are commonly encountered by the practitioner and possible approaches which may be applicable to them are considered to some extent below.

COUPLES WITH ADULT CHILDREN

19.4 In the case of a married couple (neither of whom have previously been widowed) with adult children who have no claims to dependency on their parents, there are three popular forms of Will.
(1) In most cases the most appropriate provision will be for each party to give the whole of his or her estate to the other with a gift over to the children equally in the event of the spouse or (where appropriate) civil partner predeceasing the testator. **Forms 19.1** and **19.2** are examples.

(2) An alternative is to give the survivor a life interest. This qualifies as an immediate post-death interest in possession (IPDI) as discussed in **chapter 15**, and spouse/civil partner exempt so that there is no tax on the first death. It also has the advantage that the nil-rate band is not used where it is left to the surviving spouse or civil partner who then benefits from an augmented nil-rate band on his or her death. **Form 19.3** is an example.

(3) A further alternative (which saw a rapid decline in popularity after the introduction of a transferable nil-rate band between spouses and civil partners) is to give the inheritance tax-free band direct to the children. This was only ever appropriate where the joint assets would result in inheritance tax being payable on the second death and it was thought that half the joint assets would provide adequately for the surviving spouse. The same considerations as to the size of the estate still apply but, in an inversion of previous thinking, a gift of the nil-rate band to the children is now considered wasteful although this will not necessarily be the case if, for example, the survivor remarries and is widowed again. **Forms 19.4** and **19.5** are examples.

COUPLES WITH MINOR CHILDREN

19.5 Another common situation is that of a married couple with children all of whom are under 18 and in full-time education. Particularly in the case of a younger couple, both husband and wife may be content that the whole of their estate should pass to the survivor and be confident that the survivor will make proper provision for the dependent children, but they may be concerned about what would happen if they both die while the children are not self-sufficient.

19.6 Prior to Finance Act 2006 this book suggested that, notwithstanding the privileged inheritance tax treatment of accumulation and maintenance trusts, a discretionary trust ought to be preferred. This is because the traditional class gift to the children with powers of advancement is somewhat inflexible whereas a discretionary trust for the children with a distribution of the unallocated funds once the reason for the discretionary trust has ceased to exist provides rather more flexibility. In the new inheritance tax environment the pendulum swung first in favour of fully discretionary trusts for the children and then, because of the introduction of the transferrable nil-rate band, towards making no provision for the children whatever. In circumstances in which there is a desire to make provision for children which overrides the advantages inherent in a transferable nil-rate band between spouses, the fully discretionary trust is now the most sensible solution. The privileged treatment of old accumulation and maintenance trusts has been phased out and the potential for creating new trusts along these lines is now limited to trusts for bereaved minors (which must vest at 18) and section 71D trusts (which must vest at 25): see **chapter 15** at **15.39** to **15.45**. The vast majority of parents will not want substantial sums to vest in their children when they are as young as 18 and many will take the view – particularly in the economic climate in which young people currently live – that it is a little early for sums to vest in their children at 25 when they might be both immature and debt-ridden. Most will lean in favour of fully discretionary trusts under which trustees will be able to make sums available to children in full-time education without them being in charge of it.

19.7 There is much sense in this because the needs of the children during their formative years will vary and, if their parents are alive, they will accommodate those needs as seems best at the time without necessarily treating the children equally. Thus, the object of the discretionary trust is, so far as practicable, to provide for the children

19.8 *Wills for married couples or civil partners with children*

in the same way as their parents would have done if they had been alive. It follows that they must have complete confidence in the trustees appointed. **Forms 19.2** to **19.5** are examples.

PENSIONS

19.8 Where one spouse (usually the husband) enjoys a substantial salary and is in pensionable employment, inheritance tax may be a relevant consideration on the first death, particularly if a large sum will be payable from his pension fund if he dies before reaching pensionable age. It is then worthwhile considering the terms of the pension scheme, which often provide that a lump sum payment on death may be paid to dependents of the deceased at the discretion of the trustees of the pension fund. It is usual to invite the employee to nominate his preferred beneficiary or beneficiaries. The lump sum payment falls outside the scope of inheritance tax, and it may be a waste of a tax-free sum for all of this sum to pass to the surviving spouse (who is an exempt beneficiary). A nomination of the death benefit in favour of the children coupled with a Will-making provision for the surviving spouse is more tax advantageous than providing for the children by Will with the pension lump sum being paid over to the surviving spouse. On the other hand, if the pension fund is needed by the surviving spouse, it may be possible for the nomination to be in favour of the trustees of a discretionary trust for spouse and children created by the testator during his lifetime (with nominal assets).

REMARRIAGE OR THE FORMATION OF A (NEW) CIVIL PARTNERSHIP

19.9 The practitioner frequently has to face the delicate problem posed by the testator who is anxious that the surviving spouse should have ample provision for his or her needs but is apprehensive that the survivor will remarry or form a (new) civil partnership and their children will be deprived of what the testator considers to be their lawful inheritance. Remarriage amongst the elderly is an increasingly common occurrence and the fear that children may be disinherited is genuine[1]. Often the problem is essentially one of human relationships and is incapable of being satisfactorily resolved by a legal formula. A provision relating to remarriage or the creation of a civil partnership may well be ineffective because the current morals of society do not inhibit cohabitation. At the same time, a provision in the Will relating to cohabitation could well prove offensive to the testator's spouse or civil partner or even to the testator himself as well as being difficult, in most certain circumstances, to establish or enforce. Both provisions might also be seen as an invitation for the surviving spouse to challenge the provision made by commencing proceedings under the Inheritance (Provision for Family and Dependants) Act 1975.

1   A further problem is that those entering into a second marriage easily forget (if they ever understood) that marriage revokes a Will.

19.10 The only obvious solution available involves the use of a life interest – which ought to be an immediate post-death interest: see **chapter 15** at **15.44**. Especially in the current economic climate, to provide a satisfactory income, however, the estate or fund supporting the life interest needs to be substantial and so the solution to one problem creates another. There may be a potentially large inheritance tax liability saved up for the future although the introduction of transferable nil-rate bands between spouses and civil partners has mitigated this problem to some extent. Further, the lifetime termination of an immediate post-death interest will be treated as a gift by the life tenant for gift with reservation purposes which can seriously reduce the flexibility of this structure. If the estate is not very large, a life interest in the matrimonial home with an absolute gift of income-producing assets may be the acceptable compromise. If the estate is sufficiently large, a gift to the children of a sum equal to the inheritance tax-free band with a gift of the residue to the survivor may provide a solution, as it gives partial protection against the children being disinherited and simultaneously constitutes a form of inheritance tax planning, albeit one that does not give the surviving spouse the right to an augmented nil-rate band so stores up an inheritance tax problem for the future. There is no entirely satisfactory solution to the problem. **Form 19.4** makes provision for a discretionary trust leaving the spouse a life interest in residue. **Form 19.6** provides another solution.

DRAFTING POINTS WHERE TRUSTS ARE CREATED

19.11 Where a trust is created, the reasons should, of course, be explained to the client, as should the extended powers of the trustees. There are pitfalls in the creation of trusts which can entrap even the experienced Will draftsman if he is not on his guard. This is not the place for a dissertation on the law relating to trusts but it is appropriate to remind the draftsman of certain important considerations.

(1) The need to draft with care the provisions relating to class gifts. Remember that a gift which confers a vested interest on the beneficiaries will have different consequences from one which confers a contingent interest.
(2) The significance of the 'immediate post-death interest'. See **chapter 15** at **15.44**.
(3) The risk of a partial intestacy where there is a residuary gift to a number of persons in equal shares with no provision as to what should happen to the share of a beneficiary who dies before the testator.
(4) The consequences of the provisions of Wills Act 1837 s 33 in respect of a gift to a child or remoter issue of the testator when the beneficiary fails to survive him.

Prior to 6 April 2010 when Perpetuities and Accumulations Act 2009 came into force, the Will draftsman had to take care to avoid offending the rule against perpetuities, particularly in the case of contingent gifts to grandchildren. It was also important to bear in mind the necessity of limiting the right to accumulate income to 21 years from the testator's death. Perpetuities and Accumulations Act 2009 has introduced a single perpetuity period of 125 years which severely limits the risk of new trusts offending that rule (there is, in any event, a wait and see provision). The Act has also removed the statutory restrictions on accumulations altogether.

PRECEDENTS

19.12

Wills for married couples or civil partners with children

Form 19.1 Will of married adult with adult children leaving everything to spouse with substitutional gift to children

Form 19.2 Will leaving everything to spouse or civil partner creating discretionary trust for children if spouse or civil partner has predeceased

Form 19.3 Will of married adult with adult children leaving everything to spouse for life with gift of remainder to children

Form 19.4 Will creating capped 21-year nil-rate band discretionary trust with residue to spouse or civil partner

Form 19.5 Will as one of reciprocal Wills creating nil-rate band discretionary trust with residue to spouse or civil partner for life

Form 19.6 Will creating trust for a disabled child with residue to the testator's spouse or civil partner

Form 19.7 Will giving testator's interest in residence to children with residue to spouse or civil partner

Form 19.8 Will for those previously married whose spouse has an enhanced nil-rate band either for use alone or as one of reciprocal Wills creating nil-rate band discretionary trust with residue to spouse or civil partner absolutely. Will including promissory note provisions

FORM 19.1

Will of married adult with adult children leaving everything to spouse with substitutional gift to children[1]

I, [*full name*] **of** [*home address*] revoke all earlier Wills and declare this to be my last Will

1. I appoint my [*wife*]/[*husband*] [*name*] as my sole [*executrix*]/[*executor*] but if [*she*]/[*he*] is unable or unwilling to act or if [*she*]/[*he*] dies before proving my Will I appoint my children [*name*] and [*name*] as my executors[2].

2. I appoint as my trustees those of my executors who obtain probate of this Will and in this Will the expression 'my Trustees' means (as the context requires) those of my executors who obtained probate and the trustees for the time being of any trust arising under this Will.

3. I give all my property to my [*wife*]/[*husband*] absolutely if [*she*]/[*he*] survives me[3] but if this gift fails the remaining clauses of my Will shall take effect.

[4. I appoint [*name*] of [*address*] and [*name*] of [*address*] as guardians of any of my children under eighteen[4].]

5. I give all my property to my Trustees to hold my estate on trust for sale with power to postpone sale to pay executorship expenses and debts including mortgages secured on real or leasehold property and any

inheritance tax in respect of property passing under this Will or which becomes payable because of my death on any lifetime transfer by me or payable because of my death on property in which I hold a beneficial interest as joint tenant. All income received after my death shall be treated as income of my estate regardless of the period to which it relates and the statutory rules concerning apportionment and the rules in *Howe v Dartmouth* and *Allhusen v Whittell* and *Re Chesterfield's Trusts* shall not apply.

6. My Trustees shall hold the residue ('my residuary estate') for those of my children who survive me [and attain the age of 25 years[5]] in equal shares.

[7. If any of my children does not attain the age of 25 years then his or her children who survive him or her and attain the age of 25[6] years shall take in equal shares per stirpes the share which he or she would otherwise have taken.[5]]

8. My Trustees shall have power:

    (1) to apply for the benefit of any beneficiary who is has a contingent interest the whole or any part of the income from any capital to which he may become entitled;

    (2) during the whole of the period in which a beneficiary has a contingent interest to accumulate such income as is not so applied and to invest that income as an addition to the capital of the share to which that beneficiary is entitled[7];

    (3) to pay or apply for the benefit of any beneficiary who has a contingent interest the whole or any part of the capital to which he may become entitled;

    (4) to pay any money to which a beneficiary under eighteen is entitled to his parent or guardian for his benefit or to the beneficiary himself once he has attained sixteen and to rely upon the receipt then given by the parent or guardian or the minor himself.

9. My Trustees shall have the following powers in addition to their powers under the general law:

    (1) Power to invest as if they were beneficially entitled and this power includes the right:

        (a) to invest in unsecured loans;

        (b) to invest in other non-income producing assets including policies of life assurance;

        (c) to purchase land anywhere in the world;

        (d) to purchase an undivided share in land;

        (e) to invest in land for the occupation or enjoyment of any beneficiary.

    (2) Power to delegate their powers of investment and management of trust property to an agent (including one of their number) on such terms including terms enabling the agent to charge remuneration, to appoint a substitute, to limit liability and to act in circumstances giving rise to a conflict of interest as my Trustees think fit.

19.12 *Precedents*

(3) Power to appoint any person (including one of their number or a beneficiary) to act as their nominee and to take such steps as are necessary to vest any property in such person on such terms including terms enabling the agent to charge remuneration, to appoint a substitute, to limit liability and to act in circumstances giving rise to a conflict of interest as my Trustees think fit.

(4) Power to make loans of capital to a beneficiary which may be interest free, repayable on demand or repayable at a rate below the market rate.

(5) Power to borrow money on such terms as they think fit including the giving of security and to use it for any purpose for which the capital of my estate may be used.

(6) Power without the restrictions imposed by Administration of Estates Act 1925 s 41:

(a) To appropriate to any beneficiary in satisfaction or partial satisfaction of the gift to him any asset forming part of my residuary estate and not subject to a specific gift.

(b) To appropriate as the assets or part of the assets of any trust created by this Will any asset forming part of my residuary estate and not subject to a specific gift.

10. (1) My Trustees shall exercise their powers of investment and carry out their duties as trustees without regard to the statutory duty of care and Trustee Act 2000 s 1 shall not apply to the trusts of my Will.

(2) My Trustees shall be under no duty to review the acts of agents, nominees and custodians appointed by them and Trustee Act 2000 s 22 shall not apply to the trusts of my Will.

(3) Section 11 Trusts of Land and Appointment of Trustees Act 1996 (consultation with beneficiaries) shall not apply.

(4) In the absence of proof of dishonesty or the wilful commission of an act known to be a breach of trust none of my Trustees shall be liable for any loss or bound to take proceedings against a co-trustee for any breach of trust.

(5) My Trustees shall be entitled to be indemnified out of the assets of my estate against all liabilities incurred in connection with the bona fide execution of their duties and powers[8].

As Witness my hand this [–] day of [———] 20[–].

Signed by the Testator in our presence and attested by us in the presence of the Testator and of each other.

1 This Will is also suitable for testators with minor children.
2 It is not appropriate to appoint the children if they are not adults.
3 The inclusion of a survivorship condition is now of no effect or even detrimental where the gift is in favour of a surviving spouse because of the transferability of the nil-rate band (discussed in **chapter 15**). In previous editions the survivorship condition appears in the following terms:
'I give all my property to my [wife]/[husband] absolutely if [she]/[he] survives me by [30 days]/[six months] but if this gift fails the remaining clauses of my Will shall take effect.'
If the survivor's Will is not in reciprocal terms or the surviving spouse has already been married and has an enhanced nil-rate band by virtue of the previous marriage there will be some justification for including the survivorship condition.

4	Only the survivor should appoint guardians. For commentary on this see **chapter 7**. This clause is, of course, unnecessary if the children are adults.
5	If the words in square brackets at the end of clause 6 are not included the whole of clause 7 should also be left out of account. These words (at the end of clause 6) settle property for bereaved minors at the age of 25 bringing the provision within s 71D: see **chapter 15** at **15.41** to **15.42**. Grandchildren taking by substitution are not bereaved minors.
6	In previous editions the age specified here was 21 years in order to avoid the need to rely on the 'wait and see rule' for perpetuity purposes. Now that there is only one perpetuity period of 125 years, this is not a serious risk so the testator is able to specify an age of 25 years for both children and grandchildren.
7	Perpetuities and Accumulations Act 2009 has removed the statutory restrictions on accumulations (see **11.18** to **11.19**) so that this power may be expressed, as in this form, to be of indefinite duration although it will, of course, expire with the trust at the end of the perpetuity period.
8	These are the powers as set out in **Form 16.2**.

FORM 19.2

Will leaving everything to spouse or civil partner creating discretionary trust for children if spouse or civil partner has predeceased[1]

I, [*full name*] **of** [*home address*] revoke all earlier Wills and declare this to be my last Will

1. If my [wife]/[husband]/[civil partner] survives me[2] I appoint [him]/[her] as my sole [executrix]/[executor] and I give the whole of my estate to my [wife]/[husband]/[civil partner] but if this gift fails the following provisions will apply.

2. (1) I appoint the partners at my death in the firm of   of   ('the Firm') as my executors and trustees and in this Will the expression 'my Trustees' means (as the context requires) my executors and the trustees for the time being of any trust arising under this Will.

    (2) In this clause:

    (a) The expression 'the Firm' means not only [*name*] but any other firm which at my death has succeeded to and carries on its practice including a firm which has been incorporated or has formed a limited liability partnership; and

    (b) The expression 'partners' means the persons commonly described as partners in the Firm including salaried partners and, in the case of an incorporated practice or limited liability partnership, the directors, members and beneficial owners of any share of the Firm.

    (3) Any of my Trustees who is a solicitor may charge fees for work done by him or his firm (whether or not the work is of a professional nature) on the same basis as if he were not one of my Trustees but employed to carry out the work on their behalf.

3. I appoint [*name*] of [*address*] and [*name*] of [*address*] as guardians of any of my children under eighteen[3].

4. I give all my property to my Trustees to hold my estate on trust for sale with power to postpone sale to pay executorship expenses and debts including mortgages secured on real or leasehold property and any inheritance tax in respect of property passing under this Will or which

becomes payable because of my death on any lifetime transfer by me or payable because of my death on property in which I hold a beneficial interest as joint tenant. All income received after my death shall be treated as income of my estate regardless of the period to which it relates and the statutory rules concerning apportionment and the rules in *Howe v Dartmouth* and *Allhusen v Whittell* and *Re Chesterfield's Trusts* shall not apply.

5. (1) In this clause[4]:

   (a) 'the Trust Fund' means my residuary estate.

   (b) 'my Beneficiaries' include my children and remoter issue and any spouse [civil partner within the meaning of the Civil Partnership Act 2004[5]] widow [or[5]] widower [or former civil partner[5]] of my children and remoter issue.

   (2) My Trustees shall hold the Trust Fund upon the following trusts:

   (a) For not more than 125 years from my death (which is the perpetuity period for these trusts) to apply the capital of the Trust Fund for the benefit of such of my Beneficiaries as my Trustees think fit.

   (b) To apply the income of the Trust Fund for the benefit of such of my Beneficiaries as my Trustees think fit or to accumulate the whole or any part of it as an addition to the capital of the Trust Fund.

   (c) Within 125 years of my death to end these trusts by distributing the Trust Fund among such of my Beneficiaries as my Trustees think fit.

   (d) To exercise their discretionary powers over capital or income when and how they think fit without having to make payments to or for the benefit of all my Beneficiaries or to ensure equality among those who have benefited.

   (3) My Trustees shall have the powers appearing in the following clauses in addition to their powers under the general law.

6. My Trustees shall have power:

   (1) to apply for the benefit of any beneficiary who is has a contingent interest the whole or any part of the income from any capital to which he may become entitled;

   (2) to pay or apply for the benefit of any beneficiary who has a contingent interest the whole or any part of the capital to which he may become entitled;

   (3) to pay any money to which a beneficiary under eighteen is entitled to his parent or guardian for his benefit or to the beneficiary himself once he has attained sixteen and to rely upon the receipt then given by the parent or guardian or the minor himself.

7. My Trustees shall have the following powers in addition to their powers under the general law:

   (1) Power to invest as if they were beneficially entitled and this power includes the right:

(a) to invest in unsecured loans;

(b) to invest in other non-income producing assets including policies of life assurance;

(c) to purchase land anywhere in the world;

(d) to purchase an undivided share in land;

(e) to invest in land for the occupation or enjoyment of any beneficiary.

(2) Power to delegate their powers of investment and management of trust property to an agent (including one of their number) on such terms including terms enabling the agent to charge remuneration, to appoint a substitute, to limit liability and to act in circumstances giving rise to a conflict of interest as my Trustees think fit.

(3) Power to appoint any person (including one of their number or a beneficiary) to act as their nominee and to take such steps as are necessary to vest any property in such person on such terms including terms enabling the agent to charge remuneration, to appoint a substitute, to limit liability and to act in circumstances giving rise to a conflict of interest as my Trustees think fit.

(4) Power to make loans of capital to a beneficiary which may be interest free, repayable on demand or repayable at a rate below the market rate.

(5) Power to borrow money on such terms as they think fit including the giving of security and to use it for any purpose for which the capital of my estate may be used.

(6) Power without the restrictions imposed by Administration of Estates Act 1925 s 41:

(a) To appropriate to any beneficiary in satisfaction or partial satisfaction of the gift to him any asset forming part of my residuary estate and not subject to a specific gift.

(b) To appropriate as the assets or part of the assets of any trust created by this Will any asset forming part of my residuary estate and not subject to a specific gift.

8. (1) My Trustees shall exercise their powers of investment and carry out their duties as trustees without regard to the statutory duty of care and Trustee Act 2000 s 1 shall not apply to the trusts of my Will.

(2) My Trustees shall be under no duty to review the acts of agents, nominees and custodians appointed by them and Trustee Act 2000 s 22 shall not apply to the trusts of my Will.

(3) Section 11 Trusts of Land and Appointment of Trustees Act 1996 (consultation with beneficiaries) shall not apply.

(4) In the absence of proof of dishonesty or the wilful commission of an act known to be a breach of trust none of my Trustees shall be liable for any loss or bound to take proceedings against a co-trustee for any breach of trust.[6]

19.12 *Precedents*

(5) My Trustees shall be entitled to be indemnified out of the assets of my estate against all liabilities incurred in connection with the bona fide execution of their duties and powers.

As Witness my hand this [–] day of [———] 20[–].

Signed by the Testator in our presence and attested by us in the presence of the Testator and of each other.

1 This form is suitable for a married couple or for civil partners of fairly modest means with younger children whose circumstances are likely to vary over time. It is intended that reciprocal Wills should be made in this form. In the first instance the surviving spouse has care of the children and receives the whole of the deceased's estate but the survivor appoints guardians and creates a discretionary trust of the whole of his or her estate for the benefit of the children.
2 The inclusion of a survivorship condition is now of no effect or even detrimental where the gift is in favour of a surviving spouse because of the transferability of the nil-rate band (discussed in **chapter 15**). In the previous edition the survivorship condition was in the following terms:
'If my [wife]/[husband]/[civil partner] survives me by [30 days]/[six months]…'
3 Only the survivor should appoint guardians. For commentary on this see **chapter 7**. This clause is, of course, unnecessary if the children are adults.
4 For a brief commentary on the use of discretionary trusts see **chapters 11** and **15**. Although this discretionary trust has a perpetuity period of 125 years it should be explained to the testator that it can be wound up at any time before then and so need not last until the end of the period.
5 Include the references to civil partners in the beneficial class if those are the testator's instructions.
6 This exoneration clause is broader than that which the Law Commission considers to be appropriate where trustees are professional. See the note to **Form 12.22**.

FORM 19.3

Will of married adult with adult children leaving everything to spouse for life with gift of remainder to children[1]

I, [*full name*] **of** [*home address*] revoke all earlier Wills and declare this to be my last Will

1. (1) I appoint my [wife]/[husband]/[civil partner] [AB] and the partners at my death in the firm of   of   ('the Firm') as my executors and trustees and in this Will the expression 'my Trustees' means (as the context requires) my executors and the trustees for the time being of any trust arising under this Will.

    (2) In this clause:

    (a) The expression 'the Firm' means not only [*name*] but any other firm which at my death has succeeded to and carries on its practice including a firm which has been incorporated or has formed a limited liability partnership; and

    (b) The expression 'partners' means the persons commonly described as partners in the Firm including salaried partners and, in the case of an incorporated practice or limited liability partnership, the directors, members and beneficial owners of any share of the Firm.

    (3) I wish my [wife]/[husband]/[civil partner] and not more than [one] of the partners in the Firm to apply for probate of this Will.

    (4) If my [wife]/[husband]/[civil partner] is unable or unwilling to act or dies before proving my Will I appoint my brother [JC] as executor in her place to act with the partners in the Firm.

(5) Any of my Trustees who is a solicitor may charge fees for work done by him or his firm (whether or not the work is of a professional nature) on the same basis as if he were not one of my Trustees but employed to carry out the work on their behalf.

2. I give to my [wife]/[husband]/[civil partner] my personal chattels as defined by Administration of Estates Act 1925 s 55(1)(x)[2].

3. I give all the rest of my property to my Trustees to hold my estate on trust for sale with power to postpone sale to pay executorship expenses and debts including mortgages secured on real or leasehold property and any inheritance tax in respect of property passing under this Will or which becomes payable because of my death on any lifetime transfer by me or payable because of my death on property in which I hold a beneficial interest as joint tenant. All income received after my death shall be treated as income of my estate regardless of the period to which it relates and the statutory rules concerning apportionment and the rules in *Howe v Dartmouth* and *Allhusen v Whittell* and *Re Chesterfield's Trusts* shall not apply.

4. My Trustees shall hold the residue of my estate ('my residuary estate') on trust to pay the income from my residuary estate to my [wife]/[husband]/[civil partner] during [her]/[his] lifetime with power to pay or apply the whole or any part of the capital of my residuary estate for the benefit of my [wife]/[husband]/[civil partner][3] and subject to any exercise of that power after [her]/[his] death to hold the capital and income of my residuary estate in equal shares to those of my children by my [wife]/[husband] who survive me in equal shares and if any of them dies before me his or her children shall take per stirpes the share of my estate which their parent would otherwise have inherited.

5. My Trustees shall have power:

   (1) to apply for the benefit of any beneficiary who is has a contingent interest the whole or any part of the income from any capital to which he may become entitled;

   (2) during the whole of the period in which a beneficiary has a contingent interest to accumulate such income as is not so applied and to invest that income as an addition to the capital of the share to which that beneficiary is entitled[4];

   (3) to pay or apply for the benefit of any beneficiary who has a contingent interest the whole or any part of the capital to which he may become entitled;

   (4) to pay any money to which a beneficiary under eighteen is entitled to his parent or guardian for his benefit or to the beneficiary himself once he has attained sixteen and to rely upon the receipt then given by the parent or guardian or the minor himself.

6. My Trustees shall have the following powers in addition to their powers under the general law:

   (1) Power to invest as if they were beneficially entitled and this power includes the right:

       (a) to invest in unsecured loans;

19.12 *Precedents*

- (b) to invest in other non-income producing assets including policies of life assurance;
- (c) to purchase land anywhere in the world;
- (d) to purchase an undivided share in land;
- (e) to invest in land for the occupation or enjoyment of any beneficiary.

(2) Power to delegate their powers of investment and management of trust property to an agent (including one of their number) on such terms including terms enabling the agent to charge remuneration, to appoint a substitute, to limit liability and to act in circumstances giving rise to a conflict of interest as my Trustees think fit.

(3) Power to appoint any person (including one of their number or a beneficiary) to act as their nominee and to take such steps as are necessary to vest any property in such person on such terms including terms enabling the agent to charge remuneration, to appoint a substitute, to limit liability and to act in circumstances giving rise to a conflict of interest as my Trustees think fit.

(4) Power to make loans of capital to a beneficiary which may be interest free, repayable on demand or repayable at a rate below the market rate.

(5) Power to borrow money on such terms as they think fit including the giving of security and to use it for any purpose for which the capital of my estate may be used.

(6) Power without the restrictions imposed by Administration of Estates Act 1925 s 41:

- (a) To appropriate to any beneficiary in satisfaction or partial satisfaction of the gift to him any asset forming part of my residuary estate and not subject to a specific gift.
- (b) To appropriate as the assets or part of the assets of any trust created by this Will any asset forming part of my residuary estate and not subject to a specific gift.

7. (1) My Trustees shall exercise their powers of investment and carry out their duties as trustees without regard to the statutory duty of care and Trustee Act 2000 s 1 shall not apply to the trusts of my Will.

(2) My Trustees shall be under no duty to review the acts of agents, nominees and custodians appointed by them and Trustee Act 2000 s 22 shall not apply to the trusts of my Will.

(3) Section 11 Trusts of Land and Appointment of Trustees Act 1996 (consultation with beneficiaries) shall not apply.

(4) In the absence of proof of dishonesty or the wilful commission of an act known to be a breach of trust none of my Trustees shall be liable for any loss or bound to take proceedings against a co-trustee for any breach of trust[5].

(5) My Trustees shall be entitled to be indemnified out of the assets of my estate against all liabilities incurred in connection with the bona fide execution of their duties and powers[6].

As Witness my hand this [–] day of [———] 20[–].

Signed by the Testator in our presence and attested by us in the presence of the Testator and of each other.

1 This Will is not suitable for the younger couple. Binding a young widow, widower or surviving civil partner to a life interest can be overly wasteful and complex. It might also lead to a claim under the Inheritance (Provision for Family and Dependants) Act 1975.
2 It is unwise to settle chattels. They deteriorate over time, require maintenance and their upkeep necessitates expense.
3 Note that this clause includes an express power to pay or apply capital to the life tenant. This could be important if a capital outlay is needed in connection with the provision of assisted accommodation. The gift of a life interest is an immediate post-death interest within Inheritance Tax Act 1984 s 49A, as added by the Finance Act 2006.
4 Perpetuities and Accumulations Act 2009 has removed the statutory restrictions on accumulations (see **11.18** to **11.19**) so that this power may be expressed without making reference to the previous limit on the duration of a power to accumulate income.
5 This exoneration clause is broader than that which the Law Commission considers to be appropriate where trustees are professional. See the note to **Form 12.22**.
6 This form deserves full powers. The STEP provisions could be incorporated in place of clauses 5 to 7 if preferred with the added deletion of subclause 1(4).

FORM 19.4

Will creating capped 21-year capped nil-rate band discretionary trust with residue to spouse or civil partner[1]

I, [*full name*] **of** [*home address*] revoke all earlier Wills and declare this to be my last Will

1. (1) I appoint as my executors the partners at my death in the firm of of ('the Firm').

   (2) In this clause:

   (a) The expression 'the Firm' means not only [*name*] but any other firm which at my death has succeeded to and carries on its practice including a firm which has been incorporated or has formed a limited liability partnership; and

   (b) The expression 'partners' means the persons commonly described as partners in the Firm including salaried partners and, in the case of an incorporated practice or limited liability partnership, the directors, members and beneficial owners of any share of the Firm.

   (3) I wish not more than two of the partners in the Firm to apply for probate of this Will.

   (4) Any of my executors who is a solicitor may charge fees for work done by him or his firm (whether or not the work is of a professional nature) on the same basis as if he were not one of my executors but employed to carry out the work on their behalf.

   (5) I appoint as my trustees those of my executors who obtain probate of this Will and in this Will the expression 'my Trustees' means (as the context requires) those of my executors who obtained probate and the trustees for the time being of any trust arising under this Will.

19.12 *Precedents*

2. I give £1,000 to each of my nephews and nieces [living at my death]/[who attains the age of 21 years][2];

3. I give to my Trustees on the trust set out in clause 4 assets equal in value to the maximum which at my death can be given to them on these trusts without inheritance tax becoming payable in respect of this gift or the sum of £250,000 if less[3].

4. (1) In this clause:

    (a) 'the Trust Fund' means the assets at any particular time held by my Trustees on the trust set out in subclause 4(2);

    (b) 'my Beneficiaries' are:

        (i) my [wife]/[husband]/[civil partner]

        (ii) my children

        (iii) the spouse [or civil partner] of any of my children

        (iv) the issue of any of my children.

   (2) My Trustees shall hold the Trust Fund on the following trust:

    (a) For not more than 21 years after my death:

        (i) to apply the capital of the Trust Fund for the benefit of such of my Beneficiaries as my Trustees think fit

        (ii) to apply the income of the Trust Fund for the benefit of such of my Beneficiaries as my Trustees think fit or to accumulate the whole or any part of it as an addition to the capital of the Trust Fund.

    (b) Not later than 21 years after my death to end this trust by distributing the Trust Fund among such of my Beneficiaries as my Trustees think fit;

    (c) My Trustees may exercise their discretionary powers when and how they think fit and need not make payments to or for the benefit of all my Beneficiaries nor ensure equality among those who have benefited.

   (3) My Trustees shall have the following powers:

    (a) To constitute the Trust Fund by appropriating to it such of my assets as they think fit;

    (b) To retain or sell any of the assets constituting the Trust Fund;

    (c) To invest as if they were beneficially entitled and this power includes the right to invest in:

        (i) unsecured interest free loans

        (ii) other non-income producing assets including policies of life assurance (with power to pay premiums out of income or capital).

    (d) To hold investments in the name of such person or body as they think fit;

(e) To borrow money on such terms as they think fit including the giving of security and to use it for any purpose for which the capital of the Trust Fund may be used;

(f) To use the income or capital of the Trust Fund for or towards the cost of maintaining or improving any property forming part of the Trust Fund;

(g) To do anything incidental to the powers they have whether given by statute or under this Will.

5. My Trustees shall hold the rest of my estate on trust for sale with power to postpone sale to pay executorship expenses and debts including mortgages secured on real or leasehold property and any inheritance tax in respect of property passing under this Will or which becomes payable because of my death on any lifetime transfer by me or payable because of my death on property in which I hold a beneficial interest as joint tenant. All income received after my death shall be treated as income of my estate regardless of the period to which it relates and the statutory rules concerning apportionment and the rules in *Howe v Dartmouth* and *Allhusen v Whittell* and *Re Chesterfield's Trusts* shall not apply.

6. My Trustees shall hold the residue ('my residuary estate') on the following trusts:

(1) To pay my residuary estate to my [wife]/[husband]/[civil partner] if [she]/[he] survives me[4];

(2) If my [wife]/[husband]/[civil [partner] does not survive me to divide my residuary estate among those of [my]/[our][5] children who survive me and attain the age of 25 years in equal shares;

(3) If any of [my]/[our][5] children die before us the share of our estate which he or she would otherwise have inherited shall be taken as to one half by his or her spouse and as to one half equally by those of his or her children who survive me;

(4) If there is no surviving spouse of any of [my]/[our][5] children who dies before me then his or her children shall take equally the whole of the share which their parent would otherwise have inherited;

(5) If any of [my]/[our][5] children dies before me leaving no children his or her spouse shall take the share of my estate which he or she would otherwise have inherited.

[*For powers take in clauses 6, 7 and 8 of* **Form 19.2**]

As Witness my hand this [–] day of [———] 20[–].

Signed by the Testator in our presence and attested by us in the presence of the Testator and of each other.

---

[1] This Will is suitable for a relatively wealthy couple with young children. The discretionary trust is capped at 21 years because there is likely to be a distribution of the whole fund within that time either to the surviving spouse or to the children. In many cases a distribution to the spouse within two years will be the most satisfactory option since, unless the spouse is left particularly well off without having recourse to the discretionary fund, there is little point in leaving it in place. In addition, it should be remembered that this precedent 'wastes' part of the nil-rate band of the first to die so that the survivor will not be entitled to the maximum enhanced nil-rate band on death.

19.12 *Precedents*

2   In previous editions the age specified here was 21 years in order to avoid the need to rely on the 'wait and see rule' for perpetuity purposes. Now that there is only one perpetuity period of 125 years this is not a serious risk so the testator is able to specify a greater age although 21 years is often considered the maximum suitable age for receipt of a modest legacy. The class-closing rules limit this gift to those grandchildren living at the testator's death but there is surely no harm in including an express provision to that effect.

3   There are a number of points to bear in mind in relation to this gift. It does not take advantage of the transferable nil-rate band between spouses or civil partners but is not entirely inheritance tax inefficient either. It is quite simply not a purely inheritance tax-driven gift: first the sum given is capped at a level below the nil-rate band and, secondly, the discretionary trust takes effect even if the testator is the second to die. In most cases there is little point in or desire to include a discretionary trust of this sort in the Will of the second to die (see the next form) but where the circumstances of the family are in flux a testator might wish to leave property on discretionary trust with guidance being provided by a letter of wishes which might be varied from time to time without the need to make a new Will on a regular basis.

The capped figure could be index-linked by using the following formula:

'I give the lesser of £250,000 increased by the percentage by which the latest available figure of the All Items Index of Retail Prices at my death exceeds that last available before today and the maximum amount (after taking Relief into account) which can be given without Inheritance Tax being payable …'

The discretionary trust in this case is limited in duration to 21 years but a different period (up to 125 years) could be employed.

4   There is little point in providing an extended survivorship period where the nil-rate band has almost been exhausted.

5   A gift to 'our children' has been held to refer to all children of all marriages of both spouses: *Re Zehr* [1944] 2 DLR 670; but as a matter of construction it may be limited to the children of the marriage, thus excluding children from a previous relationship. Where the family relationships include step-children it is more precise to refer to 'my children and step-children'. If the testator does not intend to include step-children or illegitimate children who might subsequently come our of the woodwork the description should be 'my children by my [wife]/[husband]' although if the testator has children by a previous relationship words will then have to be used to include them. In such a case it might be better to name them.

FORM 19.5

Will as one of reciprocal Wills creating nil-rate band discretionary trust with residue to spouse or civil partner for life[1]

I, [*full name*] **of** [*home address*] revoke all earlier Wills and declare this to be my last Will

[1.   *Appointment of executors as in clause 1 of **Form 19.4**.*]

2.   If my [wife]/[husband]/[civil partner] survives me by [30 days]/[six months][2] I give to my Trustees on the trust set out in clause 4 assets equal in value to the maximum which at my death can be given to them on my death without inheritance tax becoming payable in respect thereof[3].

3.   If my [wife]/[husband]/[civil partner] does not survive me by [30 days]/[six months] I appoint [*name*] of [*address*] and [*name*] of [*address*] as guardians of any of my children under eighteen[4].

4.   I give to my Trustees on the trust set out in clause 5 assets equal in value to the maximum which at my death can be given to them on these trusts without inheritance tax becoming payable in respect of this gift.

5.   (1)   In this clause:

(a)   'the Trust Fund' means the assets at any particular time held by my Trustees on the trust set out in subclause 5(2);

(b) 'my Beneficiaries' are:

    (i) my [wife]/[husband]/[civil partner]

    (ii) my children

    (iii) the spouse [or civil partner] of any of my children

    (iv) the issue of any of my children.

(2) My Trustees shall hold the Trust Fund upon the following trusts:

    (a) For not more than 125 years from my death (which is the perpetuity period for these trusts) to apply the capital of the Trust Fund for the benefit of such of my Beneficiaries as my Trustees think fit.

    (b) To apply the income of the Trust Fund for the benefit of such of my Beneficiaries as my Trustees think fit or to accumulate the whole or any part of it as an addition to the capital of the Trust Fund.

    (c) Within 125 years of my death to end these trusts by distributing the Trust Fund among such of my Beneficiaries as my Trustees think fit.

    (d) To exercise their discretionary powers over capital or income when and how they think fit without having to make payments to or for the benefit of all my Beneficiaries or to ensure equality among those who have benefited.

(3) My Trustees shall have the powers appearing in the following clauses in addition to their powers under the general law:

    (a) To constitute the Trust Fund by appropriating to it such of my assets as they think fit;

    (b) To retain or sell any of the assets constituting the Trust Fund;

    (c) To invest as if they were beneficially entitled and this power includes the right to invest in:

        (i) unsecured interest free loans

        (ii) other non-income producing assets including policies of life assurance (with power to pay premiums out of income or capital).

    (d) To hold investments in the name of such person or body as they think fit;

    (e) To borrow money on such terms as they think fit including the giving of security and to use it for any purpose for which the capital of the Trust Fund may be used;

    (f) To use the income or capital of the Trust Fund for or towards the cost of maintaining or improving any property forming part of the Trust Fund;

    (g) To do anything incidental to the powers they have whether given by statute or under this Will.

19.12 *Precedents*

6. My Trustees shall hold the rest of my estate on trust for sale with power to postpone sale to pay executorship expenses and debts including mortgages secured on real or leasehold property and any inheritance tax in respect of property passing under this Will or which becomes payable because of my death on any lifetime transfer by me or payable because of my death on property in which I hold a beneficial interest as joint tenant. All income received after my death shall be treated as income of my estate regardless of the period to which it relates and the statutory rules concerning apportionment and the rules in *Howe v Dartmouth* and *Allhusen v Whittell* and *Re Chesterfield's Trusts* shall not apply.

7. My Trustees shall hold the residue of my estate ('my residuary estate') on trust to pay the income from my residuary estate to my [wife]/[husband]/[civil partner] during [her]/[his] lifetime with power to pay or apply the whole or any part of the capital of my residuary estate for the benefit of my [wife]/[husband]/[civil partner][5] and subject to any exercise of that power after [her]/[his] death:

   (1) to divide my residuary estate among those of [my]/[our][6] children who survive me and attain the age of 25 years in equal shares;

   (2) if any of [my]/[our][6] children die before us the share of our estate which he or she would otherwise have inherited shall be taken as to one half by his or her spouse and as to one half equally per stirpes by those of his or her children who survive me;

   (3) if there is no surviving spouse of any of [my]/[our][6] children who dies before me then his or her children shall take equally per stirpes the whole of the share which their parent would otherwise have inherited;

   (4) if any of [my]/[our][6] children dies before me leaving no children his or her spouse shall take the share of my estate which he would otherwise have inherited.

[*For powers take in clauses 6, 7 and 8 of* **Form 19.2**]

As Witness my hand this [–] day of [———] 20[–].

Signed by the Testator in our presence and attested by us in the presence of the Testator and of each other.

1 This Will was previously recommended for a relatively wealthy couple with young children but makes use of the nil-rate band of the first to die so that the transferable nil-rate band will be lost between the spouses it is therefore less inheritance tax efficient than was previously the case but may be considered useful where the wealth of the couple is such that the nil-rate band is not especially significant or where the couple accept the possibility that the survivor might well remarry.
2 Unlike the nil-rate band gift in the previous form this one only takes effect on the death of the first spouse to die.
3 It should be remembered that if there is business or agricultural property in the estate this uncapped gift could be very valuable indeed.
4 Only the survivor should appoint guardians.
5 Note that this clause includes an express power to pay or apply capital to the life tenant.
6 See footnote 5 to the previous form.

FORM 19.6

Will creating trust for a disabled child with residue to the testator's spouse or civil partner[1]

I, [*full name*] **of** [*home address*] revoke all earlier Wills and declare this to be my last Will

1. I appoint my [*wife*]/[*husband*]/[*civil partner*] [*name*] and my children [AB] and [CD] as my executors and if my [*wife*]/[*husband*]/[*civil partner*] is unable or unwilling to act or dies before proving my Will I appoint my son [EF] to be an additional executor in [*her*]/[*his*] place.

2. I appoint as my trustees those of my executors who obtain probate of this Will and in this Will the expression 'my Trustees' means (as the context requires) those of my executors who obtained probate and the trustees for the time being of any trust arising under this Will.

3. If my [*wife*]/[*husband*]/[*civil partner*] does not survive me I appoint [*name*] of [*address*] and [*name*] of [*address*] as guardians of any of my children under eighteen.[2]

4. I give to my Trustees the sum of £[......] to be held by my Trustees on the following trusts:

    (1) In this clause:

        (a) 'the Trust Fund' means the assets at any particular time held by my Trustees on the trusts of this clause;

        (b) 'the Primary Beneficiary' means my son [GB];

        (c) 'my other Beneficiaries' are:

            my [wife]/[husband]/[civil partner]

            my children other than the Primary Beneficiary

            my grandchildren.

    (2) My Trustees shall hold the Trust Fund on the following trusts:

        (a) During the lifetime of the Primary Beneficiary:

            (i) to apply the capital of the Trust Fund for the benefit of the Primary Beneficiary and my other Beneficiaries as my Trustees think fit so long as not less than half of any capital appointed is applied for the benefit of the Primary Beneficiary;

            (ii) to accumulate the whole or any part of the income arising from the Trust Fund as an addition to the capital of the Trust Fund and to apply any income not accumulated solely for the benefit of the Primary Beneficiary.

        (b) After the death of the Primary Beneficiary:

            (i) to apply the capital of the Trust Fund for the benefit of such of my other Beneficiaries as my Trustees think fit;

19.12 *Precedents*

        (ii)   to apply the income of the Trust Fund for the benefit of such of my other Beneficiaries as my Trustees think fit or to accumulate the whole or any part of it;

        (iii)   within 12 months of the Primary Beneficiary's death to end these trusts by distributing the Trust Fund among such of my other Beneficiaries as my Trustees think fit.

    (3)   My Trustees shall have the following powers:

        (a)   To retain or sell any of the assets constituting the Trust Fund;

        (b)   To invest as if they were beneficially entitled and this power includes the right to invest in non-income producing assets including policies of life assurance;

        (c)   To hold investments in the name of such person or body as they think fit;

        (d)   To borrow money on such terms as they think fit and to use it for any purpose for which the capital of the Trust Fund may be used;

        (e)   In exercising the statutory power of appointing new trustees to appoint a professional person and give him the right to charge for work done by him or his firm;

        (f)   To make retentions for any taxes for which they may be liable;

        (g)   To appropriate to the Trust Fund any asset forming part of my residuary estate;

        (h)   To do anything incidental to the powers which my Trustees have whether given by statute or under these trusts.

5.   My Trustees shall hold the rest of my estate on trust for sale with power to postpone sale to pay executorship expenses and debts including mortgages secured on real or leasehold property and any inheritance tax in respect of property passing under this Will or which becomes payable because of my death on any lifetime transfer by me or payable because of my death on property in which I hold a beneficial interest as joint tenant. All income received after my death shall be treated as income of my estate regardless of the period to which it relates and the statutory rules concerning apportionment and the rules in *Howe v Dartmouth* and *Allhusen v Whittell* and *Re Chesterfield's Trusts* shall not apply.

6.   My Trustees shall hold the residue ('my residuary estate') on the following trusts:

    (1)   To pay my residuary estate to my [wife]/[husband]/[civil partner] if [she]/[he] survives me;

    (2)   If my [wife]/[husband]/[civil partner] does not survive me to divide my residuary estate among those of [my]/[our][3] children who survive me in equal shares;

    (3)   If any of [my]/[our] children dies before me his or her children shall take equally the share which their parent would otherwise have inherited.

*[For powers take in clauses 6, 7 and 8 of **Form 19.4**]*

As Witness my hand this [–] day of [———] 20[–].

Signed by the Testator in our presence and attested by us in the presence of the Testator and of each other.

1   A trust for a disabled person created during the lifetime of the settlor has inheritance tax and capital gains tax advantages but a trust created by Will has no inheritance tax advantage. A disabled person is defined in Inheritance Tax Act 1984 s 89(4). Stated shortly, he is a person who, because of mental disorder, is incapable of managing his affairs or a person in receipt of disability living allowance or an attendance allowance or would have been in receipt of those allowances in the manner prescribed by Inheritance Tax Act 1984 s 89(5) and (6). The trustees of a settlement created by Will can obtain the capital gains tax exemption available to individuals (instead of the one-half allowed to trustees) if:
  (i)   the disability of the beneficiary existed during the relevant year of assessment;
  (ii)   under the trust not less than half the capital of the trust fund which is applied is applied for the benefit of the disabled person; and
  (iii)   that person is entitled to not less than half of the income arising from the trust fund or no such income may be applied for the benefit of any other person.
The object of a trust for the disabled is to preserve the state benefits received by the disabled person but to make available income and, if necessary, capital to supplement those benefits. A discretionary trust is usually preferred to granting the disabled person a life interest in the trust fund. The terms of the trust, in effect, create a discretionary trust during the lifetime of the disabled person with a gift over on his death. The trust fund may be a specific sum which is settled by the testator or the whole or part of the residue.
    Unless the trust fund is substantial it will be preferable in many cases to use an ordinary discretionary trust although both actual and deemed interests in possession may qualify as disabled person's interests under Inheritance Tax Act 1984 s 89B(1) introduced by Finance Act 2006.
2   Only the survivor should appoint guardians.
3   See footnote 5 to **Form 19.5**.

FORM 19.7

Will giving testator's interest in residence to children with residue to spouse or civil partner[1]

I, [*full name*] **of** [*home address*] revoke all earlier Wills and declare this to be my last Will

1. I appoint my [*wife*]/[*husband*]/[*civil partner*] [*name*] and my children [*AB*] and [*CD*] as my executors.

2. I appoint as my trustees those of my executors who obtain probate of this Will and in this Will the expression 'my Trustees' means (as the context requires) those of my executors who obtained probate and the trustees for the time being of any trust arising under this Will.

3. I give in equal shares to those of my children who survive me my share and beneficial interest in the house known as [   ] or the house that constitutes the home of my [wife]/[husband]/[civil partner] and me at my death.

4. If my [wife]/[husband]/[civil partner] survives me I give the rest of my estate to [him]/[her].

5. If my [wife]/[husband]/[civil partner] does not survive me I give the rest of my estate in equal shares to those of my children who survive me and if any of them dies before me his or her children shall take the share of my estate which their parent would otherwise have inherited.

19.12 *Precedents*

As Witness my hand this [–] day of [——] 20[–].

Signed by the Testator in our presence and attested by us in the presence of the Testator and of each other.

1   This is a useful vehicle for the older couple in, say, a case in which the survivor might have to be moved to a nursing home in the future and face having their interest in the matrimonial home charged with the nursing fees. It is not a Will for those whose principal aim is to minimise inheritance tax although if the surviving spouse does not survive for very long, the loss of a transferable nil-rate band need not be serious. It is not suitable for couples with young children and so does not include an appointment of guardians.

FORM 19.8

Will for those previously married whose spouse has an enhanced nil-rate band either for use alone or as one of reciprocal Wills creating nil-rate band discretionary trust with residue to spouse or civil partner absolutely. Will including promissory note provisions[1]

I, [*full name*] of [*home address*] revoke all earlier Wills and declare this to be my last Will

[1. *Appointment of executors as in clause 1 of* ***Form 19.5***.[2]]

2. If my [wife]/[husband]/civil partner] survives me[3] I give to my Trustees on the trust set out in clause 4 assets equal in value to the maximum which at my death can be given to them on my death without inheritance tax becoming payable in respect thereof[4].

3. If my [wife]/[husband]/[civil partner] does not survive me I appoint [*name*] of [*address*] and [*name*] of [*address*] as guardians of any of my children under eighteen[5].

4. (1) In this clause:

    (a) 'the Trust Fund' means the assets at any particular time held by the Discretionary Trustees on the trust set out in subclause 4(2) subject to the powers set out in subclauses 4(3) and 4(4);

    (b) 'my Beneficiaries' are:

    (i) my [wife]/[husband]/[civil partner]

    (ii) my children

    (iii) the spouse [or civil partner] of any of my children

    (iv) the issue of any of my children.

    (c) 'the Discretionary Trustees' means the trustees for the time being of the Trust Fund.

    (2) My Trustees shall hold the Trust Fund on the following trust:

    (a) For not more than 21 years after my death:

    (i) to apply the capital of the Trust Fund for the benefit of such of my Beneficiaries as my Trustees think fit;

(ii) to apply the income of the Trust Fund for the benefit of such of my Beneficiaries as my Trustees think fit or to accumulate the whole or any part of it;

(b) Not later than 21 years after my death to end this trust by distributing the Trust Fund among such of my Beneficiaries as my Trustees think fit;

(c) My Trustees may exercise their discretionary powers when and how they think fit and need not make payments to or for the benefit of all my Beneficiaries nor ensure equality among those who have benefited.

(3) My Trustees shall have the following powers:

(a) To constitute the Trust Fund by appropriating to it such of my assets as they think fit;

(b) To retain or sell any of the assets constituting the Trust Fund;

(c) To invest as if they were beneficially entitled and this power includes the right to invest in:

(i) unsecured interest free loans;

(ii) other non-income producing assets including policies of life assurance (with power to pay premiums out of income or capital).

(d) To hold investments in the name of such person or body as they think fit;

(e) To borrow money on such terms as they think fit including the giving of security and to use it for any purpose for which the capital of the Trust Fund may be used;

(f) To use the income or capital of the Trust Fund for or towards the cost of maintaining or improving any property forming part of the Trust Fund;

(g) To do anything incidental to the powers they have whether given by statute or under this Will.

(4) My Trustees may require the Discretionary Trustees to accept from them in full or partial satisfaction of the Trust Fund a promise on the part of my [wife]/[husband]/[civil partner] to pay the Trust Fund on demand or a charge of any part of my Residue with payment when demanded of all or part of the Trust Fund[6].

(a) The promise or charge may include whatever terms my Trustees think fit including terms:

(i) relating to the provision of fixed or floating security;

(ii) requiring the payment of interest; and

(iii) making the sum payable linked to the All Items Index of Retail Prices or any other index.

(b) The Discretionary Trustees:

19.12 *Precedents*

        (i)   may refrain from calling in or exercising any rights in relation to any sum the subject of the promise or charge for as long as they think fit;

        (ii)   will not be liable for any loss which may occur through the exercise of any power under this clause if my Trustees are unable to make payment in full or any security given becomes inadequate.

    (c)   The powers given under this clause are exercisable even though the Discretionary Trustees and my Trustees are one and the same provided that my [wife]/[husband]/[civil partner] must not be the only trustee in either case.

[5.   *Administration trusts of residue as in clause 6 of **Form 19.5**.*]

6.   My Trustees shall hold the residue ('my residuary estate') on the following trusts:

    (1)   To pay my residuary estate to my [wife]/[husband]/[civil partner] if [she]/[he] survives me;

    (2)   If my [wife]/[husband]/[civil partner] does not survive me to divide my residuary estate among those of [my]/[our][7] children who survive me and attain the age of 25 years in equal shares;

    (3)   If any of [my]/[our][7] children die before us the share of our estate which he or she would otherwise have inherited shall be taken as to one half by his or her spouse [or civil partner] and as to one half equally by those of his or her children who survive me;

    (4)   If there is no surviving spouse [or civil partner] of any of [my]/[our][7] children who dies before me then his or her children shall take equally the whole of the share which their parent would otherwise have inherited;

    (5)   If any of [my]/[our][7] children dies before me leaving no children his or her spouse [or civil partner] shall take the share of my estate which he or she would otherwise have inherited.

[*For powers take in clauses 6, 7 and 8 of **Form 19.2***]

As Witness my hand this [–] day of [———] 20[–].

Signed by the Testator in our presence and attested by us in the presence of the Testator and of each other.

1   This Will is principally driven by an interest in inheritance tax planning where the other spouse already has an enhanced nil-rate band as a result of previously being widowed. The intention is to employ the promissory note scheme described in **chapter 15**.
2   The surviving spouse should not be a sole trustee.
3   Unlike the nil-rate band gift in the previous form this one only takes effect on the death of the first spouse to die.
4   It should be remembered that if there is business or agricultural property in the estate this gift could be very valuable indeed.
5   Only the survivor should appoint guardians.
6   See **chapter 15**.
7   See footnote 5 to **Form 19.4**.

20 Unmarried couples with children

20.1 The concerns of unmarried couples are similar to those of married couples (although there is less opportunity for inheritance tax mitigation). The provision of life interests and rights of residence are often favoured. **Forms 20.1** and **20.2** cater exclusively for unmarried couples but the earlier forms can be adapted with little difficulty.

PRECEDENTS

20.2

Wills for unmarried couples with children

Form 20.1 Legacies; residue equally between children and partner
Form 20.2 Will providing for right of residence and legacy for partner with residue to children

FORM 20.1

Legacies; residue equally between children and partner[1]

I, [*full name*] **of** [*home address*] revoke all earlier Wills and declare this to be my last Will

1. (1) I appoint as my executors the partners at my death in the firm of of ('the Firm').

    (2) In this clause:

    (a) The expression 'the Firm' means not only [*name*] but any other firm which at my death has succeeded to and carries on its practice including a firm which has been incorporated or has formed a limited liability partnership; and

    (b) The expression 'partners' means the persons commonly described as partners in the Firm including salaried partners and, in the case of an incorporated practice or limited liability partnership, the directors, members and beneficial owners of any share of the Firm.

    (3) I wish not more than two of the partners in the Firm to apply for probate of this Will.

    (4) Any of my Trustees who is a solicitor may charge fees for work done by him or his firm (whether or not the work is of a professional nature) on the same basis as if he were not one of my Trustees but employed to carry out the work on their behalf.

2. I appoint as my trustees those of my executors who obtain probate of this Will and in this Will the expression 'my Trustees' means (as the context requires) those of my executors who obtained probate and the trustees for the time being of any trust arising under this Will.

3. [If my partner [LL] does not survive me] I appoint [*name*] of [*address*] and [*name*] of [*address*] as guardians of any of my children under eighteen[2].

4. I give to [LL] my personal chattels as defined by Administration of Estates Act 1925 s 55(1)(x)[3].

5. I give my stamp collection to my friend [AB].

6. I give legacies of £5,000 each to my friends:

> [CD] of
>
> [EF] of
>
> [GH] of

7. My Trustees shall hold the rest of my estate on trust for sale with power to postpone sale to pay executorship expenses and debts including mortgages secured on real or leasehold property and any inheritance tax in respect of property passing under this Will or which becomes payable because of my death on any lifetime transfer by me or payable because of my death on property in which I hold a beneficial interest as joint tenant. All income received after my death shall be treated as income of my estate regardless of the period to which it relates and the statutory rules concerning apportionment and the rules in *Howe v Dartmouth* and *Allhusen v Whittell* and *Re Chesterfield's Trusts* shall not apply.

8. My Trustees shall hold the residue ('my residuary estate') on the following trusts:

    (1) To pay one half of the residue to [LL] who has been my companion for over 25 years;

    (2) To divide the other half of the residue equally among such of [my]/[our][4] children as survive me in equal shares;

    (3) If any of [my]/[our][4] children die before us the share of our estate which he or she would otherwise have inherited shall be taken as to one half by his or her spouse [or civil partner] and as to one half equally by those of his or her children who survive me;

    (4) If there is no surviving spouse [or civil partner] of any of [my]/[our][4] children who dies before me then his or her children shall take equally the whole of the share which their parent would otherwise have inherited;

    (5) If any of [my]/[our][4] children dies before me leaving no children his or her spouse [or civil partner] shall take the share of my estate which he or she would otherwise have inherited.

9. My Trustees shall have power:

    (1) to apply for the benefit of any beneficiary who has a contingent interest the whole or any part of the income from any capital to which he may become entitled;

    (2) during the whole of the period in which a beneficiary has a contingent interest to accumulate such income as is not so applied and to invest that income as an addition to the capital of the share to which that beneficiary is entitled;

    (3) to pay or apply for the benefit of any beneficiary who has a contingent interest the whole or any part of the capital to which he may become entitled;

    (4) to pay any money to which a beneficiary under eighteen is entitled to his parent or guardian for his benefit or to the beneficiary himself once he has attained sixteen and to rely upon the receipt then given by the parent or guardian or the minor himself.

20.2 *Precedents*

10. My Trustees shall have the following powers in addition to their powers under the general law:

    (1) Power to invest as if they were beneficially entitled and this power includes the right:

    (a) to invest in unsecured loans;

    (b) to invest in other non-income producing assets including policies of life assurance;

    (c) to purchase land anywhere in the world;

    (d) to purchase an undivided share in land;

    (e) to invest in land for the occupation or enjoyment of any beneficiary.

    (2) Power to delegate their powers of investment and management of trust property to an agent (including one of their number) on such terms including terms enabling the agent to charge remuneration, to appoint a substitute, to limit liability and to act in circumstances giving rise to a conflict of interest as my Trustees think fit.

    (3) Power to appoint any person (including one of their number or a beneficiary) to act as their nominee and to take such steps as are necessary to vest any property in such person on such terms including terms enabling the agent to charge remuneration, to appoint a substitute, to limit liability and to act in circumstances giving rise to a conflict of interest as my Trustees think fit.

    (4) Power to make loans of capital to a beneficiary which may be interest free, repayable on demand or repayable at a rate below the market rate.

    (5) Power to borrow money on such terms as they think fit including the giving of security and to use it for any purpose for which the capital of my estate may be used.

    (6) Power without the restrictions imposed by Administration of Estates Act 1925 s 41:

    (a) To appropriate to any beneficiary in satisfaction or partial satisfaction of the gift to him any asset forming part of my residuary estate and not subject to a specific gift.

    (b) To appropriate as the assets or part of the assets of any trust created by this Will any asset forming part of my residuary estate and not subject to a specific gift.

11. (1) My Trustees shall exercise their powers of investment and carry out their duties as trustees without regard to the statutory duty of care and Trustee Act 2000 s 1 shall not apply to the trusts of my Will.

    (2) My Trustees shall be under no duty to review the acts of agents, nominees and custodians appointed by them and Trustee Act 2000 s 22 shall not apply to the trusts of my Will.

    (3) Section 11 Trusts of Land and Appointment of Trustees Act 1996 (consultation with beneficiaries) shall not apply.

(4) In the absence of proof of dishonesty or the wilful commission of an act known to be a breach of trust none of my Trustees shall be liable for any loss or bound to take proceedings against a co-trustee for any breach of trust[5].

(5) My Trustees shall be entitled to be indemnified out of the assets of my estate against all liabilities incurred in connection with the bona fide execution of their duties and powers[6].

As Witness my hand this [–] day of [———] 20[–].

Signed by the Testator in our presence and attested by us in the presence of the Testator and of each other.

1 This Will, for the unmarried couple ([LL] being the partner), simply splits residue between the partner and the children. It is an easy solution but not necessarily one which is morally justifiable.
2 Only the survivor should appoint guardians but the question of the parental responsibility of the survivor may need investigation. For example, if the father does not have parental responsibility, the mother should appoint him even if she is the first to die. To adapt the form in order to cater for this situation, the mother's Will should not include the words in square brackets at the start of the clause.
3 This express gift is not essential but may be seen as desirable.
4 See footnote 6 to **Form 19.2**. It is particularly important, in the context of unmarried couples (where it is possible that only one name appears on a child's birth certificate), to ensure that the beneficiaries are described accurately. Clause 8(2) could be adapted to read '... our children [*name*], [*name*] and [*name*] ...' in order to avoid uncertainty.
5 This exoneration clause is broader than that which the Law Commission considers to be appropriate where trustees are professional. See the note to **Form 12.22**.
6 This form deserves full powers. The STEP provisions could be incorporated in place of clauses 9 to 11 if preferred with the added deletion of subclause 1(4).

FORM 20.2

Will providing for right of residence and legacy for partner with residue to children[1]

I, [*full name*] **of** [*home address*] revoke all earlier Wills and declare this to be my last Will

1. (1) I appoint as my executors the partners at my death in the firm of   of   ('the Firm').

   (2) In this clause:

   (a) The expression 'the Firm' means not only [*name*] but any other firm which at my death has succeeded to and carries on its practice including a firm which has been incorporated or has formed a limited liability partnership; and

   (b) The expression 'partners' means the persons commonly described as partners in the Firm including salaried partners and, in the case of an incorporated practice or limited liability partnership, the directors, members and beneficial owners of any share of the Firm.

   (3) I wish not more than two of the partners in the Firm to apply for probate of this Will.

20.2 *Precedents*

       (4) Any of my Trustees who is a solicitor may charge fees for work done by him or his firm (whether or not the work is of a professional nature) on the same basis as if he were not one of my Trustees but employed to carry out the work on their behalf.

2. I appoint as my trustees those of my executors who obtain probate of this Will and in this Will the expression 'my Trustees' means (as the context requires) those of my executors who obtained probate and the trustees for the time being of any trust arising under this Will.

3. [If my partner [LL] does not survive me] I appoint [*name*] of [*address*] and [*name*] of [*address*] as guardians of any of my children under eighteen[2].

4. I give to [LL] my personal chattels as defined by Administration of Estates Act 1925 s 55(1)(x)[3].

5. I give my house known as [*postal address*] ('the House') to my Trustees on trust on the following terms[4]:

       (1) My Trustees shall permit [LL] to live in the House free of charge so long as [she]/[he] wishes.

       (2) While [LL] is living in the House my Trustees shall not sell it without [her]/[his] consent.

       (3) When [LL] has ceased to live in the House my Trustees shall hold it as part of my residuary estate.

       (4) At [LL]'s request my Trustees may sell the House and buy another to be held on trust [for sale] on the same terms as the House.

       (5) In purchasing a replacement in accordance with the previous power my Trustees may join with any person in purchasing an undivided share of land.

6. I give [LL] the sum of [£250,000].

7. My Trustees shall hold the rest of my estate on trust for sale with power to postpone sale to pay executorship expenses and debts including mortgages secured on real or leasehold property and any inheritance tax in respect of property passing under this Will or which becomes payable because of my death on any lifetime transfer by me or payable because of my death on property in which I hold a beneficial interest as joint tenant. All income received after my death shall be treated as income of my estate regardless of the period to which it relates and the statutory rules concerning apportionment and the rules in *Howe v Dartmouth* and *Allhusen v Whittell* and *Re Chesterfield's Trusts* shall not apply.

8. My Trustees shall hold the residue on trust for such of [my]/[our][5] children as survive me in equal shares.

[*For powers take in clauses 9, 10 and 11 of* **Form 20.1**]

As Witness my hand this [–] day of [———] 20[–].

Signed by the Testator in our presence and attested by us in the presence of the Testator and of each other.

1	This Will makes provision for the unmarried partner by way of a right of residence and a substantial gift. Inheritance tax planning is not a concern for this couple: there will be an inheritance tax charge on the death of the testator and probably on the death of the surviving partner. If they want to minimise inheritance tax and are able to do so they should get married/form a civil partnership.
2	Only the survivor should appoint guardians but the question of the parental responsibility of the survivor may need investigation. For example, if the father does not have parental responsibility, the mother should appoint him even if she is the first to die. To adapt the form in order to cater for this situation, the mother's Will should not include the words in square brackets at the start of the clause.
3	This express gift is not essential but may be seen as desirable.
4	For a discussion of the grant of rights of residence by Will see **10.19** to **10.22**.
5	See footnote 6 to **Form 19.2**. It is particularly important, in the context of unmarried couples (where it is possible that only one name appears on a child's birth certificate), to ensure that the beneficiaries are described accurately. Clause 8 could be adapted to read '… our children [*name*], [*name*] and [*name*] …' in order to avoid uncertainty.

21 Second marriages or civil partnerships

21.1 A similar problem arises where the testator has remarried or formed a (new) civil partnership and there are children of the first marriage or civil partnership in existence. Often, the problem is less acute because a second spouse or civil partner usually recognises as natural the desire of the testator to make provision for the children of his first marriage or civil partnership. However, there can sometimes be terrible animosity between the children and their step-parent which a testator would be wise to defuse by careful dispositions. Some suggested approaches are contained in **Forms 21.1 to 21.2**.

21.2 The draftsman should also be careful in cases of second marriages to ascertain how the first marriage ended. A marriage which ended with the death of the former spouse may result in the testator being entitled to an enhanced nil-rate band on his death (see **chapter 15**). This will depend upon the disposition of the estate of the former spouse (which ought to be investigated while there is still an opportunity to do so). Where the testator is entitled to an enhanced nil-rate band adequate provision might be made for the children of the first marriage by means of a nil-rate band gift as in **Forms 19.5** or **19.8**. It is, however, up to the personal representatives of the testator to claim the enhanced nil-rate band. Enlarging a nil-rate band gift at the expense of residue is contrary to the interests of the surviving second spouse and so, in such cases, it would not be wise to appoint the second spouse as one of the executors because of the conflict that would naturally arise.

PRECEDENTS

21.3

Wills where there is a second marriage or civil partnership

Form 21.1 Will giving legacies to children of first marriage and residue to spouse or civil partner
Form 21.2 Will giving residence to surviving spouse or civil partner with half residue to spouse and half residue to children of first marriage or civil partnership
Form 21.3 Will giving right of residence to surviving spouse or civil partner with half residue to spouse and half residue to children of first marriage etc
Form 21.4 Will giving right of residence and life interest in residue to surviving spouse or civil partner; remainder to children
Form 21.5 Two-thirds to wife or civil partner; one-third to in-laws

FORM 21.1

Will in favour of testator's second spouse with legacies to children of first marriage[1]

I, [*full name*] **of** [*home address*] revoke all earlier Wills and declare this to be my last Will

1. I appoint my [*wife*]/[*husband*]/[*civil partner*] [*name*] to be my [*executrix*]/[*executor*] but if my [*wife*]/[*husband*]/[*civil partner*] is unable or unwilling to act or dies before proving my Will I appoint as my executors those of my children who survive me but it is my wish that not more than two of them obtain probate of my Will.

2. I give legacies of £5,000 to each of my[2] children.

3. If my [*wife*]/[*husband*]/[*civil partner*] does not survive me I appoint [*name*] of [*address*] and [*name*] of [*address*] as guardians of any of my children under eighteen[3].

4. If my [*wife*]/[*husband*]/[*civil partner*] survives me[4] I give the rest of my estate to [*him*]/[*her*]. If the gift made by this clause fails I give the rest of my estate to those of my[2] children who survive me in equal shares.

5. A gift to any of my children shall lapse if he or she dies before me[5].

As Witness my hand this [–] day of [———] 20[–].

Signed by the Testator in our presence and attested by us in the presence of the Testator and of each other.

1 This Will, for the less wealthy testator, makes only limited provision for the children.
2 A gift to 'our children' has been held to refer to all children of all marriages of both spouses: *Re Zehr* [1944] 2 DLR 670; but as a matter of construction it may be limited to the children of the marriage, thus excluding children from a previous relationship. Where the family relationships include step-children it is more precise to refer to 'my children and step-children'. If the testator does not intend to include step-children or illegitimate children who might subsequently come out of the

21.3 *Precedents*

woodwork the description should be 'my children by my [wife]/[husband]', although if the testator has children by a previous relationship words will then have to be used to include them. In such a case it might be better to name them.

3   Only the survivor should appoint guardians but the question of the parental responsibility of the survivor may need investigation.

4   The inclusion of a survivorship condition is now of no effect or even detrimental where the gift is in favour of a surviving spouse because of the transferability of the nil-rate band (discussed in chapter 15). In the previous editions the survivorship condition appears in the following terms:
'If my [wife]/[husband]/[civil partner] survives me by [30 days]/[six months] ...'
If the survivor's will is not in reciprocal terms or the surviving spouse has already been married and has an enhanced nil-rate band by virtue of the previous marriage there will be some justification for including the survivorship condition.

5   This is intended to override Wills Act 1837 s 33.

FORM 21.2

Will giving residence to surviving spouse with half residue to spouse or civil partner and half residue to children of first marriage or civil partnership

I, [*full name*] **of** [*home address*] revoke all earlier Wills and declare this to be my last Will

1. I appoint my [*wife*]/[*husband*]/[*civil partner*] [*name*] and my children [AB] and [CD] as my executors.

2. I appoint as my trustees those of my executors who obtain probate of this Will and in this Will the expression 'my Trustees' means (as the context requires) those of my executors who obtained probate and the trustees for the time being of any trust arising under this Will.

3. I appoint [*name*] of [*address*] and [*name*] of [*address*] as guardians of any of my children under eighteen[1].

4. If [she]/[he] survives me by [30 days]/[six months] I give to my [wife]/[husband]/[civil partner] the house that constitutes at my death our matrimonial home.

5. My Trustees shall hold the rest of my estate on trust for sale with power to postpone sale to pay executorship expenses and debts including mortgages secured on real or leasehold property and any inheritance tax in respect of property passing under this Will or which becomes payable because of my death on any lifetime transfer by me or payable because of my death on property in which I hold a beneficial interest as joint tenant. All income received after my death shall be treated as income of my estate regardless of the period to which it relates and the statutory rules concerning apportionment and the rules in *Howe v Dartmouth* and *Allhusen v Whittell* and *Re Chesterfield's Trusts* shall not apply.

6. My Trustees shall hold the residue ('my residuary estate') on the following trusts:

    (1) As to one half of my residuary estate for my [wife]/[husband]/[civil partner] if [she]/[he] survives me by [30 days]/[six months] but if my [wife]/[husband] does not survive me by [30 days]/[six months] my Trustees shall hold this half of my residuary estate upon the trusts of subclause 6(2) of my Will;

(2) As to the other half of my residuary estate to those of my children [and stepchildren][2] who survive me in equal shares and if any of them dies before me his or her children shall take the share of my estate which their parent would otherwise have inherited.

7. My Trustees shall have power:

   (1) to apply for the benefit of any beneficiary who is has a contingent interest the whole or any part of the income from any capital to which he may become entitled;

   (2) during the whole of the period in which a beneficiary has a contingent interest to accumulate such income as is not so applied and to invest that income as an addition to the capital of the share to which that beneficiary is entitled;

   (3) to pay or apply for the benefit of any beneficiary who has a contingent interest the whole or any part of the capital to which he may become entitled;

   (4) to pay any money to which a beneficiary under eighteen is entitled to his parent or guardian for his benefit or to the beneficiary himself once he has attained sixteen and to rely upon the receipt then given by the parent or guardian or the minor himself.

8. My Trustees shall have the following powers in addition to their powers under the general law:

   (1) Power to invest as if they were beneficially entitled and this power includes the right:

      (a) to invest in unsecured loans;

      (b) to invest in other non-income producing assets including policies of life assurance;

      (c) to purchase land anywhere in the world;

      (d) to purchase an undivided share in land;

      (e) to invest in land for the occupation or enjoyment of any beneficiary.

   (2) Power to delegate their powers of investment and management of trust property to an agent (including one of their number) on such terms including terms enabling the agent to charge remuneration, to appoint a substitute, to limit liability and to act in circumstances giving rise to a conflict of interest as my Trustees think fit.

   (3) Power to appoint any person (including one of their number or a beneficiary) to act as their nominee and to take such steps as are necessary to vest any property in such person on such terms including terms enabling the agent to charge remuneration, to appoint a substitute, to limit liability and to act in circumstances giving rise to a conflict of interest as my Trustees think fit.

   (4) Power to make loans of capital to a beneficiary which may be interest free, repayable on demand or repayable at a rate below the market rate.

21.3 *Precedents*

        (5)   Power to borrow money on such terms as they think fit including the giving of security and to use it for any purpose for which the capital of my estate may be used.

        (6)   Power without the restrictions imposed by Administration of Estates Act 1925 s 41:

                (a)   To appropriate to any beneficiary in satisfaction or partial satisfaction of the gift to him any asset forming part of my residuary estate and not subject to a specific gift.

                (b)   To appropriate as the assets or part of the assets of any trust created by this Will any asset forming part of my residuary estate and not subject to a specific gift.

9.   (1)   My Trustees shall exercise their powers of investment and carry out their duties as trustees without regard to the statutory duty of care and Trustee Act 2000 s 1 shall not apply to the trusts of my Will.

        (2)   My Trustees shall be under no duty to review the acts of agents, nominees and custodians appointed by them and Trustee Act 2000 s 22 shall not apply to the trusts of my Will.

        (3)   Section 11 Trusts of Land and Appointment of Trustees Act 1996 (consultation with beneficiaries) shall not apply.

        (4)   In the absence of proof of dishonesty or the wilful commission of an act known to be a breach of trust none of my Trustees shall be liable for any loss or bound to take proceedings against a co-trustee for any breach of trust[3].

        (5)   My Trustees shall be entitled to be indemnified out of the assets of my estate against all liabilities incurred in connection with the bona fide execution of their duties and powers[4].

As Witness my hand this [–] day of [———] 20[–].

Signed by the Testator in our presence and attested by us in the presence of the Testator and of each other.

1   This clause presupposes that the children of the first marriage are adults or that the former spouse is responsible for appointing guardians etc. If it is desired that appointments should be made in respect of the children of both marriages but that different appointments are desired in respect of each class of child then the clause needs to be split so that one set of guardians is appointed in respect of the children of the first marriage and another appointed in respect of children of the second marriage. Thus:

    'I appoint [*name*] of [*address*] and [*name*] of [*address*] as guardians of any of my children by [X] under eighteen and I appoint [*name*] of [*address*] and [*name*] of [*address*] as guardians of any of my children by [Y] under eighteen.'

In either case only the survivor should appoint guardians but the question of the parental responsibility of the survivor may need investigation.

2   See footnote 2 to **Form 21.1**.
3   This exoneration clause is broader than that which the Law Commission considers to be appropriate where trustees are professional. See the note to **Form 12.22**.
4   This form deserves full powers. The STEP provisions could be incorporated in place of clauses 7 to 9 if preferred with the added deletion of subclause 1(4).

FORM 21.3

Will giving right of residence to surviving spouse with half residue to spouse or civil partner and half residue to children of first marriage etc[1]

I, [full name] of [home address] revoke all earlier Wills and declare this to be my last Will

1. I appoint my [wife]/[husband]/[civil partner] [name] and my children [AB] and [CD] as my executors.

2. I appoint as my trustees those of my executors who obtain probate of this Will and in this Will the expression 'my Trustees' means (as the context requires) those of my executors who obtained probate and the trustees for the time being of any trust arising under this Will.

3. If my [wife]/[husband]/[civil partner] does not survive me I appoint [name] of [address] and [name] of [address] as guardians of any of my children under eighteen[2].

4. I give my house known as [postal address] ('the House') to my Trustees on trust on the following terms[3]:

    (1) My Trustees shall permit my [wife]/[husband]/[civil partner] to live in the House free of charge so long as [she]/[he] wishes.

    (2) While my [wife]/[husband]/[civil partner] is living in the House my Trustees shall not sell it without [her]/[his] consent.

    (3) When my [wife]/[husband]/[civil partner] has ceased to live in the House my Trustees shall hold it [as part of my residuary estate] or [appropriate gift over].

    (4) [At my [wife]/[husband]/[civil partner]'s request my Trustees may sell the House and buy another to be held on trust [for sale] on the same terms as the House.]

    (5) In purchasing a replacement in accordance with the previous power my Trustees may join with any person in purchasing an undivided share of land.

5. I give to my [wife]/[husband]/[civil partner] my personal chattels as defined by Administration of Estates Act 1925 s 55(1)(x)[4].

6. My Trustees shall hold the rest of my estate on trust for sale with power to postpone sale to pay executorship expenses and debts including mortgages secured on real or leasehold property and any inheritance tax in respect of property passing under this Will or which becomes payable because of my death on any lifetime transfer by me or payable because of my death on property in which I hold a beneficial interest as joint tenant. All income received after my death shall be treated as income of my estate regardless of the period to which it relates and the statutory rules concerning apportionment and the rules in *Howe v Dartmouth* and *Allhusen v Whittell* and *Re Chesterfield's Trusts* shall not apply.

7. My Trustees shall hold the residue ('my residuary estate') on the following trusts:

21.3 *Precedents*

    (1)   As to one half of my residuary estate for my [wife]/[husband]/[civil partner] if [she]/[he] survives me but if my [wife]/[husband]/[civil partner] does not survive me my Trustees shall hold this half of my residuary estate upon the trusts of subclause 7(2) of my Will;

    (2)   As to the other half of my residuary estate to those of our[5] children who survive me in equal shares and if any of them dies before me his or her children shall take the share of my estate which their parent would otherwise have inherited.

[*For powers take in clauses 7, 8 and 9 except 9(3) (exclusion of consultation with occupying beneficiary) of* **Form 21.2**]

As Witness my hand this [–] day of [———] 20[–].

Signed by the Testator in our presence and attested by us in the presence of the Testator and of each other.

1   A variation on the previous form giving only a right of residence and half the residue to the spouse.
2   See **Form 21.2** footnote 1.
3   For a discussion of the grant of rights of residence by Will see **10.19** to **10.22**. Instead of a gift of 'my house' the testator could give 'my beneficial share and interest in the house' with the remainder of the clause unchanged. This will cater for the situation in which the testator and another own as tenants in common but it should be noted that the Will will not override the interests of the co-owner.
4   Often a desirable thing to do in these family circumstances.
5   See footnote 2 to **Form 21.1**.

FORM 21.4

Will giving right of residence and life interest in residue to surviving spouse or civil partner with remainder to children of first marriage etc[1]

I, [*full name*] **of** [*home address*] revoke all earlier Wills and declare this to be my last Will

    1.   I appoint my [*wife*]/[*husband*]/[*civil partner*] [*name*] and my children [AB] and [CD] as my executors.

    2.   I appoint as my trustees those of my executors who obtain probate of this Will and in this Will the expression 'my Trustees' means (as the context requires) those of my executors who obtained probate and the trustees for the time being of any trust arising under this Will.

    3.   I give my house known as [*postal address*] ('the House') to my Trustees on trust on the following terms[2]:

    (1)   My Trustees shall permit my [wife]/[husband]/[civil partner] to live in the House free of charge so long as [she]/[he] wishes.

    (2)   While my [wife]/[husband]/[civil partner] is living in the House my Trustees shall not sell it without [her]/[his] consent.

    (3)   When my [wife]/[husband]/[civil partner] has ceased to live in the House my Trustees shall hold it upon trust for my children in equal shares.

    (4)   At my [wife]/[husband]/[civil partner]'s request my Trustees may sell the House and buy another to be held on trust [for sale] on the same terms as the House[3].

> (5) In purchasing a replacement in accordance with the previous power my Trustees may join with any person in purchasing an undivided share of land.
>
> 4. I give to [wife]/[husband]/[civil partner] my personal chattels as defined by Administration of Estates Act 1925 s 55(1)(x)[3].
>
> 5. My Trustees shall hold the rest of my estate on trust for sale with power to postpone sale to pay executorship expenses and debts including mortgages secured on real or leasehold property and any inheritance tax in respect of property passing under this Will or which becomes payable because of my death on any lifetime transfer by me or payable because of my death on property in which I hold a beneficial interest as joint tenant. All income received after my death shall be treated as income of my estate regardless of the period to which it relates and the statutory rules concerning apportionment and the rules in *Howe v Dartmouth* and *Allhusen v Whittell* and *Re Chesterfield's Trusts* shall not apply.
>
> 6. My Trustees shall hold the residue of my estate ('my residuary estate') on trust to pay the income from my residuary estate to my [wife]/[husband]/[civil partner] during [her]/[his] lifetime with power to pay or apply the whole or any part of the capital of my residuary estate for the benefit of my [wife]/[husband]/[civil partner][4] and subject to any exercise of that power after [her]/[his] death for my[5] children in equal shares.

[*Adapt clauses 7, 8 and 9 (except 9(3) (exclusion of consultation with occupying beneficiary)) of **Form 21.2***]

As Witness my hand this [–] day of [———] 20[–].

Signed by the Testator in our presence and attested by us in the presence of the Testator and of each other.

1   Another variation, this time only giving the spouse a right of residence and a life interest in the residue. This is suitable for the older couple.
2   For a discussion of the grant of rights of residence by Will see **10.19** to **10.22**. Instead of a gift of 'my house' the testator could give 'my beneficial share and interest in the house' with the remainder of the clause unchanged. This will cater for the situation in which the testator and another own as tenants in common but it should be noted that the Will will not override the interests of the co-owner.
3   Often a desirable thing to do in these family circumstances. Since the spouse takes a life interest in residue a separate gift of chattels ought to be included. The older testator will probably want to include specific legacies of items of sentimental value to the children of his first marriage.
4   Note that this clause includes an express power to pay or apply capital to the life tenant.
5   See footnote 2 to **Form 21.1**.

FORM 21.5

Will sharing estate between the testator's second spouse or civil partner and the brothers and sisters of his first spouse or civil partner[1]

I, [*full name*] **of** [*home address*] revoke all earlier Wills and declare this to be my last Will

> 1. I appoint my [wife]/[husband]/[civil partner] [*name*] to be my [executrix]/[executor] but if my [wife]/[husband]/[civil partner] is unable or unwilling to act or dies before proving my Will I appoint my brother-in-law CD to be my executor.

21.3 Precedents

2. I appoint as my trustees those of my executors who obtain probate of this Will and in this Will the expression 'my Trustees' means (as the context requires) those of my executors who obtained probate and the trustees for the time being of any trust arising under this Will.

3. If my [wife]/[husband]/[civil partner] does not survive me I give the whole of my estate to the brothers and sisters of my late [wife]/[husband]/[civil partner] who survive me in equal shares.

4. If my [wife]/[husband]/[civil partner] survives me I give two thirds of my net estate to my [wife]/[husband]/[civil partner] absolutely and the remaining one-third of my estate shall be shared equally by those of the brothers and sisters of my late [wife]/[husband]/[civil partner] [*name of first spouse or civil partner*] who survive me.

As Witness my hand this [–] day of [———] 20[–].

Signed by the Testator in our presence and attested by us in the presence of the Testator and of each other.

1 This Will is suitable for childless testators with an ongoing relationship with the relatives of their previous spouse.

22 Variations after death

22.1 The disposition of the deceased's estate may be varied by a Deed of Variation or by disclaimer. For inheritance tax and capital gains tax purposes the variation or disclaimer can take effect as if the dispositions effected by it were made by the deceased provided the requirements of the legislation are satisfied.

22.2 To take advantage of Inheritance Tax Act 1984 s 142(1)[1] and Taxation of Chargeable Gains Act 1992 s 62(6)[2], the variation or disclaimer must be in writing and made within two years of the death by the persons who benefit or would benefit under the dispositions affected.

1 See **appendix 28.5**.
2 See **appendix 28.10**.

22.3 Note that a variation or disclaimer is only effective both as a matter of general law and fiscally if made by all of the persons who benefit or would benefit under the dispositions affected. If any of them is not sui juris (ie of full age and mental capacity) then they cannot join in. In an appropriate case the court, exercising the special jurisdiction of the Variation of Trusts Act 1958, might approve a variation on behalf of persons who are not sui juris but it has no power to compel persons who are able to consent to do so.

22.4 If a variation is to be effective for inheritance tax and capital gains tax purposes the instrument (usually a deed) should also contain a statement that Inheritance Tax Act 1984 s 142(1) and Taxation of Chargeable Gains Act 1992 s 62(6) are intended to take effect. If additional inheritance tax will be payable the personal representatives must be parties unless they hold insufficient assets to pay that tax. The property the subject of the variation or disclaimer will then be treated for inheritance tax and capital gains tax purposes as if it passed to the recipient under the Will or intestacy of the deceased. There will be no transfer of value for the purpose of inheritance tax and no capital gains tax charge will arise.

22.5 Where a variation results in the payment of additional inheritance tax any of the parties or the personal representatives must, within six months after the day on which the instrument is made, deliver a copy to HMRC and notify it of the amount of the additional tax[1]. There is otherwise no longer an obligation to report variations to HMRC.

1 Inheritance Tax Act 1984 s 218A.

22.6 Inheritance Tax Act 1984 s 142(1) does not apply to a variation or disclaimer made for any consideration in money or money's worth, other than consideration consisting of the making in respect of another of the deceased's dispositions of a

22.7 *Variations after death*

variation or disclaimer to which s 142(1) applies[1]. Difficult questions can arise in connection with this provision and the practitioner should seek specialist advice where necessary.

1   Inheritance Tax Act 1984 s 142(3), see **appendix 28.5**.

22.7 There is no income tax equivalent of Inheritance Tax Act 1984 s 142 so that if one of the parties to a variation gives up an interest under the Will or intestacy and the variation settles that interest that will be a settlement of which the party is settlor so if any of the property or related property in the settlement will or may be payable or applicable to or for the benefit of him or his spouse or civil partner the income will be taxed as his under Income Tax (Trading and Other Income) Act 2005 ss 624 and 625. If his minor children or step-children (who are not married or in a civil partnership) benefit (although he does not) the income will still be taxed as his under s 629. It is thought that HMRC does not take the same view of a disclaimer.

Disclaimer

22.8 A beneficiary may disclaim a benefit obtained by Will, under an intestacy or by survivorship. The result of his disclaiming a gift under a Will is that it falls into residue or, if the gift is of the residue or part of it, there is a partial intestacy. A gift may not be disclaimed in part so that, if a Will contains a gift of £5,000, the beneficiary cannot disclaim £2,000 of it. He must disclaim it in its entirety or not at all. If, however, there are two separate gifts in the Will it is possible for the same beneficiary to disclaim one and retain the other. Similarly, subject to the unresolved question whether it is possible to disclaim an interest under an intestacy at all, it is thought that a beneficiary under an intestacy may only disclaim the whole of his entitlement. A gift cannot be disclaimed after it has been accepted by the beneficiary, for example, after paying into his bank account a cheque which he has received from the executors in satisfaction or on account of his benefit under the Will.

22.9 A disclaimer is usually effected by deed (although it need not be). It does not require to be stamped or contain any statement for Inheritance Tax Act 1984 s 142(1) and Taxation of Chargeable Gains Act 1992 s 62(6) to apply. For an example, see **Form 22.1**.

Deed of Variation

22.10 A Deed of Variation can relate to property passing under the deceased's Will, his intestacy or by survivorship. If the statutory requirements are complied with, the property to which the variation relates will pass to the beneficiary receiving it under the variation as if he had been entitled under the Will or intestacy. In the case of a variation affecting property passing by survivorship the deceased's half share in the property will be treated as part of his estate and not passing to the surviving joint owner. The variation will not be treated as a transfer of value between the original and the substituted beneficiary.

22.11 Both Inheritance Tax Act 1984 s 142(1)[1] and Taxation of Chargeable Gains Act 1992 s 62(6) refer to variations of 'dispositions' and it is believed that HMRC is not prepared to accept a Deed of Variation which merely introduces new or additional administrative powers and provisions without altering the disposition of property.

1   See **appendix 28.5**.

22.12 On the other hand, the ability to employ a Deed of Variation completely to rewrite a Will by, for example, appointing different or additional personal representatives is doubtful. In such a case the persons making the variation undermine their authority to do so by the deed itself.

22.13 It is usual for the variation to be effected by deed, with the personal representatives, the original beneficiary and the substituted beneficiary as parties and for the necessary statement under Inheritance Tax Act s 142(2) and Taxation of Chargeable Gains Act s 62(7) to be included as a clause in the deed. Inclusion of the substituted beneficiary as a party is not essential; for example, a variation can be made in favour of a person under a disability through immaturity or mental incapacity.

22.14 Unlike a disclaimer, a Deed of Variation can be concluded after the property to which it relates has been distributed to the original beneficiary. This is not recommended. Indeed, the variation can be effected by the personal representative of the original beneficiary within two years of the testator's death, although HMRC requires written evidence of the consent of any beneficiaries of the original beneficiary who are affected by the variation.

22.15 Thus, where two spouses die within two years of one another and the first has not made full use of his nil-rate band it is possible to vary the disposition of the estate of the first to die in order to make maximum use of his nil-rate band. Such variations were once the most common type of what is referred to as a 'double death variation' but now that the nil-rate band is transferrable between spouses the cases in which it may be desirable to maximise use of the nil-rate band of the first to die will be limited to those where the survivor already has an enhanced nil-rate band by virtue of a previous marriage or civil partnership that has terminated by death. (It is not possible to eliminate a nil-rate band discretionary trust by deed of variation because a discretionary trust almost invariably involves the interests of persons who are not sui juris.) The personal representatives of the second spouse to die should be parties to the deed but they must have the consent of such of the beneficiaries of the second to die whose interests are affected. It should be noted that if a variation of this sort is contemplated it is the nil-rate band of the first to die at the date of his or her death, not at the date of the variation, that is substituted[1]. (It is not possible to eliminate a nil-rate band discretionary trust by deed of variation because a discretionary trust almost invariably involves the interests of persons who not sui juris: see **22.22**.)

1   This was the error made in *Martin v Nicholson* [2005] WTLR 175.

22.16 However, HMRC has expressed the view[1] that a variation must be implemented in the real world:

> 'It is perhaps not immediately obvious that a variation must be implemented in the real world. S. 17(a) IHTA expressly provides that a variation or disclaimer to which s. 142(1) applies is not a transfer of value, so the instrument in writing must be more than an empty piece of paper. That provision and s. 142, in previous incarnations, were in effect a form of relief from double charges under the CTT regime. It is a pre-requisite if the provisions are to have any impact that a "real life" disposition or transfer took place, so that the transferor can decide whether or not to make an election in order to trigger the deeming provisions.
>
> As Mr R T Oerton put it in Capital Tax Planning July 1992 "In the real world of property law, where questions about ownership and the transfer of ownership are decided, the deceased does not make the

22.17 *Variations after death*

changes: the beneficiaries do. And the deceased cannot be deemed in the true world to bring about effects which the beneficiaries cannot, or do not, bring about in the real world."

Let us take the situation in which, under the will of A, B has an interest in possession in settled property, and on its cesser the beneficial interest in possession passes to C. In other words A leaves a life interest in property to B, with remainder to C. Following B's death within two years of A, C makes a deed of variation – still within that two year period – which purports to vary the will of A by redirecting B's interest to C or to extinguish it totally. In the real world B's interest does not exist, there is nothing for the deed to bite upon, and so s. 142 simply cannot apply. If the situation had been that it was possible for B's executors to disclaim his life interest as a matter of general law, then that should fall within the protection of s. 142.

It has been found that some of these inoperative deeds have been accepted as effective variations. The inconsistency of treatment is regretted, and assurances that have been given in the past will be binding upon the Revenue.'

As a result, HMRC no longer accepts that it is possible to claim that Inheritance Tax Act 1984 s 142(1) applies to a double death variation which purports to redirect or extinguish an interest terminable on the death of the second to die[2].

1   Capital Taxes Office *IHT Newsletter*, December 2001, p 5.
2   See the decision of the Scottish Special Commissioner in *Soutter's Executry v IRC* [2002] STC (SCD) 385.

22.17 Deeds of Variation ceased to be subject to stamp duty following the Stamp Duty (Exempt Instruments) Regulations 1987 (SI 1987/516) provided that they were certified under category M of the Regulations. The Regulations somewhat stubbornly remain in force but, for practical purposes, stamp duty has been abolished and replaced with stamp duty land tax except in relation to stock or marketable securities. HMRC had very sensibly advised that, except in the highly unusual case of a variation actually amounting to a stock transfer form (which should continue to be certified), no stamp duty certificate is required in the Deed of Variation[1]. The stock transfer form should incorporate a certificate instead. However, scope for confusion remains because the *Inheritance Tax Manual*[2] now states that the appropriate certificate (usually category M) *should* be included if the parties are relying on the instrument to reduce the liability to inheritance tax. The forms in this chapter continue to include optional Stamp Duty Certificates.

1   See Capital Taxes Office *IHT Newsletter*, August 2004.
2   IHTM35060 (*Has Stamp Duty exemption been claimed?*).

22.18 Following the enactment of Finance Act 2003 s 49 variations carried out within two years of death for no consideration in money or money's worth other than the making of a variation of another disposition are exempt from charge to stamp duty land tax under Sch 3 para 4. It is not necessary to include any certificate or statement to that effect in the deed itself.

22.19 It is possible to have more than one variation in respect of the same estate but not in respect of the same property in the same estate[1]. A Deed of Variation cannot be the subject of a further variation within Inheritance Tax Act 1984 s 142. It is always sensible to try to include all variations in one document if at all possible[2] although failure to do so is less likely to excite the interest of HMRC now that tax neutral or tax saving variations no longer need to be reported.

1   *Russell v IRC* [1988] STC 195.
2   See Inland Revenue statement (*Law Society Gazette*, 22 May 1985, p 1454).

22.20 **Form 22.1** is an example of a simple disclaimer. **Form 22.2** is designed for a comparatively simple variation and **Form 22.3** for a variation which is more detailed, by which the Will is virtually re-written in a schedule.

22.21 **Form 22.4** is an example of a 'double death' variation intended to be used where the original beneficiary has died within two years of the testator. In this case the original beneficiary has died intestate.

22.22 Prior to the 2007 Pre-Budget Report and the introduction of transferrable nil-rate bands between spouses and civil partners one very common variation was to be rid of a widow's absolute interest to utilise the tax-free inheritance tax band. In most cases the trend will now be reversed with the tendency being to maximise the surviving spouse's or civil partner's interest in order to avoid 'wasting' the nil-rate band. Where the will of the first to die includes a nil-rate band discretionary trust a deed of variation cannot be used to do away with it because the potential beneficiaries of the trust are often numerous and include persons who cannot enter into the variation either because they are minors or because they are not ascertained. In such a case, the trust can usually be wound up by the trustees exercising a power of appointment in favour of the surviving spouse (if such a power is available) within two years of the death. This will fall within IHTA 1984 s 144[1] and be read back into the will in the same way as a variation. Note, however, that an appointment under s 144 cannot be used in this way after the death of the surviving spouse or civil partner. There will still be cases in which such a trust is appropriate. For example, where the survivor has been married before and that marriage ended with death there may already be an enhanced nil-rate band available. **Form 22.5** provides a simple example appropriate for use in such cases.

1   See Appendix **28.7**.

22.23 **Form 22.6** is a simple example of a Deed of Variation in the event of an intestacy. It is difficult to supply a precedent of general application because there are so many possible alternatives even when the deceased has died intestate. Indeed, Deeds of Variation, though often quite straightforward (as in **Form 22.5**), should not be settled by the inexperienced or by anyone without giving the deed and its ramifications careful thought. It is not possible, for inheritance tax purposes, to correct a Deed of Variation by making another variation of the same property although rectification[1] may be a possibility if things go wrong.

1   As in *Martin v Nicholson* [2005] WTLR 175.

22.24 Where the variation includes assets which have passed by survivorship, **Form 22.7** can be used. The Capital Taxes Office takes the view that a deed of disclaimer is inappropriate but accepts a variation effecting deemed severance of the joint tenancy immediately before the death. The joint tenancy may be of leasehold and freehold property or a joint account, joint shareholding or the like.

PRECEDENTS

22.25

FORM 22.1

Deed of Disclaimer

This Deed of Disclaimer dated the   day of [*month*] 201* is made by [*name*] of [*address*] ('the Beneficiary')

    1.1   [*Name*] ('the Testator') died on [*date*] [and probate of his Will was granted to [*name(s)*] ('the Executors') by the [Principal]/[District] Probate Registry on [*date*]][1].

    1.2   By his Will the Testator gave [*specified gift disclaimed or use a schedule*] ('the Gift(s)') to the Beneficiary.

    2.1   By this deed the Beneficiary disclaims the Gift(s) in [its]/[their] entirety.

    2.2   The Beneficiary has not [entered into possession of the Gift(s) nor] done anything which would constitute an acceptance of the Gift(s).

Signed as a Deed by [*the Beneficiary*]

in the presence of:

[1] A disclaimer can be effected before a grant of probate has been obtained. In such a case the words included in square parenthesis here should be omitted.

FORM 22.2

Simple Deed of Variation

THIS DEED OF VARIATION is made the   day of [*month*] 201* BY [*names and addresses of Executors*] ('the Executors') [*name and address of Original Beneficiary*] ('the Donor') [*name and address of donee*] ('the Donee')[1]

Recitals:

    1.1   [*Name of testator*] late of [*address*] ('the Testator') died on [*date of death*] having made his last Will dated [*date of will*] ('the Will') by which he appointed the Executors to be his Executors and Trustees.

    [1.2   The Executors obtained a grant of Probate out of the [Principal]/[   ] District] Probate Registry on [*date of grant*]][2]

    1.3   By clause [6][3] of the Will the Testator gave the whole of his residuary estate to the Donor absolutely[3].

    1.4   The Donor has a [nephew][3] ('the Donee') [*name and address of nephew*][3].

    1.5   The Donor and the Executors wish to vary the disposition of the Testator's estate effected by his Will for the benefit of the Donee in the following manner.

Operative Variation:

2.1 The parties to this deed vary the disposition of the Testator's estate effected by his Will as follows:

2.1.1 The Will shall be varied and the Testator's estate administered as if from the death of the Testator clause [6][3] of the Will had provided that the Testator's residuary estate should be held by the Executors on trust for the Donor and the Donee in equal shares absolutely.

2.1.2 In accordance with section 142(2) of the Inheritance Tax Act 1984 and Section 62(7) of the Taxation of Chargeable Gains Act 1992 the parties hereto make a statement that they intend that the provisions of Section 142(1) of the Inheritance Tax Act 1984 and of Section 62(6) of the Taxation of Chargeable Gains Act 1992 shall apply in relation to the variation effected by this deed to the intent that such variation shall be treated as if it were made by the Testator for the purposes of inheritance tax and capital gains tax[4].

[Stamp Duty Certificate:

2.2 The parties certify that this instrument falls within Category M in the Schedule to the Stamp Duty (Exempt Instruments) Regulations 1987.][5]

IN WITNESS whereof the parties hereto have executed these presents as their deed the day and year first above written

SIGNED and DELIVERED as a deed by the said

[*name of first Executor*] in the presence of:

SIGNED and DELIVERED as a deed by the said

[*name of second Executor*] in the presence of:

SIGNED and DELIVERED as a deed by the said

[*name of Donor*] in the presence of:

SIGNED and DELIVERED as a deed by the said

[*name of Donee*] in the presence of:

1 The donee does not normally need to be a party but is commonly included.
2 A grant is not a prerequisite although an intention to obtain a grant ought to be recited if it has not been obtained.
3 These are, of course, only examples.
4 See **22.4**.
5 See **22.17**.

FORM 22.3

Deed of Variation – longer alternative

THIS DEED OF VARIATION is made the   day of [*month*] 201* BY [*names and addresses of Executors*] ('the Executors') [*name and address of Original Beneficiary*] ('the Donor') and [*names and addresses of Trustees*] ('the Trustees')[1]

22.25 Precedents

Recitals:

1.1 [*Name of testator*] late of [*address*] ('the Testator') died on [*date of death*] having made his last Will dated [*date of will*] ('the Will') by which he appointed the Executors to be his Executors and Trustees.

[1.2 The Executors obtained a grant of Probate out of the [Principal]/[ ] District] Probate Registry on [*date of grant*]][2].

1.3 In the events which have occurred the Testator gave the whole of his estate to the Donor absolutely[3].

1.4 The Donor and the Executors wish to vary the disposition of the Testator's estate effected by his Will for the benefit of the persons described below in the following manner.

Operative Variation:

2.1 The parties to this deed vary the disposition of the Testator's estate effected by his Will as follows:

2.1.1 The Will shall be varied and the Testator's estate administered as if from his death the Testator had given the whole of his estate to the Trustees to hold on the trusts set out in the Schedule hereto.

2.1.2 In accordance with Section 142(2) of the Inheritance Tax Act 1984 and Section 62(7) of the Taxation of Chargeable Gains Act 1992 the parties hereto make a statement that they intend that the provisions of Section 142(1) of the Inheritance Tax Act 1984 and of Section 62(6) of the Taxation of Chargeable Gains Act 1992 shall apply in relation to the variation effected by this deed to the intent that such variation shall be treated as if it were made by the Testator for the purposes of inheritance tax and capital gains tax[4].

[Stamp Duty Certificate:

2.2 The parties certify that this instrument falls within Category M in the Schedule to the Stamp Duty (Exempt Instruments) Regulations 1987.][5]

IN WITNESS whereof the parties hereto have executed these presents as their deed the day and year first above written.

SCHEDULE

[*Terms of substitute provisions*]

SIGNED and DELIVERED etc[6].

1 The intended ultimate donees do not need to be parties where the gift is to trustees. In the sort of case contemplated by this deed there might well be only one executor who could also be the donor.
2 A grant is not a prerequisite although an intention to obtain a grant ought to be recited if it has not been obtained.
3 This is only an example but the most common case in which a substitute Will is to be written is that in which the whole estate is left to one beneficiary.
4 See **22.4**.
5 See **22.17**.
6 See **Form 22.2**.

FORM 22.4

Deed of Variation – original beneficiary surviving but subsequently dying intestate

THIS DEED OF VARIATION is made the   day of [*month*] 201* BY [*names and addresses of Executors*] ('the Executors') [*names and addresses of Administrators of Original Beneficiary*] ('the Administrators') [*name and address of the Donor*] ('the Donor') and [*names and addresses of Trustees*] ('the Trustees')[1]

Recitals:

1.1   [*Name of testator*] late of [*address*] ('the Testator') died on [*date of death*] having made his last Will dated [*date of will*] ('the Will') by which he appointed the Executors to be his Executors and Trustees.

[1.2   The Executors obtained a grant of Probate out of the [Principal]/[   ] District] Probate Registry on [*date of grant*]][2].

1.3   By clause [#] of his Will the Testator gave the whole of his estate to the [*name of the Original Beneficiary*] ('the Original Beneficiary') absolutely[3].

1.4   The Original Beneficiary died on [*date of death*] intestate without issue[3].

1.5   Letters of administration to the estate of the Original Beneficiary were issued out of the [Principal]/[   ] District] Probate Registry on [*date of grant*] to the Administrators.

1.6   Under the rules relating to intestacy under the Administration of Estates Act 1925 the Original Beneficiary's estate is held for the Donor absolutely[3].

1.7   The Donor the Administrators the Executors and the Trustees wish to vary the disposition of the Testator's estate effected by his Will in the following manner.

Operative Variation:

2.1   The parties to this deed vary the disposition of the Testator's estate effected by his Will as follows:

   2.1.1   The Will shall be varied and the Testator's estate administered as if from his death the Testator had given the whole of his estate to the Trustees to hold on the trusts set out in the Schedule hereto.

   2.1.2   In accordance with Section 142(2) of the Inheritance Tax Act 1984 and Section 62(7) of the Taxation of Chargeable Gains Act 1992 the parties hereto make a statement that they intend that the provisions of Section 142(1) of the Inheritance Tax Act 1984 and of Section 62(6) of the Taxation of Chargeable Gains Act 1992 shall apply in relation to the variation effected by this deed to the intent that such variation shall be treated as if it were made by the Testator for the purposes of inheritance tax and capital gains tax[4].

[Stamp Duty Certificate:

2.2   The parties certify that this instrument falls within Category M in the Schedule to the Stamp Duty (Exempt Instruments) Regulations 1987.][5]

22.25 *Precedents*

IN WITNESS whereof the parties hereto have executed these presents as their deed the day and year first above written

SCHEDULE

[*Terms of substitute provisions*]

SIGNED and DELIVERED etc[6].

1 The intended ultimate donees do not need to be parties. The trustees stand in their place.
2 A grant is not a prerequisite although an intention to obtain a grant ought to be recited if it has not been obtained.
3 This is only an example.
4 See **22.4**.
5 See **22.17**.
6 See **Form 22.2**.

FORM 22.5

Deed of Variation – use of nil-rate band where previously married widow with enhanced nil-rate band has absolute interest

THIS DEED OF VARIATION is made the   day of [*month*] 201* BY [*names and addresses of Executors*] ('the Executors') [*name and address of the widow*] ('the Widow') and [*names and addresses of testator's children*] ('the Children')[1]

Recitals:

1.1 [*Name of testator*] late of [*address*] ('the Testator') died on [*date of death*] having made his last Will dated [*date of will*] ('the Will') by which he appointed the Executors to be his Executors and Trustees.

[1.2 The Executors obtained a grant of Probate out of the [Principal]/[   ] District] Probate Registry on [*date of grant*]][2].

1.3 In the events which have occurred the Testator gave the whole of his estate to the Widow absolutely[3].

1.4 The Widow the Executors and the Children wish to vary the disposition of the Testator's estate effected by his Will in the following manner.

Operative Variation:

2.1 The parties to this deed vary the disposition of the Testator's estate effected by his Will as follows:

2.1.1 The Will shall be varied and the Testator's estate administered as if from his death the Testator had given by his Will a pecuniary legacy of [£325,000[4]]/[*the maximum amount which could be given without any inheritance tax being payable*[5]] to the Children in equal shares and given the whole of the residue of his estate to the Widow absolutely.

2.1.2 In accordance with Section 142(2) of the Inheritance Tax Act 1984 and Section 62(7) of the Taxation of Chargeable Gains Act 1992 the parties hereto make a statement that they intend that the provisions of Section 142(1) of the Inheritance Tax Act 1984 and of Section 62(6) of the Taxation of Chargeable Gains Act 1992 shall apply in relation to the variation effected by this deed to the intent that such variation shall be treated as if it were made by the Testator for the purposes of inheritance tax and capital gains tax[6].

[Stamp Duty Certificate:

2.2 The parties certify that this instrument falls within Category M in the Schedule to the Stamp Duty (Exempt Instruments) Regulations 1987.][7]

IN WITNESS whereof the parties hereto have executed these presents as their deed the day and year first above written

SCHEDULE

[*Terms of substitute provisions*]

SIGNED and DELIVERED etc[8].

1. The intended donees (the children) do not need to be parties but they are usually included. If they are not parties they will need to be defined elsewhere in the deed.
2. A grant is not a prerequisite although an intention to obtain a grant ought to be recited if it has not been obtained.
3. This is probably the most common case.
4. This is the current nil-rate band. The variation should refer to the nil-rate band at the date of death. This is fixed at £325,000 at present.
5. In the case of post-death variations where the sum available is known the deed need only specify a pecuniary legacy as in the first alternative. Where, however, there remains uncertainty as to the value of lifetime gifts or legacies to non-exempt beneficiaries and the like it is more sensible to include an ambulatory provision defining the nil-rate gift since the sum available free of inheritance tax will not be known at the date of the variation and the second alternative should be chosen.
6. See **22.4**.
7. See **22.17**.
8. See **Form 22.2**.

FORM 22.6

Deed of Variation – intestacy, simple form

THIS DEED OF VARIATION is made the   day of [*month*] 201* BY [*names and addresses of Administrators*] ('the Administrators') [*name and address of Original Beneficiary*] ('the Donor') and [*names and addresses of Trustees*] ('the Trustees')[1]

Recitals:

1.1 [*Name of deceased*] late of [*address*] ('the Intestate') died on [*date of death*] survived by his sister, the Donor.

1.2 Letters of administration to the estate of the Original Beneficiary were issued out of the [Principal]/[   ] District] Probate Registry on [*date of issue*] to the Administrators[2].

1.3 Under the rules relating to intestacy under the Administration of Estates Act 1925 the Original Beneficiary's estate is held for the Donor absolutely[3].

22.25 *Precedents*

    1.4   The Donor the Administrators and the Trustees wish to vary the disposition of the Intestate's estate effected by his intestacy in the following manner.

Operative Variation:

    2.1   The parties to this deed vary the disposition of the Intestate's estate effected by his intestacy as follows:

        2.1.1 The Will shall be varied and the Intestate's estate administered from the date of his death as if after the payment of all debts, taxes and other administration expenses he had given a legacy of £20,000 to the Donor absolutely and given the residue of his estate to the Trustees to hold on the trusts set out in the Schedule hereto[4].

        2.1.2 In accordance with Section 142(2) of the Inheritance Tax Act 1984 and Section 62(7) of the Taxation of Chargeable Gains Act 1992 the parties hereto make a statement that they intend that the provisions of Section 142(1) of the Inheritance Tax Act 1984 and of Section 62(6) of the Taxation of Chargeable Gains Act 1992 shall apply in relation to the variation effected by this deed to the intent that such variation shall be treated as if it were made by the Intestate for the purposes of inheritance tax and capital gains tax[5].

[Stamp Duty Certificate:

    2.2   The parties certify that this instrument falls within Category M in the Schedule to the Stamp Duty (Exempt Instruments) Regulations 1987.][6]

IN WITNESS whereof the parties hereto have executed these presents as their deed the day and year first above written

SCHEDULE

[*Terms of substitute provisions*]

SIGNED and DELIVERED etc[7].

1   The intended donees do not need to be parties. The trustees stand in their place.
2   A grant is not a prerequisite although an intention to obtain a grant ought to be recited if it has not been obtained.
3   This is only an example.
4   In this example the donor has held back £20,000 for herself but wishes to vary the disposition of the remainder of the estate. This cannot be done by way of disclaimer.
5   See **22.4**.
6   See **22.17**.
7   See **Form 22.2**.

FORM 22.7

Deed of Variation – where some of the property passes by survivorship

THIS DEED OF VARIATION is made the   day of [*month*] 201* BY [*names and addresses of Administrators*] ('the Administrators') [*name and address of surviving joint tenant*] ('the Donor') and [*name and address of Donee*] ('the Donee')[1]

Precedents **22.25**

Recitals:

1.1 [*Name of deceased*] late of [*address*] ('the Deceased') died on [*date of death*] survived by the Donor.

1.2 Prior to the death of the Deceased the matrimonial home at [*address of matrimonial home*] ('the Property') was vested in the joint names of the Deceased and the Donor as beneficial joint tenants[2].

1.3 Under the law of survivorship the legal estate and the Deceased's severable share and interest in the Property passed to the Donor by survivorship[2].

1.4 Letters of administration to the estate of the Deceased were issued out of the [Principal]/[ ] District] Probate Registry on [*date of issue*] to the Administrators.

1.5 Under the rules relating to intestacy under the Administration of Estates Act 1925 the Deceased's estate is held for the Donor absolutely[3].

1.6 The Donor the Administrators and the Donee wish to vary the disposition of the severable share of the Deceased in the Property which passed to the Donee by survivorship in the following manner.

Operative Variation:

2.1 The parties to this deed vary the disposition of the Property effected by the Deceased's death by right of survivorship as follows:

2.1.1 It shall be deemed and the Deceased's estate shall be administered as if the joint tenancy in equity of the Deceased and the Donor in the Property had been severed immediately before the death of the Deceased.

2.1.2 The severable share in equity deemed to be held by the Deceased in the Property immediately before his death shall be treated as having devolved on the Donee (instead of to the Donor under the law of survivorship) as if the Deceased had made a will to that effect with the result that the Donor holds the Property upon trust for the Donor and the Donee as tenants in common in equal shares[4].

2.1.3 In accordance with Section 142(2) of the Inheritance Tax Act 1984 and Section 62(7) of the Taxation of Chargeable Gains Act 1992 the parties hereto make a statement that they intend that the provisions of Section 142(1) of the Inheritance Tax Act 1984 and of Section 62(6) of the Taxation of Chargeable Gains Act 1992 shall apply in relation to the variation effected by this deed to the intent that such variation shall be treated as if it were made by the Deceased for the purposes of inheritance tax and capital gains tax[5].

[Stamp Duty Certificate:

2.2 The parties certify that this instrument falls within Category M in the Schedule to the Stamp Duty (Exempt Instruments) Regulations 1987.[6]]

IN WITNESS whereof the parties hereto have executed these presents as their deed the day and year first above written,

22.25 *Precedents*

SCHEDULE

[*Terms of substitute provisions*]

SIGNED and DELIVERED etc[7].

1 The intended donees do not need to be parties.
2 This presupposes that the Property comprises the matrimonial home but other property such as an interest in joint bank accounts could be specified. In such a case it might be better to list the joint assets in a schedule.
3 This is only an example but probably the most common case encountered in practice.
4 In this example the severable share is simply held by the donor and a particular donee for themselves as tenants in common in equity. As an alternative, the severable share could be given to trustees to hold on the trusts set out in a schedule or perhaps to the executors to hold on the trusts of the Will.
5 See **22.4**.
6 See **22.17**.
7 See **Form 22.2**.

23 Oaths for executors

Need for an oath

23.1 The proving executor or executors must swear an oath in the form of an affidavit to identify the Will, the deceased and the death and in this way the executors prove their entitlement to take a grant. In doing so they promise to administer the estate of the deceased according to law.

Reference to Registries

23.2 'The Principal Registry', 'The Probate Registry of Wales' or a District Registry will be specified according to the Registry applied to. The name of the solicitor's firm or probate practitioner and postcode must be given on the Oath as they are entered onto the Probate Registry's computer. The DX number and postal address other than the postcode are optional but it is understood that Registries prefer DX to the post.

23.3 The Probate Registries will deal by fax on request, for instance, in the covering letter lodging the probate papers. It is also possible to send a draft Oath with a copy of the Will to a Probate Registry in advance to seek its comments on the Oath, the Will's validity[1] or aspects of it which may require further details. At the time of going to press there is a £10 per document settling fee[2].

1   The Probate registry will not be able to comment on questions of capacity, want of knowledge and approval and undue influence which will not appear on the face of the Will.
2   Non-Contentious Probate Fees Order 2004 (SI 2004/3120) Sch. 1.

Description by address

23.4 It is not usually necessary to give a former address in a testamentary document or in an Oath. If it is, put it in the Will and state why it is given. Questions of identity generally can be dealt with in a clause of the Oath, for instance, if the deceased was known by more than one name in any connection. A statement of relationship should only be included where this is necessary to establish identity.

23.5 For example, if the Will appoints: 'my husband [AB]' as executor, 'I am the sole executor named in the Will of the deceased' suffices. Whereas if the Will appoints: 'my husband' as executor the oath should read 'I am the sole executor named

23.6 *Oaths for executors*

in the deceased's Will, being her lawful husband at the date of her Will and today'. This wording can be adapted in other cases of the also rare case where executors are not named but described.

Female deponents

23.6 Where the deponent is a woman none of *Mrs*, *Miss*, or *Ms* should appear before the name.

23.7 A woman deponent can be described as 'executor' or 'executrix' if she alone proves although the latter is the proper description. In the plural 'executors' or 'executrices' may be used, but the term 'executrices' is only appropriate where there is more than one executrix, not where a man is also appointed.

Power reserved

23.8 Where power is reserved to an executor appointed by the Will he should be given notice (as in **Form 23.7**) of the application for the grant, except where power is to be reserved to executors who are appointed by reference to their being partners in a firm and the application is by another partner in that firm. See Non-Contentious Probate Rules 1987 r 27(1A). This provision applies to all the forms of Oath except **Form 23.6**.

Size of the estate

23.9 Supreme Court Act 1981 s 109 requires that on applying for a grant an applicant must pay and account for inheritance tax if any is due. An account is not necessary in the case of an excepted estate, defined by the Inheritance Tax (Delivery of Accounts) (Excepted Estates) Regulations 2004 (SI 2004/2543) in rather complicated terms, which might be summarised as follows:
(a) the deceased was domiciled in the UK at the date of death;
(b) the estate consists only of property passing under the deceased's will or intestacy or under a trust, nominated property, or joint property passing by survivorship;
(c) where any trust assets were held in a single trust in which the deceased had an interest in possession with a value not exceeding £150,000;
(d) not more than £100,000 represents the value of property situated outside the UK;
(e) the deceased is not a person by reason of whose death one of the alternatively secured pension fund provisions applies.
(f) the deceased died without having made any chargeable transfer in the seven years before his death except cash, quoted shares or quoted securities, or land and buildings (and contents), with a total gross value not exceeding £150,000. For this purpose business property relief and agricultural property relief shall not apply; and
(g) the gross value of the estate plus transfer within seven years of death plus exempt transfers to spouse/civil partner, charities etc within seven years of death do not exceed the nil-rate threshold at death.

An estate is also excepted where paragraphs (a) to (f) apply and the gross value of chargeable assets of the estate (before deducting liabilities, reliefs or exemptions), when added to the cumulative chargeable gifts made in the seven years before death, does not exceed £1,000,000 and the net chargeable estate after deduction of spouse/civil partner and charity exemptions only does not exceed the nil-rate threshold.

The estate is also exempt if the deceased was never domiciled (or deemed domiciled) in the UK, the estate consists only of cash or quoted shares the alternative pension fund provisions do not apply and the gross value does not exceed £150,000.

Where the estate is an excepted estate the requirement for an account is relaxed. Further guidance can be found in HMRC's Customer Guide to Inheritance Tax.

Drafting variants

23.10 The drafting of the commonly used form of Oath with which Registries are familiar could be greatly improved. Wordings may be changed (provided the meaning is not changed and is clear) as may the order of clauses, but the scope is limited. For instance, despite Wills Act 1837 s 1 some Registries still desire a reference to 'Last Will and Testament'.

PRECEDENTS

23.11

FORM 23.1

Oaths for Sole Executor; Sole Surviving Executor; Sole Proving Executor (Power reserved to the other)

IN THE HIGH COURT OF JUSTICE Extracting Solicitors:
[*name, address, (postcode, DX number, fax number) Telephone number and reference of Extracting Solicitors*]

FAMILY DIVISION

[THE PRINCIPAL REGISTRY][1]

[THE PROBATE REGISTRY OF WALES][1]

[[*NAME*] DISTRICT PROBATE REGISTRY][1]

IN THE ESTATE of [AB][2] deceased

I, [CD][3] of [*full names and address (including postcode)*] make oath and say that:

1. I believe the paper writing now produced to and marked by me to contain the true and original last Will and Testament of [AB] ('the deceased') of [*address at date of death*] [and [*number*] Codicil(s)].

2. The deceased was born on [*date*] and died on [*date*] domiciled in England and Wales.

3. To the best of my knowledge, information and belief there was no land vested in the deceased which was settled previously to [his]/[her] death (and not by [his]/[her] Will) and which remained settled land notwithstanding [his]/[her] death.

   CHOOSE ONE ALTERNATIVE

   Either

   Sole executor

4. I am the sole [executor]/[executrix] named in the deceased's Will.

   Or

   Sole surviving executor

4. [EF][4] having died during the deceased's lifetime I am the sole surviving [executor]/[executrix] named in the deceased's Will.

   Or

   One of two executors – power reserved to the other

4. I am one of the executors named in the deceased's Will and notice of this application has been given to [EF][4], the other executor, to whom power is to be reserved.

   In any event

5. I will:

   5.1 collect, get in and administer according to the law the deceased's real and personal estate;

   5.2 when required to do so by the Court, exhibit on oath in the Court a full inventory of the estate of the deceased;

   5.3 when required to do so by the High Court, deliver up the grant of Probate to that Court[5].

6. To the best of my knowledge, information and belief the gross estate passing under the grant does not exceed £1,000,000 and the net estate does not exceed £[325,000] and that this is not a case in which an account is required to be delivered to HMRC.

SWORN by the above named Deponent [CD]

At [*place*]

On [*date*]

Before me,

Commissioner for Oaths

A Solicitor authorised to administer Oaths

1 These are, of course, alternatives.

2 This is the name of the deceased.

3 Names of the proving executors.

4 Name of non-proving executor(s).

5 These are the words of Administration of Estate Act 1925 s 25.

FORM 23.2

Oath for two named Executors and two Executors – power reserved to a third

IN THE HIGH COURT OF JUSTICE   Extracting Solicitors:
[*name, address, (postcode, DX number, fax number) Telephone number and reference of Extracting Solicitors*]

FAMILY DIVISION

[THE PRINCIPAL REGISTRY][1]

23.11 *Precedents*

[THE PROBATE REGISTRY OF WALES][1]

[[*NAME*] DISTRICT PROBATE REGISTRY][1]

IN THE ESTATE of [*AB*][2] deceased

We, [CD][3] of [*full names and address (including postcode)*] and [EF][3] [*full names and address (including postcode)*] of make oath and say that:

1. We believe the paper writing now produced to and marked by us to contain the true and original last Will and Testament of [AB] ('the deceased') of [*address at date of death*] [and [*number*] Codicil(s)].

2. The deceased was born on [*date*] and died on [*date*] domiciled in England and Wales.

3. To the best of our knowledge, information and belief there was no land vested in the deceased which was settled previously to [his]/[her] death (and not by [his]/[her] Will) and which remained settled land notwithstanding [his]/[her] death).

CHOOSE ONE ALTERNATIVE

Either

Two executors

4. We are the executors named in the deceased's Will.

Or

Two of three executors – power reserved to the other

4. We are two of the executors named in the deceased's Will and notice of this application has been given to [GH][4], the other executor, to whom power is to be reserved.

In any event

5. We will:

    5.1 collect, get in and administer according to the law the deceased's real and personal estate;

    5.2 when required to do so by the Court, exhibit on oath in the Court a full inventory of the estate of the deceased;

    5.3 when required to do so by the High Court, deliver up the grant of Probate to that Court.[5]

6. To the best of our knowledge, information and belief the gross estate passing under the grant does not exceed £1,000,000 and the net estate does not exceed £[325,000] and that this is not a case in which an account is required to be delivered to HMRC.

SWORN by the above named Deponent [CD]

At [*place*]

On [*date*]

Before me,

Commissioner for Oaths

A Solicitor authorised to administer Oaths

SWORN by the above named Deponent [EF]

At [place]

On [date]

Before me,

Commissioner for Oaths

A Solicitor authorised to administer Oaths

1   These are, of course, alternatives.
2   This is the name of the deceased.
3   Names of the proving executors.
4   Name of non-proving executor(s).
5   These are the words of Administration of Estate Act 1925 s 25.

FORM 23.3

Oath for Partner in Solicitors' firm or its successor[1]

IN THE HIGH COURT OF JUSTICE	**Extracting Solicitors:** [*name, address, (postcode, DX number, fax number) Telephone number and reference of Extracting Solicitors*]

FAMILY DIVISION

[THE PRINCIPAL REGISTRY][2]

[THE PROBATE REGISTRY OF WALES][2]

[[*NAME*]   DISTRICT PROBATE REGISTRY][2]

IN THE ESTATE of [AB][3] **deceased**

I, [CD][4] of [*full names and business address*] make oath and say that:

1. I believe the paper writing now produced to and marked by me to contain the true and original last Will and Testament of [AB] ('the deceased') of [*address at date of death*] [and [*number*] Codicil(s)].

2. The deceased was born on [*date*] and died on [*date*] domiciled in England and Wales.

3. To the best of my knowledge, information and belief there was no land vested in the deceased which was settled previously to [his]/[her] death (and not by [his]/[her] Will) and which remained settled land notwithstanding [his]/[her] death.

   CHOOSE ONE ALTERNATIVE

   Either

23.11 *Precedents*

Original firm

4. The deceased's Will appointed the Partners at [his]/[her] death in the firm of [BC & Co].

5. At the date of the deceased's death:

    5.1 I was one of the Partners in [BC & Co] and consequently one of the Executors appointed by the Will.

    5.2 Power is to be reserved to the other Partners in the firm of [BC & Co].

Or

Successor firm

4. The deceased's Will appointed the Partners at [his]/[her] death in the firm of [BC & Co] or any other firm which had at [his]/[her] death succeeded to and was carrying on its practice.

5. On [*date*] [XY & Co] succeeded to and since then has carried on the practice of [BC & Co] and at the date of the deceased's death:

    5.1 I was one of the Partners in [XY & Co] and consequently one of the Executors appointed by the Will.

    5.2 Power is to be reserved to the other Partners in the firm of [XY & Co].

In any event

6. I will:

    6.1 collect, get in and administer according to the law the deceased's real and personal estate;

    6.2 when required to do so by the Court, exhibit on oath in the Court a full inventory of the estate of the deceased;

    6.3 when required to do so by the High Court, deliver up the grant of Probate to that Court[5].

7. To the best of my knowledge, information and belief the gross estate passing under the grant does not exceed £1,000,000 and the net estate does not exceed £[325,000] and that this is not a case in which an account is required to be delivered to HMRC.

SWORN by the above named Deponent [CD]

At [*place*]

On [*date*]

Before me,

Commissioner for Oaths

A Solicitor authorised to administer Oaths

1   It would be unusual for one partner only in a firm to be the executor, except where there are separate appointments of executor and trustees, but this does happen.
2   These are, of course, alternatives.

3   This is the name of the deceased.
4   Names of the proving executors.
5   These are the words of Administration of Estate Act 1925 s 25.

FORM 23.4

Oath for Two Partners in firm of Solicitors and two Partners in its successor firm

IN THE HIGH COURT OF JUSTICE   Extracting Solicitors:
                                 [*name, address, (postcode,*
                                 DX number, fax number)
                                 Telephone number and
                                 reference of Extracting Solicitors]

FAMILY DIVISION

[THE PRINCIPAL REGISTRY][1]

[THE PROBATE REGISTRY OF WALES][1]

[[*NAME*]   DISTRICT PROBATE REGISTRY][1]

IN THE ESTATE of [AB][2] **deceased**

We, [BP][3] of [*full names and business address*] and [LD][3] of [*full names and business address*] make oath and say that:

1. We believe the paper writing now produced to and marked by us to contain the true and original last Will and Testament of [AB] ('the deceased') of [*address at date of death*] [and [*number*] Codicil(s)].

2. The deceased was born on [*date*] and died on [*date*] domiciled in England and Wales.

3. To the best of our knowledge, information and belief there was no land vested in the deceased which was settled previously to [his]/[her] death (and not by [his]/[her] Will) and which remained settled land notwithstanding [his]/[her] death).

    CHOOSE ONE ALTERNATIVE

    Either

    Original Firm

4. The deceased's Will appointed the Partners at [his]/[her] death in the firm of [BC & Co].

5. At the date of the deceased's death:

    5.1   We were two of the Partners in [BC & Co] and consequently two of the Executors appointed by the Will.

    5.2   Power is to be reserved to the other Partners in the firm of [BC & Co].

    Or

    Successor firm

23.11 *Precedents*

4. The deceased's Will appointed the Partners at [his]/[her] death in the firm of [BC & Co] or any other firm which had at [his]/[her] death succeeded to and was carrying on its practice.

5. On [*date*] [XY & Co] succeeded to and since then has carried on the practice of [BC & Co] and at the date of the deceased's death:

   5.1 We were two of the Partners in [XY & Co] and consequently two of the Executors appointed by the Will.

   5.2 Power is to be reserved to the other Partners in the firm of [XY & Co].

   In any event

6. We will:

   6.1 collect, get in and administer according to the law the deceased's real and personal estate;

   6.2 when required to do so by the Court, exhibit on oath in the Court a full inventory of the estate of the deceased;

   6.3 when required to do so by the High Court, deliver up the grant of Probate to that Court.[4]

7. To the best of our knowledge, information and belief the gross estate passing under the grant does not exceed £1,000,000 and the net estate does not exceed £[325,000] and that this is not a case in which an account is required to be delivered to HMRC.

SWORN by the above named Deponent [BP]

At [*place*]

On [*date*]

Before me,

Commissioner for Oaths

A Solicitor authorised to administer Oaths

SWORN by the above named Deponent [LD]

At [*place*]

On [*date*]

Before me,

Commissioner for Oaths

A Solicitor authorised to administer Oaths

1 These are, of course, alternatives.
2 This is the name of the deceased.
3 Names of the proving executors.
4 These are the words of Administration of Estate Act 1925 s 25.

Precedents **23.11**

FORM 23.5

Oath for a Partner in each of a Solicitors' and an Accountants' firm or a Partner in a Solicitors' firm and a layman appointed, power reserved to either the Accountant or the layman

IN THE HIGH COURT OF JUSTICE   Extracting Solicitors:
[*name, address, (postcode, DX number, fax number) Telephone number and reference of Extracting Solicitors*]

FAMILY DIVISION

[**THE PRINCIPAL REGISTRY**][1]

[**THE PROBATE REGISTRY OF WALES**][1]

[[*NAME*]   **DISTRICT PROBATE REGISTRY**][1]

IN THE ESTATE of [AB][2] **deceased**

We, [PC][3] of [*full names and business address*] and [JC]/[GG][3] of [*full names and business address*] make oath and say that:

1. We believe the paper writing now produced to and marked by us to contain the true and original last Will and Testament of [AB] ('the deceased') of [*address at date of death*] [and [*number*] Codicil(s)].

2. The deceased was born on [*date*] and died on [*date*] domiciled in England and Wales.

3. To the best of our knowledge, information and belief there was no land vested in the deceased which was settled previously to [his]/[her] death (and not by [his]/[her] Will) and which remained settled land notwithstanding [his]/[her] death.

4. The deceased's Will appointed as Executors:

    4.1   the Partners at [his]/[her] death in the firm of [BC & Co]; and

    Either

    4.2   the Partners at [his]/[her] death in the firm of [CT & Co].

    Or

    4.2   [GG] (layman).

5. At the date of the deceased's death:

    Either

    5.1   [PC] was one of the Partners in [BC & Co] and consequently one of the Executors appointed by the Will with power being reserved to the other Partners.

    Or

    Accountants firm not involved

229

23.11 *Precedents*

        5.1   [JC] was one of the Partners in the firm of [CT & Co] [to whom power is to be reserved].

       Or

       Layman – 5 and 5.1 become a single clause with appropriate adjustments

6.   We will:

        6.1   collect, get in and administer according to the law the deceased's real and personal estate;

        6.2   when required to do so by the Court, exhibit on oath in the Court a full inventory of the estate of the deceased;

        6.3   when required to do so by the High Court, deliver up the grant of Probate to that Court.[4]

7.   To the best of our knowledge, information and belief the gross estate passing under the grant does not exceed £1,000,000 and the net estate does not exceed £[325,000] and that this is not a case in which an account is required to be delivered to HMRC.

SWORN by the above named Deponent [PC]

At [*place*]

On [*date*]

Before me,

Commissioner for Oaths

A Solicitor authorised to administer Oaths

SWORN by the above named Deponent [JC]/[GG]

At [*place*]

On [*date*]

Before me,

Commissioner for Oaths

A Solicitor authorised to administer Oaths

1   These are, of course, alternatives.
2   This is the name of the deceased.
3   Names of the proving executors.
4   These are the words of Administration of Estate Act 1925 s 25.

FORM 23.6

Oath for Minor contingently appointed with an adult: having attained eighteen; still not having attained eighteen

IN THE HIGH COURT OF JUSTICE   Extracting Solicitors:
[*name, address, (postcode, DX number, fax number) Telephone number and reference of Extracting Solicitors*]

FAMILY DIVISION

[THE PRINCIPAL REGISTRY][1]

[THE PROBATE REGISTRY OF WALES][1]

[[*NAME*]   DISTRICT PROBATE REGISTRY][1]

IN THE ESTATE of [AB][2] **deceased**

We, [CD][3] of [*full names and address*] and [EF][3] [*full names and address*] make oath and say that:

1. We believe the paper writing now produced to and marked by us to contain the true and original last Will and Testament of [AB] ('the deceased') of [*address at date of death*] [and [*number*] Codicil(s)].

2. The deceased was born on [*date*] and died on [*date*] domiciled in England and Wales.

3. To the best of our knowledge, information and belief there was no land vested in the deceased which was settled previously to [his]/[her] death (and not by [his]/[her] Will) and which remained settled land notwithstanding [his]/[her] death.

   CHOOSE ONE ALTERNATIVE

   Either

   Another, [GH][4]**, a minor not having attained 18**

4. We are the Executors named in the Deceased's Will [GH] not having attained 18 at the date of the Deceased's death.

   Or

   [EF][4]**, the minor having attained 18**

4. We are the two Executors named in the Deceased's Will [EF] having attained 18 in the Deceased's lifetime.

   In any event

5. We will:

   5.1   collect, get in and administer according to the law the deceased's real and personal estate;

   5.2   when required to do so by the Court, exhibit on oath in the Court a full inventory of the estate of the deceased;

23.11 *Precedents*

      5.3   when required to do so by the High Court, deliver up the grant of Probate to that Court.[5]

      6.   To the best of our knowledge, information and belief the gross estate passing under the grant does not exceed £1,000,000 and the net estate does not exceed £[325,000] and that this is not a case in which an account is required to be delivered to HMRC.

SWORN by the above named Deponent [CD]

At [*place*]

On [*date*]

Before me,

Commissioner for Oaths

A Solicitor authorised to administer Oaths

SWORN by the above named Deponent [EF]/[GH]

At [*place*]

On [*date*]

Before me,

Commissioner for Oaths

A Solicitor authorised to administer Oaths

1   These are, of course, alternatives.
2   This is the name of the deceased.
3   Names of the proving executors.
4   Name of the minor in question.
5   These are the words of Administration of Estate Act 1925 s 25.

FORM 23.7

Notice to Non-Proving Executor(s)[1]

IN THE HIGH COURT OF JUSTICE	**Extracting Solicitors:** [*name, address, (postcode, DX number, fax number) Telephone number and reference of Extracting Solicitors*]

FAMILY DIVISION

[THE PRINCIPAL REGISTRY][2]

[THE PROBATE REGISTRY OF WALES][2]

[[*NAME*]   DISTRICT PROBATE REGISTRY][2]

To [*full names and address of each Executor to whom it is intended that power will be reserved*]

Precedents **23.11**

IN THE ESTATE of [AB]³ deceased who died on [*date*] having made a Will dated * [[with] [a codicil]/[codicils] dated *]/[and [*date*]]

We [*full names of proving Executors*] being [one]/[two]/[three] of the Executors named in that Will [and Codicil/s] intend to make an application for a grant of Probate in the estate in which power to apply for a like grant is to be reserved to you.

DATED   20[ ]

Name and address of Solicitors for the proving Executors

[I]/[We] acknowledge receipt of a notice of which the above is a copy

DATED   20[ ]

....

[*full names*]

....

[*full names*]

....

[*full names*]

1   Not necessary in relation to a firm or its non-proving partners.
2   These are, of course, alternatives.
3   This is the name of the deceased.

FORM 23.8

Deposition for non-believers and non-Christians

Affirmation: I do solemnly, sincerely and truly declare and affirm that:

Muslims (swearing on the Koran):	I swear by Allah that:
Hindus (swearing on the Gita):	I swear by the Gita that:
Sikhs (swearing on the Adi Granth):	I swear by the Guru Nanak that:

Other faiths swear on the appropriate Holy Book

In the case of an Affirmation the jurat should substitute *DECLARED AND AFFIRMED* for *SWORN*. It need not be changed in the case of persons swearing on a holy book other than the Bible.

24 Letters and other support materials

1.	Basic procedure note	24.1
Wills and related matters:		
2.	Will draftsman's Guidance Notes	24.2
3.	Will and related matters – checklist	24.3
4.	Matters to be considered at interview and beyond	24.4
5.	Letter about a life interest trust	24.5
6.	Letter about a discretionary trust	24.6
7.	Letter submitting a draft Will and Notice of Severance	24.7
8.	Notice of Severance	24.8
9.	Letter enclosing Wills for completion	24.9
10.	Will enabling Promissory Note – procedure after completion of the administration of the Estate	24.10
11.	Promissory Note	24.11
12.	Appointment ending a discretionary trust within two years of death	24.12

1. Basic procedure note

24.1

1. First interview (or incoming letter or telephone call):
    1.1 Obtain thorough instructions from the testator[1]. Record these in writing. In an emergency ensure that an additional witness can be present and ask the testator to execute the instructions as a Will[2].
    1.2 Where appropriate (including where the position is uncertain) deal with Notice of Severance[3].
2. Either:
    2.1 submit draft Will(s) for approval with comments and (where appropriate) Notice of Severance for signature. (See **24.7** and **24.8**.)
    Or
    2.2 (Where 2.1 can be dispensed with and geography so requires) Submit Will(s) for completion with comments and (where appropriate) Notice of Severance.
3. Make a computer or diary note no more than four weeks ahead of submission of draft or signature copy to contact the clients if they have not replied[4].
4. Once final instructions are received submit Will(s) for completion[5].
5. When completed Will(s) is/are received check them carefully, send copies to the client(s) and deal with the original(s) as directed.

1   For a discussion of the so-called 'golden rule' (the steps which a Will draftsman should take to ensure that a testator has capacity) see **2.25**.

2   The Will draftsman will serve as one witness (unless he or she is also a beneficiary). The other witness must be somebody who is not a beneficiary under the Will.
3   See the commentary at **24.8**.
4   The covering letter should, of course, ask the client to respond sooner.
5   In most cases the Will draftsman will feel most comfortable ensuring that he or she has attended personally to supervise the proper execution of the Will. Where the Will is attested without any proper supervision the chances of something going wrong are vastly increased.

2. Will draftsman's Guidance Notes

24.2

1. Concentrate on finding out what the client(s) think he/they need and what, subject to his/their personal wishes, he/they in fact require. This is best done by asking 'open' questions such as 'who ...', 'what ...' and 'how much ...'. It helps to enquire as to whether there is a previous Will and, if possible, to have a copy of it available so that any radical changes of intention can be discussed with the client.
2. On the other hand, remember that many theoretical points may not be relevant to his/their circumstances. Also, the client(s) might well have missed important points which ought to be covered.
3. Back up a meeting or other dealing to prepare for the next, with one-word/line prompts as relevant.
4. Where applicable remember to delve into the peculiarities of non-mainstream assets if this requires work which cannot be done at interview.

3. Will and related matters – checklist

24.3 The following form, which may be sent to the client(s) for completion before a meeting or telephone conversation or be used as a basic checklist during a meeting has been updated. The author is grateful for the assistance of the Institute of Professional Willwriters.

Detail can be dealt with at the meeting or in the advisory/confirmatory letter about the drafted Will which you should normally write.

Every client is different. A checklist is merely the starting point and not the be all and the end all and should not be used as a substitute for proper questioning of the testator at a meeting. A questionnaire might or might not serve as a basis of notes of a meeting.

A   CONTACT AND OTHER PERSONAL DETAILS

Full Name(s):..

Address (including postcode): ....

....

Telephone Numbers (home): ....

(work): ....

(mobile): ....

Other contact details (fax/e-mail): ....

24.3 *Letters and other support materials*

Date of Birth: ....

Occupation/Profession: ....

Marital status (delete as appropriate): Single/Married/Civil Partnership/Co-habiting/Widowed or widower/Divorced/Dissolved Civil Partnership/Separated/Contemplating Marriage or Civil Partnership.

Previous name(s): ....

B   PERSONAL FAMILY AND FINANCIAL BACKGROUND

Have you previously been married/had a Civil Partnership? ....

If so, when did that marriage/Civil Partnership end and is there any ongoing obligation to pay maintenance? Please give details: ....

....

....

If you are a widow, widower or the survivor of civil partners please answer the following questions as accurately as possible:

A   When did your spouse or civil partner die? ....

B   What happened to his or her estate? In particular, did your spouse or civil partner leave any property by Will, on intestacy or to the survivor of property held on a joint tenancy to anyone other than yourself or a charity?

....

....

....

C   If the answer to B is yes, please say how much property (what value) was left to others?

....

Do you have any children? If so please provide details of their names and ages: ....

....

....

....

Are all of your children the children of your relationship with your current spouse/partner? If not please give further details: ....

....

....

....

Are any children maintained by a former spouse/partner? Please give details if appropriate.

....

....

236

Do you have a pension? If so please give details: ....

....

....

Do you have any life assurance policies? Are these written in trust? Please give details:
....

....

Do you own any property (investments and interests in land) outside England and Wales? If so, please provide details: ....

....

Do you have a business or do you farm any land? If so, is this something which could continue after your death? ....

....

Do you own your own home? ....

If you own your own home:

    Do you own it with anyone else? ....

    If it is owned with another, do you know if the house is owned by you as joint tenants or as tenants in common? ....

    What is your house worth (approximately)? ....

    Is there a mortgage? If so, how much is outstanding (approximately)? ....

....

    Are there any policies of life assurance linked to the mortgage? ....

....

What is the approximate value of any other property (land, investments, bank and building accounts and policies) which you own? Please give details if possible. ....

....

C APPOINTMENT OF EXECUTORS/TRUSTEES AND GUARDIANS

EXECUTORS/TRUSTEES

(You should not appoint more than four executors and trustees. The order in which they are appointed is irrelevant to their powers and duties.)

If Married, in a Civil Partnership or other relationship as a couple do you want your spouse/partner to be one of your executors and trustees? ....

Other executors:

Name: ....

Relationship to you: ....

Address: ....

24.3 Letters and other support materials

....

Is this executor to be appointed with your spouse/partner or only if you are the survivor? ....

Name: ....

Relationship to you: ....

Address: ....

....

Is this executor to be appointed with your spouse /partner or only if you are the survivor? ....

Name: ....

Relationship to you: ....

Address: ....

....

Is this executor to be appointed with your spouse/partner or only if you are the survivor? ....

GUARDIANS

If you are responsible for children under the age of 18? Who is to take responsibility for them until they are 18? (Children also includes illegitimate children, adopted children but not step-children unless adopted)

Name: ....

Relationship to you: ....

Address: ....

....

Name: ....

Relationship to you: ....

Address: ....

....

Name: ....

Relationship to you: ....

Address: ....

....

D   FUNERAL WISHES

Would you like to express any particular desires concerning your funeral and the disposal of your body? If you have a pre-paid funeral plan please give details ....

....

E   SPECIFIC GIFTS AND LEGACIES

Are there any specific gifts or sums of money that either client would like to leave?

Name of Beneficiary: ....

Relationship to you: ....

Is this beneficiary under 18 years old? ....

Address: ....

....

Description of Gift/Sum of Money: ....

....

Is this to be free of inheritance tax? (The tax will be met out of residue) ....

Name of Beneficiary: ....

Relationship to you: ....

Is this beneficiary under 18 years old? ....

Address: ....

....

Description of Gift/Sum of Money: ....

....

Is this to be free of inheritance tax? (The tax will be met out of residue) ....

Name of Beneficiary: ....

Relationship to you: ....

Is this beneficiary under 18 years old? ....

Address: ....

....

Description of Gift/Sum of Money: ....

....

Is this to be free of inheritance tax? (The tax will be met out of residue) ....

Name of Beneficiary: ....

Relationship to you: ....

Is this beneficiary under 18 years old? ....

Address: ....

....

Description of Gift/Sum of Money: ....

....

Is this to be free of inheritance tax? (The tax will be met out of residue) ....

24.3 *Letters and other support materials*

F   GIFT OF THE REST OF YOUR ESTATE (YOUR RESIDUARY ESTATE)

If you are single or if you are a couple (married/civil partners etc) what would you like to happen to your estate if you are the first to die? ....

....

....

....

....

....

.... etc.

If you are a couple (married/civil partners etc) what would you like to happen to your estate if you survive your spouse/partner? ....

....

....

.... etc.

G   ANY OTHER POINTS RELEVANT TO YOUR ESTATE OR YOUR WILL

For instance:

i.   any problems which may arise about your Will(s) or in the family generally

ii.   would you like to grant Powers of Attorney so that members of the family or others whom you choose could deal with your affairs in your later years?

iii. an insurance policy on your life or your life and the life of another which would mature on the survivor's death could be written in trust to fund Inheritance Tax (or provide other Inheritance Tax-free money) for your children

....

....

....

.... etc.

H   ANY OTHER PROBLEMS, POSSIBLE PROBLEMS OR UNUSUAL POINTS FOR EXAMPLE, IS THERE SOMEBODY WHO YOU DO NOT WISH TO INCLUDE AS A BENEFICIARY WHO MIGHT CLAIM THAT YOU OUGHT TO MAKE PROVISION FOR THEM?

....

....

....

....

.... etc.

Letters and other support materials **24.4**

I DO YOU OWN PROPERTY OVERSEAS, SUCH AS A TIMESHARE APPARTMENT? IF SO, HAVE YOU TAKEN ADVICE FROM A LOCAL LAWYER?

....

....

.... etc.

4. MATTERS TO BE CONSIDERED AT INTERVIEW AND BEYOND

24.4 Particular points to be investigated at interview are likely to include the following:

1. Are some assets likely to be difficult to realise?

2. Does the estate include business assets? If so, what steps can or should be taken to secure their future?

3. Inheritance tax considerations:

3.1 Is the client married? Have either the client or his/her spouse/civil partner been married before? Is there the potential to draw a will taking advantage of the nil-rate band transfer provisions?

3.2 Have any steps been taken to mitigate inheritance tax such as through the use of life assurance or property related schemes sold by financial advisors? What effect, if any, do these have on the ability of this particular testator to entertain any further inheritance tax planning during his lifetime or through his Will?

3.3 Is Business or Agricultural Relief available? What steps can be taken to ensure that any such relief is utilised?

3.4 Can assets be so rearranged that they come to attract Business Relief?

3.5 What non-exempt gifts have been made to date?

3.6 What lifetime gifts can be made now or in the future? When considering this remember that the client might be able to effect estate planning using a combination of lifetime action and the Will and remember that the rate-tapering provisions only come into play on the excess over the tax free allowance of gifts made in the seven years before death.

3.7 What if any assets are not part of the client's estate but will be aggregable with it for inheritance tax (e.g. interests settled property) and can anything be done about this?

3.8 What use can be made of inheritance tax exemptions or what potentially exempt transfers can be made without attracting capital gains tax or, importantly, leaving the client short of capital? Remember that in many cases there are two clients, a husband and wife, whose inheritance tax planning should be viewed together. Gifts to a spouse (but not a former spouse) are inheritance tax exempt. This gives flexibility in equalising estates.

3.9 If there is property which attracts an inheritance tax relief, such as business or agricultural property is there a way of ensuring that the relief is not wasted, which it will be if the property is used for the benefit of a spouse?

24.4 *Letters and other support materials*

4. Considerations other than those relating to inheritance tax:

4.1 Married and unmarried couples do not invariably have easy or, in this sort of context, well-defined relationships. Clients should be encouraged to discuss the provisions of their Wills and related points fully and frankly.

4.2 Is it possible to make provision, perhaps lifetime provision as well as by Will, for the survivor and children who may not be self-sufficient.

4.3 Where there are two clients, have they considered the effect if both are killed together in an accident?

4.4 Many couples share concern for the survivor being adequately provided for but one or both could be equally anxious about the survivor remarrying and the children being deprived of an inheritance. The only satisfactory theoretical answer to the latter point is to limit the survivor's benefit until remarriage but realistically the draftsman should try to rule out any alternative or additional provision related to co-habitation. Enforcement is impossible and there will be personal problems while the Wills are being made, at any rate if only one of the couple holds that view. Equally, an income and enjoyment entitlement may be inadequate[1]. An interest in residue until death or remarriage will be the answer in the case of larger estates.

1   Failure to make adequate provision may result in a claim under the Inheritance (Provision for Family and Dependants) Act 1975: see **chapter 2**. In the case of the smaller estate the answer may be an interest in the matrimonial home (or its replacement) until death or remarriage and an outright gift of the other (income-producing) assets to the survivor.

Once the client has given instructions, the draftsman's mind should turn to the following:

5.1 Consider the possibilities in the narrative of **chapter 15**.

5.2 Are there relevant documents which may restrict the client's powers over his property? For example, a partnership agreement may include provisions which undermine the intent of the Will. The Articles of a company can have a similar effect. If the client has a significant shareholding, the Articles may permanently affect it. Consider whether those provisions might be amended in a helpful way.

5.3 Are there capital gains tax and income tax consequences of inheritance tax mitigation provisions? These are easily overlooked but can have important consequences.

5.4 Where inheritance tax is likely to be payable do not forget to consider the incidence of the tax. Inheritance tax is payable out of residue unless the Will directs otherwise[1]. Where there are to be substantial legacies draw the client's attention to the prospective amount of residue and the effect of the inheritance tax payable out of it[2], including any effect which this might have on the legacies. Remember *Benham*[3]!

1   Try to avoid creating a situation in which legacies have to be grossed-up.
2   It is best to avoid a direction that each gift is to bear its own inheritance tax and, more particularly, a direction that some gifts are to bear their own inheritance tax while inheritance tax on other gifts are to be borne by residue. This can produce results which the client did not envisage and of a subtlety which his solicitor might miss.
3   *Re Benham's Will Trusts* [1995] STC 210.

5.5 Does the client understand that future legislative changes may ruin a well-devised inheritance tax mitigation plan[1]? This is a fact of life with which both clients and solicitors have to cope but it is important to warn the client of this possibility. Many clients are conscious of this but remind the client that his Will has been drafted on the basis of the law when he makes his Will and his existing or reasonably foreseeable circumstances.

1   So long as it continues to be possible to vary a Will after death for inheritance tax it may be possible to resolve some, but not all, of the problems which legislative changes create.

5.6   After the death of the first of a couple consider the possibility of a variation of the Will.

5.7   Make sure that the client is aware that, apart from possible changes in taxation, changes in family circumstances may require him to review his Will periodically. Not all clients realise that they can review and change their Wills from time to time. A Will is not for life but for death[1].

1   Subject, of course, to any post-death variation.

5.8   Failure to make adequate provision may result in a claim under the Inheritance (Provision for Family and Dependants) Act 1975. Do the client's instructions create that risk? There is not a lot that can be done about that but the client's attention should be drawn to the point whenever appropriate.

5.9   Where a trust is to be created, have the trustees' powers been explained to the client and the reasons for extended powers or exoneration provisions been given?

5.10 If the instructions contemplate settled gifts, take care to guard against the following pitfalls:
–   Draft class gifts with care. Pay attention to the possibility (thrown up by the Gender Recognition Act 2004) that a gift to 'sons' might accidentally include a person who is currently a 'daughter' and vice versa.
–   Remember that a gift which gives the beneficiaries a vested interest will have different consequences from one giving a contingent interest.
–   Consider the notes to **chapter 15** for the significance of the taxation of trusts.
–   Avoid the risk of a partial intestacy where there is a residuary gift to a number of persons in equal shares by substitution or accruer provisions or both.
–   Avoid the effect of Wills Act 1837 s 33 on a gift to a descendant who fails to survive the client if that is not what the client intends.

5. Letter about a Life Interest Trust

24.5   Dear *

After taking advice you have decided to include a gift to [*your spouse*] 'the Life Tenant') on trust for life. The effect of this is that the Life Tenant will be entitled to receive the income produced by the property in which the life interest subsists but will not be entitled to be paid the capital. In order to ensure that the interests of both the Life Tenant and those who take the capital after [*his/her*] death (the remaindermen) are protected it is important that there are trustees who are able to balance both interests. That is best done by appointing at least one professional person to be a trustee and always ensuring that there are at least two trustees.

The trustees will hold the trust property on trust to pay income to the Life Tenant. They also have a power to pay capital to the remaindermen. Doing this will diminish the fund from which income is produced for the Life Tenant and so the Life Tenant has to consent to any such payment. In other respects the trustees are expected to weigh the interests of all parties in the balance before making investments.

24.6 *Letters and other support materials*

Administration of a trust can sometimes be expensive and professional trustees can be expected to charge for their time and services. Annual accounts and tax returns have to be completed and tax has to be paid on trust income. Further, trustees can be expected to take legal, accountancy and investment advice when necessary or appropriate. Whatever advice they receive your trustees still have duties, powers and discretions to follow. However, for the reasons discussed with you, it is desirable that you should make provision for the Life Tenant in this way and the likely expense is justified in order to make the provision which you intend to make.

If you have any further queries about this trust please do not hesitate to ask. We should be pleased to explain the matter further if necessary.

Yours sincerely

6. Letter about a Discretionary Trust

24.6 This letter concerns the creation of a discretionary trust by Will. There will be situations in which a discretionary trust is thought to be a sensible inclusion in a Will even after the introduction of transferable nil-rate bands. However, most Wills for married couples will now leave the whole of the estate of the first to die to the survivor either absolutely or on an immediate post-death interest in possession and so in those cases the inclusion of a discretionary trust will be quite rare.

Dear *

We have advised you to take advantage of the Nil-Rate Band, an amount which you can leave Inheritance Tax-free to your family.

We suggested that the vehicle for this should be a 'Discretionary Trust' which means what it says. The Trustees will hold property on trust to pay income and sometimes capital to the beneficiaries but at their discretion. No beneficiary has any absolute right to receive income or capital or to control the trustees.

Trustees can be expected to take legal, accountancy and investment advice when necessary or appropriate. Whatever advice they receive your trustees still have duties, powers and discretions, particularly in relation to how they dispose of capital and income.

It would be a good idea to write a letter about your wishes for the trust's future to your trustees so that all concerned have guidance as to how capital and income ought to be spent and there is no doubt how you see things. However, such a letter expressing your wishes will not be binding on the trustees. They will be entitled to ignore it and may well be obliged to do so if the circumstances envisaged by you have changed. It is therefore absolutely crucial that you should have the fullest confidence in your trustees.

The relevant tax and general law in this area and therefore the trust provisions themselves are complex. Further, administration can sometimes be expensive. Annual accounts and tax returns have to be completed and tax has to be paid on trust income currently at 42.5% for dividends and 50% for other income over £1,000 in the first place. A repayment claim then has to be made for a beneficiary to whom income is distributed for the difference between that rate and the top rate at which the beneficiary pays tax. Inheritance and capital gains tax might also have to be paid from time to time.

However, the total value of your estates justifies the expense and because the trustees, of whom the survivor of you will be one, have a discretion as to how capital and income are dealt with the flexibility of this arrangement is advantageous. Thus, income could be paid out to your grandchildren to take advantage of their personal allowances for income tax purposes.

The survivor of you can also be among the class of beneficiaries as well as a trustee and the trust can be made up of a variety of different kinds of property although, in the light of HMRC's views on the subject, it would be prudent not to include the half share in your home of the first of you to die in the trust.

Yours sincerely

7. Letter submitting a draft Will and Notice of Severance

24.7   Dear *

Further to [your letter]/[our discussion] we enclose a draft of the Will which we suggest for [Mr A]. It is intended that [Mrs A] will make a similar Will. Some of the clauses should not require further comment. Our brief comments on the other ones are:

For example[1]:

2 & 3   Your [children]/[sons]/[daughters] inherit the Nil-Rate Amount which is currently [£325,000][2]. That is what can be left to them free of Inheritance Tax.

It is a matter for you what capital they have until you are both dead [and each in turn attains 25].

[The executors and trustees of your Will] could let the [children] [sons] [daughters] have a Promissory Note (under *) and in return the entire estate and not just the residue after the Nil Rate Amount could be transferred to [the survivor of you]/[the trustees for the survivor's benefit].]

4.1   The survivor has [an outright entitlement to]/[a life interest in]/[an interest until death or remarriage in] the residue.

4.2   On the survivor's death or remarriage your children share everything equally on attaining 25.

The trustees have powers to make capital and income available to them in the meantime.

5.   Orphaned grandchildren would inherit the share which their deceased parent would have taken.

Again, the executors could make capital and income available for them.

(Any other appropriate specific comments)

*.   The Standard Provisions referred to cover a wide range of administrative provisions, Trustees' powers, other points about the Trustees' position and some technical points. A copy is enclosed and should be kept with your Will if it is not to be retained by us.

We will be pleased to explain the meaning of any particular clauses to you.

We also enclose the Notice which we explained to you which will have the effect that, on the death of one of you, his or her half share in your home will pass by Will and not automatically to the survivor.

24.8 *Letters and other support materials*

[Mr A] should sign the Notice first followed by [Mrs A], both where indicated. You should insert the dates of your signatures.

Please return the signed Notice to us.

Yours truly

[Mr and Mrs A]

1 For commentary on the inheritance tax significance of nil-rate band gifts and gifts contingent on beneficiaries attaining an age such as 25 years see **chapter 15**.
2 This is the current rate and presupposes that no chargeable lifetime gifts are made.

8. Notice of Severance

24.8 Severance of a joint tenancy is discussed in **Chapter 2** at **2.3** to **2.6**. As mentioned there, the most common (and by far the most certain) means of severing a joint tenancy in equity is by means of a notice given by one joint owner to the other. The following is an adequate form for such a notice of severance but it is by no means unique. This form contemplates that one joint tenant will sign and give notice of severance and the other will then sign to acknowledge receipt. The second signature is not necessary to effect a severance (which may be done unilaterally and without the consent of a co-owner) but the presence of both signatures helps to avoid future disputes that may not be predictable at the time.

Ordinarily, in friendly situations, the two joint tenants will be making Wills together and the notice will be explained to both of them and 'given' by one to the other in the presence of the solicitor or will draftsman. There are, however, situations in which the joint tenants are not both making Wills at the same time or where relations are hostile whether or not they are living apart. Where relations between the joint tenants are hostile a joint tenant who wishes to sever might not want to exacerbate an already difficult relationship by giving notice of severance. In the ordinary course of things there is no means of effecting severance in secret; the party who wishes to effect a severance of a beneficial joint tenancy must give notice. They need not do this in person and evidentially personal service by one of the joint tenants is problematic since the survivor might well deny that service took place.

In such situations service is usually effected by post and this is recommended for all cases in which the joint tenants are not present before the solicitor or Will draftsman. The use of ordinary post will not do, however, because if the recipient subsequently denies receipt the severance will not be presumed. The proper course is to send the notice of severance by registered post. If the notice is not returned undelivered it will be deemed to have been served by Law of Property Act 1925 s 196(4) and this is so even where the addressee never sees the notice (even if that is because the sender intercepts it after delivery): *Kinch v Bullard* [1998] 4 All ER 650. A record of the posting should be kept so that disputes about severance do not subsequently arise.

After severance a form RX1 should be submitted to the Land Registry in order to enter a restriction on the title to the property preventing disposal by a sole proprietor. Form RX1 is available from the Land Registry online at www.landregistry.gov.uk. The appropriate restriction is in Form A to Sch 4 to the Land Registration Rules 2003, SI 2003/1417 and is in the following terms: 'No disposition by a sole proprietor of the registered estate (except a trust corporation) under which capital money arises is to be registered unless authorised by an order of the court'.

Letters and other support materials **24.9**

NOTICE OF SEVERANCE OF JOINT TENANCY[1]

To:

*
—

I give you notice to sever the joint tenancy in equity of the property which we have previously owned as joint tenants at law and in equity.

Dated 20[   ]

....

(*one joint owner*)

RECEIVED this Notice on   20[   ]

....

(*the other joint owner*)

1 Only one notice is necessary: Law of Property Act 1925 s 36(2). There is no prescribed form. For a further discussion of severance of a joint tenancy see **Chapter 2** at **2.3** to **2.6**.

9. Letter enclosing Wills for completion

24.9 For commentary on a Will draftsman's duty in relation to attestation see **14.8** to **14.13**. The authorities are slightly inconsistent. At the very least a solicitor is under a duty to take proper care in advising the testator as to the procedure to be followed for the valid execution of his Will and where he is not going to be present at that execution the solicitor is under a duty, when the Will is returned to him after execution, to examine it and consider whether it appears to be properly executed. If it is not then it is his duty to raise the question with his client in order to check that the Will has been properly executed or, if not, to advise him that it should be re-executed.

In *Gray and Ors v Richards Butler (a firm)*[1] Lloyd J found that the solicitor was not put on inquiry by the minor irregularities in attestation apparent on the face of the Will. That latter finding appears to have been made on the solicitor giving evidence to the effect that if he had noticed the irregularity in execution he would have taken comfort from the fact that one of the witnesses was an employee of Coutts & Co and so ought to have known what was required of him. The authors consider that Lloyd J was extremely generous in his assessment. Experience suggests that the strict formal requirements of Wills Act 1837 s 9 are not understood by non-lawyers such as bankers, sub-postmasters and other pillars of the community to whom testators regularly turn in order to have their Wills witnessed. Indeed, if anything, there may be a bias against proper attestation where the testator asks his banker to witness his Will because he may then defer to his banker's ill-informed view of the formalities and pay no regard to his solicitor's carefully phrased instructions.

1 [2000] WTLR 143.

Dear *

Your Wills

We enclose:

1. your [Will]/[Wills] for/each of/you to complete/if you are indeed happy with [it]/[them]. Otherwise please get in touch with us as soon as possible with any queries or to request further information.

24.9 *Letters and other support materials*

You and two witnesses who are over 18 and are not (and are not the husband or wife of) anybody who will or may receive a gift or other benefit under the Will and not professional advisers named as executors or their partners should be present together throughout.

On the last page of the Will:

- date the Will in words in your usual handwriting;
- then sign your usual signature where your initials are pencilled. Do so in the simultaneous presence of both witnesses;
- the witnesses should then sign their usual signatures and (legibly) add their addresses and occupations where indicated.

It is vital that nothing is ever attached to the Will and that no amendments are made to the Will.

Our duty extends to doing what we can to ensure that a Will is properly executed.

EITHER (*non-local clients*)

It is impractical for you to complete your Will(s) here but please ensure that you comply with the necessary formalities.

Then let us have [it]/[them] so that we might check [it]/[them] and either retain photocopies for our records or, if you prefer, make arrangements to store the original(s).

OR (*local clients*)

Therefore it is important that even if you wish to hold the Will(s) yourselves/and do not come here to complete them/, you should let us have sight of them so that we might check [it]/[them] and retain photocopies for our records.

Ideally you should complete your Will(s) here. If however, this is not practical for you please ensure that you comply with the necessary formalities as described above.

Then let us have [it]/[them] so that we might check [it]/[them] and either retain photocopies for our records or, if you prefer, make arrangements to store the original(s).

2. envelope for your use.
3. (*not if Notice has been previously completed*) for each of you to sign where indicated the Notice further to which your half shares in your home will pass under your Wills. Insert the date of your signature in the two places.

Will you or would you like us to hold the Will(s)? If so, we would let you have complete copies.

Tell your Executors where the Will(s) [is]/[are].

(*Where appropriate*) The original Notice should be placed with your Will(s) [but copies should go on the old file relating to your purchase and with the Title documents].

We will deal with this when you return it to us.

Yours faithfully,

10. Will enabling Promissory Note – Procedure after completion of administration of the estate

24.10 Surviving spouse (if outright gift of residue) or trustees of residue give to the beneficiaries under or trustees of the nil-rate band gift a promissory note for the amount otherwise payable under the nil-rate band gift.

Transfers in return (which must be for at least the full amount of the promissory note):

1. Cash or cheque.
2. To avoid complication existing accounts in the executors' names should be used. None should be transferred to the surviving spouse.
3. A property. This transfer will be registrable.
4. A share in a property. It will not be registrable but it may be appropriate for it to be followed by a registrable transfer of the legal estate.
5. Transfers of investments.

11. Promissory Note

24.11   (*Address of surviving spouse or Trustees of residue*)

To: [(*names of nil-rate band beneficiaries*)] [(*executors' names*) (as Executors of YZ Deceased)]

YZ Deceased

[(*surviving spouse's full names*) I SZ]/[(*executors' full names*) as Trustees of YZ's (*date*) Will] promise to pay you:

1. on demand [£   [1]] increased by the percentage by which the latest figure of the All Items Index of Retail Prices published by the Office for National Statistics or its successor available before the date of repayment exceeds that last available before today.
2. interest at the annual rate of 1% payable annually in arrear and taking into account any fluctuations in the debt during the year.

DATED   20[ ]

EITHER

....

SZ

OR

....

....

....

YZ's Executors as Trustees of his Will

1   Insert amount of legacy as provided for the Will.

24.12 *Letters and other support materials*

12. Appointment ending a discretionary trust within two years of death

THIS DEED OF APPOINTMENT is made the   day of [*month*] 20** BY [*names and addresses of Trustees*] ('the Trustees')

Recitals:

1.1   [*Name of testator*] late of [*address*] ('the Testator') died on [*date of death*] having made his last Will dated [*date of Will*] ('the Will')

1.2   By clause [...] of the Will the Testator gave to the Trustees to hold on the discretionary trusts described in that clause.

1.3   [*Name*] is the Widow of the Testator and is one of the persons named as beneficiary of the trusts of clause [...] of the Will.

1.4   The Trustees are the persons appointed trustees of the trusts of clause [...].

1.3   The Trustees desire that the trusts of clause [...] be brought to an end and the whole of the trust property be appointed to the Testator's widow [*Name*] absolutely.

Operative provisions:

2.1   The Trustees in exercise of the power of appointment given to them by clause [...] of the Will and each and every other power them enabling by this Deed appoint the property subject to the trusts of clause [...] of the Will to [*Name*] absolutely.

IN WITNESS whereof the parties hereto have executed these presents as their deed the day and year first above written

SIGNED and DELIVERED etc.

[*As in* **Form 22.2**]

Appendix

PART 1: ATTESTATION, CONSTRUCTION AND INTERPRETATION
WILLS ACT 1837

s 1	Meaning of certain words in this Act	25.1
s 7	No will of a person under age valid	25.2
s 9	Signing and attestation of wills	25.3
s 15	Gifts to an attesting witness, or his or her wife or husband, to be void	25.4
s 18	Wills to be revoked by marriage, except in certain cases	25.5
s 18A	Effect of dissolution or annulment of marriage on wills	25.6
s 18B	Wills to be revoked by civil partnership, except in certain cases	25.7
s 18C	Effect of dissolution or annulment of civil partnership on wills	25.8
s 20	No will to be revoked otherwise than as aforesaid or by another will or codicil, or by destruction thereof	25.9
s 21	No alteration in a will after execution except in certain cases, shall have any effect unless executed as a will	25.10
s 22	No revoked will shall be revived otherwise than by re-execution or a codicil, etc	25.11
s 24	Wills shall be construed, as to the estate comprised, to speak from the death of the testator	25.12
s 29	The words "die without issue", or "die without leaving issue", shall be construed to mean die without issue living at the death	25.13
s 33	Gifts to children or other issue who leave issue living at the testator's death shall not lapse	25.14

LAW OF PROPERTY ACT 1925

s 184	Presumption of survivorship in regard to claims to property	25.15

ADMINISTRATION OF ESTATES ACT 1925

s 35	Charges on property of deceased to be paid primarily out of the property charged	25.16
s 55	Definitions	25.17

WILLS ACT 1968

s 1	Restriction of operation of Wills Act 1837	25.18

ADMINISTRATION OF JUSTICE ACT 1982

s 20	Rectification	25.19
s 21	Interpretation of wills—general rules as to evidence	25.20

MENTAL CAPACITY ACT 2005

s 16	Powers to make decisions and appoint deputies: general	25.21
s 18	Section 16 powers: property and affairs	25.22
Sch 2	Property and affairs: supplementary provisions	25.23

FAMILY LAW REFORM ACT 1987

s 1	General principle	25.24

Appendix

s 19	Dispositions of property	25.25

LEGITIMACY ACT 1976

s 5	Rights of legitimated persons and others to take interests in property	25.26

ADOPTION AND CHILDREN ACT 2002

s 66	Meaning of adoption in Chapter 4	25.27
s 67	Status conferred by adoption	25.28
s 68	Adoptive relatives	25.29
s 69	Rules of interpretation for instruments concerning property	25.30
s 70	Dispositions depending on date of birth	25.31
s 72	Protection of trustees and personal representatives	25.32
s 73	Meaning of disposition	25.33

PART 2: POWERS

TRUSTEE ACT 1925

s 19	Power to insure	26.1
s 31	Power to apply income for maintenance and to accumulate surplus income during a minority	26.2
s 32	Power of advancement	26.3
s 33	Protective trusts	26.4

PERPETUITIES AND ACCUMULATIONS ACT 1964

s 1	Power to specify perpetuity period	26.5

PERPETUITIES AND ACCUMULATIONS ACT 2009

s 1	Application of the rule	26.6
s 5	Perpetuity period	26.7
s 6	Start of perpetuity period	26.8
s 7	Wait and see rule	26.9
s 8	Exclusion of class of members to avoid remoteness	26.10
s 11	Powers of appointment	26.11
s 15	Application of this Act	26.12
s 20	Interpretation	26.13

TRUSTS OF LAND AND APPOINTMENT OF TRUSTEES ACT 1996

s 1	Meaning of "trust of land"	26.14
s 2	Trusts in place of settlements	26.15
s 3	Abolition of doctrine of conversion	26.16
s 4	Express trusts for sale as trusts of land	26.17
s 5	Implied trusts for sale as trusts of land	26.18
s 6	General powers of trustees	26.19
s 7	Partition by trustees	26.20
s 8	Exclusion and restriction of powers	26.21
s 9	Delegation by trustees	26.22
s 9A	Duties of trustees in connection with delegation etc	26.23
s 10	Consents	26.24
s 11	Consultation with beneficiaries	26.25
s 12	The right to occupy	26.26
s 13	Exclusion and restriction of right to occupy	26.27
s 18	Application of part to personal representatives	26.28

SCHEDULES

Sch 1	Provisions consequential on section 2	26.29

TRUSTEE ACT 2000

PART I THE DUTY OF CARE

s 1	The duty of care	26.30
s 2	Application of duty of care	26.31

PART II INVESTMENT

s 3	General power of investment	26.32

s 4	Standard investment criteria	26.33
s 5	Advice	26.34
s 6	Restriction or exclusion of this part etc	26.35

PART III ACQUISITION OF LAND

s 8	Power to acquire freehold and leasehold land	26.36
s 9	Restriction or exclusion of this part etc	26.37

PART IV AGENTS, NOMINEES AND CUSTODIANS

AGENTS

s 11	Power to employ agents	26.38
s 12	Persons who may act as agents	26.39
s 13	Linked functions etc	26.40
s 14	Terms of agency	26.41
s 15	Asset management: special restrictions	26.42

NOMINEES AND CUSTODIANS

s 16	Power to appoint nominees	26.43
s 17	Power to appoint custodians	26.44
s 18	Investment in bearer securities	26.45
s 19	Persons who may be appointed as nominees or custodians	26.46
s 20	Terms of appointment of nominees and custodians	26.47

REVIEW OF AND LIABILITY FOR AGENTS, NOMINEES AND CUSTODIANS ETC

s 21	Application of sections 22 and 23	26.48
s 22	Review of agents, nominees and custodians etc	26.49
s 23	Liability for agents, nominees and custodians etc	26.50

SUPPLEMENTARY

s 24	Effect of trustees exceeding their powers	26.51
s 25	Sole trustees	26.52
s 26	Restriction or exclusion of this part etc	26.53

PART V REMUNERATION

s 28	Trustee's entitlement to payment under trust instrument	26.54
s 29	Remuneration of certain trustees	26.55
s 31	Trustees' expenses	26.56
s 32	Remuneration and expenses of agents, nominees and custodians	26.57

PART VI MISCELLANEOUS AND SUPPLEMENTARY

s 34	Power to insure	26.58
s 35	Personal representatives	26.59
s 39	Interpretation	26.60
SCHEDULE 1 Application of duty of care		26.61

PART 3: INTESTACY RULES

ADMINISTRATION OF ESTATES ACT 1925

s 46	Succession to real and personal estate on intestacy	27.1
s 47	Statutory trusts in favour of issue and other classes of relatives of intestate	27.2
s 47A	Right of surviving spouse to have his own life interest redeemed	27.3

PART 4: INHERITANCE TAX AND CAPITAL GAINS TAX

INHERITANCE TAX ACT 1984

s 8A	Transfer of unused nil-rate band between spouses and civil partners	28.1
s 8B	Claims under section 8A	28.2
s 8C	Section 8A and subsequent charges	28.3

FINANCE ACT 2008

s 10	Sch 4 Inheritance Tax: Transfer of Nil-rate Band etc	28.4

INHERITANCE TAX ACT 1984

s 142	Alteration of dispositions taking effect on death	28.5

Appendix

s 143	Compliance with testator's request	**28.6**
s 144	Distribution etc from property settled by will	**28.7**
Inland Revenue statement of practice 10/79		**28.8**
Inland Revenue press release 6 August 1975		**28.9**
TAXATION OF CHARGEABLE GAINS ACT 1992		
s 62	Death: general provisions	**28.10**

Appendix Part 1: Attestation, construction and interpretation

WILLS ACT 1837 ss 1, 7, 9, 15, 18, 18A (as amended by the Law Reform (Succession) Act 1995 s 3), 24 and 33

1 Meaning of certain words in this Act

25.1 ... the words and expressions herein-after mentioned, which in their ordinary signification have a more confined or a different meaning, shall in this Act, except where the nature of the provision or the context of the Act shall exclude such construction, be interpreted as follows; (that is to say,) the word "will" shall extend to a testament, and to a codicil, and to an appointment by will or by writing in the nature of a will in exercise of a power, [and also to an appointment by will of a guardian of a child], [and also to an appointment by will of a representative under section 4 of the Human Tissue Act 2004,] ... and to any other testamentary disposition; and the words "real estate" shall extend to manors, advowsons, messuages, lands, tithes, rents, and hereditaments, ... whether corporeal, incorporeal, or personal, ... and to any estate, right, or interest (other than a chattel interest) therein; and the words "personal estate" shall extend to leasehold estates and other chattels real, and also to monies, shares of government and other funds, securities for money (not being real estates), debts, choses in action, rights, credits, goods, and all other property whatsoever which by law devolves upon the executor or administrator, and to any share or interest therein; and every word importing the singular number only shall extend and be applied to several persons or things as well as one person or thing; and every word importing the masculine gender only shall extend and be applied to a female as well as a male[1].

1   The words omitted were repealed by the Statute Law Revision Act 1893, the Statute Law (Repeals) Act 1969 and the Trusts of Land and Appointment of Trustees Act 1990 s 25(2), Sch 4 and the words in square brackets were (a) substituted by the Children Act 1989 s 108(5), Sch 13 para 1 and (b) inserted by the Human Tissue Act 2004 s 56, Sch 6 para 1 (with effect from 1 September 2006).

7 No Will of a person under age valid

25.2   ... no will made by any person under the age of [eighteen years] shall be valid[1].

1   Words omitted repealed by the Statute Law Revision (No 2) Act 1888; words in square brackets substituted by the Family Law Reform Act 1969 s 3(1)(a).

25.3 *Appendix Part 1: Attestation, construction and interpretation*

9 Signing and attestation of Wills[1]

25.3 No will shall be valid unless—

(*a*) it is in writing, and signed by the testator, or by some other person in his presence and by his direction; and

(*b*) it appears that the testator intended by his signature to give effect to the Will; and

(*c*) the signature is made or acknowledged by the testator in the presence of two or more witnesses present at the same time; and

(*d*) each witness either—
 (i) attests and signs the Will; or
 (ii) acknowledges his signature,
in the presence of the testator (but not necessarily in the presence of any other witness),

but no form of attestation shall be necessary.

1 This section was substituted by Administration of Justice Act 1982 s 17 with effect from 1 January 1983.

15 Gifts to an attesting witness, or his or her wife or husband, to be void[1]

25.4 ... if any person shall attest the execution of any Will for whom or to whose wife or husband any beneficial devise, legacy, estate, interest, gift, or appointment, of or affecting any real or personal estate (other than and except charges and directions for the payment of any debt or debts), shall be thereby given or made, such devise, legacy, estate, interest, gift, or appointment shall, so far as concerns such person attesting the execution of such Will, or the wife or husband of such person, or any person claiming under such person or wife or husband, be utterly null and void, and such person so attesting shall be admitted as a witness to prove the execution of such Will, or to prove the validity or invalidity thereof, notwithstanding such devise, legacy, estate, interest, gift, or appointment mentioned in such Will[2].

1 See Wills Act 1968 s 1 for exception.
2 Words omitted repealed by the Statute Law Revision (No 2) Act 1888. This section applies in relation to the attestation of a Will by a person to whose civil partner there is given or made any such disposition as is here described as it apples in relation to a person to whose spouse is given or made any such disposition: Civil Partnership Act 2004 s 71, Sch 4 Part 1 para 3; a piece of parliamentary drafting, the incomprehensibility of which matches the Prescription Act 1832.

18 Wills to be revoked by marriage, except in certain cases[1]

25.5 (1) Subject to subsections (2) to (4) below, a Will shall be revoked by the testator's marriage.

(2) A disposition in a Will in exercise of a power of appointment shall take effect notwithstanding the testator's subsequent marriage unless the property so appointed would in default of appointment pass to his personal representatives.

(3) Where it appears from a Will that at the time it was made the testator was expecting to be married to a particular person and that he intended that the Will should not be revoked by the marriage, the Will shall not be revoked by his marriage to that person.

(4) Where it appears from a Will that at the time it was made the testator was expecting to be married to a particular person and that he intended that a disposition in the Will should not be revoked by his marriage to that person—
(a) that disposition shall take effect notwithstanding the marriage; and
(b) any other disposition in the Will shall take effect also, unless it appears from the Will that the testator intended the disposition to be revoked by the marriage.

1   This section was substituted by Administration of Justice Act 1982 s 18(1) with effect from 1 January 1983.

18A Effect of dissolution or annulment of marriage on Wills[1]

25.6 (1) Where, after a testator had made a Will [an order or decree[2]] of a court [of civil jurisdiction in England and Wales] dissolves or annuls his marriage [or his marriage is dissolved or annulled and the divorce or annulment is entitled to recognition in England and Wales by virtue of Part II of the Family Law Act 1986[3]],—
(a) provisions of the Will Appointing executors or trustees or conferring a power of appointment, if they appoint or confer the power on the former spouse, shall take effect as if the former spouse had died on the date on which the marriage is dissolved or annulled, and
(b) any property which, or an interest in which, is devised or bequeathed to the former spouse shall pass as if the former spouse had died on that date, except in so far as a contrary intention appears by the Will.[4]

(2) Subsection (1)(b) above is without prejudice to any right of the former spouse to apply for financial provision under the Inheritance (Provision for Family and Dependants) Act 1975.

1   This section was added by Administration of Justice Act 1982 s 18(2) with effect from 1 January 1983.
2   These words were substituted for 'a decree' by Family Law Act 1996 s 66(1), Sch 8 para 1 to take effect from a date to be appointed.
3   As amended by Family Law Act 1986 s 53.
4   Paras (a) and (b) substituted by Law Reform Succession Act 1995 s 3 and original subsection (3) repealed by s 5 of that Act.

18B Will to be revoked by civil partnership[1]

25.7 (1) Subject to subsections (2) to (6), a will is revoked by the formation of a civil partnership between the testator and another person.

(2) A disposition in a will in exercise of a power of appointment takes effect despite the formation of a subsequent civil partnership between the testator and another person unless the property so appointed would in default of appointment pass to the testator's personal representatives.

(3) If it appears from a will—
(a) that at the time it was made the testator was expecting to form a civil partnership with a particular person, and
(b) that he intended that the will should not be revoked by the formation of the civil partnership,

the will is not revoked by its formation.

25.8 *Appendix Part 1: Attestation, construction and interpretation*

(4) Subsections (5) and (6) apply if it appears from a will—

(*a*) that at the time it was made the testator was expecting to form a civil partnership with a particular person, and

(*b*) that he intended that a disposition in the will should not be revoked by the formation of the civil partnership.

(5) The disposition takes effect despite the formation of the civil partnership.

(6) Any other disposition in the will also takes effect, unless it appears from the will that the testator intended the disposition to be revoked by the formation of the civil partnership.

1   This section was added by Civil Partnership Act 2004 s 71, Sch 4 para 2 with effect from 5 December 2005.

18C Effect of dissolution or annulment of civil partnership on wills[1]

25.8 (1) This section applies if, after a testator has made a will—

(*a*) a court of civil jurisdiction in England and Wales dissolves his civil partnership or makes a nullity order in respect of it, or

(*b*) his civil partnership is dissolved or annulled and the dissolution or annulment is entitled to recognition in England and Wales by virtue of Chapter 3 of Part 5 of the Civil Partnership Act 2004.

(2) Except in so far as a contrary intention appears by the will—

(*a*) provisions of the will appointing executors or trustees or conferring a power of appointment, if they appoint or confer the power on the former civil partner, take effect as if the former civil partner had died on the date on which the civil partnership is dissolved or annulled, and

(*b*) any property which, or an interest in which, is devised or bequeathed to the former civil partner shall pass as if the former civil partner had died on that date.

(3) Subsection (2)(b) does not affect any right of the former civil partner to apply for financial provision under the Inheritance (Provision for Family and Dependants) Act 1975.

1   This section was added by Civil Partnership Act 2004 s 71, Sch 4 para 2 with effect from 5 December 2005.

20 No will to be revoked otherwise than as aforesaid or by another will or codicil, or by destruction thereof

25.9 … no will or codicil, or any part thereof, shall be revoked otherwise than as aforesaid, or by another will or codicil executed in manner herein-before required, or by some writing declaring an intention to revoke the same and executed in the manner in which a will is herein-before required to be executed, or by the burning, tearing, or otherwise destroying the same by the testator, or by some person in his presence and by his direction, with the intention of revoking the same.

21 No alteration in a will after execution except in certain cases, shall have any effect unless executed as a will

25.10 ... no obliteration, interlineation, or other alteration made in any will after the execution thereof shall be valid or have any effect, except so far as the words or effect of the will before such alteration shall not be apparent, unless such alteration shall be executed in like manner as herein-before is required for the execution of the will; but the will, with such alteration as part thereof, shall be deemed to be duly executed if the signature of the testator and the subscription of the witnesses be made in the margin or on some other part of the will opposite or near to such alteration, or at the foot or end of or opposite to a memorandum referring to such alteration, and written at the end or some other part of the will.

22 No revoked will shall be revived otherwise than by re-execution or a codicil, etc

25.11 ... no will or codicil, or any part thereof, which shall be in any manner revoked, shall be revived otherwise than by the re-execution thereof or by a codicil executed in manner herein-before required and showing an intention to revive the same; and when any will or codicil which shall be partly revoked, and afterwards wholly revoked, shall be revived, such revival shall not extend to so much thereof as shall have been revoked before the revocation of the whole thereof, unless an intention to the contrary shall be shown.

24 Wills shall be construed, as to the estate comprised, to speak from the death of the testator

25.12 ... every Will shall be construed, with reference to the real estate and personal estate comprised in it, to speak and take effect as if it had been executed immediately before the death of the testator, unless a contrary intention shall appear by the Will[1].

1   Words omitted repealed by the Statute Law Revision (No 2) Act 1888.

29 The words "die without issue", or "die without leaving issue", shall be construed to mean die without issue living at the death

25.13 ... in any devise or bequest of real or personal estate the words "die without issue," or "die without leaving issue," or "have no issue," or any other words which may import either a want or failure of issue of any person in his lifetime or at the time of his death, or an indefinite failure of his issue, shall be construed to mean a want or failure of issue in the lifetime or at the time of the death of such person, and not an indefinite failure of his issue, unless a contrary intention shall appear by the will, by reason of such person having a prior estate tail, or of a preceding gift, being, without any implication arising from such words, a limitation of an estate tail to such person or issue, or otherwise: Provided, that this Act shall not extend to cases where such words as aforesaid import if no issue described in a preceding gift shall be born, or if there shall be no issue who shall live to attain the age or otherwise answer the description required for obtaining a vested estate by a preceding gift to such issue.

33 Gifts to children or other issue who leave issue living at the testator's death shall not lapse[1]

25.14 (1) Where—
(a) a Will contains a devise or bequest to a child or remoter descendant of the testator; and
(b) the intended beneficiary dies before the testator, leaving issue; and
(c) issue of the intended beneficiary are living at the testator's death,

then, unless a contrary intention appears by the Will, the devise or bequest shall take effect as a devise or bequest to the issue living at the testator's death.

(2) Where—
(a) a Will contains a devise or bequest to a class of person consisting of children or remoter descendants of the testator; and
(b) a member of the class dies before the testator, leaving issue; and
(c) issue of that member are living at the testator's death,

then, unless a contrary intention appears by the Will, the devise or bequest shall take effect as if the class included the issue of its deceased member living at the testator's death.

(3) Issue shall take under this section through all degrees, according to their stock, in equal shares if more than one, any gift or share which their parent would have taken and so that no issue shall take whose parent is living at the testator's death and that no issue shall take whose parent is living at the testator's death and so capable of taking.

(4) For the purposes of this section—
(a) the illegitimacy of any person is to be disregarded; and
(b) a person conceived before the testator's death and born living thereafter is to be taken to have been living at the testator's death.

1 This section was substituted by Administration of Justice Act 1982 s 19 with effect from 1 January 1983.

LAW OF PROPERTY ACT 1925 s 184

184 Presumption of survivorship in regard to claims to property

25.15 In all cases where, after the commencement of this Act, two or more persons have died in circumstances rendering it uncertain which of them survived the other or others, such deaths shall (subject to any order of the court), for all purposes affecting the title to property, be presumed to have occurred in order of seniority, and accordingly the younger shall be deemed to have survived the elder.

ADMINISTRATION OF ESTATES ACT 1925 ss 35 and 55

35 Charges on property of deceased to be paid primarily out of the property charged

25.16 (1) Where a person dies possessed of, or entitled to, or, under a general power of appointment (including the statutory power to dispose of entailed interests) by his will disposes of, an interest in property, which at the time of his death is charged with the payment of money, whether by way of legal mortgage, equitable charge or otherwise (including a lien for unpaid purchase money), and the deceased has not by will deed or other document signified a contrary or other intention, the interest so charged, shall as between the different persons claiming through the deceased, be primarily liable for the payment of the charge; and every part of the said interest, according to its value, shall bear a proportionate part of the charge on the whole thereof.

(2) Such contrary or other intention shall not be deemed to be signified—
(a) by a general direction for the payment of debts or of all the debts of the testator out of his personal estate, or his residuary real and personal estate, or his residuary real estate; or
(b) by a charge of debts upon any such estate;

unless such intention is further signified by words expressly or by necessary implication referring to all or some part of the charge.

(3) Nothing in this section affects the right of a person entitled to the charge to obtain payment or satisfaction thereof either out of the other assets of the deceased or otherwise.

55 DEFINITIONS

25.17 In this Act, unless the context otherwise requires, the following expressions have the meanings hereby assigned to them respectively, that is to say—

(1)—
(i) "Administration" means, with reference to the real and personal estate of a deceased person, letters of administration whether general or limited, or with the will annexed or otherwise;
(ii) "Administrator" means a person to whom administration is granted;
(iii) "Conveyance" includes a mortgage, charge by way of legal mortgage, lease, assent, vesting, declaration, vesting instrument, disclaimer, release and every other assurance of property or of an interest therein by any instrument, except a will, and convey has a corresponding meaning, and disposition includes a conveyance also a devise bequest and an appointment of property contained in a will, and dispose of has a corresponding meaning;
[(iiiA) "the County Court limit", in relation to any enactment contained in this Act, means the amount for the time being specified by an Order in Council under section 145 of the County Courts Act 1984 as the county court limit for the purposes of that enactment (or, where no such Order in Council has been made, the corresponding limit specified by Order in Council under section 192 of the County Courts Act 1959);[1]]
(iv) "the Court" means the High Court and also the county court, where that court has jurisdiction ...[2];
(v) "Income" includes rents and profits;
(vi) "Intestate" includes a person who leaves a will but dies intestate as to some beneficial interest in his real or personal estate;
[(via) "Land" has the same meaning as in the Law of Property Act 1925;[3]]
(vii) "Legal estates" mean the estates charges and interests in or over land (subsisting or created at law) which are by statute authorised to subsist or to be created at law; and equitable interests mean all other interests and charges in or over land ...[4];

25.17 *Appendix Part 1: Attestation, construction and interpretation*

(viii) ...[5];

(ix) "Pecuniary legacy" includes an annuity, a general legacy, a demonstrative legacy so far as it is not discharged out of the designated property, and any other general direction by a testator for the payment of money, including all death duties free from which any devise, bequest, or payment is made to take effect;

(x) "Personal chattels" mean carriages, horses, stable furniture and effects (not used for business purposes), motor cars and accessories (not used for business purposes), garden effects, domestic animals, plate, plated articles, linen, china, glass, books, pictures, prints, furniture, jewellery, articles of household or personal use or ornament, musical and scientific instruments and apparatus, wines, liquors and consumable stores, but do not include any chattels used at the death of the intestate for business purposes nor money or securities for money;

(xi) "Personal representative" means the executor, original or by representation, or administrator for the time being of a deceased person, and as regards any liability for the payment of death duties includes any person who takes possession of or intermeddles with the property of a deceased person without the authority of the personal representatives or the court, and executor includes a person deemed to be appointed executor as respects settled land;

(xii) "Possession" includes the receipt of rents and profits or the right to receive the same, if any;

(xiii) "Prescribed" means prescribed by rules of court ...[6];

(xiv) "Probate" means the probate of a will;

(xv) ...[7]

(xvi) ...[8]

(xvii) "Property" includes a thing in action and any interest in real or personal property;

(xviii) "Purchaser" means a lessee, mortgagee, or other person who in good faith acquires an interest in property for valuable consideration, also an intending purchaser and valuable consideration includes marriage [and formation of a civil partnership[9]], but does not include a nominal consideration in money;

(xix) "Real estate" save as provided in Part IV of this Act means real estate, including chattels real, which by virtue of Part I of this Act devolves on the personal representative of a deceased person;

(xx) "Representation" means the probate of a will and administration, and the expression taking out representation refers to the obtaining of the probate of a will or of the grant of administration;

(xxi) "Rent" includes a rent service or a rentcharge, or other rent, toll, duty, or annual or periodical payment in money or moneys worth, issuing out of or charged upon land, but does not include mortgage interest; and rentcharge includes a fee farm rent;

(xxii) ...[10]

(xxiii) "Securities" include stocks, funds, or shares;

(xxiv) "Tenant for life", "statutory owner", ...[10] "settled land", "settlement", "trustees of the settlement", "term of years absolute", "death duties", and "legal mortgage", have the same meanings as in the Settled Land Act 1925, and "entailed interest" and "charge by way of legal mortgage" have the same meanings as in the Law of Property Act 1925;

(xxv) "Treasury solicitor" means the solicitor for the affairs of His Majesty's Treasury, and includes the solicitor for the affairs of the Duchy of Lancaster;

(xxvi) ..."Trust corporation" means the public trustee or a corporation either appointed by the court in any particular case to be a trustee or entitled by

Appendix Part 1: Attestation, construction and interpretation **25.19**

rules made under subsection (3) of section four of the Public Trustee Act 1906, to act as custodian trustee;

(xxvii) …[11]

(xxviii) "Will" includes codicil.

(2) References to a child or issue living at the death of any person include child or issue en ventre sa mère at the death.

(3) References to the estate of a deceased person include property over which the deceased exercises a general power of appointment (including the statutory power to dispose of entailed interests) by his will.

1 Inserted by County Courts Act 1984 s 148(1), Sch 2 Part III para 15.
2 Word omitted repealed by Courts Act 1971 s 56(4), Sch 11 Part II.
3 Inserted by Trusts of Land and Appointment of Trustees Act 1996 s 25(1), Sch 3 para 6(5).
4 Words omitted repealed by Trusts of Land and Appointment of Trustees Act 1996 s 25(2), Sch 4.
5 Whole of (viii) repealed by Mental Capacity Act 2005 s 67(1), Sch 6 para 5 from 1 October 2007.
6 Words omitted repealed by Supreme Court Act 1981 s 152(4), Sch 7.
7 Repealed by Law of Property (Miscellaneous Provisions) Act 1994 s 21(2), Sch 2.
8 Repealed by Supreme Court Act 1981 s 152(4), Sch 7.
9 Words in square brackets inserted by Civil Partnership Act 2004 s 71, Sch 4 Part 2 para 12 with effect from 5 December 2005.
10 Repealed by Supreme Court Act 1981 s 152(4), Sch 7.
10 Words omitted repealed by Trusts of Land and Appointment of Trustees Act 1996 s 25(2), Sch 4.
11 Repealed by Trusts of Land and Appointment of Trustees Act 1996 s 25(2), Sch 4.

WILLS ACT 1968 s 1

1. Restriction of operation of Wills Act 1837 s 15

25.18 (1) For the purposes of section 15 of the Wills Act 1837 (avoidance of gifts to attesting witnesses and their spouses) the attestation of a Will by a person to whom or to whose spouse there is given or made any such disposition as is described in that section shall be disregarded if the Will is duly executed without his attestation and without that of any other such person.

(2) This section applies to the Will of any person dying after the passing of this Act, whether executed before or after the passing of this Act[1].

1 This section applies in relation to the attestation of a Will by a person to whose civil partner there is given or made any such disposition as is here described as it apples in relation to a person to whose spouse is given or made any such disposition: Civil Partnership Act 2004 s 71, Sch 4 Part 1 para 3; a piece of parliamentary drafting, the incomprehensibility of which matches the Prescription Act 1832.

ADMINISTRATION OF JUSTICE ACT 1982 ss 20 and 21

20 Rectification

25.19 (1) If a court is satisfied that a Will is so expressed that it fails to carry out the testator's intentions, in consequence—

(a) of a clerical error; or

(b) of a failure to understand his instructions,

25.20 *Appendix Part 1: Attestation, construction and interpretation*

it may order that the Will shall be rectified so as to carry out his intentions.

(2) An application for an order under this section shall not, except with the permission of the court, be made after the end of the period of six months from the date on which representation with respect to the estate of the deceased is first taken out.

(3) The provisions of this section shall not render the personal representatives of a deceased person liable for having distributed any part of the estate of the deceased, after the end of the period of six months from the date on which representation with respect to the estate of the deceased is first taken out, on the ground that they ought to have taken into account the possibility that the court might permit the making of an application for an order under this section after the end of that period; but this subsection shall not prejudice any power to recover, by reason of the making of an order under this section, any part of the estate so distributed.

(4) In considering for the purposes of this section when representation with respect to the estate of a deceased person was first taken out, a grant limited to settled land or to trust property shall be left out of account, and a grant limited to real estate or to personal estate shall be left out of account unless a grant limited to the remainder of the estate has previously been made or is made at the same time.

21 Interpretation of wills—general rules as to evidence

25.20 (1) This section applies to a Will—
(a) in so far as any part of it is meaningless;
(b) in so far as the language used in any part of it is ambiguous on the face of it;
(c) in so far as evidence, other than evidence of the testator's intention, shows that the language used in any part of it is ambiguous in the light of surrounding circumstances.

(2) In so far as this section applies to a will extrinsic evidence, including evidence of the testator's intention, may be admitted to assist in its interpretation.

MENTAL CAPACITY ACT 2005, ss 16, 18 and sch 2 paras 1 to 4

16 Powers to make decisions and appoint deputies: general

25.21 (1) This section applies if a person ("P") lacks capacity in relation to a matter or matters concerning—
...
(b) P's property and affairs.

(2) The court may—
(a) by making an order, make the decision or decisions on P's behalf in relation to the matter or matters, or
(b) appoint a person (a "deputy") to make decisions on P's behalf in relation to the matter or matters.

(3) The powers of the court under this section are subject to the provisions of this Act and, in particular, to sections 1 (the principles) and 4 (best interests).

...

18 Section 16 powers: property and affairs

25.22 (1) The powers under section 16 as respects P's property and affairs extend in particular to—

...

(j) the execution for P of a will;

...

(2) No will may be made under subsection (1)(i) at a time when P has not reached 18.

...

(4) Schedule 2 supplements the provisions of this section.

SCHEDULE 2
PROPERTY AND AFFAIRS: SUPPLEMENTARY PROVISIONS

Wills: general

25.23

1

Paragraphs 2 to 4 apply in relation to the execution of a will, by virtue of section 18, on behalf of P

Provision that may be made in will

2

The will may make any provision (whether by disposing of property or exercising a power or otherwise) which could be made by a will executed by P if he had capacity to make it.

Wills: requirements relating to execution

3

(1) Sub-paragraph (2) applies if under section 16 the court makes an order or gives directions requiring or authorising a person ("the authorised person") to execute a will on behalf of P.

(2) Any will executed in pursuance of the order or direction—
(a) must state that it is signed by P acting by the authorised person,
(b) must be signed by the authorised person with the name of P and his own name, in the presence of two or more witnesses present at the same time,
(c) must be attested and subscribed by those witnesses in the presence of the authorised person, and
(d) must be sealed with the official seal of the court.

Wills: effect of execution

4

(1) This paragraph applies where a will is executed in accordance with paragraph 3.

25.24 *Appendix Part 1: Attestation, construction and interpretation*

(2) The Wills Act 1837 has effect in relation to the will as if it were signed by P by his own hand, except that—

(a) section 9 of the 1837 Act (requirements as to signing and attestation) does not apply, and

(b) in the subsequent provisions of the 1837 Act any reference to execution in the manner required by the previous provisions is to be read as a reference to execution in accordance with paragraph 3.

(3) The will has the same effect for all purposes as if—

(a) P had had the capacity to make a valid will, and

(b) the will had been executed by him in the manner required by the 1837 Act.

(4) But sub-paragraph (3) does not have effect in relation to the will—

(a) in so far as it disposes of immovable property outside England and Wales, or

(b) in so far as it relates to any other property or matter if, when the will is executed—

(i) P is domiciled outside England and Wales, and

(ii) the condition in sub-paragraph (5) is met.

(5) The condition is that, under the law of P's domicile, any question of his testamentary capacity would fall to be determined in accordance with the law of a place outside England and Wales.

FAMILY LAW REFORM ACT 1987 ss 1 and 19

Part I
General Principle

1. General principle

25.24 (1) In this Act and enactments passed and instruments made after the coming into force of this section, references (however expressed) to any relationship between two persons shall, unless the contrary intention appears, be construed without regard to whether or not the father and mother of either of them, or the father and mother of any person through whom the relationship is deduced, have or had been married to each other at any time.

(2) In this Act and enactments passed after the coming into force of this section, unless the contrary intention appears—

(a) references to a person whose father and mother were married to each other at the time of his birth include; and

(b) references to a person whose father and mother were not married to each other at the time of his birth do not include, references to any person to whom subsection (3) below applies, and cognate references shall be construed accordingly.

(3) This subsection applies to any person who—

(a) is treated as legitimate by virtue of section 1 of the Legitimacy Act 1976;

(b) is a legitimated person within the meaning of section 10 of that Act;

Appendix Part 1: Attestation, construction and interpretation **25.25**

[(ba) has a parent by virtue of section 42 of the Human Fertilisation and Embryology Act 2008 (which relates to treatment provided to a woman who is at the time of treatment a party to a civil partnership or, in certain circumstances, a void civil partnership);
(bb) has a parent by virtue of section 43 of that Act (which relates to treatment provided to woman who agrees that second woman to be parent) who—
(i) is the civil partner of the child's mother at the time of the child's birth, or
(ii) was the civil partner of the child's mother at any time during the period beginning with the time mentioned in section 43(b) of that Act and ending with the child's birth;][1]
[(c) is an adopted person within the meaning of Chapter 4 of Part 1 of the Adoption of Children Act 2002]; or
(d) is otherwise treated in law as legitimate.

(4) For the purpose of construing references falling within subsection (2) above, the time of a person's birth shall be taken to include any time during the period beginning with—
(a) the insemination resulting in his birth; or
(b) where there was no such insemination, his conception,

and (in either case) ending with his birth.

[(5) A child whose parents are parties to a void civil partnership shall, subject to subsection (6), be treated as falling within subsection (3)(bb) if at the time when the parties registered as civil partners of each other both or either of the parties reasonably believed that the civil partnership was valid.

(6) Subsection (5) applies only where the woman who is a parent by virtue of section 43 was domiciled in England and Wales at the time of the birth or, if she died before the birth, was so domiciled immediately before her death.

(7) Subsection (5) applies even though the belief that the civil partnership was valid was due to a mistake as to law.

(8) It shall be presumed for the purposes of subsection (5), unless the contrary is shown, that one of the parties to a void civil partnership reasonably believed at the time of the formation of the civil partnership that the civil partnership was valid.][1]

1   Inserted by Human Fertilisation and Embryology Act 2008 ss 56, 139 and Sch 6 Pt 1 paras 24(1) to (3).

19 Dispositions of property

25.25   (1)   In the following dispositions, namely—
(a) dispositions inter vivos made on or after the date on which this section comes into force; and
(b) dispositions by will or codicil where the will or codicil is made on or after that date,

references (whether express or implied) to any relationship between two persons shall be construed in accordance with section 1 above.

(2) It is hereby declared that the use, without more, of the word "heir" or "heirs" or any expression [purporting to create] an entailed interest in real or personal property does not show a contrary intention for the purposes of section 1 as applied by subsection (1) above.

25.26 *Appendix Part 1: Attestation, construction and interpretation*

(3) In relation to the dispositions mentioned in subsection (1) above, section 33 of the Trustee Act 1925 (which specifies the trust implied by a direction that income is to be held on protective trusts for the benefit of any person) shall have effect as if any reference (however expressed) to any relationship between two persons were construed in accordance with section 1 above.

(4) Where under any disposition of real or personal property, any interest in such property is limited (whether subject to any preceding limitation or charge or not) in such a way that it would, apart from this section, devolve (as nearly as the law permits) along with a dignity or title of honour, then—
 (a) whether or not the disposition contains an express reference to the dignity or title of honour; and
 (b) whether or not the property or some interest in the property may in some event become severed from it,

nothing in this section shall operate to sever the property or any interest in it from the dignity or title, but the property or interest shall devolve in all respects as if this section had not been enacted.

(5) This section is without prejudice to section 42 of the Adoption Act 1976 [or section 69 of the Adoption and Children Act 2002] (construction of dispositions in cases of adoption).

(6) In this section "disposition" means a disposition, including an oral disposition, of real or personal property whether inter vivos or by will or codicil.

(7) notwithstanding any rule of law, a disposition made by will or codicil executed before the date on which this section comes into force shall not be treated for the purposes of this section as made on or after that date by reason only that the will or codicil is confirmed by a codicil executed on or after that date.

Legitimacy Act 1976 s 5

5 Rights of legitimated persons and others to take interests in property

25.26 (1) Subject to any contrary indication, the rules of construction contained in this section apply to any instrument other than an existing instrument, so far as the instrument contains a disposition of property.

(2) For the purposes of this section, provisions of the law of intestate succession applicable to the estate of a deceased person shall be treated as if contained in an instrument executed by him (while of full capacity) immediately before his death.

(3) A legitimated person, and any other person, shall be entitled to take any interest as if the legitimated person had been born legitimate.

(4) A disposition which depends on the date of birth of a child or children of the parent or parents shall be construed as if—
 (a) a legitimated child had been born on the date of legitimation,
 (b) two or more legitimated children legitimated on the same date had been born on that date in the order of their actual births,

but this does not affect any reference to the age of a child.

(5) Examples of phrases in wills on which subsection (4) above can operate are—

Appendix Part 1: Attestation, construction and interpretation **25.27**

1. Children of A "living at my death or born afterwards".

2. Children of A "living at my death or born afterwards before any one of such children for the time being in existence attains a vested interest, and who attain the age of 21 years".

3. As in example 1 or 2, but referring to grandchildren of A, instead of children of A.

4. A for life "until he has a child" and then to his child or children.

Note. Subsection (4) above will not affect the reference to the age of 21 years in example 2.

(6) If an illegitimate person or a person adopted by one of his natural parents dies, or has died before the commencement of this Act, and—

(a) after his death his parents marry or have married; and

(b) the deceased would, if living at the time of the marriage, have become a legitimated person,

this section shall apply for the construction of the instrument so far as it relates to the taking of interests by, or in succession to, his spouse, children and remoter issue as if he had been legitimated by virtue of the marriage.

(7) In this section "instrument" includes a private Act settling property, but not any other enactment.

ADOPTION AND CHILDREN ACT 2002 ss 66 to 73

Status of Adopted Children

66 Meaning of adoption in Chapter 4

25.27 (1) In this Chapter "adoption" means—

(a) adoption by an adoption order or a Scottish or Northern Irish adoption order,

(b) adoption by an order made in the Isle of Man or any of the Channel Islands,

(c) an adoption effected under the law of a Convention country outside the British Islands, and certified in pursuance of Article 23(1) of the Convention (referred to in this Act as a "Convention adoption"),

(d) an overseas adoption, or

(e) an adoption recognised by the law of England and Wales and effected under the law of any other country;

and related expressions are to be interpreted accordingly.

(2) But references in this Chapter to adoption do not include an adoption effected before the day on which this Chapter comes into force (referred to in this Chapter as "the appointed day").

(3) Any reference in an enactment to an adopted person within the meaning of this Chapter includes a reference to an adopted child within the meaning of Part 4 of the Adoption Act 1976 (c 36).

67 Status conferred by adoption

25.28 (1) An adopted person is to be treated in law as if born as the child of the adopters or adopter.

(2) An adopted person is the legitimate child of the adopters or adopter and, if adopted by—

(a) a couple, or

(b) one of a couple under section 51(2),

is to be treated as the child of the relationship of the couple in question.

(3) An adopted person—
(a) if adopted by one of a couple under section 51(2), is to be treated in law as not being the child of any person other than the adopter and the other one of the couple, and
(b) in any other case, is to be treated in law, subject to subsection (4), as not being the child of any person other than the adopters or adopter;

but this subsection does not affect any reference in this Act to a person's natural parent or to any other natural relationship.

(4) In the case of a person adopted by one of the person's natural parents as sole adoptive parent, subsection (3)(b) has no effect as respects entitlement to property depending on relationship to that parent, or as respects anything else depending on that relationship.

(5) This section has effect from the date of the adoption.

(6) Subject to the provisions of this Chapter and Schedule 4, this section—
(a) applies for the interpretation of enactments or instruments passed or made before as well as after the adoption, and so applies subject to any contrary indication, and
(b) has effect as respects things done, or events occurring, on or after the adoption.

68 Adoptive relatives

25.29 (1) A relationship existing by virtue of section 67 may be referred to as an adoptive relationship, and—

(a) an adopter may be referred to as an adoptive parent or (as the case may be) as an adoptive father or adoptive mother,

(b) any other relative of any degree under an adoptive relationship may be referred to as an adoptive relative of that degree.

(2) Subsection (1) does not affect the interpretation of any reference, not qualified by the word "adoptive", to a relationship.

(3) A reference (however expressed) to the adoptive mother and father of a child adopted by—
(a) a couple of the same sex, or
(b) a partner of the child's parent, where the couple are of the same sex,

is to be read as a reference to the child's adoptive parents.

69 Rules of interpretation for instruments concerning property

25.30 (1) The rules of interpretation contained in this section apply (subject to any contrary indication and to Schedule 4) to any instrument so far as it contains a disposition of property.

(2) In applying section 67(1) and (2) to a disposition which depends on the date of birth of a child or children of the adoptive parent or parents, the disposition is to be interpreted as if—
(a) the adopted person had been born on the date of adoption,
(b) two or more people adopted on the same date had been born on that date in the order of their actual births;

but this does not affect any reference to a person's age.

(3) Examples of phrases in wills on which subsection (2) can operate are—
1 Children of A "living at my death or born afterwards".
2 Children of A "living at my death or born afterwards before any one of such children for the time being in existence attains a vested interest and who attain the age of 21 years".
3 As in example 1 or 2, but referring to grandchildren of A instead of children of A.
4 A for life "until he has a child", and then to his child or children.

Note Subsection (2) will not affect the reference to the age of 21 years in example 2.

(4) Section 67(3) does not prejudice—
(a) any qualifying interest, or
(b) any interest expectant (whether immediately or not) upon a qualifying interest.
"Qualifying interest" means an interest vested in possession in the adopted person before the adoption.

(5) Where it is necessary to determine for the purposes of a disposition of property effected by an instrument whether a woman can have a child—
(a) it must be presumed that once a woman has attained the age of 55 years she will not adopt a person after execution of the instrument, and
(b) if she does so, then (in spite of section 67) that person is not to be treated as her child or (if she does so as one of a couple) as the child of the other one of the couple for the purposes of the instrument.

(6) In this section, "instrument" includes a private Act settling property, but not any other enactment.

70 Dispositions depending on date of birth

25.31 (1) Where a disposition depends on the date of birth of a person who was born illegitimate and who is adopted by one of the natural parents as sole adoptive parent, section 69(2) does not affect entitlement by virtue of Part 3 of the Family Law Reform Act 1987 (dispositions of property).

(2) Subsection (1) applies for example where—
(a) a testator dies in 2001 bequeathing a legacy to his eldest grandchild living at a specified time,
(b) his unmarried daughter has a child in 2002 who is the first grandchild,
(c) his married son has a child in 2003,

(d) subsequently his unmarried daughter adopts her child as sole adoptive parent.

In that example the status of the daughter's child as the eldest grandchild of the testator is not affected by the events described in paragraphs (c) and (d).

72 Protection of trustees and personal representatives

25.32 (1) A trustee or personal representative is not under a duty, by virtue of the law relating to trusts or the administration of estates, to enquire, before conveying or distributing any property, whether any adoption has been effected or revoked if that fact could affect entitlement to the property.

(2) A trustee or personal representative is not liable to any person by reason of a conveyance or distribution of the property made without regard to any such fact if he has not received notice of the fact before the conveyance or distribution.

(3) This section does not prejudice the right of a person to follow the property, or any property representing it, into the hands of another person, other than a purchaser, who has received it.

73 Meaning of disposition

25.33 (1) This section applies for the purposes of this Chapter.

(2) A disposition includes the conferring of a power of appointment and any other disposition of an interest in or right over property; and in this subsection a power of appointment includes any discretionary power to transfer a beneficial interest in property without the furnishing of valuable consideration.

(3) This Chapter applies to an oral disposition as if contained in an instrument made when the disposition was made.

(4) The date of death of a testator is the date at which a will or codicil is to be regarded as made.

(5) The provisions of the law of intestate succession applicable to the estate of a deceased person are to be treated as if contained in an instrument executed by him (while of full capacity) immediately before his death.

Appendix Part 2: Powers

TRUSTEE ACT 1925 (as amended) ss 19, 31 and 32

19 Power to insure[1]

26.1 (1) A trustee may—
(a) insure any property which is subject to the trust against risks of loss or damage due to any event, and
(b) pay the premiums out of the trust funds.

(2) In the case of property held on a bare trust, the power to insure is subject to any direction given by the beneficiary or each of the beneficiaries—
(a) that any property specified in the direction is not to be insured,
(b) that any property specified in the direction is not to be insured except on such conditions as may be so specified.

(3) Property is held on a bare trust if it is held on trust for—
(a) a beneficiary who is of full age and capacity and absolutely entitled to the property subject to the trust, or
(b) beneficiaries each of whom is of full age and capacity and who (taken together) are absolutely entitled to the property subject to the trust.

(4) If a direction under subsection (2) of this section is given, the power to insure, so far as it is subject to the direction, ceases to be a delegable function for the purposes of section 11 of the Trustee Act 2000 (power to employ agents).

(5) In this section "trust funds" means any income or capital funds of the trust.

1 This section was substituted by Trustee Act 2000 s 34(1) with effect from 1 February 2001.

31 Power to apply income for maintenance and to accumulate surplus income during a minority

26.2 (1) Where any property is held by trustees in trust for any person for any interest whatsoever, whether vested or contingent, then, subject to any prior interests or charges affecting that property—
(i) during the infancy of any such person, if his interest so long continues, the trustees may, at their sole discretion, pay to his parent or guardian, if any, or otherwise apply for or towards his maintenance, education, or benefit, the

26.2 Appendix Part 2: Powers

whole or such part, if any, of the income of that property as may, in all the circumstances, be reasonable, whether or not there is—

(a) any other fund applicable to the same purpose, or

(b) any person bound by law to provide for his maintenance or education, and

(ii) if such person on attaining the age of [eighteen years[1]] has not a vested interest in such income, the trustees shall thenceforth pay the income of that property and of any accretion thereto under subsection (2) of this section to him, until he either attains a vested interest therein or dies, or until failure of his interest:

Provided that, in deciding whether the whole or any part of the income of the property is during a minority to be paid or applied for the purposes aforesaid, the trustees shall have regard to the age of the infant and his requirements and generally to the circumstances of the case, and in particular to what other income, if any, is applicable for the same purposes; and where trustees have notice that the income of more than one fund is applicable for those purposes, then, so far as practicable, unless the entire income of the funds is paid or applied as aforesaid or the court otherwise directs, a proportionate part only of the income of each fund shall be so paid or applied.

(2) During the infancy of any such person, if his interest so long continues, the trustees shall accumulate all the residue of that income [by investing it, and any profits from so investing it[2]] from time to time in authorised investments, and shall hold those accumulations as follows:—

(i) If any such person—

(a) attains the age of [eighteen years[1]], or marries under that age [or forms a civil partnership under that age[3]], and his interest in such income during his infancy[, or until his marriage or his formation of a civil partnership,[4]] is a vested interest; or

(b) on attaining the age of [eighteen years[1]] or on marriage[, or formation of a civil partnership,[5]] under that age becomes entitled to the property from which such income arose in fee simple, absolute or determinable, or absolutely, or for an entailed interest;

the trustees shall hold the accumulations in trust for such person absolutely, but without prejudice to any provision with respect thereto contained in any settlement by him made under any statutory powers during his infancy, and so that the receipt of such person after marriage [or formation of a civil partnership[6]], and though still an infant, shall be a good discharge; and

(ii) In any other case the trustees shall, notwithstanding that such person had a vested interest in such income, hold the accumulations as an accretion to the capital of the property from which such accumulations arose, and as one fund with such capital for all purposes, and so that, if such property is settled land, such accumulations shall be held upon the same trusts as if the same were capital money arising therefrom;

but the trustees may, at any time during the infancy of such person if his interest so long continues, apply those accumulations, or any part thereof, as if they were income arising in the then current year[2].

(3) This section applies in the case of a contingent interest only if the limitation or trust carries the intermediate income of the property, but it applies to a future or contingent legacy by the parent of, or a person standing in loco parentis to, the legatee, if and for such period as, under the general law, the legacy carries interest for the maintenance of the legatee, and in any such case as last aforesaid the rate of interest

shall (if the income available is sufficient, and subject to any rules of court to the contrary) be five pounds per centum per annum.

(4) This section applies to a vested annuity in like manner as if the annuity were the income of property held by trustees in trust to pay the income thereof to the annuitant for the same period for which the annuity is payable, save that in any case accumulations made during the infancy of the annuitant shall be held in trust for the annuitant or his personal representatives absolutely.

(5) This section does not apply where the instrument, if any, under which the interest arises came into operation before the commencement of this Act.

1 Words in square brackets substituted by Family Law Reform Act 1969 s 1(3), Sch 1 Part I.
2 Words in square brackets substituted by Trustee Act 2000 s 40(1), Sch 2 Part II para 25 with effect from 1 February 2001.
4 Words in square brackets substituted by Civil Partnership Act 2004 s 261(1), Sch 27 para 5(1), (2)(b) with effect from 5 December 2005.
5 Words in square brackets inserted by Civil Partnership Act 2004 s 261(1), Sch 27 para 5(1), (3) with effect from 5 December 2005.
6 Words in square brackets inserted by Civil Partnership Act 2004 s 261(1), Sch 27 para 5(1), (5) with effect from 5 December 2005.

32 Power of advancement

26.3 (1) Trustees may at any time or times pay or apply any capital money subject to a trust, for the advancement or benefit, in such manner as they may, in their absolute discretion, think fit, of any person entitled to the capital of the trust property or of any share thereof, whether absolutely or contingently on his attaining any specified age or on the occurrence of any other event, or subject to a gift over on his death under any specified age or on the occurrence of any other event, and whether in possession or in remainder or reversion, and such payment or application may be made notwithstanding that the interest of such person is liable to be defeated by the exercise of a power of appointment or revocation, or to be diminished by the increase of the class to which he belongs:

Provided that—

(a) the money so paid or applied for the advancement or benefit of any person shall not exceed altogether in amount one-half of the presumptive or vested share or interest of that person in the trust property, and

(b) if that person is or becomes absolutely and indefeasibly entitled to a share in the trust property the money so paid or applied shall be brought into account as part of such share, and

(c) no such payment or application shall be made so as to prejudice any person entitled to any prior life or other interest, whether vested or contingent, in the money paid or applied unless such person is in existence and of full age and consents in writing to such payment or application.

[(2) This section does not apply to capital money arising under the Settled Land Act, 1925.[1]]

(3) This section does not apply to trusts constituted or created before the commencement of this Act.

1 Words in square brackets substituted by Trusts of Land and Appointment of Trustees Act 1996 s 25(1), Sch 3 para 3(8).

33 Protective trusts

26.4 (1) Where any income, including an annuity or other periodical income payment, is directed to be held on protective trusts for the benefit of any person (in this section called "the principal beneficiary") for the period of his life or for any less period, then, during that period (in this section called the "trust period") the said income shall, without prejudice to any prior interest, be held on the following trusts, namely:—

(i) Upon trust for the principal beneficiary during the trust period or until he, whether before or after the termination of any prior interest, does or attempts to do or suffers any act or thing, or until any event happens, other than an advance under any statutory or express power, whereby, if the said income were payable during the trust period to the principal beneficiary absolutely during that period, he would be deprived of the right to receive the same or any part thereof, in any of which cases, as well as on the termination of the trust period, whichever first happens, this trust of the said income shall fail or determine;

(ii) If the trust aforesaid fails or determines during the subsistence of the trust period, then, during the residue of that period, the said income shall be held upon trust for the application thereof for the maintenance or support, or otherwise for the benefit, of all or any one or more exclusively of the other or others of the following persons (that is to say)—

 (a) the principal beneficiary and his or her [spouse or civil partner][1], if any, and his or her children or more remote issue, if any, or

 (b) if there is no [spouse or civil partner] or issue of the principal beneficiary in existence, the principal beneficiary and the persons who would, if he were actually dead, be entitled to the trust property or the income thereof or to the annuity fund, if any, or arrears of the annuity, as the case may be,

as the trustees in their absolute discretion, without being liable to account for the exercise of such discretion, think fit.

(2) This section does not apply to trusts coming into operation before the commencement of this Act, and has effect subject to any variation of the implied trusts aforesaid contained in the instrument creating the trust.

(3) Nothing in this section operates to validate any trust which would, if contained in the instrument creating the trust, be liable to be set aside.

[(4) In relation to the dispositions mentioned in section 19(1) of the Family Law Reform Act 1987, this section shall have effect as if any reference (however expressed) to any relationship between two persons were construed in accordance with section 1 of that Act.][2]

1 Words in square brackets substituted by Civil Partnership Act 2004 s 261(1), Sch 27 para 6 with effect from 5 December 2005.
2 Subsection (4) inserted by Family Law Reform Act 1987 s 33(1), Sch 2 para 2 Sch 3 para 1.

PERPETUITIES AND ACCUMULATIONS ACT 1964 s 1

1 Power to specify perpetuity period

26.5 (1) Subject to section 9(2) of this Act and subsection (2) below, where the instrument by which any disposition is made so provides, the perpetuity period applicable to the disposition under the rule against perpetuities, instead of being of any other duration, shall be of a duration equal to such number of years not exceeding eighty as is specified in that behalf in the instrument.

(2) Subsection (1) above shall not have effect where the disposition is made in exercise of a special power of appointment, but where a period is specified under that subsection in the instrument creating such a power the period shall apply in relation to any disposition under the power as it applies in relation to the power itself.

PERPETUITIES AND ACCUMULATIONS ACT 2009

Application of rule against perpetuities

1 Application of the rule

26.6 (1) The rule against perpetuities applies (and applies only) as provided by this section.

(2) If an instrument limits property in trust so as to create successive estates or interests the rule applies to each of the estates or interests.

(3) If an instrument limits property in trust so as to create an estate or interest which is subject to a condition precedent and which is not one of successive estates or interests, the rule applies to the estate or interest.

(4) If an instrument limits property in trust so as to create an estate or interest subject to a condition subsequent the rule applies to—

(a) any right of re-entry exercisable if the condition is broken, or

(b) any equivalent right exercisable in the case of property other than land if the condition is broken.

(5) If an instrument which is a will limits personal property so as to create successive interests under the doctrine of executory bequests, the rule applies to each of the interests.

(6) If an instrument creates a power of appointment the rule applies to the power.

(7) For the purposes of subsection (2) an estate or interest includes an estate or interest—

(a) which arises under a right of reverter on the determination of a determinable fee simple, or

(b) which arises under a resulting trust on the determination of a determinable interest.

(8) This section has effect subject to the exceptions made by section 2 and to any exceptions made under section 3.

(9) In section 4(3) of the Law of Property Act 1925 (c 20) (rights of entry affecting a legal estate) omit the words from 'but' to the end.

26.7 *Appendix Part 2: Powers*

Perpetuity period

5 Perpetuity period

26.7 (1) The perpetuity period is 125 years (and no other period).

(2) Subsection (1) applies whether or not the instrument referred to in section 1(2) to (6) specifies a perpetuity period; and a specification of a perpetuity period in that instrument is ineffective.

Perpetuities: miscellaneous

6 Start of perpetuity period

26.8 (1) The perpetuity period starts when the instrument referred to in section 1(2) to (6) takes effect; but this is subject to subsections (2) and (3).

(2) If section 1(2), (3) or (4) applies and the instrument is made in the exercise of a special power of appointment the perpetuity period starts when the instrument creating the power takes effect; but this is subject to subsection (3).

(3) If section 1(2), (3) or (4) applies and—
(a) the instrument nominates benefits under a relevant pension scheme, or
(b) the instrument is made in the exercise of a power of advancement arising under a relevant pension scheme,

the perpetuity period starts when the member concerned became a member of the scheme.

(4) The member concerned is the member in respect of whose interest in the scheme the instrument is made.

7 Wait and see rule

26.9 (1) Subsection (2) applies if (apart from this section and section 8) an estate or interest would be void on the ground that it might not become vested until too remote a time.

(2) In such a case—
(a) until such time (if any) as it becomes established that the vesting must occur (if at all) after the end of the perpetuity period the estate or interest must be treated as if it were not subject to the rule against perpetuities, and
(b) if it becomes so established, that does not affect the validity of anything previously done (whether by way of advancement, application of intermediate income or otherwise) in relation to the estate or interest.

(3) Subsection (4) applies if (apart from this section) any of the following would be void on the ground that it might be exercised at too remote a time—
(a) a right of re-entry exercisable if a condition subsequent is broken,
(b) an equivalent right exercisable in the case of property other than land if a condition subsequent is broken,
(c) a special power of appointment.

(4) In such a case—

Appendix Part 2: Powers **26.11**

(a) the right or power must be treated as regards any exercise of it within the perpetuity period as if it were not subject to the rule against perpetuities, and
(b) the right or power must be treated as void for remoteness only if and so far as it is not fully exercised within the perpetuity period.

(5) Subsection (6) applies if (apart from this section) a general power of appointment would be void on the ground that it might not become exercisable until too remote a time.

(6) Until such time (if any) as it becomes established that the power will not be exercisable within the perpetuity period, it must be treated as if it were not subject to the rule against perpetuities.

8 Exclusion of class members to avoid remoteness

26.10 (1) This section applies if—
(a) it is apparent at the time an instrument takes effect or becomes apparent at a later time that (apart from this section) the inclusion of certain persons as members of a class would cause an estate or interest to be treated as void for remoteness, and
(b) those persons are potential members of the class or unborn persons who at birth would become members or potential members of the class.

(2) From the time it is or becomes so apparent those persons must be treated for all the purposes of the instrument as excluded from the class unless their exclusion would exhaust the class.

(3) If this section applies in relation to an estate or interest to which section 7 applies, this section does not affect the validity of anything previously done (whether by way of advancement, application of intermediate income or otherwise) in relation to the estate or interest.

(4) For the purposes of this section—
(a) a person is a member of a class if in that person's case all the conditions identifying a member of the class are satisfied, and
(b) a person is a potential member of a class if in that person's case some only of those conditions are satisfied but there is a possibility that the remainder will in time be satisfied.

11 Powers of appointment

26.11 ...

(3) Subsection (4) applies to a power of appointment exercisable by will (whether or not it is also exercisable otherwise than by will).

(4) For the purposes of the rule against perpetuities the power is a special power unless—
(a) the instrument creating it expresses it to be exercisable by one person only, and
(b) that person could exercise it so as to transfer to that person's personal representatives the whole of the estate or interest to which it relates.

(5) Subsection (6) applies to a power of appointment exercisable by will or otherwise.

26.12 *Appendix Part 2: Powers*

(6) If for the purposes of the rule against perpetuities the power would be a special power under one but not both of subsections (2) and (4), for the purposes of the rule it is a special power.

Application of statutory provisions

15 Application of this Act

26.12 (1) Sections 1, 2, 4 to 11, 13 and 14 apply in relation to an instrument taking effect on or after the commencement day, except that—
(a) those sections do not apply in relation to a will executed before that day, and
(b) those sections apply in relation to an instrument made in the exercise of a special power of appointment only if the instrument creating the power takes effect on or after that day.
(2) Section 12 applies (except as provided by subsection (3)) in relation to—
(a) a will executed before the commencement day (whether or not it takes effect before that day),
(b) an instrument, other than a will, taking effect before that day.
(3) Section 12 does not apply if—
(a) the terms of the trust were exhausted before the commencement day, or
(b) before that day the property became held on trust for charitable purposes by way of a final disposition of the property.
(4) The commencement day is the day appointed under section 22(2).

20 Interpretation

26.13 ...

(6) An instrument which is a will takes effect at the testator's death.
(7) A reference to a will includes a reference to a codicil.

TRUSTS OF LAND AND APPOINTMENT OF TRUSTEES ACT 1996 ss 1 to 13, 18 and Sch 1

PART I

TRUSTS OF LAND

1 MEANING OF "TRUST OF LAND"

26.14 (1) In this Act—
(a) "trust of land" means (subject to subsection (3)) any trust of property which consists of or includes land, and
(b) "trustees of land" means trustees of a trust of land.

(2) The reference in subsection (1)(a) to a trust—
(a) is to any description of trust (whether express, implied, resulting or constructive), including a trust for sale and a bare trust, and
(b) includes a trust created, or arising, before the commencement of this Act.

(3) The reference to land in subsection (1)(a) does not include land which (despite section 2) is settled land or which is land to which the Universities and College Estates Act 1925 applies.

2 TRUSTS IN PLACE OF SETTLEMENTS

26.15 (1) No settlement created after the commencement of this Act is a settlement for the purposes of the Settled Land Act 1925; and no 1925 c. 18. settlement shall be deemed to be made under that Act after that commencement.

(2) Subsection (1) does not apply to a settlement created on the occasion of an alteration in any interest in, or of a person becoming entitled under, a settlement which—
(a) is in existence at the commencement of this Act, or
(b) derives from a settlement within paragraph (a) or this paragraph.

(3) But a settlement created as mentioned in subsection (2) is not a settlement for the purposes of the Settled Land Act 1925 if provision to the effect that it is not is made in the instrument, or any of the instruments, by which it is created.

(4) Where at any time after the commencement of this Act there is in the case of any settlement which is a settlement for the purposes of the Settled Land Act 1925 no relevant property which is, or is deemed to be, subject to the settlement, the settlement permanently ceases at that time to be a settlement for the purposes of that Act.

In this subsection "relevant property" means land and personal chattels to which section 67(1) of the Settled Land Act 1925 (heirlooms) applies.

(5) No land held on charitable, ecclesiastical or public trusts shall be or be deemed to be settled land after the commencement of this Act, even if it was or was deemed to be settled land before that commencement.

(6) Schedule 1 has effect to make provision consequential on this section (including provision to impose a trust in circumstances in which, apart from this section, there would be a settlement for the purposes of the Settled Land Act 1925 (and there would not otherwise be a trust)).

3 ABOLITION OF DOCTRINE OF CONVERSION

26.16 (1) Where land is held by trustees subject to a trust for sale, the land is not to be regarded as personal property; and where personal property, is subject to a trust for sale in order that the trustees may acquire land, the personal property is not to be regarded as land.

(2) Subsection (1) does not apply to a trust created by a will if the testator died before the commencement of this Act.

(3) Subject to that, subsection (1) applies to a trust whether it is created, or arises, before or after that commencement.

26.17 *Appendix Part 2: Powers*

4 EXPRESS TRUSTS FOR SALE AS TRUSTS OF LAND

26.17 (1) In the case of every trust for sale of land created by a disposition there is to be implied, despite any provision to the contrary made by the disposition, a power for the trustees to postpone sale of the land; and the trustees are not liable in any way for postponing sale of the land, in the exercise of their discretion, for an indefinite period.

(2) Subsection (1) applies to a trust whether it is created, or arises, before or after the commencement of this Act.

(3) Subsection (1) does not affect any liability incurred by trustees before that commencement.

5 IMPLIED TRUSTS FOR SALE AS TRUSTS OF LAND

26.18 (1) Schedule 2 has effect in relation to statutory provisions which impose a trust for sale of land in certain circumstances so that in those circumstances there is instead a trust of the land (without a duty to sell).

(2) Section 1 of the Settled Land Act 1925 does not apply to land held on any trust arising by virtue of that Schedule (so that any such land is subject to a trust of land).

6 GENERAL POWERS OF TRUSTEES

26.19 (1) For the purpose of exercising their functions as trustees, the trustees of land have in relation to the land subject to the trust all the powers of an absolute owner.

(2) Where in the case of any land subject to a trust of land each of the beneficiaries interested in the land is a person of full age and capacity who is absolutely entitled to the land, the powers conferred on the trustees by subsection (1) include the power to convey the land to the beneficiaries even though they have not required the trustees to do so; and where land is conveyed by virtue of this subsection—
(a)   the beneficiaries shall do whatever is necessary to secure that it vests in them, and
(b)   if they fail to do so, the court may make an order requiring them to do so.

(3) The trustees of land have power to [acquire land under the power conferred by section 8 of the Trustee Act 2000][1].

(4)   ...[1]

(5) In exercising the powers conferred by this section trustees shall have regard to the rights of the beneficiaries.

(6) The powers conferred by this section shall not be exercised in contravention of, or of any order made in pursuance of, any other enactment or any rule of law or equity.

(7) The reference in subsection (6) to an order includes an order of any court or of the [Charity Commission][2].

(8) Where any enactment other than this section confers on trustees authority to act subject to any restriction, limitation or condition, trustees of land may not exercise the powers conferred by this section to do any act which they are prevented from doing under the other enactment by reason of the restriction, limitation or condition.

[(9) The duty of care under section 1 of the Trustee Act 2000 applies to trustees of land when exercising the powers conferred by this section[1].]

1   Words in square brackets substituted or inserted and subsection (4) repealed by Trustee Act 2000 Sch 2 Part II para 45 with effect from 1 February 2001.
2   Words in square brackets substituted by Charities Act 2006 s 75(1), Sch 8 para 182.

7 PARTITION BY TRUSTEES

26.20 (1) The trustees of land may, where beneficiaries of full age are absolutely entitled in undivided shares to land subject to the trust, partition the land, or any part of it, and provide (by way of mortgage or otherwise) for the payment of any equality money.

(2) The trustees shall give effect to any such partition by conveying the partitioned land in severalty (whether or not subject to any legal mortgage created for raising equality money), either absolutely or in trust, in accordance with the rights of those beneficiaries.

(3) Before exercising their powers under subsection (2) the trustees shall obtain the consent of each of those beneficiaries.

(4) Where a share in the land is affected by an incumbrance, the trustees may either give effect to it or provide for its discharge from the property allotted to that share as they think fit.

(5) If a share in the land is absolutely vested in a minor, subsections (1) to (4) apply as if he were of full age, except that the trustees may act on his behalf and retain land or other property representing his share in trust for him.

[(6) Subsection (1) is subject to sections 21 (part-unit: interests) and 22 (part-unit: charging) of the Commonhold and Leasehold Reform Act 2002[1].]

1   Words in square brackets inserted by Commonhold and Leasehold Reform Act 2002 s 68, Sch 5 para 8 with effect from 27 September 2004.

8 EXCLUSION AND RESTRICTION OF POWERS

26.21 (1) Sections 6 and 7 do not apply in the case of a trust of land created by a disposition in so far as provision to the effect that they do not apply is made by the disposition.

(2) If the disposition creating such a trust makes provision requiring any consent to be obtained to the exercise of any power conferred by sections 6 or 7, the power may not be exercised without that consent.

(3) Subsection (1) does not apply in the case of charitable, ecclesiastical or public trusts.

(4) Subsections (1) and (2) have effect subject to any enactment which prohibits or restricts the effect of provision of the description mentioned in them.

9 DELEGATION BY TRUSTEES

26.22 (1) The trustees of land may, by power of attorney, delegate to any beneficiary or beneficiaries of full age and beneficially entitled to an interest in possession in land subject to the trust any of their functions as trustees which relate to the land.

26.23 *Appendix Part 2: Powers*

(2) Where trustees purport to delegate to a person by a power of attorney under subsection (1) functions relating to any land and another person in good faith deals with him in relation to the land, he shall be presumed in favour of that other person to have been a person to whom the functions could be delegated unless that other person has knowledge at the time of the transaction that he was not such a person.

And it shall be conclusively presumed in favour of any purchaser whose interest depends on the validity of that transaction that that other person dealt in good faith and did not have such knowledge if that other person makes a statutory declaration to that effect before or within three months after the completion of the purchase.

(3) A power of attorney under subsection (1) shall be given by all the trustees jointly and (unless expressed to be irrevocable and to be given by way of security) may be revoked by any one or more of them; and such a power is revoked by the appointment as a trustee of a person other than those by whom it is given (though not by any of those persons dying or otherwise ceasing to be a trustee).

(4) Where a beneficiary to whom functions are delegated by a power of attorney under subsection (1) ceases to be a person beneficially entitled to an interest in possession in land subject to the trust—
(a) if the functions are delegated to him alone, the power is revoked,
(b) if the functions are delegated to him and to other beneficiaries to be exercised by them jointly (but not separately), the power is revoked if each of the other beneficiaries ceases to be so entitled (but otherwise functions exercisable in accordance with the power are so exercisable by the remaining beneficiary or beneficiaries), and
(c) if the functions are delegated to him and to other beneficiaries to be exercised by them separately (or either separately or jointly), the power is revoked in so far as it relates to him.

(5) A delegation under subsection (1) may be for any period or indefinite.

(6) A power of attorney under subsection (1) cannot be *an enduring power within the meaning of the Enduring Powers of Attorney Act 1985* [an enduring power of attorney or lasting power of attorney within the meaning of the Mental Capacity Act 2005][1].

(7) Beneficiaries to whom functions have been delegated under subsection (1) are, in relation to the exercise of the functions, in the same position as trustees (with the same duties and liabilities); but such beneficiaries shall not be regarded as trustees for any other purposes (including, in particular, the purposes of any enactment permitting the delegation of functions by trustees or imposing requirements relating to the payment of capital money).

(8) …[2]

(9) Neither this section nor the repeal by this Act of section 29 of the Law of Property Act 1925 (which is superseded by this section) affects the operation after the commencement of this Act of any delegation effected before that commencement.

1 Words in italics repealed and words in square brackets inserted by Mental Capacity Act 2005 s 67(1), Sch 6 para 42(1) and (2) with effect from a date as yet to be appointed.
2 Repealed by Trustee Act 2000 Sch 2 Part II para 46.

9A DUTIES OF TRUSTEES IN CONNECTION WITH DELEGATION ETC[1]

26.23 (1) The duty of care under section 1 of the Trustee Act 2000 applies to trustees of land in deciding whether to delegate any of their functions under section 9.

(2) Subsection (3) applies if the trustees of land
(a) delegate any of their functions under section 9, and
(b) the delegation is not irrevocable.

(3) While the delegation continues, the trustees
(a) must keep the delegation under review,
(b) if the circumstances make it appropriate to do so, must consider whether there is a need to exercise any power of intervention that they have, and
(c) if they consider that there is a need to exercise such a power, must do so.

(4) "Power of intervention" includes
(a) a power to give directions to the beneficiary,
(b) a power to revoke the delegation.

(5) The duty of care under section 1 of the 2000 Act applies to trustees in carrying out any duty under subsection (3).

(6) A trustee of land is not liable for any act or default of the beneficiary, or beneficiaries, unless the trustee fails to comply with the duty of care in deciding to delegate any of the trustees' functions under section 9 or in carrying out any duty under subsection (3).

(7) Neither this section nor the repeal of section 9(8) by the Trustee Act 2000 affects the operation after the commencement of this section of any delegation effected before that commencement.

1 Inserted by Trustee Act 2000 s 40(1), Sch 2 para 47.

10 CONSENTS

26.24 (1) If a disposition creating a trust of land requires the consent of more than two persons to the exercise by the trustees of any function relating to the land, the consent of any two of them to the exercise of the function is sufficient in favour of a purchaser.

(2) Subsection (1) does not apply to the exercise of a function by trustees of land held on charitable, ecclesiastical or public trusts.

(3) Where at any time a person whose consent is expressed by a disposition creating a trust of land to be required to the exercise by the trustees of any function relating to the land is not of full age—
(a) his consent is not, in favour of a purchaser, required to the exercise of the function, but
(b) the trustees shall obtain the consent of a parent who has parental responsibility for him (within the meaning of the Children Act 1989) or of a guardian of his.

11 CONSULTATION WITH BENEFICARIES

26.25 (1) The trustees of land shall in the exercise of any function relating to land subject to the trust—
(a) so far as practicable, consult the beneficiaries of full age and beneficially entitled to an interest in possession in the land, and

26.26 *Appendix Part 2: Powers*

(b) so far as consistent with the general interest of the trust, give effect to the wishes of those beneficiaries, or (in case of dispute) of the majority (according to the value of their combined interests).

(2) Subsection (1) does not apply—
(a) in relation to a trust created by a disposition in so far as provision that it does not apply is made by the disposition,
(b) in relation to a trust created or arising under a will made before the commencement of this Act, or
(c) in relation to the exercise of the power mentioned in section 6(2).

(3) Subsection (1) does not apply to a trust created before the commencement of this Act by a disposition, or a trust created after that commencement by reference to such a trust, unless provision to the effect that it is to apply is made by a deed executed—
(a) in a case in which the trust was created by one person and he is of full capacity, by that person, or
(b) in a case in which the trust was created by more than one person, by such of the persons who created the trust as are alive and of full capacity.

(4) A deed executed for the purposes of subsection (3) is irrevocable.

12 THE RIGHT TO OCCUPY

26.26 (1) A beneficiary who is beneficially entitled to an interest in possession in land subject to a trust of land is entitled by reason of his interest to occupy the land at any time if at that time—
(a) the purposes of the trust include making the land available for his occupation (or for the occupation of beneficiaries of a class of which he is a member or of beneficiaries in general), or
(b) the land is held by the trustees so as to be so available.

(2) Subsection (1) does not confer on a beneficiary a right to occupy land if it is either unavailable or unsuitable for occupation by him.

(3) This section is subject to section 13.

13 EXCLUSION AND RESTRICTION OF RIGHT TO OCCUPY

26.27 (1) Where two or more beneficiaries are (or apart from this subsection would be) entitled under section 12 to occupy land, the trustees of land may exclude or restrict the entitlement of any one or more (but not all) of them.

(2) Trustees may not under subsection (1)—
(a) unreasonably exclude any beneficiary's entitlement to occupy land, or
(b) restrict any such entitlement to an unreasonable extent.

(3) The trustees of land may from time to time impose reasonable conditions on any beneficiary in relation to his occupation of land by reason of his entitlement under section 12.

(4) The matters to which trustees are to have regard in exercising the powers conferred by this section include—
(a) the intentions of the person or persons (if any) who created the trust,
(b) the purposes for which the land is held, and

(c) the circumstances and wishes of each of the beneficiaries who is (or apart from any previous exercise by the trustees of those powers would be) entitled to occupy the land under section 12.

(5) The conditions which may be imposed on a beneficiary under subsection (3) include, in particular, conditions requiring him—
(a) to pay any outgoings or expenses in respect of the land, or
(b) to assume any other obligation in relation to the land or to any activity which is or is proposed to be conducted there.

(6) Where the entitlement of any beneficiary to occupy land under section 12 has been excluded or restricted, the conditions which may be imposed on any other beneficiary under subsection (3) include, in particular, conditions requiring him to—
(a) make payments by way of compensation to the beneficiary whose entitlement has been excluded or restricted, or
(b) forgo any payment or other benefit to which he would otherwise be entitled under the trust so as to benefit that beneficiary.

(7) The powers conferred on trustees by this section may not be exercised—

so as prevent any person who is in occupation of land (whether or not by reason of an entitlement under section 12) from continuing to occupy the land, or
(a) in a manner likely to result in any such person ceasing to occupy the land,
(b) unless he consents or the court has given approval.

(8) The matters to which the court is to have regard in determining whether to give approval under subsection (7) include the matters mentioned in subsection (4)(a) to (c).

18 APPLICATION OF PART TO PERSONAL REPRESENTATIVES

26.28 (1) The provisions of this Part relating to trustees, other than sections 10, 11 and 14, apply to personal representatives, but with appropriate modifications and without prejudice to the functions of personal representatives for the purposes of administration.

(2) The appropriate modifications include—
(a) the substitution of references to persons interested in the due administration of the estate for references to beneficiaries, and
(b) the substitution of references to the will for references to the disposition creating the trust.

(3) Section 3(1) does not apply to personal representatives if the death occurs before the commencement of this Act.

SCHEDULE 1

PROVISIONS CONSEQUENTIAL ON SECTION 2

Minors

26.29 1.—(1) Where after the commencement of this Act a person purports to convey a legal estate in land to a minor, or two or more minors, alone, the conveyance—

26.30 *Appendix Part 2: Powers*

(a) is not effective to pass the legal estate, but
(b) operates as a declaration that the land is held in trust for the minor or minors (or if he purports to convey it to the minor or minors in trust for any persons, for those persons).

(2) Where after the commencement of this Act a person purports to convey legal estate in land to—
(a) a minor or two or more minors, and
(b) another person who is, or other persons who are, of full age,

the conveyance operates to vest the land in the other person or persons in trust for the minor or minors and the other person or persons (or if he purports it convey it to them in trust for any persons, for those persons).

(3) Where immediately before the commencement of this Act a conveyance operating (by virtue of section 27 of the Settled Land Act 1925) as an agreement to execute a settlement in favour of a minor or minors—
(a) the agreement ceases to have effect on the commencement of this Act, and
(b) the conveyance subsequently operates instead as a declaration that the land is held in trust for the minor or minors.

2 Where after the commencement of this Act a legal estate in land would, by reason of intestacy or in any other circumstances not dealt with in paragraph 1, vest in a person who is a minor if he were a person of full age, the land is held trust for the minor.

...

TRUSTEE ACT 2000

Part I
The Duty of Care

1 THE DUTY OF CARE

26.30 (1) Whenever the duty under this subsection applies to a trustee, he must exercise such care and skill as is reasonable in the circumstances, having regard in particular—
(a) to any special knowledge or experience that he has or holds himself out as having, and
(b) if he acts as trustee in the course of a business or profession, to any special knowledge or experience that it is reasonable to expect of a person acting in the course of that kind of business or profession.

(2) In this Act the duty under subsection (1) is called "the duty of care".

2 APPLICATION OF DUTY OF CARE

26.31 Schedule 1 makes provision about when the duty of care applies to a trustee.

PART II
INVESTMENT

3 GENERAL POWER OF INVESTMENT

26.32 (1) Subject to the provisions of this Part, a trustee may make any kind of investment that he could make if he were absolutely entitled to the assets of the trust.

(2) In this Act the power under subsection (1) is called "the general power of investment".

(3) The general power of investment does not permit a trustee to make investments in land other than in loans secured on land (but see also section 8).

(4) A person invests in a loan secured on land if he has rights under any contract under which—
(a) one person provides another with credit, and
(b) the obligation of the borrower to repay is secured on land.

(5) "Credit" includes any cash loan or other financial accommodation.

(6) "Cash" includes money in any form.

4 STANDARD INVESTMENT CRITERIA

26.33 (1) In exercising any power of investment, whether arising under this Part or otherwise, a trustee must have regard to the standard investment criteria.

(2) A trustee must from time to time review the investments of the trust and consider whether, having regard to the standard investment criteria, they should be varied.

(3) The standard investment criteria, in relation to a trust, are—
(a) the suitability to the trust of investments of the same kind as any particular investment proposed to be made or retained and of that particular investment as an investment of that kind, and
(b) the need for diversification of investments of the trust, in so far as is appropriate to the circumstances of the trust.

5 ADVICE

26.34 (1) Before exercising any power of investment, whether arising under this Part or otherwise, a trustee must (unless the exception applies) obtain and consider proper advice about the way in which, having regard to the standard investment criteria, the power should be exercised.

(2) When reviewing the investments of the trust, a trustee must (unless the exception applies) obtain and consider proper advice about whether, having regard to the standard investment criteria, the investments should be varied.

(3) The exception is that a trustee need not obtain such advice if he reasonably concludes that in all the circumstances it is unnecessary or inappropriate to do so.

(4) Proper advice is the advice of a person who is reasonably believed by the trustee to be qualified to give it by his ability in and practical experience of financial and other matters relating to the proposed investment.

26.35 *Appendix Part 2: Powers*

6 RESTRICTION OR EXCLUSION OF THIS PART ETC

26.35 (1) The general power of investment is—

(a) in addition to powers conferred on trustees otherwise than by this Act, but

(b) subject to any restriction or exclusion imposed by the trust instrument or by any enactment or any provision of subordinate legislation.

(2) For the purposes of this Act, an enactment or a provision of subordinate legislation is not to be regarded as being, or as being part of, a trust instrument.

(3) In this Act "subordinate legislation" has the same meaning as in the Interpretation Act 1978.

PART III
ACQUISITION OF LAND

8 POWER TO ACQUIRE FREEHOLD AND LEASEHOLD LAND

26.36 (1) A trustee may acquire freehold or leasehold land in the United Kingdom—

(a) as an investment,

(b) for occupation by a beneficiary, or

(c) for any other reason.

(2) "Freehold or leasehold land" means—

(a) in relation to England and Wales, a legal estate in land,

(b) in relation to Scotland—

    (i) the estate or interest of the proprietor of the dominium utile or, in the case of land not held on feudal tenure, the estate or interest of the owner, or

    (ii) a tenancy, and

(c) in relation to Northern Ireland, a legal estate in land, including land held under a fee farm grant.

(3) For the purpose of exercising his functions as a trustee, a trustee who acquires land under this section has all the powers of an absolute owner in relation to the land.

9 RESTRICTION OR EXCLUSION OF THIS PART ETC

26.37 The powers conferred by this Part are—

(a) in addition to powers conferred on trustees otherwise than by this Part, but

(b) subject to any restriction or exclusion imposed by the trust instrument or by any enactment or any provision of subordinate legislation.

PART IV
AGENTS, NOMINEES AND CUSTODIANS

AGENTS

11 POWER TO EMPLOY AGENTS

26.38 (1) Subject to the provisions of this Part, the trustees of a trust may authorise any person to exercise any or all of their delegable functions as their agent.

(2) In the case of a trust other than a charitable trust, the trustees' delegable functions consist of any function other than—
(a) any function relating to whether or in what way any assets of the trust should be distributed,
(b) any power to decide whether any fees or other payment due to be made out of the trust funds should be made out of income or capital,
(c) any power to appoint a person to be a trustee of the trust, or
(d) any power conferred by any other enactment or the trust instrument which permits the trustees to delegate any of their functions or to appoint a person to act as a nominee or custodian.

(3) In the case of a charitable trust, the trustees' delegable functions are—
(a) any function consisting of carrying out a decision that the trustees have taken,
(b) any function relating to the investment of assets subject to the trust (including, in the case of land held as an investment, managing the land and creating or disposing of an interest in the land),
(c) any function relating to the raising of funds for the trust otherwise than by means of profits of a trade which is an integral part of carrying out the trust's charitable purpose,
(d) any other function prescribed by an order made by the Secretary of State.

(4) For the purposes of subsection (3)(c) a trade is an integral part of carrying out a trust's charitable purpose if, whether carried on in the United Kingdom or elsewhere, the profits are applied solely to the purposes of the trust and either—
(a) the trade is exercised in the course of the actual carrying out of a primary purpose of the trust, or
(b) the work in connection with the trade is mainly carried out by beneficiaries of the trust.

(5) The power to make an order under subsection (3)(d) is exercisable by statutory instrument which shall be subject to annulment in pursuance of a resolution of either House of Parliament.

12 PERSONS WHO MAY ACT AS AGENTS

26.39 (1) Subject to subsection (2), the persons whom the trustees may under section 11 authorise to exercise functions as their agent include one or more of their number.

(2) The trustees may not authorise two (or more) persons to exercise the same function unless they are to exercise the function jointly.

26.40 *Appendix Part 2: Powers*

(3) The trustees may not under section 11 authorise a beneficiary to exercise any function as their agent (even if the beneficiary is also a trustee).

(4) The trustees may under section 11 authorise a person to exercise functions as their agent even though he is also appointed to act as their nominee or custodian (whether under section 16, 17 or 18 or any other power).

13 LINKED FUNCTIONS ETC

26.40 (1) Subject to subsections (2) and (5), a person who is authorised under section 11 to exercise a function is (whatever the terms of the agency) subject to any specific duties or restrictions attached to the function.

For example, a person who is authorised under section 11 to exercise the general power of investment is subject to the duties under section 4 in relation to that power.

(2) A person who is authorised under section 11 to exercise a power which is subject to a requirement to obtain advice is not subject to the requirement if he is the kind of person from whom it would have been proper for the trustees, in compliance with the requirement, to obtain advice.

(3) Subsections (4) and (5) apply to a trust to which section 11(1) of the Trusts of Land and Appointment of Trustees Act 1996 (duties to consult beneficiaries and give effect to their wishes) applies.

(4) The trustees may not under section 11 authorise a person to exercise any of their functions on terms that prevent them from complying with section 11(1) of the 1996 Act.

(5) A person who is authorised under section 11 to exercise any function relating to land subject to the trust is not subject to section 11(1) of the 1996 Act.

14 TERMS OF AGENCY

26.41 (1) Subject to subsection (2) and sections 15(2) and 29 to 32, the trustees may authorise a person to exercise functions as their agent on such terms as to remuneration and other matters as they may determine.

(2) The trustees may not authorise a person to exercise functions as their agent on any of the terms mentioned in subsection (3) unless it is reasonably necessary for them to do so.

(3) The terms are—
(a) a term permitting the agent to appoint a substitute,
(b) a term restricting the liability of the agent or his substitute to the trustees or any beneficiary,
(c) a term permitting the agent to act in circumstances capable of giving rise to a conflict of interest.

15 ASSET MANAGEMENT: SPECIAL RESTRICTIONS

26.42 (1) The trustees may not authorise a person to exercise any of their asset management functions as their agent except by an agreement which is in or evidenced in writing.

(2) The trustees may not authorise a person to exercise any of their asset management functions as their agent unless—
(a) they have prepared a statement that gives guidance as to how the functions should be exercised ("a policy statement"), and
(b) the agreement under which the agent is to act includes a term to the effect that he will secure compliance with—
   (i) the policy statement, or
   (ii) if the policy statement is revised or replaced under section 22, the revised or replacement policy statement.

(3) The trustees must formulate any guidance given in the policy statement with a view to ensuring that the functions will be exercised in the best interests of the trust.

(4) The policy statement must be in or evidenced in writing.

(5) The asset management functions of trustees are their functions relating to—
(a) the investment of assets subject to the trust,
(b) the acquisition of property which is to be subject to the trust, and
(c) managing property which is subject to the trust and disposing of, or creating or disposing of an interest in, such property.

NOMINEES AND CUSTODIANS

16 POWER TO APPOINT NOMINEES

26.43 (1) Subject to the provisions of this Part, the trustees of a trust may—
(a) appoint a person to act as their nominee in relation to such of the assets of the trust as they determine (other than settled land), and
(b) take such steps as are necessary to secure that those assets are vested in a person so appointed.

(2) An appointment under this section must be in or evidenced in writing.

(3) This section does not apply to any trust having a custodian trustee or in relation to any assets vested in the official custodian for charities.

17 POWER TO APPOINT CUSTODIANS

26.44 (1) Subject to the provisions of this Part, the trustees of a trust may appoint a person to act as a custodian in relation to such of the assets of the trust as they may determine.

(2) For the purposes of this Act a person is a custodian in relation to assets if he undertakes the safe custody of the assets or of any documents or records concerning the assets.

(3) An appointment under this section must be in or evidenced in writing.

(4) This section does not apply to any trust having a custodian trustee or in relation to any assets vested in the official custodian for charities.

26.45　*Appendix Part 2: Powers*

18 INVESTMENT IN BEARER SECURITIES

26.45　(1)　If trustees retain or invest in securities payable to bearer, they must appoint a person to act as a custodian of the securities.

(2)　Subsection (1) does not apply if the trust instrument or any enactment or provision of subordinate legislation contains provision which (however expressed) permits the trustees to retain or invest in securities payable to bearer without appointing a person to act as a custodian.

(3)　An appointment under this section must be in or evidenced in writing.

(4)　This section does not apply to any trust having a custodian trustee or in relation to any securities vested in the official custodian for charities.

19 PERSONS WHO MAY BE APPOINTED AS NOMINEES OR CUSTODIANS

26.46　(1)　A person may not be appointed under section 16, 17 or 18 as a nominee or custodian unless one of the relevant conditions is satisfied.

(2)　The relevant conditions are that—
(a)　the person carries on a business which consists of or includes acting as a nominee or custodian,
(b)　the person is a body corporate which is controlled by the trustees,
(c)　the person is a body corporate recognised under section 9 of the Administration of Justice Act 1985.

(3)　The question whether a body corporate is controlled by trustees is to be determined in accordance with section 1124 of the Corporation Tax Act 2010[1].

(4)　The trustees of a charitable trust which is not an exempt charity must act in accordance with any guidance given by the [Charity Commission][2] concerning the selection of a person for appointment as a nominee or custodian under section 16, 17 or 18.

(5)　Subject to subsections (1) and (4), the persons whom the trustees may under section 16, 17 or 18 appoint as a nominee or custodian include—
(a)　one of their number, if that one is a trust corporation, or
(b)　two (or more) of their number, if they are to act as joint nominees or joint custodians.

(6)　The trustees may under section 16 appoint a person to act as their nominee even though he is also—
(a)　appointed to act as their custodian (whether under section 17 or 18 or any other power), or
(b)　authorised to exercise functions as their agent (whether under section 11 or any other power).

(7)　Likewise, the trustees may under section 17 or 18 appoint a person to act as their custodian even though he is also—
(a)　appointed to act as their nominee (whether under section 16 or any other power), or
(b)　authorised to exercise functions as their agent (whether under section 11 or any other power).

1   Words s 1124 of the Corporation Tax Act 2010 substituted for s 840 of the Income and Corporation Taxes Act 1988.
2   Words in square brackets substituted by Charities Act 2006 s 75(1), Sch 8 para 197.

20 TERMS OF APPOINTMENT OF NOMINEES AND CUSTODIANS

26.47 (1) Subject to subsection (2) and sections 29 to 32, the trustees may under section 16, 17 or 18 appoint a person to act as a nominee or custodian on such terms as to remuneration and other matters as they may determine.

(2) The trustees may not under section 16, 17 or 18 appoint a person to act as a nominee or custodian on any of the terms mentioned in subsection (3) unless it is reasonably necessary for them to do so.

(3) The terms are—
(a) a term permitting the nominee or custodian to appoint a substitute,
(b) a term restricting the liability of the nominee or custodian or his substitute to the trustees or to any beneficiary,
(c) a term permitting the nominee or custodian to act in circumstances capable of giving rise to a conflict of interest.

REVIEW OF AND LIABILITY FOR AGENTS, NOMINEES AND CUSTODIANS ETC

21 APPLICATION OF SECTIONS 22 AND 23

26.48 (1) Sections 22 and 23 apply in a case where trustees have, under section 11, 16, 17 or 18—
(a) authorised a person to exercise functions as their agent, or
(b) appointed a person to act as a nominee or custodian.

(2) Subject to subsection (3), sections 22 and 23 also apply in a case where trustees have, under any power conferred on them by the trust instrument or by any enactment or any provision of subordinate legislation—
(a) authorised a person to exercise functions as their agent, or
(b) appointed a person to act as a nominee or custodian.

(3) If the application of section 22 or 23 is inconsistent with the terms of the trust instrument or the enactment or provision of subordinate legislation, the section in question does not apply.

22 REVIEW OF AGENTS, NOMINEES AND CUSTODIANS ETC

26.49 (1) While the agent, nominee or custodian continues to act for the trust, the trustees—
(a) must keep under review the arrangements under which the agent, nominee or custodian acts and how those arrangements are being put into effect,
(b) if circumstances make it appropriate to do so, must consider whether there is a need to exercise any power of intervention that they have, and

(c) if they consider that there is a need to exercise such a power, must do so.

(2) If the agent has been authorised to exercise asset management functions, the duty under subsection (1) includes, in particular—

(a) a duty to consider whether there is any need to revise or replace the policy statement made for the purposes of section 15,

(b) if they consider that there is a need to revise or replace the policy statement, a duty to do so, and

(c) a duty to assess whether the policy statement (as it has effect for the time being) is being complied with.

(3) Subsections (3) and (4) of section 15 apply to the revision or replacement of a policy statement under this section as they apply to the making of a policy statement under that section.

(4) "Power of intervention" includes—

(a) a power to give directions to the agent, nominee or custodian,

(b) a power to revoke the authorisation or appointment.

23 LIABILITY FOR AGENTS, NOMINEES AND CUSTODIANS ETC

26.50 (1) A trustee is not liable for any act or default of the agent, nominee or custodian unless he has failed to comply with the duty of care applicable to him, under paragraph 3 of Schedule 1—

(a) when entering into the arrangements under which the person acts as agent, nominee or custodian, or

(b) when carrying out his duties under section 22.

(2) If a trustee has agreed a term under which the agent, nominee or custodian is permitted to appoint a substitute, the trustee is not liable for any act or default of the substitute unless he has failed to comply with the duty of care applicable to him, under paragraph 3 of Schedule 1—

(a) when agreeing that term, or

(b) when carrying out his duties under section 22 in so far as they relate to the use of the substitute.

SUPPLEMENTARY

24 EFFECT OF TRUSTEES EXCEEDING THEIR POWERS

26.51 A failure by the trustees to act within the limits of the powers conferred by this Part—

(a) in authorising a person to exercise a function of theirs as an agent, or

(b) in appointing a person to act as a nominee or custodian,

does not invalidate the authorisation or appointment.

25 SOLE TRUSTEES

26.52 (1) Subject to subsection (2), this Part applies in relation to a trust having a sole trustee as it applies in relation to other trusts (and references in this Part to trustees—except in sections 12(1) and (3) and 19(5)—are to be read accordingly).

(2) Section 18 does not impose a duty on a sole trustee if that trustee is a trust corporation.

26 RESTRICTION OR EXCLUSION OF THIS PART ETC

26.53 The powers conferred by this Part are—
(a) in addition to powers conferred on trustees otherwise than by this Act, but
(b) subject to any restriction or exclusion imposed by the trust instrument or by any enactment or any provision of subordinate legislation.

PART V
REMUNERATION

28 TRUSTEE'S ENTITLEMENT TO PAYMENT UNDER TRUST INSTRUMENT

26.54 (1) Except to the extent (if any) to which the trust instrument makes inconsistent provision, subsections (2) to (4) apply to a trustee if—
(a) there is a provision in the trust instrument entitling him to receive payment out of trust funds in respect of services provided by him to or on behalf of the trust, and
(b) the trustee is a trust corporation or is acting in a professional capacity.

(2) The trustee is to be treated as entitled under the trust instrument to receive payment in respect of services even if they are services which are capable of being provided by a lay trustee.

(3) Subsection (2) applies to a trustee of a charitable trust who is not a trust corporation only—
(a) if he is not a sole trustee, and
(b) to the extent that a majority of the other trustees have agreed that it should apply to him.

(4) Any payments to which the trustee is entitled in respect of services are to be treated as remuneration for services (and not as a gift) for the purposes of—
(a) section 15 of the Wills Act 1837 (gifts to an attesting witness to be void), and
(b) section 34(3) of the Administration of Estates Act 1925 (order in which estate to be paid out).

(5) For the purposes of this Part, a trustee acts in a professional capacity if he acts in the course of a profession or business which consists of or includes the provision of services in connection with—
(a) the management or administration of trusts generally or a particular kind of trust, or
(b) any particular aspect of the management or administration of trusts generally or a particular kind of trust,

26.55 *Appendix Part 2: Powers*

and the services he provides to or on behalf of the trust fall within that description.

(6) For the purposes of this Part, a person acts as a lay trustee if he—
(a) is not a trust corporation, and
(b) does not act in a professional capacity.

29 REMUNERATION OF CERTAIN TRUSTEES

26.55 (1) Subject to subsection (5), a trustee who—
(a) is a trust corporation, but
(b) is not a trustee of a charitable trust,

is entitled to receive reasonable remuneration out of the trust funds for any services that the trust corporation provides to or on behalf of the trust.

(2) Subject to subsection (5), a trustee who—
(a) acts in a professional capacity, but
(b) is not a trust corporation, a trustee of a charitable trust or a sole trustee,

is entitled to receive reasonable remuneration out of the trust funds for any services that he provides to or on behalf of the trust if each other trustee has agreed in writing that he may be remunerated for the services.

(3) "Reasonable remuneration" means, in relation to the provision of services by a trustee, such remuneration as is reasonable in the circumstances for the provision of those services to or on behalf of that trust by that trustee and for the purposes of subsection (1) includes, in relation to the provision of services by a trustee who is an authorised institution under the Banking Act 1987 and provides the services in that capacity, the institution's reasonable charges for the provision of such services.

(4) A trustee is entitled to remuneration under this section even if the services in question are capable of being provided by a lay trustee.

(5) A trustee is not entitled to remuneration under this section if any provision about his entitlement to remuneration has been made—
(a) by the trust instrument, or
(b) by any enactment or any provision of subordinate legislation.

(6) This section applies to a trustee who has been authorised under a power conferred by Part IV or the trust instrument—
(a) to exercise functions as an agent of the trustees, or
(b) to act as a nominee or custodian,

as it applies to any other trustee.

31 TRUSTEES' EXPENSES

26.56 (1) A trustee—
(a) is entitled to be reimbursed from the trust funds, or
(b) may pay out of the trust funds,

expenses properly incurred by him when acting on behalf of the trust.

(2) This section applies to a trustee who has been authorised under a power conferred by Part IV or any other enactment or any provision of subordinate legislation, or by the trust instrument—

(a) to exercise functions as an agent of the trustees, or
(b) to act as a nominee or custodian,

as it applies to any other trustee.

32 REMUNERATION AND EXPENSES OF AGENTS, NOMINEES AND CUSTODIANS

26.57 (1) This section applies if, under a power conferred by Part IV or any other enactment or any provision of subordinate legislation, or by the trust instrument, a person other than a trustee has been—
(a) authorised to exercise functions as an agent of the trustees, or
(b) appointed to act as a nominee or custodian.

(2) The trustees may remunerate the agent, nominee or custodian out of the trust funds for services if—
(a) he is engaged on terms entitling him to be remunerated for those services, and
(b) the amount does not exceed such remuneration as is reasonable in the circumstances for the provision of those services by him to or on behalf of that trust.

(3) The trustees may reimburse the agent, nominee or custodian out of the trust funds for any expenses properly incurred by him in exercising functions as an agent, nominee or custodian.

PART VI
MISCELLANEOUS AND SUPPLEMENTARY

34 POWER TO INSURE[1]

26.58 1 This section substitutes a new Trustee Act 1925 s 19. The text is reproduced (as substituted) at **26.1**.

35 PERSONAL REPRESENTATIVES

26.59 (1) Subject to the following provisions of this section, this Act applies in relation to a personal representative administering an estate according to the law as it applies to a trustee carrying out a trust for beneficiaries.

(2) For this purpose this Act is to be read with the appropriate modifications and in particular—
(a) references to the trust instrument are to be read as references to the will,
(b) references to a beneficiary or to beneficiaries, apart from the reference to a beneficiary in section 8(1)(b), are to be read as references to a person or the persons interested in the due administration of the estate, and
(c) the reference to a beneficiary in section 8(1)(b) is to be read as a reference to a person who under the will of the deceased or under the law relating to intestacy is beneficially interested in the estate.

(3) Remuneration to which a personal representative is entitled under section 28 or 29 is to be treated as an administration expense for the purposes of—

26.60   *Appendix Part 2: Powers*

(a) section 34(3) of the Administration of Estates Act 1925 (order in which estate to be paid out), and
(b) any provision giving reasonable administration expenses priority over the preferential debts listed in Schedule 6 to the Insolvency Act 1986.

(4) Nothing in subsection (3) is to be treated as affecting the operation of the provisions mentioned in paragraphs (a) and (b) of that subsection in relation to any death occurring before the commencement of this section.

39 INTERPRETATION

26.60   (1) In this Act—
"asset" includes any right or interest;
"charitable trust" means a trust under which property is held for charitable purposes and "charitable purposes" has the same meaning as in the Charities Act 1993;
"custodian trustee" has the same meaning as in the Public Trustee Act 1906;
"enactment" includes any provision of a Measure of the Church Assembly or of the General Synod of the Church of England;
"exempt charity" has the same meaning as in the Charities Act 1993;
"functions" includes powers and duties;
"legal mortgage" has the same meaning as in the Law of Property Act 1925;
"personal representative" has the same meaning as in the Trustee Act 1925;
"settled land" has the same meaning as in the Settled Land Act 1925;
"trust corporation" has the same meaning as in the Trustee Act 1925;
"trust funds" means income or capital funds of the trust.

(2) In this Act the expressions listed below are defined or otherwise explained by the provisions indicated—

asset management functions	section 15(5)
custodian	section 17(2)
the duty of care	section 1(2)
the general power of investment	section 3(2)
lay trustee	section 28(6)
power of intervention	section 22(4)
the standard investment criteria	section 4(3)
subordinate legislation	section 6(3)
trustee acting in a professional capacity	section 28(5)
trust instrument	sections 6(2) and 35(2)(a)

SCHEDULE 1
APPLICATION OF DUTY OF CARE

Section 2

INVESTMENT

26.61   1   The duty of care applies to a trustee—

(a) when exercising the general power of investment or any other power of investment, however conferred;
(b) when carrying out a duty to which he is subject under section 4 or 5 (duties relating to the exercise of a power of investment or to the review of investments).

Acquisition of land

2   The duty of care applies to a trustee—

(a) when exercising the power under section 8 to acquire land;
(b) when exercising any other power to acquire land, however conferred;
(c) when exercising any power in relation to land acquired under a power mentioned in sub-paragraph (a) or (b).

Agents, nominees and custodians

3   (1)   The duty of care applies to a trustee—
(a) when entering into arrangements under which a person is authorised under section 11 to exercise functions as an agent,
(b) when entering into arrangements under which a person is appointed under section 16 to act as a nominee,
(c) when entering into arrangements under which a person is appointed under section 17 or 18 to act as a custodian,
(d) when entering into arrangements under which, under any other power, however conferred, a person is authorised to exercise functions as an agent or is appointed to act as a nominee or custodian,
(e) when carrying out his duties under section 22 (review of agent, nominee or custodian, etc).

(2)   For the purposes of sub-paragraph (1), entering into arrangements under which a person is authorised to exercise functions or is appointed to act as a nominee or custodian includes, in particular—
(a) selecting the person who is to act,
(b) determining any terms on which he is to act, and
(c) if the person is being authorised to exercise asset management functions, the preparation of a policy statement under section 15.

Compounding of liabilities

4   The duty of care applies to a trustee—
(a) when exercising the power under section 15 of the Trustee Act 1925 to do any of the things referred to in that section,
(b) when exercising any corresponding power, however conferred.

Insurance

5   The duty of care applies to a trustee—
(a) when exercising the power under section 19 of the Trustee Act 1925 to insure property,
(b) when exercising any corresponding power, however conferred.

26.61 *Appendix Part 2: Powers*

Reversionary interests, valuations and audit

6   The duty of care applies to a trustee—
(a)   when exercising the power under section 22(1) or (3) of the Trustee Act 1925 to do any of the things referred to there,
(b)   when exercising any corresponding power, however conferred.

Exclusion of duty of care

7   The duty of care does not apply if or in so far as it appears from the trust instrument that the duty is not meant to apply.

Appendix Part 3: Intestacy Rules

ADMINISTRATION OF ESTATES ACT 1925 SS 46, 47 AND 47A

46 SUCCESSION TO REAL AND PERSONAL ESTATE ON INTESTACY

27.1 (1) The residuary estate of an intestate shall be distributed in the manner or be held on the trusts mentioned in this section, namely:—

(i) If the intestate leaves a [spouse or civil partner][1], then in accordance with the following Table:

TABLE

If the intestate—
(1) leaves—
(a) no issue, and
(b) no parent, or brother or sister of the whole blood, or issue of a brother or sister of the whole blood

the residuary estate shall be held in trust for the surviving [spouse or civil partner][1] absolutely.

(2) leaves issue (whether or not persons mentioned in subparagraph (b) above also survive)

the surviving [spouse or civil partner[1]] shall take the personal chattels absolutely and, in addition, the residuary estate of the intestate (other than the personal chattels) shall stand charged with the payment of a [fixed net sum[2]], free of death duties and costs, to the surviving [spouse or civil partner[1]] with interest thereon from the date of the death ... [at such rate as the Lord Chancellor may specify by order[3]] until paid or appropriated, and, subject to providing for that sum and the interest thereon, the residuary estate (other than the personal chattels) shall be held—
(a) as to one half upon trust for the surviving [spouse or civil partner[1]] during his or her life, and, subject to such life interest, on the statutory trusts for the issue of the intestate, and
(b) as to the other half, on the statutory trusts for the issue of the intestate.

27.1 *Appendix Part 3: Intestacy Rules*

TABLE

(3) leaves one or more of the following, that is to say, a parent, a brother or sister of the whole blood, or issue of a brother or sister of the whole blood, but leaves no issue	the surviving [spouse or civil partner[1]] shall take the personal chattels absolutely and, in addition, the residuary estate of the intestate (other than the personal chattels) shall stand charged with the payment of a [fixed net sum[4]], free of death duties and costs, to the surviving [spouse or civil partner[1]] with interest thereon from the date of the death ... [at such rate as the Lord Chancellor may specify by order[5]] until paid or appropriated, and, subject to providing for that sum and the interest thereon, the residuary estate (other than the personal chattels) shall be held— (a) as to one half in trust for the surviving [spouse or civil partner[1]] absolutely, and (b) as to the other half— (i) where the intestate leaves one parent or both parents (whether or not brothers or sisters of the intestate or their issue also survive) in trust for the parent absolutely or, as the case may be, for the two parents in equal shares absolutely (ii) where the intestate leaves no parent, on the statutory trusts for the brothers and sisters of the whole blood of the intestate.

[The fixed net sums referred to in paragraphs (2) and (3) of this Table shall be of the amounts provided by or under section 1 of the Family Provision Act 1966]

(ii) If the intestate leaves issue but no [spouse or civil partner[1]] the residuary estate of the intestate shall be held on the statutory trusts for the issue of the intestate;

(iii) If the intestate leaves no [spouse or civil partner[1]] and no issue but both parents, then the residuary estate of the intestate shall be held in trust for the father and mother in equal shares absolutely;

(iv) If the intestate leaves no [spouse or civil partner[1]] and no issue but one parent, then the residuary estate of the intestate shall be held in trust for the surviving father or mother absolutely;

(v) If the intestate leaves no [spouse or civil partner[1]] and no issue and no parent, then the residuary estate of the intestate shall be held in trust for the following persons living at the death of the intestate, and in the following order and manner, namely:—

First, on the statutory trusts for the brothers and sisters of the whole blood of the intestate; but if no person takes an absolutely vested interest under such trusts; then

Secondly, on the statutory trusts for the brothers and sisters of the half blood of the intestate, but if no person takes an absolutely vested interest under such trusts; then

Thirdly, for the grandparents of the intestate and, if more than one survive the intestate, in equal shares; but if there is no member of this class; then

Fourthly, on the statutory trusts of the uncles and aunts of the intestate (being brothers or sisters of the whole blood of a parent of the intestate); but if no person takes an absolutely vested interest under such trusts; then

Fifthly, on the statutory trusts for the uncles and aunts of the intestate (being brothers or sisters of the half blood of a parent of the intestate);

(vi) In default of any person taking an absolute interest under the foregoing provisions, the residuary estate of the intestate shall belong to the Crown or to

Appendix Part 3: Intestacy Rules **27.2**

the Duchy of Lancaster or to the Duke of Cornwall for the time being, as the case may be, as bona vacantia, and in lieu of any right to escheat.

The Crown or the said Duchy or the said Duke may (without prejudice to the powers reserved by section nine of the Civil List Act 1910, or any other powers), out of the whole or any part of the property devolving on them respectively, provide, in accordance with the existing practice, for dependants, whether kindred or not, of the intestate, and other persons for whom the intestate might reasonably have been expected to make provision.

(1A) The power to make orders under subsection (1) above shall be exercisable by statutory instrument subject to annulment in pursuance of a resolution of either House of Parliament; and any such order may be varied or revoked by a subsequent order made under the power[6].

(2) A husband and wife shall for all purposes of distribution or division under the foregoing provisions of this section be treated as two persons.

(2A) Where the intestate's [spouse or civil partner][1] survived the intestate but died before the end of the period of 28 days beginning with the day on which the intestate died, this section shall have effect as respects the intestate as if the [spouse or civil partner][1] had not survived the intestate[7].

(3) Where the intestate and the intestate's [spouse or civil partner][1] have died in circumstances rendering it uncertain which of them survived the other and the intestate's [spouse or civil partner][1] is by virtue of section one hundred and eighty-four of the Law of Property Act 1925 deemed to have survived the intestate, this section shall, nevertheless, have effect as respects the intestate as if the [spouse or civil partner][1] had not survived the intestate.

(4) The interest payable on the [fixed net sum[8]] payable to a surviving [spouse or civil partner][1] shall be primarily payable out of income.

1 Words in square brackets substituted by Civil Partnership Act 2004 s 71, Sch 4 Part 2 para 7 with effect from 5 December 2005.
2 Words in square brackets substituted by Family Provisions Act 1966 s 1(2). In relation to deaths on or after 1 February 2009 this 'fixed net sum' is currently set at £250,000 where the deceased leaves a spouse or civil partner and children (Family Provision (Intestate Succession) Order 1993 (SI 1993/2906)). With effect from 1 December 1993 this was £125,000.
3 Words omitted repealed by the Statute Law (Repeals) Act 1981 and words in square brackets substituted by Administration of Justice Act 1977 s 28(1) for the rate of per cent per annum. The rate of interest is currently 6% per annum: Intestate Succession (Interest and Capitalisation) Order 1977 (SI 1977/1491) art 2, as amended by SI 1983/1374.
4 Words in square brackets substituted by Family Provisions Act 1966 s 1(2). This fixed net sum is currently set at £450,000 in relation to deaths on or after 1 February 2009. This was previously £200,000. The relevant statutory instruments are the same as those relating to the other fixed net sum; see note 2.
5 The words omitted were repealed by the Statute Law (Repeals) Act 1981. See note 3 for the rates of interest.
6 Sub-s (1A) was inserted by Administration of Justice Act 1977 s 28(1).
7 Sub-s (2A) was inserted by Law Reform (Succession) Act 1995 s 1(1), as respects an intestate dying on or after 1 January 1996.
8 Words in square brackets substituted by Family Provisions Act 1966 s 1(2). See note 2.

47 STATUTORY TRUSTS IN FAVOUR OF ISSUE AND OTHER CLASSES OF RELATIVES OF INTESTATE

27.2 (1) Where under this Part of this Act the residuary estate of an intestate, or any part thereof, is directed to be held on the statutory trusts for the issue of the intestate, the same shall be held upon the following trusts, namely:—

27.2 Appendix Part 3: Intestacy Rules

(i) In trust, in equal shares if more than one, for all or any of the children or child of the intestate, living at the death of the intestate, who attain the age of [eighteen] years[1] or marry under that age [or form a civil partnership under that age[2]], and for all or any of the issue living at the death of the intestate who attain the age of [eighteen] years[1] or marry [or form a civil partnership[3]] under that age of any child of the intestate who predeceases the intestate, such issue to take through all degrees, according to their stocks, in equal shares if more than one, the share which their parent would have taken if living at the death of the intestate, and so that no issue shall take whose parent is living at the death of the intestate and so capable of taking;

(ii) The statutory power of advancement, and the statutory provisions which relate to maintenance and accumulation of surplus income, shall apply, but when an infant marries or [forms a civil partnership[4]] such infant shall be entitled to give valid receipts for the income of the infant's share or interest;

(iii) ...[5]

(iv) The personal representatives may permit any infant contingently interested to have the use and enjoyment of any personal chattels in such manner and subject to such conditions (if any) as the personal representatives may consider reasonable, and without being liable to account for any consequential loss.

(2) If the trusts in favour of the issue of the intestate fail by reason of no child or other issue attaining an absolutely vested interest—

(a) the residuary estate of the intestate and the income thereof and all statutory accumulations, if any, of the income thereof, or so much thereof as may not have been paid or applied under any power affecting the same, shall go, devolve and be held under the provisions of this Part of this Act as if the intestate had died without leaving issue living at the death of the intestate;

(b) references in this Part of this Act to the intestate "leaving no issue" shall be construed as "leaving no issue who attain an absolutely vested interest";

(c) references in this Part of this Act to the intestate "leaving issue" or "leaving a child or other issue" shall be construed as 'leaving issue who attain an absolutely vested interest'.

(3) Where under this Part of this Act the residuary estate of an intestate or any part thereof is directed to be held on the statutory trusts for any class of relatives of the intestate, other than issue of the intestate, the same shall be held on trusts corresponding to the statutory trusts for the issue of the intestate (other than the provision for bringing any money or property into account) as if such trusts (other than as aforesaid) were repeated with the substitution of references to the members or member of that class for references to the children or child of the intestate.

(4) References in paragraph (i) of subsection (1) of the last foregoing section to the intestate leaving, or not leaving, a member of the class consisting of brothers or sisters of the whole blood of the intestate and issue of brothers or sisters of the whole blood of the intestate shall be construed as references to the intestate leaving, or not leaving, a member of that class who attains an absolutely vested interest.

(5) ...[6]

1 Words substituted by Family Law Reform Act 1969 s 3(2).
2 Words in square brackets inserted by Civil Partnership Act 2004 s 71, Sch 4 Part 2 para 8(2) with effect from 5 December 2005.
3 Words in square brackets inserted by Civil Partnership Act 2004 s 71, Sch 4 Part 2 para 8(3) with effect from 5 December 2005.

4   Words in square brackets inserted by Civil Partnership Act 2004 s 71, Sch 4 Part 2 para 8(4) with effect from 5 December 2005.
5   Repealed by Law Reform (Succession) Act 1995 ss 1(2)(a), 5, Sch, as respects intestates dying on or after 1 January 1996.
6   Repealed by Family Provision Act 1966 ss 9, 10, Sch 2.

47A RIGHT OF SURVIVING SPOUSE TO HAVE HIS OWN LIFE INTEREST REDEEMED

27.3 (1) Where a surviving [spouse or civil partner][1] is entitled to a life interest in part of the residuary estate, and so elects, the personal representative shall purchase or redeem the life interest by paying the capital value thereof to the tenant for life, or the persons deriving title under the tenant for life, and the costs of the transaction; and thereupon the residuary estate of the intestate may be dealt with and distributed free from the life interest.

(2) ...[2]

(3) An election under this section shall only be exercisable if at the time of the election the whole of the said part of the residuary estate consists of property in possession, but, for the purposes of this section, a life interest in property partly in possession and partly not in possession shall be treated as consisting of two separate life interests in those respective parts of the property.

(3A) The capital value shall be reckoned in such manner as the Lord Chancellor may by order direct, and an order under this subsection may include transitional provisions.

(3B) The power to make orders under subsection (3A) above shall be exercisable by statutory instrument subject to annulment in pursuance of a resolution of either House of Parliament; and any such order may be varied or revoked by a subsequent order made under the power[3],

(4) ...[2]

(5) An election under this section shall be exercisable only within the period of twelve months from the date on which representation with respect to the estate of the intestate is first taken out:

Provided that if the surviving [spouse or civil partner[1]] satisfies the court that the limitation to the said period of twelve months will operate unfairly—
(a)   in consequence of the representation first taken out being probate of a will subsequently revoked on the ground that the will was invalid, or
(b)   in consequence of a question whether a person had an interest in the estate, or as to the nature of an interest in the estate, not having been determined at the time when representation was first taken out, or
(c)   in consequence of some other circumstances affecting the administration or distribution of the estate,

the court may extend the said period.

(6) An election under this section shall be exercisable, except where the tenant for life is the sole personal representative, by notifying the personal representative (or, where there are two or more personal representatives of whom one is the tenant for life, all of them except the tenant for life) in writing; and a notification in writing under this subsection shall not be revocable except with the consent of the personal representative.

27.3 Appendix Part 3: Intestacy Rules

(7) Where the tenant for life is the sole personal representative an election under this section shall not be effective unless written notice thereof is given to the [Senior Registrar of the Family Division of the High Court[4]] within the period within which it must be made; and provision may be made by probate rules for keeping a record of such notices and making that record available to the public.

In this subsection the expression 'probate rules' means rules [of court made under section 127 of the Supreme Court Act 1981[5]].

(8) An election under this section by a tenant for life who is an infant shall be as valid and binding as it would be if the tenant for life were of age; but the personal representative shall, instead of paying the capital value of the life interest to the tenant for life, deal with it in the same manner as with any other part of the residuary estate to which the tenant for life is absolutely entitled.

(9) In considering for the purposes of the foregoing provisions of this section the question when representation was first taken out, a grant limited to settled land or to trust property shall be left out of account and a grant limited to real estate or to personal estate shall be left out of account unless a grant limited to the remainder of the estate has previously been made or is made at the same time.

1   Words in square brackets inserted by Civil Partnership Act 2004 s 71, Sch 4 Part 2 para 9 with effect from 5 December 2005.
2   Repealed by Administration of Justice Act 1977 s 32, Sch 5 Part VI. Rules replacing those formerly enacted by s 47A(2) to calculate the capital value of a life interest in favour of a surviving spouse in the residuary estate are prescribed by Intestate Succession (Interest and Capitalisation) Order 1977 (SI 1977/1491) art 3.
3   Inserted by Administration of Justice Act 1977 s 28(3).
4   Words in brackets substituted by Administration of Justice Act 1970 s 1, Sch 2 and Supreme Court Act 1981 s 152(1), Sch 5. Reference to the Supreme Court Act 1981 amended to the Senior Courts Act 1981 by Constitutional Reform Act 2005 s 59(5), Sch 11 Part 1 from a date to be appointed.
5   Words in brackets substituted by Supreme Court Act 1981 s 152(1), Sch 5. Reference to the Supreme Court Act 1981 amended to the Senior Courts Act 1981 by Constitutional Reform Act 2005 s 59(5), Sch 11 Part 1 from a date to be appointed.

Appendix Part 4: Inheritance tax and capital gains tax

INHERITANCE TAX ACT 1984 ss 8A to 8C and FINANCE ACT 2008 SCH 4

8A Transfer of unused nil-rate band between spouses and civil partners

28.1 (1) This section applies where—

(a) immediately before the death of a person (a "deceased person"), the deceased person had a spouse or civil partner ("the survivor"), and

(b) the deceased person had unused nil-rate band on death.

(2) A person has unused nil-rate band on death if—

$$M > VT$$

where—

M is the maximum amount that could be transferred by a chargeable transfer made (under section 4 above) on the person's death if it were to be wholly chargeable to tax at the rate of nil per cent. (assuming, if necessary, that the value of the person's estate were sufficient but otherwise having regard to the circumstances of the person); and

VT is the value actually transferred by the chargeable transfer so made (or nil if no chargeable transfer is so made).

(3) Where a claim is made under this section, the nil-rate band maximum at the time of the survivor's death is to be treated for the purposes of the charge to tax on the death of the survivor as increased by the percentage specified in subsection (4) below (but subject to subsection (5) and section 8C below).

(4) That percentage is—

$$(E \div NRBMD) \times 100$$

where—

E is the amount by which M is greater than VT in the case of the deceased person; and

NRBMD is the nil-rate band maximum at the time of the deceased person's death.

28.2 *Appendix Part 4: Inheritance tax and capital gains tax*

(5) If (apart from this subsection) the amount of the increase in the nil-rate band maximum at the time of the survivor's death effected by this section would exceed the amount of that nil-rate band maximum, the amount of the increase is limited to the amount of that nil-rate band maximum.

(6) Subsection (5) above may apply either—
(*a*) because the percentage mentioned in subsection (4) above (as reduced under section 8C below where that section applies) is more than 100 because of the amount by which M is greater than VT in the case of one deceased person, or
(*b*) because this section applies in relation to the survivor by reference to the death of more than one person who had unused nil-rate band on death.

(7) In this Act "nil-rate band maximum" means the amount shown in the second column in the first row of the Table in Schedule 1 to this Act (upper limit of portion of value charged at rate of nil per cent.) and in the first column in the second row of that Table (lower limit of portion charged at next rate).]

8B Claims under section 8A

28.2 (1) A claim under section 8A above may be made—
(*a*) by the personal representatives of the survivor within the permitted period, or
(*b*) (if no claim is so made) by any other person liable to the tax chargeable on the survivor's death within such later period as an officer of Revenue and Customs may in the particular case allow.

(2) If no claim under section 8A above has been made in relation to a person (P) by reference to whose death that section applies in relation to the survivor, the claim under that section in relation to the survivor may include a claim under that section in relation to P if that does not affect the tax chargeable on the value transferred by the chargeable transfer of value made on P's death.

(3) In subsection (1)(*a*) above "the permitted period" means—
(*a*) the period of two years from the end of the month in which the survivor dies or (if it ends later) the period of three months beginning with the date on which the personal representatives first act as such, or
(*b*) such longer period as an officer of Revenue and Customs may in the particular case allow.

(4) A claim made within either of the periods mentioned in subsection (3)(*a*) above may be withdrawn no later than one month after the end of the period concerned.

8C Section 8A and subsequent charges

28.3 (1) This section applies where—
(*a*) the conditions in subsection (1)(*a*) and (*b*) of section 8A above are met, and
(*b*) after the death of the deceased person, tax is charged on an amount under any of sections 32, 32A and 126 below by reference to the rate or rates that would have been applicable to the amount if it were included in the value transferred by the chargeable transfer made (under section 4 above) on the deceased person's death.

Appendix Part 4: Inheritance tax and capital gains tax **28.4**

(2) If the tax is charged before the death of the survivor, the percentage referred to in subsection (3) of section 8A above is (instead of that specified in subsection (4) of that section)—

$$((E \div NRBMD) - (TA \div NRBME)) \times 100$$

where—

E and NRBMD have the same meaning as in subsection (4) of that section;

TA is the amount on which tax is charged; and

NRBME is the nil-rate band maximum at the time of the event occasioning the charge.

(3) If this section has applied by reason of a previous event or events, the reference in subsection (2) to the fraction—

$$TA \div NRBME$$

is to the aggregate of that fraction in respect of the current event and the previous event (or each of the previous events).

(4) If the tax is charged after the death of the survivor, it is charged as if the personal nil-rate band maximum of the deceased person were appropriately reduced.

(5) In subsection (4) above—
"the personal nil-rate band maximum of the deceased person" is the nil-rate band maximum which is treated by Schedule 2 to this Act as applying in relation to the deceased person's death, increased in accordance with section 8A above where that section effected an increase in that nil-rate band maximum in the case of the deceased person (as survivor of another deceased person), and
"appropriately reduced" means reduced by the amount (if any) by which the amount on which tax was charged at the rate of nil per cent. on the death of the survivor was increased by reason of the operation of section 8A above by virtue of the position of the deceased person.

FINANCE ACT 2008

SCHEDULE 4 Inheritance Tax: Transfer of Nil-rate Band etc

Section 10 Amendments of IHTA 1984

28.4 ...*Commencement*

9(1) The amendments made by paragraphs 2, 3 and 4(4)[1] have effect in relation to cases where the survivor's death occurs on or after 9 October 2007.

(2) The amendments made by paragraphs 4(2) and (3) have effect in relation to deaths, cases where scheme administrators become aware of deaths and cessations of dependency occurring on or after 6 April 2008.

(3) ...

Modifications for cases where deceased person died before 25 July 1986

28.4 *Appendix Part 4: Inheritance tax and capital gains tax*

10

(1)   Section 8A of IHTA 1984 (as inserted by paragraph 2) has effect in relation to cases where the deceased person died before 25 July 1986 (and the survivor dies on or after 9 October 2007) subject as follows.

(2)   Where the deceased person died on or after 1 January 1985—
(a)   the references in subsection (2) to a chargeable transfer made under section 4 of IHTA 1984 is to a chargeable transfer made under section 4 of CTTA 1984, and
(b)   the reference in subsection (4) to the nil-rate band maximum is to the amount shown in the second column of the first row, and the first column of the second row, of the First Table in Schedule 1 to that Act.

(3)   Where the deceased person died on or after 13 March 1975 and before 1 January 1985—
(a)   the references in subsection (2) to a chargeable transfer made under section 4 of IHTA 1984 is to a chargeable transfer made under section 22 of FA 1975, and
(b)   the reference in subsection (4) to the nil-rate band maximum is to the amount shown in the second column of the first row, and in the first column of the second row, of the First Table in section 37 of that Act.

(4)   Where the deceased person died on or after 16 April 1969 and before 13 March 1975, section 8A applies as if—
(a)   M were the amount specified in paragraph (a) in Part 1 of Schedule 17 to FA 1969 at the time of the deceased person's death,
(b)   VT were the aggregate principal value of all property comprised in the estate of the deceased person for the purposes of estate duty, and
(c)   the reference in subsection (4) to the nil-rate band maximum were to the amount mentioned in paragraph (a).

(5)   Where the deceased person died before 16 April 1969, section 8A applies as if—
(a)   M were the amount specified as the higher figure in the first line, and the lower figure in the second line, in the first column of the scale in section 17 of FA 1894 at the time of the deceased person's death,
(b)   VT were the principal value of the estate of the deceased person for the purposes of estate duty, and
(c)   the reference in subsection (4) to the nil-rate band maximum were to the figure mentioned in paragraph (a).

11 (1)   Section 8C of IHTA 1984 (as inserted by paragraph 2) has effect in relation to cases where the deceased person died before 25 July 1986 but on or after 13 March 1975 (and the survivor dies on or after 9 October 2007) subject as follows.

(2)   Where the deceased person died on or after 1 January 1985—
(a)   the reference in subsection (1) to sections 32, 32A and 126 of IHTA 1984 includes sections 32, 32A and 126 of CTTA 1984,
(b)   the reference in that subsection to section 4 of IHTA 1984 is to section 4 of CTTA 1984,
(c)   the reference in subsection (2) to the nil-rate band maximum includes the amount shown in the second column of the first row, and the first column of the second row, of the First Table in Schedule 1 to that Act,
(d)   the first reference in subsection (5) to the nil-rate band maximum is to that amount, and

(e) the reference in subsection (5) to Schedule 2 to IHTA 1984 includes Schedule 2 to CTTA 1984.

(3) Where the deceased person died on or after 7 April 1976 and before 1 January 1985—
(a) the reference in subsection (1) to sections 32, 32A and 126 of IHTA 1984 includes sections 32, 32A and 126 of CTTA 1984, section 78 of FA 1976 and paragraph 2 of Schedule 9 to FA 1975,
(b) the reference in that subsection to section 4 of IHTA is to section 22 of FA 1975,
(c) the reference in subsection (2) to the nil-rate band maximum includes the amount shown in the second column of the first row, and the first column of the second row, of the First Table in Schedule 1 to CTTA 1984 and the amount shown in the second column of the first row, and in the first column of the second row, of the First Table in section 37 of FA 1975,
(d) the first reference in subsection (5) to the nil-rate band maximum is to that amount, and
(e) the reference in subsection (5) to Schedule 2 to IHTA 1984 includes Schedule 2 to CTTA 1984, Schedule 15 to FA 1980 and section 62 of FA 1978;

but, if the event occasioning the charge occurred before 27 October 1977, the reference in subsection (4) to the personal nil-rate band maximum is to the amount shown in the second column of the first row, and in the first column of the second row, of the First Table in section 37 of FA 1975 at the time of the deceased person's death.

(4) Where the deceased person died on or after 13 March 1975 and before 7 April 1976—
(a) the reference in subsection (1) to sections 32, 32A and 126 of IHTA 1984 includes paragraph 1 of Schedule 5 to that Act, section 126 of CTTA 1984 and paragraph 2 of Schedule 9 to FA 1975,
(b) the reference in that subsection to section 4 of IHTA is to section 22 of FA 1975,
(c) the reference in subsection (2) to the nil-rate band maximum includes the amount shown in the second column of the first row, and the first column of the second row, of the First Table in Schedule 1 to CTTA 1984 and the amount shown in the second column of the first row, and in the first column of the second row, of the First Table in section 37 of FA 1975, and
(d) the reference in subsection (4) to the personal nil-rate band maximum is to the amount shown in the second column of the first row, and in the first column of the second row, of the First Table in section 37 of FA 1975 at the time of the deceased person's death.

1   I.e. the insertion of sections 8A, 8B and 8C.

INHERITANCE TAX ACT 1984 ss 142, 143 and 144

142 Alteration of dispositions taking effect on death

28.5 (1) Where within the period of two years after a person's death[1]—
(*a*) any of the dispositions (whether effected by will, under the law relating to intestacy or otherwise) of the property comprised in his estate immediately before his death are varied, or
(*b*) the benefit conferred by any of those dispositions is disclaimed,

28.6 *Appendix Part 4: Inheritance tax and capital gains tax*

by an instrument in writing made by the persons or any of the persons who benefit or would benefit under the dispositions, this Act shall apply as if the variation had been effected by the deceased or, as the case may be, the disclaimed benefit had never been conferred.

[(2) Subsection (1) above shall not apply to a variation unless the instrument contains a statement, made by all the relevant persons, to the effect that they intend the subsection to apply to the variation.

(2A) For the purposes of subsection (2) above the relevant persons are—

(*a*) the person or persons making the instrument, and
(*b*) where the variation results in additional tax being payable, the personal representatives;

Personal representatives may decline to make a statement under subsection (2) above only if no, or no sufficient, assets are held by them in that capacity for discharging the additional tax.][2]

(3) Subsection (1) above shall not apply to a variation or disclaimer made for any consideration in money or money's worth other than consideration consisting of the making, in respect of another of the dispositions, of a variation or disclaimer to which that subsection applies.

(4) Where a variation to which subsection (1) above applies results in property being held in trust for a person for a period which ends not more than two years after the death, this Act shall apply as if the disposition of the property that takes effect at the end of the period had had effect from the beginning of the period; but this subsection shall not affect the application of this Act in relation to any distribution or application of property occurring before that disposition takes effect.

(5) For the purposes of subsection (1) above the property comprised in a person's estate includes any excluded property but not any property to which he is treated as entitled by virtue of section 49(1) above [or section 102 of the Finance Act 1986][3].

(6) Subsection (1) above applies whether or not the administration of the estate is complete or the property concerned has been distributed in accordance with the original dispositions.

(7) In the application of subsection (4) above to Scotland, property which is subject to a proper liferent shall be deemed to be held in trust for the liferenter.

1 Sub-ss (1) to (6) derived from Finance Act 1978 s 68(1) to (5); sub-s (7) derived from the Finance Act 1978 s 68(4) and Finance Act 1980 s 93(3).
2 Sub-ss (2) and (2A) substituted by Finance Act 2002 s 120.
3 Sub-s (5): words in square brackets added by Finance Act 1986 s 101, Sch 19 Part I para 24, in relation to transfers of value made, and other events occurring, on or after 18 March 1986.

143 Compliance with testator's request

28.6 Where a testator expresses a wish that property bequeathed by his will should be transferred by the legatee to other persons, and the legatee transfers any of the property in accordance with that wish within the period of two years after the death of the testator, this Act shall have effect as if the property transferred had been bequeathed by the will to the transferee.

144 Distribution etc from property settled by will

28.7 (1) [Subsection (2) below applies]¹ where property comprised in a person's estate immediately before his death is settled by his will and, within the period of two years after his death and before any interest in possession has subsisted in the property, there occurs—
(a) an event on which tax would ([apart from subsection (2) below]¹) be chargeable under any provision, other than section 64 or 79, of Chapter III of Part III of this Act, or
(b) an event on which tax would be so chargeable but for section 75 or 76 above or paragraph 16(1) of Schedule 4 to this Act.

[(1A) Where the testator dies on or after 22nd March 2006, subsection (1) above shall have effect as if the reference to any interest in possession were a reference to any interest in possession that is—
(a) an immediate post-death interest, or
(b) a disabled person's interest².]

(2) Where this section applies by virtue of an event within paragraph (a) of subsection (1) above, tax shall not be charged under the provision in question on that event; and in every case in which [this subsection¹] applies in relation to an event, this Act shall have effect as if the will had provided that on the testator's death the property should be held as it is held after the event.

[(3) Subsection (4) below applies where—
(a) a person dies on or after 22nd March 2006,
(b) property comprised in the person's estate immediately before his death is settled by his will, and
(c) within the period of two years after his death, but before an immediate post-death interest or a disabled person's interest has subsisted in the property, there occurs an event that involves causing the property to be held on trusts that would, if they had in fact been established by the testator's will, have resulted in—
   (i) an immediate post-death interest subsisting in the property, or
   (ii) section 71A or 71D above applying to the property.

(4) Where this subsection applies by virtue of an event—
(a) this Act shall have effect as if the will had provided that on the testator's death the property should be held as it is held after the event, but
(b) tax shall not be charged on that event under any provision of Chapter 3 of Part 3 of this Act.

(5) Subsection (4) above also applies where—
(a) a person dies before 22nd March 2006,
(b) property comprised in the person's estate immediately before his death is settled by his will,
(c) an event occurs—
   (i) on or after 22nd March 2006, and
   (ii) within the period of two years after the testator's death,
   that involves causing the property to be held on trusts within subsection (6) below,
(d) no immediate post-death interest, and no disabled person's interest, subsisted in the property at any time in the period beginning with the testator's death and ending immediately before the event, and

28.8 *Appendix Part 4: Inheritance tax and capital gains tax*

(e) no other interest in possession subsisted in the property at any time in the period beginning with the testator's death and ending immediately before 22nd March 2006.

(6) Trusts are within this subsection if they would, had they in fact been established by the testator's will and had the testator died at the time of the event mentioned in subsection (5)(c) above, have resulted in—

(a) an immediate post-death interest subsisting in the property, or

(b) section 71A or 71D above applying to the property.][2]

1 Words in sub-ss (1), (2) substituted by Finance Act 2006 s 156, Sch 20 paras 7, 27.
2 Sub-ss (1A), (3)–(6) inserted by Finance Act 2006 s 156, Sch 20 paras 7, 27.

INLAND REVENUE STATEMENT OF PRACTICE 10/79

Power for trustees to allow a beneficiary to occupy dwelling-house

28.8 Many wills and settlements contain a clause empowering the trustees to permit a beneficiary to occupy a dwelling-house which forms part of the trust property as they think fit. The Board do not regard the existence of such a power as excluding any interest in possession of the property.

When there is no interest in possession in the property in question, the Board do not regard the exercise of power as creating one if the effect is merely to allow non-exclusive occupation or to create a contractual tenancy for full consideration. The Board also take the view that no interest in possession arises on the creation of a lease for a term or a periodic tenancy for less than full consideration, though this will normally give rise to a charge for tax under IHTA 1984 s 65(1)(b) (formerly FA 1982 s 108(1)(b)). On the other hand if the power is drawn in terms wide enough to cover the creation of an exclusive or joint residence, albeit revocable, for a definite or indefinite period, and is exercised with the intention of providing a particular beneficiary with a permanent home, the Revenue will normally regard the exercise of the power as creating an interest in possession. And if the trustees in exercise of their powers grant a lease for life for less than full consideration, this will be regarded as creating an interest in possession in view of IHTA 1984 ss 43(3), 50(6) (formerly FA 1975 Sch 5 paras 1(3), 3(6)).

A similar view will be taken where the power is exercised over property in which another beneficiary had an interest in possession up to the time of the exercise.

INLAND REVENUE PRESS RELEASE 6 AUGUST 1975

Power to allow beneficiary to occupy house

28.9 "Commonly such a power is ancillary to a primary trust created by the will and we should not regard its presence as affecting any interest in possession existing under that trust. If there is no such interest it could perhaps be argued that the exercise of the power might create one, but in the ordinary case we should not take this view unless the trustees were empowered to, and did, grant a lease for life within the terms of FA 1975 Sch 5 para 1(3) [now Inheritance Tax Act 1984 s 43(3)]."

"If the exercise of the power reduces the value of the settled property, as it would if the trustees could and did grant a lease for a fixed term at less than a rack rent, we should in practice seek the alternative charge given by para 6(3) [repealed 1982] or 4(9) [now Inheritance Tax Act 1984 s 52(3),(4)] of the Schedule."

TAXATION OF CHARGEABLE GAINS ACT 1992 s 62

62 Death: general provisions

28.10 (1) For the purposes of this Act the assets of which a deceased person was competent to dispose—

(*a*) shall be deemed to be acquired on his death by the personal representatives or other person on whom they devolve for a consideration equal to their market value at the date of the death, but

(*b*) shall not be deemed to be disposed of by him on his death (whether or not they were the subject of a testamentary disposition).

(2) Allowable losses sustained by an individual in the year of assessment in which he dies may, so far as they cannot be deducted from chargeable gains accruing in that year, be deducted from chargeable gains accruing to the deceased in the three years of assessment preceding the year of assessment in which the death occurs, taking chargeable gains accruing in a later year before those accruing in an earlier year.

[(2A) Amounts deductible from chargeable gains for any year in accordance with subsection (2) above shall not be so deductible from any such gains so far as they are gains that are [treated as accruing by virtue of section 87 or 89(2) (read, where appropriate, with section 10A)]³.

(3) In relation to property forming part of the estate of a deceased person the personal representatives shall for the purposes of this Act be treated as being a single and continuing body of persons (distinct from the persons who may from time to time be the personal representatives), and that body shall be treated as having the deceased's residence, ordinary residence, and domicile at the date of death.

(4) On a person acquiring any asset as legatee (as defined in section 64)—

(*a*) no chargeable gain shall accrue to the personal representatives, and

(*b*) the legatee shall be treated as if the personal representatives' acquisition of the asset had been his acquisition of it.

(5) Notwithstanding section 17(1) no chargeable gain shall accrue to any person on his making a disposal by way of donatio mortis causa.

(6) Subject to subsections (7) and (8) below, where within the period of two years after a person's death any of the dispositions (whether effected by will, under the law relating to intestacy or otherwise) of the property of which he was competent to dispose are varied, or the benefit conferred by any of those dispositions is disclaimed, by an instrument in writing made by the persons or any of the persons who benefit or would benefit under the dispositions—

(*a*) the variation or disclaimer shall not constitute a disposal for the purposes of this Act, and

(*b*) this section shall apply as if the variation had been effected by the deceased or, as the case may be, the disclaimed benefit had never been conferred.

28.10 *Appendix Part 4: Inheritance tax and capital gains tax*

(7) Subsection (6) above does not apply to a variation [unless the instrument contains a statement by the persons making the instrument to the effect that they intend the subsection to apply to the variation²].

(8) Subsection (6) above does not apply to a variation or disclaimer made for any consideration in money or money's worth other than consideration consisting of the making of a variation or disclaimer in respect of another of the dispositions.

(9) Subsection (6) above applies whether or not the administration of the estate is complete or the property has been distributed in accordance with the original dispositions.

(10) In this section references to assets of which a deceased person was competent to dispose are references to assets of the deceased which (otherwise than in right of a power of appointment or of the testamentary power conferred by statute to dispose of entailed interests) he could, if of full age and capacity, have disposed of by his will, assuming that all the assets were situated in England and, if he was not domiciled in the United Kingdom, that he was domiciled in England, and include references to his severable share in any assets to which, immediately before his death, he was beneficially entitled as a joint tenant.

1   Subsections inserted by Finance Act 1998 s 121(3), Sch 21 para 5.
2   Words substituted by Finance Act 2002 s 52.
3   Words in sub-s (2A) substituted and the whole of s (2B) repealed by Finance Act 2008 s 8 Sch 2 paras 23, 29 with effect from tax year 2008/09.

Index

[references are to paragraph numbers]

A

Accountants
  appointment as executors 6.18
Accrual
  equal shares 13.2
  proportional 13.2
Accumulation of income 12.3, 26.2
  age contingent gifts 11.19, 11.23, 12.3
  minor, for 12.3
  restrictions on 26.5
    changes to 1.14, 11.19, 12.3, 26.6
Ademption 10.5
  excluding 13.2
Administration trusts 11.1–11.3
Adopted children 13.2
Adoption
  disposition
    date of birth, depending on 25.31
    meaning 25.33
  meaning 25.27
  protection of trustees and personal representatives 25.32
  rules of interpretation 25.30
  status conferred by 25.28
Adoptive relatives 25.29
Advancement 12.4, 12.23, 26.3
Advances
  account to be taken of 13.2
  no account to be taken of 13.2
Affidavit of due execution 14.5
Age
  under-age will 25.2
Age contingent gifts 11.14–11.24
  age greater than 18 11.18
  capital gains tax, and 11.21
  income accumulation 11.19, 11.23, 12.3
  income tax, and 11.22, 11.23

Age contingent gifts 11.14–11.24 – *contd*
  inheritance tax, and 11.20
  nil-rate tax band, of amount of 15.65
  perpetuity rule and changes to 11.15–11.19, 26.5–26.13
  variation of trust, scope for 11.24
  'wait and see' provisions 11.15, 11.16, 26.9
Agents 26.38–26.42
  appointment 12.13
  asset management restrictions 26.42
  expenses 26.56
  liability for 12.17, 12.18, 26.48–26.50
  remuneration 26.57
  trustees, of 12.13
Alteration
  attestation 14.2
  executed as a will 25.10
Appointment, power of
  rule against perpetuities, for 26.11
Appropriation 12.23
Assets see also Chattels
  contingent, account of 1.5
  custodian of 12.15, 12.16
  management 12.14, 26.42
  nominee for 12.15, 12.16
  sale, restriction precedent 13.2
  trust assets, purchase by trustees 12.23
Attestation 14.1–14.14, 25.3 see also Witnesses
  alterations, and 14.2
  beneficiary as witness 14.4
  capacity 2.26
  witnesses 14.3
  clause, standard form 14.14
  codicil 14.14
  draftsman's duty relating to 14.7–14.10
  formalities 14.1

Index

Attestation 14.1–14.14, 25.3 see also Witnesses – *contd*
  precedents 14.14
  provisions 25.3
  testator unable to read or write 14.6, 14.14
  valid clause 14.5
  will made by authorised person under Mental Capacity Act 2005 14.14
Attorney, power of
  delegation to beneficiary by trustee 26.22

B

Bank
  appointment as executors and trustees 6.20
Bearer securities 26.45
Beneficiaries
  child see Child
  consultation with 10.13, 10.14, 26.25
  delegation to 10.12, 26.22
  occupation right 26.26, 26.27
    Inland Revenue Press Release 28.9
    Inland Revenue Statement of Practice 28.8
  residence right 10.19–10.22, 10.23
Bereaved minors, trust for 15.39–15.42
Body, donation of see Donation of body
Borrowing power 12.23
Burial
  direction for 5.9
Business
  chattel 9.7
  family, gift of 9.16–9.19
  farming, option to purchase 9.20
  power to carry on business 12.23
  sole proprietor, gift by 9.16, 9.20

C

Capacity of testator
  allegations 2.17
  attestation clause 2.26
  doubt as to 2.25
  draftsman's duty relating to 14.11–14.13
  'functional' approach 2.22
  meaning 2.19–2.29
  Mental Capacity Act Code of Practice 2.21

Capacity of testator – *contd*
  powers of court to make decisions and appoint deputies 25.21–25.23
  probate claims, and 2.16–2.29
  test of 2.19, 2.20
Capital gains tax
  age contingent gifts, and 11.21
  death: general provisions 28.10
  variations after death, and 22.4
Care, duty of see Trustees
Charge
  chattel subject to 9.12, 9.13
  land subject to mortgage 10.2–10.4
  payment out of property charged 25.16
  trustees' power 6.4–6.7
Charities
  gifts to 8.9–8.12
    business use 9.7
    charge, subject to 9.12, 9.13
    collections 9.8
    credit sale, subject to 9.12, 9.13
    debts, of 9.14
    family business 9.16–9.19
    general 9.6
    hire purchase, subject to 9.12, 9.13
    inflation-proof 8.13
    inheritance tax, and 9.3
    need for 9.1, 9.2
    personal 9.4–9.7
    precedents 8.13, 9.20
    releases, and 9.14
    schemes of distribution 9.9–9.11
    selection right 9.9–9.11
    settled 9.2
    shares 9.15
    similar items 9.5
Chattels
  gift of 9.1–9.20
    business use 9.7
    charge, subject to 9.12, 9.13
    collections 9.8
    debts 9.14
    disputes about 9.9
    family business 9.16–9.19
    inheritance tax issues 9.3
    personal 9.4, 9.6, 9.7
    precedent clauses 9.20
    selection right 9.9–9.11
    separate gift 9.1

Chattels – *contd*
  gift of 9.1–9.20 – *contd*
    settled 9.2
    shares 9.15
    wording to avoid ambiguity 9.4, 9.5
    payment out of property charged 25.16
Checklist 1.7, 24.3
Child
  adopted 13.2
  age, gift contingent on see Age contingent gifts
  bereaved minor, trust for 15.39–15.42
  complete wills
    married couples with children 19.1–19.12
    unmarried couples with children 20.1, 20.2
  conveyance of land, trust on 26.29
  disabled, trust for 19.12
  discretionary trust of residue for 11.30
  executor, as 6.20
  gifts of real property to 10.6
  guardian for see Testamentary guardians
  illegitimate 13.2
  inheritance tax nil-rate band, example gifts using 15.65
  legitimated 13.2, 25.26
  maintenance and advancement 12.3, 12.4, 12.23
  receipts 12.23
  trusts for 15.65, 19.11
  'without issue', construction 25.13
Civil partnerships 1.12, 16.1
  child of, construction of references to 25.24
  complete wills
    no children 18.1, 18.2
    precedents 18.2, 19.11
    second civil partnership 21.1–21.3
    with children 19.1–19.12
  dissolution or annulment, effect of 25.8
  inheritance tax nil-rate band, application to 15.9, 15.10
  intestacy rules, and surviving partner 27.1–27.3
  revocation of will by 25.7

Civil partnerships 1.12, 16.1 – *contd*
  void, child of 25.24
Class closing rules 11.27
Codicil
  examples 16.6
  revival of will, by 25.11
Cohabitees
  complete wills, couples with children 20.1, 20.2
  inheritance tax 15.3
  life interest 20.1
Complete wills
  date 16.5
  five situations 16.1
  married couple/civil partner, no children 18.1, 18.2
  married couple/civil partner, with children 19.1–19.11
  second marriages or civil partnerships 21.1–21.3
  single adults, precedents 17.1
  STEP standard provisions 16.2, 16.3
  unmarried couples with children 20.1, 20.2
Consents 26.24
Construction of will
  speaking from death of testator 25.12
Consultation with beneficiaries 10.13, 10.14, 26.25
Contingent assets 1.5
Contingent gifts see Age contingent gifts
Conversion
  abolition of doctrine 26.16
Cremation 5.6
  ashes scattered 5.9
  deposit of ashes 5.9
  funeral service followed by 5.9
  objection to 5.9
Custodians 12.15, 12.16
  expenses 26.56
  liability for 21.48–21.50
  persons who may be appointed 26.46
  power to employ 26.44
  remuneration 26.57
  terms of appointment 26.47

D

Debts
  gifts of 9.14
Declarations 5.1–5.9, 13.1–13.2
  exclusion 5.2, 5.9

Index

Declarations 5.1–5.9, 13.1–13.2 – *contd*
  foreign element 5.9
  jurisdiction 5.2
Deed of variation 22.10–22.24
  distribution, after 22.14
  further variation, and 22.19
  implementation in real world 22.16
  intestacy, and 22.23, 22.25
  nil-rate band, and 22.15
  scope 22.10–22.12
  stamp duty, and 22.17
  stamp duty land tax 22.18
  survivorship, and 22.24
Definitions 25.17
Delegation see also Agents
  beneficiaries, to 10.12, 26.22, 26.23
Deputy
  court appointment of 25.21
    property and affairs 25.22, 25.23
Destruction of will
  revocation by 25.9
Devises 10.1
Die without issue
  meaning 25.13
Disclaimer 15.57, 15.58, 22.1–22.25 see also Variations after death
  deed, by 22.9 , 22.25
  effect 22.8
  formalities 22.2
  made by all beneficiaries 22.3
  precedents 22.25
Discretionary trusts 11.28, 11.29
  appointment ending within two years of death 24.12
  letter about 24.6
  matrimonial home share, as asset of 15.48–15.57
    charge scheme 15.55–15.57
    debt scheme 15.51–15.54, 15.57
    immediate post-death interest, avoiding 15.50, 15.54
    promissory note scheme see Promissory note
  nil-rate band 15.37, 15.38, 15.50, 15.48–15.57
    examples, beneficiaries other than spouse 15.65
    short-term 15.60–15.64
  residue, of 11.30

Discretionary trusts 11.28, 11.29 – *contd*
  short-term, gift of nil-rate on 15.60–15.64
Disposal of body 5.3–5.8
Domicile 2.39–2.41
  fiscal 2.41
  obvious 2.39
Donation of body 5.7, 5.8, 5.9
  Human Tissue Act 2004 5.7, 5.8
  Human Tissue Authority, abolition 5.7
Draft will
  letter submitting 24.7
Drafting 1.10–1.15
  clarity, need for 1.10,1.11
  set forms, and 1.10

E

Evidence
  general rules 25.20
Execution
  affidavit of due execution 14.5
  alteration after 14.2
Executors 6.1–6.20 see also Trustees
  accountants 6.18
  appointment 6.1–6.20
    accountants 6.18, 6.20
    bank 6.20
    beneficiaries 6.20
    members of solicitors' firm 6.20
    minor, contingent appointment 6.20
    precedents 6.20
    professional charges clause 6.20
    Public Trustee 6.20
    sole with alternative provision 6.20
    solicitors 6.8–6.10
    surviving civil partner with friend as alternative 6.20
    testator's widow with children as alternatives 6.20
    trust, where 6.20
    two executors where no possibility of trust 6.20
    two others as trustees, with 6.20
  charge, power to 6.4–6.7
    professional charges clause 6.20
  common appointments 6.15–6.19

Executors 6.1–6.20 see also **Trustees** – *contd*
   conflict of interest, possibility of 6.17
   different from trustees 6.3
   oath see Oaths for executors
   powers 12.1–12.23
   principal beneficiary 6.16, 6.17
   solicitors
      accountants appointed alongside 6.18
      appointment of 6.8–6.10
      fees 6.4–6.7, 6.20
Expenses
   charges clause for executor 6.4–6.7, 6.20
   trustees' 26.56

F

Family business
   gift of 9.16–9.19
Foreign issues 2.38–2.43
Foreign property 2.42–2.44
   English private international law 2.42
   legal advice, need for 2.44
   moveable and immovable property 2.43
Fraud 2.29
Funeral arrangements 5.3–5.8
   expenses 5.5
   prepaid funeral 5.9
Funeral service
   direction for 5.9

G

Gender Recognition Act 2004 1.13
Grandchild
   legacy to, precedents 8.13
      great grandchild 8.13
   substitutional gift to 11.15, 11.26
Guardian, testamentary see Testamentary guardians

H

Heir
   disposition to, construction 25.25
House, gift of 10.1, 10.23 see also **Matrimonial home**

I

Identity of testator 3.2–3.4
   alias 3.2
Illegitimate children 13.2

Immovable property see also **Land**
   gift of 10.23
   settled gift 10.23
Improvement of property 12.23
Incapacity see Capacity of testator
Income
   accumulation see Accumulation of income
   contingent beneficiary
      accumulation for 11.19
      distribution to 11.23
   minor, payment or application for 12.3
Income tax
   age contingent gifts, and 11.22
   variations after death, and 22.7
Inheritance (Provision for Family and Dependants Act) 1975 2.30–2.37
   discretionary trust, and 2.37
   factors taken into account 2.34, 2.35
   identity of applicant 2.35
   intestacy, claims in 2.30
   possibility of claim 2.31
   potential claimants 2.32, 2.33
   reasonable financial provision 2.33, 2.34
   record of advice given 2.31
Inheritance tax 10.4, 15.1–15.65, 28.1–28.9
   age contingent gifts 11.20, 15.65
   equalisation of estates, planning through 15.7, 15.24–15.33
      object of 15.28
   gift of nil-rate band on short-term discretionary trusts 15.60–15.64, 15.65
   gifts free of 8.6–8.8
      precedent 8.13
   gifts of chattels, and 9.3
   gifts, planning through 15.24–15.33
      moral obligation 15.25, 15.26
   ineffective schemes 15.4
   lifetime planning 15.6
   mitigation 15.1–15.65
   nil-rate band 15.3
      discretionary trust using 15.37, 15.38, 15.48–15.57, 15.57–15.60
      first to die directing to persons other than spouse 15.65

Index

Inheritance tax 10.4, 15.1–15.65, 28.1–28.9
— *contd*
nil-rate band 15.3 — *contd*
  gift to children of 15.65
  precedents clauses 15.65
  transferable 15.4, 15.7,
    15.8–15.22, 28.1–28.3,
    and see below
  'wasted' 15.18–15.20, 15.46,
    15.47
oaths for executors, and 23.9
pension benefits 15.33
post-death rearrangements 15.7,
  15.58, 15.59
precedents 15.65
residue, payable out of 10.4
share of matrimonial home an
  asset of discretionary trust
  15.48–15.57
survivorship clauses, and
  11.4–11.13
testamentary trusts, use of 15.7,
  15.34–15.45
  bereaved minors, for
    15.39–15.42
  discretionary (nil-rate band)
    15.37
  interest in possession trusts
    15.36
  IPDIs 15.44, 15.45
  three kinds 15.35
testators of moderate wealth 15.5
  transfer between spouses and
    civil partners 15.9–15.17,
    28.1–28.3
  unused, regarded as 15.21
topics 15.7
transferable nil-rate band 15.2,
  15.4, 15.7, 15.8–15.22, 28.1
  et seq
  capped at 100% 15.18–15.20,
    28.1
  current provisions, first death
    before 15.17
  formula and examples
    15.11–15.13, 15.15, 15.16
  permitted period 15.13
  record of unused amount, PRs
    to keep 15.14
  transfer between spouses and
    civil partners 15.9–15.22
unmarried couples 15.3

Inheritance tax 10.4, 15.1–15.65, 28.1–28.9
— *contd*
variations after death, and
  22.4–22.6, 28.5–28.7
  alteration of dispositions
    within two years of death
    28.5
  property settled by will,
    distribution of 28.7
  testator's request, compliance
    with 28.6
Issue see also Child
dying without, meaning 25.13
**Instructions see also Capacity of
testator**
checklist 24.3
client details 24.3
first interview 24.1
guidance notes 24.2
particular points for investigation
  24.4
Insurance 12.19
power to insure 12.19, 26.1
Intermediate income 1.32
Interview
matters to considered at 24.4
Intestacy
deed of variation, and 22.23,
  22.25
succession on, rules 2.7–2.15,
  27.1–27.3
  alteration of dispositions
    taking effect on death
    28.5
  children 2.14, 27.2
  inheritance claims 2.30
  partial intestacy 2.9–2.11
  residuary estate 2.12–2.14
  review by Law Commission
    2.7
  spouse/civil partner 27.1, 27.3
**Investment, statutory powers
12.5–12.11, 12.23, 26.32–26.35**
bearer securities 26.45
delegation to investment
  managers and nominees
  12.11, 26.38, 26.40
duty of care 12.20, 12.21, 26.61
duty to have regard to standard
  investment criteria 12.7,
  12.8
duty to take advice 12.9, 12.10
general power 12.6, 26.32
statutory power to delegate 12.12

Index

J
Joint tenancy 2.1–2.6
  drafting issues 2.5, 2.6
  severance 2.3–2.6
    notice of 24.8
  survivorship 2.3
Joint wills 4.1
  problems which may arise 4.5

L
Land
  acquisition powers of trustees 26.36, 26.37
  gifts of 10.1 *et seq*
  joint ownership 2.5
  management powers 10.9–10.11
  matrimonial home see Matrimonial home
  occupation of see Occupation, right of
  residence right, see Residence, right of
  settled gift of 10.7, 10.8, 10.23
  trusts of see Trusts of land
Lapse 13.2
  class gifts, and 11.25–11.27
  gifts to children or issue leaving issue living at testator's death 25.14
  Legacies 8.1–8.13
  accruer, provision for 8.13
  charities, to 8.9–8.12
  demonstrative 8.5
  general 8.3
  identity of legatees 8.1, 8.2
  inheritance tax, free of 8.6–8.8
  pecuniary 8.3, 8.5, 8.8, 8.13
  precedents 8.13
  priority 8.13
  specific 8.4
    gift over by specific legatee 9.11
  types 8.3–8.5
  unmarried couples with children, precedents 20.2
Legislative changes
  will drafting, and 1.8, 1.9
Legitimated persons 13.2, 25.24
  construction of references to 25.24
  rights to take interests in property 25.26
Letters 24.1–24.12
  basic procedure 24.1
  discretionary trust 24.6

Letters 24.1–24.12 – *contd*
  draft will, submitting 24.7
  life interest trust 24.5
  notice of severance, submitting 24.7
  wills for completion, enclosing 24.9
Life assurance 1.3, 1.4
Life interest 10.20
  advancement of capital to 10.20
  cohabitee/unmarried couple 20.1
  flexible life interest trust 15.36, 15.38
  intestacy, for spouse on 27.1, 27.3
  occupation right contrasted 10.21
  remarriage of spouse, provision for 19.9
  residence right, and 10.20
  tax position of life tenant 15.36
  tenant for life 25.17
Life interest trust
  letter about 24.5
  loans to 12.23
Limited liability partnerships
  solicitors 6.11–6.14

M
Maintenance power 12.3, 12.23, 26.2
Management of land, powers of 10.9–10.11
Marriage
  dissolution or annulment, effect of 25.6
  remarriage, provision for 19.9
  revocation of will by 25.5
Married couple
  childless, complete wills 18.1, 18.2
  children, with, complete wills 19.1
    adult children 19.4, 19.12
    minor children 19.5–19.7
  pensions 19.8
  points for draftsman 19.1–19.3, 19.11
  remarriage 19.9, 19.10
  trusts, creation of 19.11
  will not valid 25.2
Matrimonial home
  gift of share or interest, tax planning 15.7
  share as asset of discretionary trust 15.48–15.57

Index

Minors see Child
Mortgages 10.2, 10.3, 10.23
Mutual wills 4.3
   agreement underpinning 4.9
   appointment as executor 6.20
   clause creating 4.9
   meaning 4.3
   moral obligation, and 4.6, 4.7
   precedents 4.9
   problems which may arise 4.5

N

Name of testator 3.2–3.4
Nephews/nieces
   single adult will leaving residue to 17.2
Nominations
   revocation, and 3.7
Nominees 12.15, 12.16
   expenses 26.57
   liability for 12.17, 12.18, 26.48–26.50
   persons who may be appointed 26.46
   power to appoint 26.43
   remuneration 26.57
   terms of appointment 26.47
   use of 12.23
Notices of severance 24.8
   letter submitting 24.7

O

Oaths for executors 23.1–23.11
   description by address 23.4, 23.5
   drafting variants 23.10
   female deponents 23.6, 23.7
   inheritance tax, and 23.9
   need for 23.1
   power reserved 23.8
   precedents 23.11
   Registries, reference to 23.2, 23.3
   size of estate 23.9
Occupation, right of 10.15–10.18
   business premises 10.16
   conditions 10.17, 10.18
   exclusion or restriction 10.17, 10.18
Opening 3.1–3.4, 31.3
   precedents 3.13
Option, gift of 9.20

P

Parent
   surviving, appointment of testamentary guardian 7.9

Parent – *contd*
   unmarried/both female
      child's guardian, as/ appointment power 7.2, 7.3
   status of child 25.24
Partial intestacy 2.9–2.11
Partnership
   gift of interest in 9.18, 9.20
Pensions 1.3, 15.33
   inheritance tax considerations 19.8
Perpetuities 26.5–26.13, see also Age contingent gifts
   application and interpretation of rule 26.6, 26.12, 26.13
   perpetuity period 11.15, 26.8–26.10
   exclusion of class members to avoid remoteness 26.10
   power to specify 26.5
   powers of appointment 26.11
   start of 26.8
   will made before 6 April 2010 11.17
   will made on/after 6 April 2010 1.14, 11.15–11.16
Personal representatives
   duties and powers 26.28, 26.59
Post-death rearrangements 15.7, 15.58, 15.59, 22.1–22.5
Precatory trust 13.2
Precedents
   use of 1.15
Probate claims 2.16–2.29
   allegations 2.17
   capacity, and 2.16–2.29
Probate Registry
   application to 23.2, 23.3
Professional charges clause 6.20
Promissory note 24.11
   discretionary trust, scheme using 15.51–15.54, 15.57, 24.11
   will enabling 15.65
   procedure after 24.10
   will including, precedent 19.12
Protective trusts 26.4
Public Trustee
   appointment as executor and trustee 6.20

R

Reciprocal wills 4.2
   clause reciting creation 4.9
   precedents 4.9

Rectification 25.19
Relative
  childless married couple, substitutional gift to 18.1, 18.2
  dispositions to, construction of 25.25
  gift of residue to, by single adult 17.2
  references to, construction of 25.24
Releases 9.14
Relationships between persons
  construction of 25.24
  dispositions of property 25.25
Remarriage see also Second marriages and civil partnerships
  precedents, married couple with children 19.9, 19.10
Remuneration see also Expenses
  trustees 26.54–26.55
Residence of testator
  gift of 10.23
Residence, right of 10.19–10.22, 10.23
  furnished accommodation 10.22
  life interest 10.20
  practical purpose 10.19
  Residuary gifts 11.1–11.29
  administration trusts 11.1–11.3
  age contingent 11.14–11.24
  death of two persons where uncertain which died first 11.11–11.13
  discretionary trusts 11.28, 11.29
  lapse 11.25–11.27
  precedents 11.30
  survivorship clause 11.4–11.13
    administrative convenience 11.7
    inheritance tax, and 11.5, 11.6
    period of survival 11.8–11.10
    transferable nil-rate band 11.5, 11.6
  trust for sale 11.2–11.3
Retention for tax liabilities 12.23
Revival
  codicil, by 25.11
  re-execution, by 25.11
Revocation 3.1–3.13
  act of testator 3.5–3.8
  another will or codicil, by 25.9
  civil partnership, by 3.9, 25.7
  decree of nullity, by 3.10, 3.11

Revocation 3.1–3.13 – *contd*
  destruction, by 25.9
  dissolution of civil partnership, by 3.10, 3.11
  divorce, by 3.10, 11
  marriage, by 3.9, 25.5
  nominations and 3.7
  precedents 3.13
  will made in expectation of marriage or civil partnership 3.12

S

Satisfaction
  excluding doctrine 13.2
Second marriages or civil partnerships
  complete wills 21.1–21.3
  inheritance claim in intestacy 2.30
Settled gifts of land 10.7, 10.8, 10.23
Settlements
  trusts in place of 26.15
Severance, notice of 24.8
  letter submitting 24.7
Shares
  gifts of 9.15
Signature see also Attestation
  testator, of 25.3
Single adult
  complete wills 17.1, 17.2
Society of Trust and Estate Practitioners 16.2–16.4
Solicitors
  appointment as executors 6.8–6.10
    accountants appointed alongside 6.18
    charges, clause for 6.4–6.7, 6.20
    incorporated practices 6.11–6.14
    limited liability partnerships 6.11–6.14
Specific property, gifts of 10.1–10.23
Spouse see also Marriage; Married couple
  death within two years of testator 22.15, 22.16
  family provision claimant 2.32
  gift to, inheritance tax nil-rate band, precedents 15.65
  intestacy rules, and surviving spouse 27.1–27.3

Index

Spouse see also **Marriage; Married couple**
– *contd*
  nil-rate band, transferability see Inheritance tax
  witness, of 25.4
Stamp duty
  deeds of variations, and 22.17
  Stamp duty land tax
  deeds of variation 22.18
STEP provisions 12.22, 16.2–16.4
  incorporations by reference 12.22
Survivorship 13.2
  presumption of 25.15
Survivorship clause 11.4–11.13

T

Tax see **Capital gains tax; Income tax; Inheritance tax**
Tenancy in common 2.4, 2.5
  drafting points 2.5
Testamentary guardians 7.1–7.9
  appointment 7.1–7.9
    precedents 7.9
    surviving parent, by 7.9
  consent 7.6
  meaning 7.4
  successor 7.7, 7.9
  unmarried father of child 7.3
Testamentary trusts see also **Trusts**
  tax see Inheritance tax
Testator
  capacity see Capacity of testator
  identity 3.2–3.4
  name and address 3.1–3.4
  signature 25.3 see also Attestation
  unable to read or write 14.6
Testimonium
  standard form 14.14
Trustees 6.1–6.20 see also **Executors**
  accumulation of surplus income see Accumulation of income
  acquisition of land 26.36, 26.37
  agents, use of 12.13, 26.38–26.42
  ancillary powers 12.23
  appointment 6.1–6.20
    accountants 6.20
    bank 6.20
    members of solicitors' firm 6.20
    professional charges clause 6.20

Trustees 6.1–6.20 see also **Executors** – *contd*
  appointment 6.1–6.20 – *contd*
    Public Trustee 6.20
    trust, where 6.20
  asset management 12.14, 26.42
    see also Assets
  consents 26.24
  consultation with beneficiaries 10.13, 10.14, 26.25
  exclusion of duty 12.23
  delegation
    agents see Agents
    beneficiaries, to 10.12, 26.22, 26.23
  different from executors 6.3
  duty of care 12.30, 12.21, 26.30, 26.31, 26.61
  exclusion 12.23, 26.61
  trustees of land 26.23
  exceeding powers 26.51
  exoneration from liability clause 12.23
  expenses 26.56
  immovable property bought by, to be held on trust for sale 13.2
  insurance 12.19, 26.1
  investment 26.32–26.35
    bearer securities 26.45
    duty of care 12.20, 12.21, 26.61
    extension of powers of 12.23
  maintenance of minor 12.3, 12.23, 26.2
  powers 12.1–12.23, 26.1 *et seq*
    charge 6.4–6.7
    insurance 12.19, 26.1
    investment see Investment, statutory powers
    management of land 10.9–10.11
    partition 26.20
    trustees of land 26.19 *et seq*
  remuneration 26.54–26.55
  sole 26.52
Trusts see also **Inheritance tax; Trustees**
  discretionary see Discretionary trusts
  drafting points 19.11
  land see Trusts of land
  life interest 12.23, 24.5
  protective 26.4
Trusts for sale 11.2–11.3

Index

Trusts of land 26.14–26.29 see also **Trustees**
  delegation, liability of trustees 26.23
  duty of care of trustees 26.23, 26.30
    application of 26.61
  express trusts for sale 26.17
  implied trusts for sale 26.18
  meaning 26.14
  occupation right of beneficiaries 26.26, 26.27
  powers of trustees 26.19 *et seq*
    exceeding, effect of 26.51

U

Undue influence
  meaning 2.28
Unmarried couples
  complete wills, couples with children 20.1, 20.2
  inheritance tax 15.3
  life interest 20.1

V

Value of estate
  underestimating 1.5

Variations after death 15.58, 22.1–22.25
  beneficiaries, made by all 22.3
  capital gains tax, and 22.4
  deed see Deed of variation
  'double death' 22.21
  formalities 22.2, 28.5
  income tax, and 22.7
  inheritance tax, and 22.4–22.6, 28.5–28.7
  precedents 22.25
  widow's absolute interest 22.22
  writing, need for 22.2, 28.5

W

Wait and see rule 11.15, 11.16, 26.9
Will draftsman
  guiding note 24.2
  role of 1.1
Will for completion
  letter enclosing 24.9
Wishes of client 1.2–1.4
Witnesses 14.3
  avoidance of gifts to 25.18
  beneficiaries as 14.4
  gifts to 25.4
  signature to will 25.3
  spouse of 25.4